THE ROAD TO MECCA

Other Works by Muhammad Asad

THE MESSAGE OF THE QUR'ĀN

ISLAM AT THE CROSSROADS

ṢAḤĪḤ AL-BUKHĀRĪ: THE EARLY YEARS
OF ISLAM

THE PRINCIPLES OF STATE AND
GOVERNMENT IN ISLAM

THIS LAW OF OURS

MEDITATIONS

HOME-COMING OF THE HEART

Muhammad Asad

THE ROAD
TO MECCA

FONS VITAE

First Published by Simon & Schuster, Inc., New York, 1954

Fourth, revised edition published 1980
by Dar al-Andalus Limited

Reprinted 1981
Reprinted 1985
Reprinted 1993

This edition reprinted by Fons Vitae Publishing
and The Book Foundation 2000, 2005
49 Mockingbird Valley Drive
Louisville, KY 40207
www.fonsvitae.com

Printed in Canada

ISBN: 1-887752-37-4

Library of Congress Card Number: 00-109390

CONTENTS

ILLUSTRATIONS

GLOSSARY
of Arabic and Persian Terms

SPELLING has been kept as close as possible to the original pronunciation, avoiding, at the same time, all signs and symbols which would unnecessarily confuse the lay reader. Terms which occur in only one place and are explained in the text have been omitted here.

abāya – a wide, woollen cloak worn by Arabs over all their other garments.

agayl – voluntary, irregular troops recruited from Central Arabia for service in Iraq, Syria and Jordan.

al- – definite article 'the' used before nouns and many proper names. If the noun begins with the consonant *d, n, r, s, t* or *z*, the *l* of *al* is 'assimilated' in sound: e.g., *Ad*-Dawish, *Az*-Zuwayy.

amīr – 'one who holds authority', e.g., governor, ruler, commander, etc.

badawi (pl. *badu*) – beduin.

bismillāh – 'in the name of God'.

burnus – hooded cloak worn by North African Arabs and Berbers.

dhow – Latin-rigged sailing vessel largely used in the Arabian Sea, the Persian Gulf and (mostly under the name *sambūk*) in the Red Sea.

faranji (Persian form, *farangi*) – European.

fellāh (pl. *fellahīn*) – peasant or farmer.

gallabiyya – long, shirtlike tunic worn in Egypt and some other Arab countries.

hajj – pilgrimage to Mecca, one of the duties enjoined upon every Muslim man and woman able to undertake it.

hājji – one who is making or has made the pilgrimage to Mecca; often used as an honorific title.

haram – 'sanctuary', especially the Holy Mosques of Mecca, Medina and Jerusalem. (Not to be confused with *harām*, which means 'forbidden by religion'.)

hazrat – lit., 'presence'; term of address roughly equivalent to 'your Honour'.

ibn – son; before a proper name, 'son of'. Frequently used in conjunction with the name of an ancestor, in which case the combination denotes a family name, or the name of a dynasty, e.g., Ibn Saud, Ibn Rashid.

igāl – a ropelike headband encircling the Arabian headcloth. It is usually made of plain black wool, but is sometimes threaded with gilded silver wire.

ihrām – white garment worn by men on pilgrimage to Mecca.

ikhwān – 'brethren', here applied to beduins settled and organized by King Ibn Saud.

imām – 'leader'; more particularly applied to the leader of a congregational prayer, but also to outstanding scholars of earlier times and to the leader of a community.

inshā-Allāh – 'God willing'.

janāb-i-āli – honorific term of address used in Persian-speaking countries.

jard – a blanketlike woollen wrap worn in western Egypt and Libya.

jihād – Holy War in the defence of Islam or Muslim liberty.

jubba – a wide, ankle-length mantle worn by many well-to-do city people, and most of the *ulamā*, in Egypt, Syria, Hijaz, Iraq, Iran, etc.

kaftān – a long, fitted gown worn throughout the Middle East under a *jubba* or an *abāya*.

khalīfa – lit., 'successor' or 'vice-gerent'; usually denoting the head of the Muslim community ('Caliph').

khān – originally the title of a Mongol prince or lord; nowadays widely used as an honorific designation in Iran, Afghanistan, etc.

kufiyya – Arabian men's headcloth.

maghrib – sunset.

marhaba – welcome.

mu'azzin – crier of the time for prayer.

mujāhid (pl. *mujāhidīn*) – one who fights in *jihād*.

nargīle – elaborate pipe for smoking tobacco, in which the smoke is filtered through water; in some countries it is also called 'hookah'.

qādi – judge.

GLOSSARY

qahwa – coffee; in Arab countries often applied also to a coffeehouse or a reception room.

rajajīl – men-at-arms, usually the bodyguards of a king or *amīr*.

riyāl – the basic silver coin in several Middle-Eastern countries.

sayyid – lit., 'lord'. Frequently used to denote a descendant of the Prophet.

sharīf – same as above. In particular applied to certain Muslim ruling dynasties; in this book to King Husayn, who ruled over the Hijaz from 1916 to 1924, and his descendants, the present dynasties of Iraq and Jordan.

shaykh – lit., 'old man'; an honorific title widely used to denote tribal chieftains as well as notables and (in Arabic-speaking countries) scholars.

shuyūkh – 'majestic plural' of *shaykh;* a designation applied in Central Arabia to the King and, occasionally, to his greatest *amīrs*.

sīdi – colloquial for *sayyidi*, 'my lord' – an honorific term especially popular in North Africa.

sūra – section, or chapter, of the Koran, which is divided into 114 *sūras*.

tarbūsh – red, brimless hat worn by men all over the Levant.

ulamā – scholars, or learned men. Especially applied to religious scholars, but often used also for those learned in other branches of knowledge.

wādi – river valley or dry river bed.

yā – interjection equivalent to 'O' used in direct address (e.g., *yā sīdi*, 'O my lord'; *yā Allāh*, 'O God').

zāwiya – lodge of a religious order or fraternity.

THE STORY OF A STORY

THE STORY I am going to tell in this book is not the autobiography of a man conspicuous for his role in public affairs; it is not a narrative of adventure – for although many strange adventures have come my way, they were never more than an accompaniment to what was happening within me; it is not even the story of a deliberate search for faith – for that faith came upon me, over the years, without any endeavour on my part to find it. My story is simply the story of a European's discovery of Islam and of his integration within the Muslim community.

I had never thought of writing it, for it had not occurred to me that my life might be of particular interest to anyone except myself. But when, after an absence of twenty-five years from the West, I came to Paris and then to New York in the beginning of 1952, I was forced to alter this view. Serving as Pakistan's Minister Plenipotentiary to the United Nations, I was naturally in the public eye and encountered a great deal of curiosity among my European and American friends and acquaintances. At first they assumed that mine was the case of a European 'expert' employed by an Eastern government for a specific purpose, and that I had conveniently adapted myself to the ways of the nation which I was serving; but when my activities at the United Nations made it obvious that I identified myself not merely 'functionally' but also emotionally and intellectually with the political and cultural aims of the Muslim world in general, they became somewhat perplexed. More and more people began to question me about my past experiences. They came to know that very early in my life I had started my career as a foreign correspondent for Continental newspapers and, after several years of extensive travels throughout the Middle East, had become a Muslim in 1926; that after my conversion to Islam I lived for nearly six years in Arabia and enjoyed the friendship of King Ibn Saud; that after leaving Arabia I went to India and there met the great

1

Muslim poet-philosopher and spiritual father of the Pakistan idea, Muhammad Iqbal. It was he who soon persuaded me to give up my plans of travelling to Eastern Turkestan, China and Indonesia and to remain in India to help elucidate the intellectual premises of the future Islamic state which was then hardly more than a dream in Iqbal's visionary mind. To me, as to Iqbal, this dream represented a way, indeed the only way, to a revival of all the dormant hopes of Islam, the creation of a political entity of people bound together not by common descent but by their common adherence to an ideology. For years I devoted myself to this ideal, studying, writing and lecturing, and in time gained something of a reputation as an interpreter of Islamic law and culture. When Pakistan was established in 1947, I was called upon by its Government to organize and direct a Department of Islamic Reconstruction, which was to elaborate the ideological, Islamic concepts of statehood and community upon which the newly born political organization might draw. After two years of this extremely stimulating activity, I transferred to the Pakistan Foreign Service and was appointed Head of the Middle East Division in the Foreign Ministry, where I dedicated myself to strengthening the ties between Pakistan and the rest of the Muslim world; and in due course I found myself in Pakistan's Mission to the United Nations at New York.

All this pointed to far more than a mere outward accommodation of a European to a Muslim community in which he happened to live: it rather indicated a conscious, wholehearted transference of allegiance from one cultural environment to another, entirely different one. And this appeared very strange to most of my Western friends. They could not quite picture to themselves how a man of Western birth and upbringing could have so fully, and apparently with no mental reservations whatever, identified himself with the Muslim world; how it had been possible for him to exchange his Western cultural heritage for that of Islam; and what it was that had made him accept a religious and social ideology which – they seemed to take for granted – was vastly inferior to all European concepts.

Now why, I asked myself, should my Western friends take this so readily for granted? Had any of them ever really bothered to gain a direct insight into Islam – or were their opinions based merely on the handful of clichés and distorted notions that had been handed down to them from previous generations? Could it perhaps be that the old Graeco-Roman mode of thought which divided the world into Greeks and Romans on one side and 'barbarians' on the other was still so thoroughly ingrained in the Western mind that it was unable to concede, even theoretically, positive value to anything that lay outside its own cultural orbit?

Ever since Greek and Roman times, European thinkers and historians have been prone to contemplate the history of the world from the standpoint and in terms of European history and Western cultural experiences alone. Non-Western civilizations enter the picture only in so far as their existence, or particular movements within them, have or had a direct influence on the destinies of Western man; and thus, in Western eyes, the history of the world and its various cultures amounts in the last resort to little more than an expanded history of the West.

Naturally, such a narrowed angle of vision is bound to produce a distorted perspective. Accustomed as he is to writings which depict the culture or discuss the problems of his own civilization in great detail and in vivid colours, with little more than side glances here and there at the rest of the world, the average European or American easily succumbs to the illusion that the cultural experiences of the West are not merely superior but out of all proportion to those of the rest of the world; and thus, that the Western way of life is the only valid norm by which other ways of life could be adjudged – implying, of course, that every intellectual concept, social institution or ethical valuation that disagrees with the Western 'norm' belongs *eo ipso* to a lower grade of existence. Following in the footsteps of the Greeks and Romans, the Occidental likes to think that all those 'other' civilizations are or were only so many stumbling experiments on the path of progress so unerringly pursued by the West; or, at best (as in the case of the 'ancestor' civilizations which preceded that of the modern West in a direct line), no more than consecutive chapters in one and the same book, of which Western civilization is, of course, the final chapter.

When I expounded this view to an American friend of mine – a man of considerable intellectual attainments and a scholarly bent of mind – he was somewhat sceptical at first.

'Granted,' he said, 'the ancient Greeks and Romans *were* limited in their approach to foreign civilizations: but was not this limitation the inevitable result of difficulties of communication between them and the rest of the world? And has not this difficulty been largely overcome in modern times? After all, we Westerners do concern ourselves nowadays with what is going on outside our own cultural orbit. Aren't you forgetting the many books about Oriental art and philosophy that have been published in Europe and America during the last quarter-century ... about the political ideas that preoccupy the minds of Eastern peoples? Surely one could not with justice overlook this desire on the part of Westerners to understand what other cultures might have to offer?'

'To some extent you may be right,' I replied. 'There is little doubt that the primitive Graeco-Roman outlook is no longer fully operative these days. Its harshness has been considerably blunted – if for no other reason, because the more mature among Western thinkers have grown disillusioned and sceptical about many aspects of their own civilization and now begin to look to other parts of the world for cultural inspiration. Upon some of them it is dawning that there may be not only one book and one story of human progress, but many: simply because mankind, in the historical sense, is not a homogeneous entity, but rather a variety of groups with widely divergent ideas as to the meaning and purpose of human life. Still, I do not feel that the West has really become less condescending toward foreign cultures than the Greeks and Romans were: it has only become more tolerant. Mind you, not toward Islam – only toward certain other Eastern cultures, which offer some sort of spiritual attraction to the spirit-hungry West and are, at the same time, too distant from the Western world-view to constitute any real challenge to its values.'

'What do you mean by that?'

'Well,' I answered, 'when a Westerner discusses, say, Hinduism or Buddhism, he is always conscious of the fundamental differences between these ideologies and his own. He may admire this or that of their ideas, but would naturally never consider the possibility of substituting them for his own. Because he *a priori* admits this impossibility, he is able to contemplate such really alien cultures with equanimity and often with sympathetic appreciation. But when it comes to Islam – which is by no means as alien to Western values as Hindu or Buddhist philosophy –

this Western equanimity is almost invariably disturbed by an emotional bias. Is it perhaps, I sometimes wonder, *because* the values of Islam are close enough to those of the West to constitute a potential challenge to many Western concepts of spiritual and social life?'

And I went on to tell him of a theory which I had conceived some years ago – a theory that might perhaps help one to understand better the deep-seated prejudice against Islam so often to be found in Western literature and contemporary thought.

'To find a truly convincing explanation of this prejudice,' I said, 'one has to look far backward into history and try to comprehend the psychological background of the earliest relations between the Western and the Muslim worlds. What Occidentals think and feel about Islam today is rooted in impressions that were born during the Crusades.'

'The Crusades!' exclaimed my friend. 'You don't mean to say that what happened nearly a thousand years ago could still have an effect on people of the twentieth century?'

'But it does! I know it sounds incredible; but don't you remember the incredulity which greeted the early discoveries of the psychoanalysts when they tried to show that much of the emotional life of a mature person – and most of those seemingly unaccountable leanings, tastes and prejudices comprised in the term "idiosyncrasies"– can be traced back to the experiences of his most formative age, his early childhood? Well, are nations and civilizations anything but collective individuals? Their development also is bound up with the experiences of their early childhood. As with children, those experiences may have been pleasant or unpleasant; they may have been perfectly rational or, alternatively, due to the child's naïve misinterpretation of an event: the *moulding* effect of every such experience depends primarily on its original intensity. The century immediately preceding the Crusades, that is, the end of the first millennium of the Christian era, might well be described as the early childhood of Western civilization . . . '

I proceeded to remind my friend – himself an historian – that this had been the age when, for the first time since the dark centuries that followed the breakup of Imperial Rome, Europe was beginning to see its own cultural way. Independently of the almost forgotten Roman heritage, new literatures were just then coming into existence in the European vernaculars; inspired by the religious experience of Western Christianity, fine arts were slowly awakening from the lethargy caused by the warlike migrations of the Goths, Huns and Avars; out of the crude conditions of the early Middle Ages, a new cultural world was emerging. It was at that critical, extremely sensitive stage of its development that Europe received its most formidable shock – in modern parlance, a 'trauma' – in the shape of the Crusades.

The Crusades were the strongest collective impression on a civilization that had just begun to be conscious of itself. Historically speaking, they represented Europe's earliest – and entirely successful – attempt to view itself under the aspect of cultural unity. Nothing that Europe has experienced before or after could compare with the enthusiasm which the First Crusade brought into being. A wave of intoxication swept over the Continent, an elation which for the first time overstepped the barriers between states and tribes and classes. Before then, there had been Franks and Saxons and Germans, Burgundians and Sicilians, Normans and Lombards–a medley of tribes and races with scarcely anything in common but the fact that most of their feudal kingdoms and principalities were remnants of the Roman Empire and that all of them professed the Christian faith: but in the Crusades, and through them, the religious bond was elevated to a new plane, a cause common to all Europeans alike – the politico-religious concept of 'Christendom', which in its turn gave birth to the cultural concept of 'Europe'. When, in his famous speech at Clermont, in November, 1095, Pope Urban II exhorted the Christians to make war upon the 'wicked race' that held the Holy Land, he enunciated – probably without knowing it himself – the charter of Western civilization.

The traumatic experience of the Crusades gave Europe its cultural awareness and its unity; but this same experience was destined henceforth also to provide the false colour in which Islam was to appear to Western eyes. Not simply because the Crusades meant war and bloodshed. So many wars have been waged between nations and subsequently forgotten, and so many animosities which in their time seemed ineradicable have later turned into friendships. The damage caused by the Crusades was not restricted to a clash of weapons: it was, first and foremost, an intellectual damage – the poisoning of the Western mind against the Muslim world through a deliberate misrepresentation of the teachings and ideals of Islam. For, if the call for a crusade was to maintain its validity, the Prophet of the Muslims had, of necessity, to be stamped as the Anti-Christ and his religion depicted in the most lurid terms as a fount of immorality and perversion. It was at the time of the Crusades that the ludicrous notion that Islam was a religion of crude sensualism and brutal violence, of an observance of ritual instead of a purification of the heart, entered the Western mind and remained there; and it was then that the name of the Prophet Muhammad – the same Muhammad who had insisted that his own followers respect the prophets of other religions – was contemptuously transformed by Europeans into 'Mahound'. The age when the spirit of independent inquiry could raise its head was as yet far distant in Europe; it was easy for the powers-that-were to sow the dark seeds of hatred for a religion and civilization that was so different from the religion and civilization of the West. Thus it was no accident that the fiery *Chanson de Roland*, which describes the legendary victory of Christendom over the Muslim 'heathen' in southern France, was composed not at the time of those battles but three centuries later – to wit, shortly before the First Crusade – immediately to become a kind of 'national anthem' of Europe; and it is no accident, either, that this warlike epic marks the beginning of a *European* literature, as distinct from the earlier, localized literatures: for hostility toward Islam stood over the cradle of European civilization.

It would seem an irony of history that the age-old Western resentment against Islam, which was religious in origin, should still persist subconsciously at a time when religion has lost most of its hold on the imagination of Western man. This, however, is not really surprising. We know that a person may completely lose the religious beliefs imparted to him in his childhood while, nevertheless, some particular emotion connected with those beliefs remains, irrationally, in force throughout his later life –

' – and this,' I concluded, 'is precisely what happened to that collective personality, Western civilization. The shadow of the Crusades hovers over the West to this day; and all its reactions toward Islam and the Muslim world bear distinct traces of that die-hard ghost . . . '

My friend remained silent for a long time. I can still see his tall, lanky figure pacing up and down the room, his hands in his coat pockets, shaking his head as if puzzled, and finally saying:

'There may be something in what you say . . . indeed, there may be, although I am not in a position to judge your "theory" offhand . . . But in any case, in the light of what you yourself have just told me, don't you realize that your life, which to you seems so very simple and uncomplicated, *must* appear very strange and unusual to Westerners? Could you not perhaps share some of your own experiences with them? Why don't you write your autobiography? I am sure it would make fascinating reading!'

Laughingly I replied: 'Well, I might perhaps let myself be persuaded to leave the Foreign Service and write such a book. After all, writing is my original profession . . . '

In the following weeks and months my joking response imperceptibly lost the aspect of a joke. I began to think seriously about setting down the story of my life and thus helping, in however small a measure, to lift the heavy veil which separates Islam and its culture from the Occidental mind. My way to Islam had been in many respects unique: I had not become a Muslim because I had lived for a long time among Muslims – on the contrary, I decided to live among them because I had embraced Islam. Might I not, by communicating my very personal experiences to Western readers, contribute more to a mutual understanding between the Islamic and Western worlds than I could by continuing in a diplomatic position which might be filled equally well by other countrymen of mine? After all, any intelligent man could be Pakistan's Minister to the United Nations – but how many men were able to talk to Westerners about Islam as I could? I was a Muslim – but I was also of Western origin: and thus I could speak the intellectual languages of both Islam and the West . . .

And so, toward the end of 1952, I resigned from the Pakistan Foreign Service and started to write this book. Whether it is as 'fascinating reading' as my American friend anticipated, I cannot say. I could do no more than try to retrace from memory – with the help of only a few old notes, disjointed diary entries and some of the newspaper articles I had written at the time – the tangled lines of a development that stretched over many years and over vast expanses of geographical space.

And here it is: not the story of all my life, but only of the years before I left Arabia for India – those exciting years spent in travels through almost all the countries between the Libyan Desert and the snow-covered peaks of the Pamirs, between the Bosporus and the Arabian Sea. It is told in the context and, it should be kept in mind, *on the time level* of my last desert journey from the interior of Arabia to Mecca in the late summer of 1932: for it was during those twenty-three days that the pattern of my life became fully apparent to myself.

The Arabia depicted in the following pages no longer exists. Its solitude and integrity have crumbled under a strong gush of oil and the gold that the oil has brought. Its great simplicity has vanished and, with it, much that was humanly unique. It is with the pain one feels for something precious, now irretrievably lost, that I remember that last, long desert trek, when we rode, rode, two men on two dromedaries, through swimming light . . .

I
THIRST

— 1 —

WE RIDE, RIDE, two men on two dromedaries, the sun flames over our heads, everything is shimmer and glimmer and swimming light. Reddish and orange-coloured dunes, dunes behind dunes beyond dunes, loneliness and burning silence, and two men on two dromedaries in that swinging gait which makes you sleepy, so that you forget the day, the sun, the hot wind and the long way. Tufts of yellow grass grow sparsely on the crests of the dunes, and here and there gnarled *hamdh* bushes wind over the sand like giant snakes. Sleepy have become the senses, you are rocking in the saddle, you perceive hardly anything beyond the crunching of the sand under the camels' soles and the rub of the saddle-peg against the crook of your knee. Your face is wrapped in your headcloth for protection against sun and wind; and you feel as if you were carrying your own loneliness, like a tangible substance, across it, right across it . . . to the wells of Tayma . . . to the dark wells of Tayma that give water to him that is thirsty . . .

'. . . right across the Nufud to Tayma . . .' I hear a voice, and do not know whether it is a dream-voice or the voice of my companion.

'Didst thou say something, Zayd?'

'I was saying,' replies my companion, 'that not many people would venture right across the Nufud just to see the wells of Tayma . . .'

. . . .

ZAYD AND I ARE returning from Qasr Athaymin on the Najd-Iraq frontier where I went at the request of King Ibn Saud. Having accomplished my mission and with plenty of leisure time at my disposal, I decided to visit the remote, ancient oasis of Tayma, nearly two hundred miles to the southwest: the *Tema* of the Old Testament of which Isaiah said, 'The inhabitants of

10

the land of Tema brought water to him that was thirsty.' The abundance of Tayma's water, its huge wells which have no like in all Arabia, made it in pre-Islamic days a great centre of caravan trade and a seat of early Arabian culture. I have long wanted to see it; and so, disregarding the circuitous caravan routes, we struck, from Qasr Athaymin, right into the heart of the Great Nufud, the reddish sand desert that stretches itself so mightily between the highlands of Central Arabia and the Syrian Desert. There is no track and no path in this part of the tremendous wasteland. The wind sees to it that no footstep of man or animal leaves a lasting trace in the soft, yielding sand and that no landmark stands out for long to guide the wayfarer's eye. Under the strokes of the wind the dunes incessantly change their outlines, flowing in a slow, imperceptible movement from form to form, hills ebbing into valleys and valleys growing into new hills dotted with dry, lifeless grass that faintly rustles in the wind and is bitter as ashes even to a camel's mouth.

Although I have crossed this desert many times in many directions, I would not trust myself to find my way through it unaided, and therefore I am glad to have Zayd with me. This country here is his homeland: he belongs to the tribe of Shammar, who live on the southern and eastern fringes of the Great Nufud and, when the heavy winter rains suddenly transform the sand dunes into lush meadows, graze their camels in its midst for a few months of the year. The moods of the desert are in Zayd's blood, and his heart beats with them.

Zayd is probably the handsomest man I have ever known: broad of forehead and slim of body, middle-sized, fine-boned, full of wiry strength. Over the narrow wheat-coloured face with its strongly moulded cheekbones and the severe and at the same time sensual mouth lies that expectant gravity which is so characteristic of the desert Arab – dignity and self-composure wedded to intimate sweetness. He is a felicitous combination of purest beduin stock and Najdi town life, having preserved within himself the beduin's sureness of instinct without the beduin's emotional lability, and acquired the practical wisdom of the townsman without falling prey to his worldly sophistication. He, like myself, enjoys adventure without running after it. Since his earliest youth his life has been filled with incident and excitement: as a boyish trooper in the irregular camel corps levied by the Turkish government for its campaign in the Sinai Peninsula during the Great War; defender of his Shammar homeland against Ibn Saud; arms-smuggler in the Persian Gulf; tempestuous lover of many women in many parts of the Arab world (all of them, of course, legitimately married to him at one time or another, and then as legitimately divorced); horsetrader in Egypt; soldier of fortune in Iraq; and lastly, for nearly five years, my companion in Arabia.

And now, in this late summer of 1932, we ride together, as so often in the past, winding our lonesome way between dunes, stopping at one or another of the widely spaced wells and resting at night under the stars; the eternal *swish-swish* of the animals' feet over the hot sand; sometimes, during the march, Zayd's husky voice chanting in rhythm with the camels' tread; night camps, cooking coffee and rice and occasional wild game; the cool sweep of the wind over our bodies as we lie at night on the sand; sunrise over sand dunes, red and violently bursting like fireworks; and sometimes, like today, the miracle of life awaking in a plant that has been watered by chance.

We had stopped for our noon prayer. As I washed my hands, face and feet from a waterskin, a few drops spilled over a dried-up tuft of grass at my feet, a miserable little plant, yellow and withered and lifeless under the harsh rays of the sun. But as the water trickled over it, a shiver went through the shrivelled blades, and I saw how they slowly, tremblingly, unfolded. A few more drops, and the little blades moved and curled and then straightened themselves slowly, hesitantly, tremblingly . . . I held my breath as I poured more water over the grass tuft. It moved more quickly, more violently, as if some hidden force were pushing it out of its dream of death. Its blades – what a delight to behold! – contracted and expanded like the arms of a starfish, seemingly overwhelmed by a shy but irrespressible delirium, a real little orgy of sensual joy: and thus life re-entered victoriously what a moment ago had been as dead, entered it visibly, passionately, overpowering and beyond understanding in its majesty.

Life in its majesty . . . you always feel it in the desert. Because it is so difficult to keep and so hard, it is always like a gift, a treasure, and a surprise. For the desert is always surprising, even though you may have known it for years. Sometimes, when you think you can see it in all its rigidity and emptiness, it awakens from its dream, sends forth its breath – and tender, pale-green grass stands suddenly where only yesterday there was nothing but sand and splintery pebbles. It sends forth its breath again – and a flock of small birds flutters through the air – from where? where to? – slim-bodied, long-winged, emerald-green; or a swarm of locusts rises up above the earth with a rush and a zoom, grey and grim and endless like a horde of hungry warriors . . .

Life in its majesty: majesty of sparseness, always surprising: herein lies the whole nameless scent of Arabia, of sand deserts like this one, and of the many other changing landscapes.

Sometimes it is lava ground, black and jagged; sometimes dunes without end; sometimes a *wadi* between rocky hills, covered with thornbushes out of which a startled hare jumps across your way; sometimes loose sand with tracks of gazelles and a few fire-blackened stones over which long-forgotten wayfarers cooked their food in long-forgotten days; sometimes a village beneath palm trees, and the wooden wheels over the wells make music and sing to you without stopping; sometimes a well in the midst of a desert valley, with beduin herdsmen bustling around it to water their thirsty sheep and camels – they chant in chorus while the water is drawn up in large leather buckets and poured with a rush into leather troughs to the delight of the excited animals. Then again, there is loneliness in steppes overcome by a sun without mercy; patches of hard, yellow grass and leafy bushes that crawl over the ground with snaky branches offer welcome pasture to your dromedaries; a solitary acacia tree spreads its branches wide against the steel-blue sky; from between earth mounds and stones appears, eyes darting right and left, and then vanishes like a ghost, the gold-skinned lizard which, they say, never drinks water. In a hollow stand black tents of goat hair; a herd of camels is being driven homeward through the afternoon, the herdsmen ride on barebacked young camels, and when they call their animals the silence of the land sucks in their voices and swallows them without echo.

Sometimes you see glimmering shadows far on the horizon: are they clouds? They float low, frequently changing their colour and position, now resembling grey-brown mountains – but in the air, somewhat above the horizon – and now, for all the world to see, shady groves of stone pines: but – in the air. And when they come down lower and change into lakes and flowing rivers which quiveringly reflect the mountains and the trees in their inviting waters, you suddenly recognize them for what they are: blandishment of the jinns, the mirage that has so often led travellers to false hopes and so to perdition: and your hand goes involuntarily toward the waterskin at your saddle . . .

And there are nights full of other dangers, when the tribes are in warlike commotion and the traveller does not light fire while camping so as not to be seen from the distance, and sits wide awake through long hours, his rifle between the knees. And those days of peace, when after a long, lonely wandering you meet a caravan and listen in the evening to the talk of the grave, sunburned men around the campfire: they talk of the simple, great things of life and death, of hunger and satiety, of pride and love and hatred, of the lust of the flesh and its appeasement, of wars, of the palm groves in the distant home village – and you never hear idle babbling: for one cannot babble in the desert . . .

And you feel the call of life in the days of thirst, when the tongue sticks to the palate like a piece of dry wood and the horizon sends no deliverance but offers flaming *samum* wind and whirling sand instead. And in yet different days, when you are a guest in beduin tents and the men bring you bowls full of milk–the milk of fat she-camels at the beginning of spring, when after strong rainfalls the steppes and dunes are green as a garden and the animals' udders heavy and round; from a corner of the tent you can hear the women laugh while they cook a sheep in your honour over an open fire.

Like red metal the sun disappears behind hills; higher than anywhere else in the world is the starry sky at night, deep and dreamless your sleep under the stars; pale-grey and cool dawn the mornings. Cold are the nights in winter, biting winds flap against the campfire around which you and your companions huddle together in search of warmth; burning the days in summer when you ride, ride on your rocking dromedary through endless hours, your face muffled in your headcloth to protect it from the searing wind, your senses lulled into sleepiness, while high above you in the noon heat a bird of prey draws its circles . . .

— 2 —

THE AFTERNOON GLIDES slowly past us with its dunes, and its silence, and its loneliness.

After a while, the loneliness is broken by a group of beduins who cross our path – four or five men and two women – mounted on dromedaries, with a beast of burden carrying a folded black tent, cooking-pots and other utensils of nomad life, with a couple of children perched on top of it all. As they come upon us, they rein in their animals:

'Peace be with you.'

And we answer: 'And with you be peace and the grace of God.'

'What is your destination, O wayfarers?'

'Tayma, *insha-Allah*.'

'And whence come you?'

'From Qasr Athaymin, brothers,' I reply; and then there is silence. One of them, a gaunt, elderly man with a sharp face and a black, pointed beard, is obviously the leader; his glance also is black and pointed when, passing over Zayd, it rests suspiciously on me, the stranger of light complexion who has so unexpectedly appeared from nowhere in this pathless wilderness; a stranger who says he is coming from the direction of British-held Iraq, and might well be (I can almost read Sharp-Face's thought) an infidel surreptitiously entering the land of the Arabs. The old man's hand plays, as if in perplexity, with the pommel of his saddle while his people, now loosely grouped around us, obviously wait for him to speak. After a few moments, he seems to be unable to bear the silence any longer, and he asks me:

'Of which Arabs art thou?' – meaning to what tribe or region I belong. But even before I am able to reply, his features light up in a sudden smile of recognition:

'Oh, I know thee now! I have seen thee with Abd al-Aziz! But that was long ago – four long years ago . . .'

And he stretches his hand in friendliness toward me and recalls the time when I was living in the royal castle at Riyadh and he came there in the retinue of a Shammar chieftain to pay the respects of the tribe to Ibn Saud, whom the beduins always call by his first name, Abd al-Aziz, without any formal, honorific title: for in their free humanity they see only a man in the King, to be honoured, no doubt, but not beyond the deserts of man. And so we go on for a while reminiscing, speaking of this man and that, exchanging anecdotes about Riyadh, in and around which up to a thousand guests live daily off the King's bounty, receiving on departure presents that vary in accordance with each man's status – from a handful of silver coins or an *abaya* to the heavy purses of golden sovereigns, horses or dromedaries which he frequently distributes among the chieftains.

But the King's generosity is not so much a matter of the purse as of the heart. Perhaps more than anything else, it is his warmth of feeling that makes the people around him, not excepting myself, love him.

In all my years in Arabia, Ibn Saud's friendship has lain like a warm shimmer over my life.

He calls me his friend, although he is a king and I a mere journalist. And I call him my friend – not merely because throughout the years that I have lived in his realm he has shown me much friendliness, for that he shows to many men: I call him my friend because on occasion he opens his innermost thoughts to me as he opens his purse to so many others. I love to call him my friend, for, despite all his faults – and there are not a few of them – he is an exceedingly good man. Not just 'kindhearted': for kindness of heart can sometimes be a cheap thing. As you would admiringly say of an old Damascene blade that it is a 'good' weapon because it has all the qualities you could demand from a weapon of its kind: thus do I consider Ibn Saud a good man. He is rounded within himself and always follows his own path; and if he often errs in his actions, it is because he never tries to be anything but himself.

.   .   .   .

MY FIRST MEETING with King Abd al-Aziz ibn Saud took place at Mecca early in 1927, a few months after my conversion to Islam.

The recent sudden death of my wife, who had accompanied me on this, my first, pilgrimage to Mecca, had made me bitter and unsocial. I was desperately striving to clamber out of darkness and utter desolation. Most of my time was spent in my lodgings; I had contact with only a few people, and for weeks I avoided even the customary courtesy call on the King. Then one day, while visiting one of Ibn Saud's foreign guests – it was, I remember, Hajji Agos Salim of Indonesia – I was informed that by order of the King my name had been entered on his guest list! He seemed to have been apprised of the reason of my reserve and to accept it with silent understanding. And so, a guest who had never yet seen the face of his host, I moved into a beautiful house at the southern end of Mecca near the rocky gorge through which the way to Yemen passes. From the terrace I could see a large part of the city: the minarets of the Great Mosque, the thousands of white cubes of houses with roof balustrades of coloured bricks, and the dead desert hills domed by skies that glared like liquid metal.

Still, I might have gone on postponing my call on the King had it not been for a chance encounter with Amir Faysal, his second son, in a library under the arcades of the Great Mosque. It was pleasant to sit in that long, narrow room surrounded by old Arabic, Persian and Turkish folios; its stillness and darkness filled me with peace. One day, however, the usual silence was broken by the swishing entry of a group of men preceded by armed bodyguards: it was Amir Faysal with his retinue passing through the library on his way to the Kaaba. He was tall and thin and of a dignity far beyond his twenty-two years and his beardless face. In spite of his youth, he had been given the important position of viceroy of the Hijaz after his father's conquest of the country two years earlier (his elder brother, Crown Prince Saud, was viceroy of Najd, while the King himself spent half the year in Mecca, the capital of the Hijaz, and the other half in the Najdi capital, Riyadh).

The librarian, a young Meccan scholar with whom I had been friendly for some time, introduced me to the Prince. He shook hands with me; and when I bowed to him, he lightly tipped my head back with his fingers and his face lit up in a warm smile.

'We people of Najd do not believe that man should bow before man; he should bow only before God in prayer.'

He seemed to be kind, dreamy and a little reserved and shy – an impression which was confirmed during the later years of our acquaintance. His air of nobility was not assumed; it seemed to glow from within. When we spoke to each other on that day in the library, I suddenly felt a strong desire to meet the father of this son.

'The King would be happy to see thee,' said Amir Faysal. 'Why dost thou shun him?'

And the next morning the *amir's* secretary fetched me in an automobile and took me to the King's palace. We passed through the bazaar street of Al-Maala, slowly making our way through a noisy throng of camels, beduins and auctioneers selling all kinds of beduin wares – camel-saddles, *abayas*, carpets, waterskins, silver-inlaid swords, tents and brass coffeepots – then through a wider, quieter and more open road, and finally reached the huge house in which the King resided. Many saddled camels filled the open space before it, and a number of armed slaves and retainers lounged about the entrance stairway. I was made to wait in a spacious, pillared room whose floor was laid with inexpensive carpets. Broad, khaki-covered divans ran along the walls, and green leaves could be seen through the windows: the beginnings of a garden which was being grown with great difficulty out of the arid soil of Mecca. A black slave appeared.

'The King invites thee.'

I entered a room like the one I had just left, except that it was rather smaller and lighter, one side opening fully onto the garden. Rich Persian carpets covered the floor; in a bay window overlooking the garden the King sat cross-legged on a divan; at his feet on the floor a secretary was taking dictation. When I entered, the King rose, extended both hands and said:

'*Ahlan wa-sahlan*' – 'Family and plain' – which means, 'You have now arrived within your family and may your foot tread on an easy plain': the most ancient and most gracious of Arabian expressions of welcome.

For just a second I was able to gaze in wonderment at Ibn Saud's gigantic height. When (by then aware of the Najdi custom) I lightly kissed the tip of his nose and his forehead, I had to stand on my toes despite my six feet, while he had to bend his head downward. Then, with an apologetic gesture in the direction of the secretary, he sat down, pulling me to his side on the divan.

'Just a minute, the letter is nearly finished.'

While he quietly continued to dictate, he also opened a conversation with me, never confusing the two themes. After a few formal sentences, I handed him a letter of introduction. He read it – which meant doing three things at once – and then, without interrupting his dictation or his inquiry after my welfare, called for coffee.

By that time I had had an opportunity to observe him more closely. He was so well proportioned that his huge size – he must have been at least six and a half feet – became apparent only

Zayd

when he stood. His face, framed in the traditional red-and-white-checked *kufiyya* and topped by a gold-threaded *igal*, was strikingly virile. He wore his beard and moustache clipped short in Najdi fashion; his forehead was broad, his nose strong and aquiline, and his full mouth appeared at times almost feminine, but without being soft, in its sensual tenderness. While he spoke, his features were enlivened by unusual mobility, but in repose his face was somehow sad, as if withdrawn in inner loneliness; the deep setting of his eyes may have had something to do with this. The superb beauty of his face was slightly marred by the vague expression of his left eye, in which a white film was discernible. In later times I learned the story of this affliction, which most people unknowingly attributed to natural causes. In reality, however, it had occurred under tragic circumstances.

Some years earlier, one of his wives, at the instigation of the rival dynasty of Ibn Rashid, had put poison into his incense vessel – a little brazier used at ceremonial gatherings in Najd – with the obvious intention of killing him. As usual, the brazier was handed first to the King before being passed around among his guests. On inhaling the first whiff, Ibn Saud immediately sensed that there was something wrong with the incense and dashed the vessel to the ground. His alertness saved his life, but not before his left eye had been affected and partially blinded. But instead of avenging himself on the faithless woman, as many another potentate in his position would surely have done, he forgave her – for he was convinced that she had been the victim of insuperable influences at the hands of her family, who were related to the House of Ibn Rashid. He merely divorced her and sent her back, richly endowed with gold and gifts, to her home at Haïl.

*   *   *   *   *   *   *   *

AFTER THAT FIRST MEETING, the King sent for me almost daily. One morning I went to him with the intention of asking, without much hope of its being granted, permission to travel into the interior of the country, for Ibn Saud did not, as a rule, allow foreigners to visit Najd. Nevertheless, I was about to bring this matter up when suddenly the King shot a brief, sharp glance in my direction – a glance which seemed to penetrate to my unspoken thoughts – smiled, and said:

'Wilt thou not, O Muhammad, come with us to Najd and stay for a few months at Riyadh?'

I was dumbfounded, and so, obviously, were the other people present. Such a spontaneous invitation to a stranger was almost unheard of.

He went on: 'I would like thee to travel by motorcar with me next month.'

I took a deep breath and answered: 'May God lengthen thy life, O Imam, but what use would that be to me? What good would it do me to whizz in five or six days from Mecca to Riyadh without having seen anything of thy country beyond the desert, some sand dunes and perhaps, somewhere on the horizon, people like shadows . . . If thou hast no objection, a dromedary would suit me better, O Long-of-Age, than all thy cars together.'

Ibn Saud laughed: 'Art thou thus tempted to look into the eyes of my beduins? I must warn thee beforehand: they are backward people, and my Najd is a desert land without charms, and the camel-saddle will be hard and the food dreary on the journey – nothing but rice and dates and occasionally meat. But so be it. If thou hast set thy heart on it, thou shalt ride. And, after all, it may well be that thou wilt not regret having come to know my people: they are poor, they know nothing and are nothing – but their hearts are full of good faith.'

And some weeks later, equipped by the King with dromedaries, provisions, a tent and a guide, I set out by a roundabout route to Riyadh, which I reached after two months. That was my first journey into the interior of Arabia; the first of many: for the few months of which the King had spoken grew into years – how easily they grew into years! – spent not only in Riyadh but in almost every part of Arabia. And the saddle is hard no longer . . .

.   .   .   .

'MAY GOD LENGTHEN the life of Abd al-Aziz,' says Sharp-Face. 'He loves the *badu* and the *badu* love him.'

And why should they not? – I ask myself. The King's open-handedness toward the beduins of Najd has become a standing feature of his administration: not a very admirable feature, perhaps, for the regular gifts of money which Ibn Saud distributes among the tribal chieftains and their followers have made them so dependent on his largesse that they are beginning to lose all incentive to improve their living conditions by their own endeavours and are gradually lapsing into the status of dole-receivers, content to remain ignorant and indolent.

Throughout my conversation with Sharp-Face, Zayd seems impatient. While he talks with one of the men, his eyes frequently rest on me, as if to remind me that there is a long way before us and that reminiscences and reflections do not quicken the camels' pace. We part. The Shammar beduins ride away toward the east and soon disappear behind dunes. From where we stand, we can hear one of them intone a nomad chant, such as a camel-rider sings to spur his beast and to break the monotony of his ride; and as Zayd and I resume our westward course toward far-off Tayma, the melody gradually fades away, and silence returns.

— 3 —

'LOOK THERE!' Zayd's voice breaks through the silence, 'a hare!'

I turn my eyes to the bundle of grey fur that has leaped out of a clump of bushes, while Zayd slides down from his saddle, unslinging the wooden mace that hangs on the pommel. He bounds after the hare and swings the mace over his head for the throw; but just as he is about to hurl it, he catches his foot in a *hamdh* root, falls flat on his face – and the hare disappears from sight.

'There goes a good supper,' I laugh as he picks himself up, ruefully eyeing the mace in his hand. 'But mind it not, Zayd: that hare was obviously not our portion . . .'

'No, it was not,' he replies, somewhat absent-mindedly; and then I see that he is limping painfully.

'Didst thou hurt thyself, Zayd?'

'Oh, it is nothing. I only twisted my ankle. It will get better in a little while.'

But it does not get better. After another hour in the saddle I can see beads of perspiration on Zayd's face; and when I take a look at his foot, I find that the ankle has been badly sprained and is angrily swollen.

'There is no use going on like this, Zayd. Let us make camp here; a night's rest will restore thee.'

.   .   .   .

ALL THROUGH THE NIGHT Zayd seems to be restless with pain. He awakens long before dawn, and his sudden movement stirs me also from my uneasy sleep.

'I see only one camel,' he says: and when we look around, we discover that one of the beasts – Zayd's – has indeed disappeared. Zayd wants to set out on mine to search for it, but his injured foot makes it difficult for him even to stand, not to speak of walking and mounting and dismounting.

'Thou rest, Zayd, and I shall go instead; it won't be difficult to find my way back by retracing my own tracks.'

And in the breaking dawn I ride away, following the tracks of the lost dromedary which wind across the sand valley and disappear behind the dunes.

I ride for one hour, and another, and a third: but the tracks of the strayed animal go on and on, as if it had pursued a deliberate course. The forenoon is well advanced when I stop for a short halt, dismount, eat a few dates and drink from the small water-skin attached to my saddle. The sun stands high, but somehow it has lost its glare. Dun-coloured clouds, unusual at this time of year, float motionless under the sky; a strangely thick, heavy air envelops the desert and softens the outlines of the dunes beyond their usual softness.

An eerie stir over the summit of the high sand hill in front of me catches my eye – is it an animal? The lost camel perhaps? But when I look more carefully, I see that the movement is not above but in the dune crest itself: the crest is moving, ever so slightly, ripplingly, forward – and then it seems to trickle down the slope toward me like the crest of a slowly breaking wave. A murky redness creeps up the sky from behind the dune; under this redness its contours lose their sharness and become blurred, as if a veil had suddenly been drawn across; and a reddish twilight begins to spread rapidly over the desert. A cloud of sand whirls against my face and around me, and all at once the wind begins to roar from all directions, crisscrossing the valley with powerful blasts. The trickling movement of the first hilltop has been taken up by all the sand hills within sight. In a matter of minutes the sky darkens to a deep, rust-brown hue and the air is filled with swirling sand dust which, like a reddish fog, obscures the sun and the day. This is a sandstorm, and no mistake.

My crouching dromedary, terrified, wants to rise. I pull it

down by the halter, struggling to keep myself upright in the wind that has now assumed the force of a gale, and manage to hobble the animal's forelegs and, to make it more secure, a hind leg as well. Then I throw myself down on the ground and draw my *abaya* over my head. I press my face against the camel's armpit so as not to be choked by the flying sand. I feel the animal press its muzzle against my shoulder, no doubt for the same reason. I can feel the sand being heaped upon me from the side where I am unprotected by the dromedary's body, and have to shift from time to time to avoid being buried.

I am not unduly worried, for it is not the first time that I have been surprised by a sandstorm in the desert. Lying thus on the ground, tightly wrapped in my *abaya*, I can do nothing but wait for the storm to abate and listen to the roar of the wind and the flapping of my cloak – flapping like a loose sail – no, like a banner in the wind – like the flapping of tribal banners carried on high poles by a beduin army on the march: just as they flapped and fluttered nearly five years ago over the host of Najdi beduin riders – thousands of them, and I among them – returning from Arafat to Mecca after the pilgrimage. It was my second pilgrimage. I had spent one year in the interior of the Peninsula and had managed to return to Mecca just in time to take part in the congregation of pilgrims on the Plain of Arafat, to the east of the Holy City; and on the way back from Arafat I found myself in the midst of a multitude of white-garbed Najdi beduins, riding in a tense gallop over the dusty plain – a sea of white-garbed men on honey-yellow, golden-brown and red-brown dromedaries – a roaring, earth-shaking gallop of thousands of dromedaries pushing forward like an irresistible wave – the tribal banners roaring in the wind and the tribal cries with which the men announced their various tribes and the warlike deeds of their ancestors surging in waves over each detachment: for to the men of Najd, men of the Central Arabian highlands, war and pilgrimage spring from the same source ... And the numberless pilgrims from other lands – from Egypt and India and North Africa and Java – unaccustomed to such wild abandon, scattered in panic before our approach: for nobody could have survived who stood in the way of the thundering host – just as instantaneous death would have been the portion of a rider who fell from the saddle in the midst of the thousands and thousands of galloping mounts.

However mad that ride, I shared the madness and abandoned myself to the hour and the whirr and the rush and the roar with a wild happiness in my heart – and the wind that rushed past my face sang out: 'Never again wilt thou be a stranger ... never again, among thy people!'

And as I lie in the sand under my flapping *abaya*, the roar of the sandstorm seems to echo: 'Never again wilt thou be a stranger ...'

I am no longer a stranger: Arabia has become my home. My Western past is like a distant dream – not unreal enough to be forgotten, and not real enough to be part of my present. Not that I have become a lotus-eater. On the contrary, whenever I happen to stay for some months in a town – as, for instance, in Medina, where I have an Arab wife and an infant son and a library full of books on early Islamic history – I grow uneasy and begin to yearn for action and movement, for the dry, brisk air of the desert, for the smell of dromedaries and the feel of the camel-saddle. Oddly enough, the urge to wander that has made me so restless for the greater part of my life (I am a little over thirty-two now) and lures me again and again into all manner of hazards and encounters, does not stem so much from a thirst for adventure as from a longing to find my own restful place in the world – to arrive at a point where I could correlate all that might happen to me with all that I might think and feel and desire. And if I understand it rightly, it is this longing for inner discovery that has driven me, over the years, into a world entirely different, both in its perceptions and its outer forms, from all to which my European birth and upbringing had seemed to destine me ...

   •   •   •   •   •   •   •

WHEN THE STORM finally subsides, I shake myself free of the sand that has been heaped around me. My dromedary is half buried in it, but none the worse for an experience that must have befallen it many times. The storm itself, it would seem at first glance, has not done us any damage apart from filling my mouth, ears and nostrils with sand and blowing away the sheepskin from my saddle. But soon I discover my error.

All the dunes around me have changed their outlines. My own tracks and those of the missing camel have been blown away. I am standing on virgin ground.

Now nothing remains but to go back to the camp – or at least to try to go back – with the help of the sun and the general sense of direction which is almost an instinct with someone accustomed to travelling in deserts. But here these two aids are not entirely reliable, for sand dunes do not allow you to go in a straight line and so to keep the direction you have chosen.

The storm has made me thirsty, but, not expecting to be away from camp for more than a few hours, I have long ago drunk the last sip from my small waterskin. However, it cannot be far to the camp; and although my dromedary has had no water since our last stop at a well some two days ago, it is an old campaigner and can be relied upon to carry me back. I set its nose toward where I think the camp must lie, and we start at a brisk pace.

An hour passes, a second, and a third, but there is no trace of Zayd or of our camping ground. None of the orange-coloured hills presents a familiar appearance; it would be difficult indeed to discover anything familiar in them even if there had been no storm.

Late in the afternoon I come upon an outcrop of granite rocks, so rare in the midst of these sand wastes, and recognize them immediately: we passed them, Zayd and I, yesterday afternoon, not long before we made camp for the night. I am greatly relieved; for though it is obvious that I am way beyond the place where I hoped to find Zayd – having probably missed him by a couple of miles or so – it seems to me that it should not now be difficult to find him by simply going in a southwesterly direction, as we did yesterday.

There were, I remember, about three hours between the rocks and our night camp: but when I now ride for three more hours, there is no sign of the camp or of Zayd. Have I missed him again? I push forward, always toward southwest, taking the movement of the sun carefully into account; two more hours pass, but still there is no camp and no Zayd. When night falls, I decide it is senseless to continue further; better rest and wait for the morning light. I dismount, hobble the dromedary, try to eat some dates but am too thirsty: and so I give them to the camel and lie down with my head against its body.

It is a fitful doze into which I fall: not quite sleep and not quite waking, but a succession of dream states brought about by fatigue, broken by a thirst that has gradually become distressing;

and, somewhere in those depths which one does not want to uncover to oneself, there is that grey, squirming mollusc of fear:
what will happen to me if I do not find my way back to Zayd and
to our waterskins? – for, as far as I know, there is no water and
no settlement for many days' journey in all directions.

At dawn I start again. During the night I calculated that I
must have gone too far to the south and that, therefore, Zayd's
camp ought to be somewhere north-northeast of the place where
I spent the night. And so toward north-northeast we go, thirsty
and tired and hungry, always threading our way in wavy lines
from valley to valley, circumventing sand hills now to the right,
now to the left. At noon we rest. My tongue sticks to the roof of
my mouth and feels like old, cracked leather; the throat is sore
and the eyes inflamed. Pressed to the camel's belly, with my *abaya*
drawn over my head, I try to sleep for a while, but cannot. The
afternoon sees us again on the march, this time in a more easter-
ly direction – for by now I know that we have gone too far west
– but still there is no Zayd and no camp.

Another night comes. Thirst has grown to be torment, and the
desire for water the one, the overpowering thought in a mind
that can no longer hold orderly thoughts. But as soon as dawn
lightens the sky, I ride on: through the morning, through noon-
day, into the afternoon of another day. Sand dunes and heat.
Dunes behind dunes, and no end. Or is this perhaps the end –
the end of all my roads, of all my seeking and finding? Of my
coming to the people among whom I would never again be a
stranger . . . ? 'O God,' I pray, 'let me not perish thus . . .'

In the afternoon I climb a tall dune in the hope of getting a
better view of the landscape. When I suddenly discern a dark
point far to the east, I could cry with joy, only I am too weak for
that: for this must be Zayd's encampment, and the waterskins,
the two big waterskins full of water! My knees shake as I remount my dromedary. Slowly, cautiously, we move in the direction of that black point which can surely be nothing but Zayd's
camp. This time I take every precaution not to miss it: I ride in a
straight line, up sand hills, down sand valleys, thus doubling,
trebling our toil, but spurred by the hope that within a short
while, within two hours at the most, I shall reach my goal. And
finally, after we have crossed the last dune crest, the goal comes
clearly within my sight, and I rein in the camel, and look down

upon the dark something less than half a mile away, and my
heart seems to stop beating: for what I see before me is the dark
outcrop of granite rocks which I passed three days ago with
Zayd and revisited two days ago alone . . .

For two days I have going in a circle.

— 4 —

WHEN I SLIDE DOWN from the saddle, I am entirely exhausted. I do not even bother to hobble the camel's legs, and indeed the beast is too tired to think of running away. I weep; but
no tears come from my dry, swollen eyes.

How long it is since I have wept . . . But, then, is not everything long past? Everything is past, and there is no present.
There is only thirst. And heat. And torment.

I have been without water for nearly three days now, and it is
five days since my dromedary has had its last drink. It could
probably carry on like this for one day more, perhaps two; but I
cannot, I know it, last that long. Perhaps I shall go mad before I
die, for the pain in my body is ensnarled with the dread in my
mind, and the one makes the other grow, searing and whispering
and tearing. . .

I want to rest, but at the same time I know that if I rest now I
shall never be able to get up again. I drag myself into the saddle
and force the dromedary with beating and kicking to get up; and
almost fall from the saddle when the animal lurches forward
while rising on its hind legs and, again, when it lurches backward, straightening its forelegs. We begin to move, slowly, painfully, due west. Due west: what a mockery! What does 'due
west' amount to in this deceptive, undulating sea of sand hills?
But I want to live. And so we go on.

We plod with the rest of our strength through the night. It
must be morning when I fall from the saddle. I do not fall hard;
the sand is soft and embracing. The camel stands still for a while,
then slides down with a sigh on its knees, then on its hind legs,
and lies crouched by my side with its neck stretched on the sand.

I lie on the sand in the narrow shadow of the dromedary's
body, wrapped in my *abaya* against the heat outside me and the
pain and thirst and dread within me. I cannot think any more. I
cannot close my eyes. Every movement of the lids is like hot
metal on the eye-balls. Thirst and heat; thirst and crushing

silence: a dry silence that swathes you in its shroud of loneliness and despair and makes the singing of blood in your ears and the camel's occasional sigh stand out, threateningly, as though these were the last sounds on earth and you two, the man and the beast, the last living beings, doomed beings, on earth.

High above us, in the swimming heat, a vulture circles slowly, without ever stopping, a pinpoint against the hard paleness of the sky, free and above all horizons . . .

My throat is swollen, constricted, and every breath moves a thousand torturing needles at the base of my tongue – that big, big tongue which should not move but cannot stop moving in pain, backward, forward, like a rasp against the dry cavity of my mouth. All my insides are hot and intertwined in one unceasing grip of agony. For seconds the steely sky becomes black to my wide-open eyes.

My hand moves, as if of its own, and strikes against the hard butt of the carbine slung on the saddle-peg. And the hand stands still, and with sudden clarity the mind sees the five good shells in the magazine and the quick end that a pressure on the trigger could bring . . . Something in me whispers: Move quickly, get the carbine before you are unable to move again!

And then I feel my lips move and shape toneless words that come from some dark recesses of my mind: 'We shall try you . . . most certainly try you . . .' and the blurred words slowly assume shape and fall into pattern – a verse from the Koran: *We shall most certainly try you with fear and hunger and with the lack of possessions and labour's fruits. But give the good tiding to those who remain steadfast and, when calamity befalls them, say: 'Behold, to God we belong and unto Him do we return.'*

Everything is hot and dark; but out of the hot darkness I sense a cooling breath of wind and hear it rustle softly – wind rustling, as if in trees – over water – and the water is the sluggish little stream between grassy banks, near the home of my childhood. I am lying on the bank, a little boy of nine or ten years, chewing a grass stalk and gazing at the white cows which graze nearby with great, dreamy eyes and the innocence of contentment. In the distance peasant women work in the field. One of them wears a red head-kerchief and a blue skirt with broad red stripes. Willow trees stand on the bank of the stream, and over its surface glides a white duck, making the water glitter in its wake. And the soft wind rustles over my face like an animal's snort: oh, yes, it is indeed an animal's snort: the big white cow with the brown spots has come quite close to me and now nudges me, snorting, with its muzzle, and I feel the movement of its legs by my side. . .

I open my eyes, and hear the snort of my dromedary, and feel the movement of its legs by my side. It has half raised itself on its hind legs with uplifted neck and head, its nostrils widened as if scenting a sudden, welcome smell in the noon air. It snorts again, and I sense the excitement rippling down its long neck toward the shoulder and the big, half-raised body. I have seen camels snuffle and snort like this when they scent water after long days of desert travel; but there is no water here. . . Or – is there? I lift my head and follow with my eyes the direction toward which the camel has turned its head. It is the dune nearest us, a low summit against the steely bleakness of the sky, empty of movement or sound. But there *is* a sound! There is a faint sound like the vibration of an old harp, very delicate and brittle, high-pitched: the high-pitched, brittle sound of a beduin voice chanting on the march in rhythm with the camel's tread – just beyond the summit of the sand hill, quite near as distances go, but – I know it in a fraction of an instant – far beyond my reach or the sound of my voice. There are people there, but I cannot reach them. I am too weak even to get up. I try to shout, but only a hoarse grunt comes from my throat. And then my hand strikes, as if of its own, against the hard butt of the carbine on the saddle . . . and with the eye of my mind I see the five good shells in the magazine. . .

With a supreme effort I manage to unsling the weapon from the saddle-peg. Drawing the bolt is like lifting a mountain, but finally it is done. I stand the carbine on its butt and fire a shot vertically into the air. The bullet whines into the emptiness with a pitifully thin sound. I draw the bolt again and fire again, and then listen. The harplike singing has stopped. For a moment there is nothing but silence. Suddenly a man's head, and then his shoulders, appear over the crest of the dune; and another man by his side. They look down for a while, then turn around and shout something to some invisible companions, and the man in front clambers over the crest and half runs, half slides down the slope toward me.

There is commotion around me: two, three men – what a

crowd after all that loneliness! – are trying to lift me up, their movements a most confusing pattern of arms and legs. . . I feel something burning-cold, like ice and fire, on my lips, and see a bearded beduin face bent over me, his hand pressing a dirty, moist rag against my mouth. The man's other hand is holding an open waterskin. I make an instinctive move toward it, but the beduin gently pushes my hand back, dunks the rag into the water and again presses a few drops onto my lips. I have to bite my teeth together to prevent the water from burning my throat; but the beduin pries my teeth apart and again drops some water into my mouth. It is not water: it is molten lead. Why are they doing this to me? I want to run away from the torture, but they hold me back, the devils. . . My skin is burning. My whole body is in flames. Do they want to kill me? Oh, if only I had the strength to get hold of my rifle to defend myself! But they do not even let me rise: they hold me down to the ground and pry my mouth open again and drip water into it, and I have to swallow it – and, strangely enough, it does not burn as fiercely as a moment ago – and the wet rag on my head feels good, and when they pour water over my body, the touch of the wet clothes brings a shudder of delight. . .

And then all goes black, I am falling, falling down a deep well, the speed of my falling makes the air rush past my ears, the rushing grows into a roar, a roaring blackness, black, black . . .

— 5 —

. . . BLACK, BLACK, a soft blackness without sound, a good and friendly darkness that embraces you like a warm blanket and makes you wish that you could always remain like this, so wonderfully tired and sleepy and lazy; and there is really no need for you to open your eyes or to move your arm; but you do move your arm and do open your eyes: only to see darkness above you, the woollen darkness of a beduin tent made of black goat hair, with a narrow opening in front that shows you a piece of starry night sky and the soft curve of a dune shimmering under the starlight. . . And then the tent-opening darkens and a man's figure stands in it, the outline of his flowing cloak sharply etched against the sky, and I hear Zayd's voice exclaim: 'He is awake, he is awake!' – and his austere face comes quite close to my own and his hand grips my shoulder. Another man enters the tent; I cannot clearly see him, but as soon as he speaks with a slow, solemn voice I know he is a Shammar beduin.

Again I feel a hot, consuming thirst and grip hard the bowl of milk which Zayd holds out toward me; but there is no longer any pain when I gulp it down while Zayd relates how this small group of beduins happened to camp near him at the time when the sandstorm broke loose, and how, when the strayed camel calmly returned by itself during the night, they became worried and went out, all of them together, to search for me; and how, after nearly three days, when they had almost given up hope, they heard my rifle shots from behind a dune. . .

And now they have erected a tent over me and I am ordered to lie in it tonight and tomorrow. Our beduin friends are in no hurry; their waterskins are full; they have even been able to give three bucketfuls to my dromedary: for they know that one day's journey toward the south will bring them, and us, to an oasis where there is a well. And in the meantime the camels have fodder enough in the *hamdh* bushes that grow all around.

After a while, Zayd helps me out of the tent, spreads a blanket on the sand, and I lie down under the stars.

.   .   .   .

A FEW HOURS LATER I awaken to the clanking of Zayd's coffeepots; the smell of fresh coffee is like a woman's embrace.

'Zayd!' I call out, and am pleasantly surprised that my voice, though still tired, has lost its croak. 'Wilt thou give me some coffee?'

'By God I will, O my uncle!' answers Zayd, following the old Arab custom of thus addressing a man to whom one wants to show respect, be he older or younger than the speaker (as it happens, I am a few years younger than Zayd). 'Thou shalt have as much coffee as thy heart desires!'

I drink my coffee and grin at Zayd's happy countenance. 'Why, brother, do we expose ourselves to such things instead of staying in our homes like sensible people?'

'Because,' Zayd grins back at me, 'it is not for the like of thee and me to wait in our homes until the limbs become stiff and old age overtakes us. And besides, do not people die in their houses as well? Does not man always carry his destiny around his neck, wherever he may be?'

The word Zayd uses for 'destiny' is *qisma* – 'that which is apportioned' – better known to the West in its Turkish form, *kismet*. And while I sip another cup of coffee, it passes through my mind that this Arabic expression has another, deeper meaning as well: 'that in which one has a share.'

That in which one has a share . . .

These words strike a faint, elusive chord in my memory . . . there was a grin that accompanied them . . . whose grin? A grin behind a cloud of smoke, pungent smoke, like the smoke of hashish: yes – it was the smoke of hashish, and the grin belonged to one of the strangest men I have ever met – and I met him after one of the strangest experiences of my life: while trying to escape from a danger that seemed – only seemed – to be imminent in its threat, I had been racing, without knowing it, into a danger far more real, far more imminent, than the one I was trying to elude: and both the unreal danger and the real one led to another escape. . .

It all happened nearly eight years ago, when I was travelling on horseback, accompanied by my Tatar servant Ibrahim, from Shiraz to Kirman in southern Iran – a desolate, thinly populated, roadless stretch near Niris Lake. Now, in winter, it was a squelchy, muddy steppe with no villages in the vicinity, hedged in to the south by Kuh-i-Gushnegan, 'the Mountains of the Hungry'; toward the north it dissolved into the swamps that bordered the lake. In the afternoon, as we circumvented an isolated hill, the lake came suddenly into view: a motionless green surface without breath or sound or life, for the water was so salty that no fish could live in it. Apart from a few crippled trees and desert shrubs, the salty soil near its shores did not allow any vegetation to grow. The ground was lightly covered with muddy snow and over it, at a distance of about two hundred yards from the shore, ran a thinly outlined path.

The evening fell and the caravanserai of Khan-i-Khet – our goal for the night – was nowhere in sight. But we had to reach it at any price; far and wide there was no other settlement, and the nearness of the swamps made progress in darkness extremely hazardous. In fact, we had been warned in the morning not to venture there alone, for one false step might easily mean sudden death. Apart from that, our horses were very tired after a long day's march over oozy ground and had to be rested and fed.

With the coming of the night heavy rain set in. We rode, wet and morose and silent, relying on the instinct of the horses rather than on our useless eyes. Hours passed: and no caravanserai appeared. Perhaps we had passed it by in the darkness and would now have to spend the night in the open under a downpour that was steadily mounting in strength... The hooves of our horses splashed through water; our sodden clothes clung heavily to our bodies. Black and opaque hung the night around us under its veils of streaming water; we were chilled to the bone; but the knowledge that the swamps were so close was even more chilling. Should the horses at any time miss the solid ground – 'then may God have mercy upon you,' we had been warned in the morning.

I rode ahead, with Ibrahim following perhaps ten paces behind. Again and again the terrifying thought: Had we left Khan--i-Khet behind us in the darkness? What an evil prospect, to have to spend the night under the cold rain; but if we proceeded farther – what about the swamps?

All of a sudden a soft, squishy sound from under my horse's hooves; I felt the animal slide in the muck, sink in a little, draw up one leg frantically, slide again – and the thought pierced my mind: the swamp! I jerked the reins hard and dug my heels into the horse's flanks. It tossed its head high and started working its legs furiously. My skin broke out in cold perspiration. The night was so black that I could not even discern my own hands, but in the convulsive heaving of the horse's body I sensed its desperate struggle against the embrace of the swamp. Almost without thinking, I grabbed the riding crop which ordinarily hung unused at my wrist and struck the horse's hindquarters with all my might, hoping thus to incite it to utmost effort – for if it stood still now, it would be sucked, and I with it, deeper and deeper into the mud... Unaccustomed to such ferocious beating, the poor beast – a Kashgai stallion of exceptional speed and power – reared on its hind legs, struck the ground with all fours again, strained gaspingly against the mud, jumped, slipped, heaved itself forward again, and slipped again – and all the time its hooves beat desperately against the soft, oozy mire...

Some mysterious object swept with a swish over my head... I raised my hand and received a hard, incomprehensible blow... what from? Time and thought tumbled over one another and

became confused. . . Through the splashing of the rain and the
panting of the horse I could hear, for seconds that were like
hours, the relentless sucking sound of the swamp. . . The end
must be near. I loosened my feet from the stirrups, ready to
jump from the saddle and try my luck alone – perhaps I could
save myself if I lay flat on the ground – when suddenly – un-
believably – the horse's hooves struck against hard ground, once,
twice . . . and, with a sob of relief, I pulled the reins and brought
the quivering animal to a standstill. We were saved. . .

Only now did I remember my companion and called out, full
of terror, 'Ibrahim!' No answer. My heart went cold.

'Ibrahim. . . !' – but there was only the black night around
me and the falling rain. Had he been unable to save himself?
With a hoarse voice I called out once again, 'Ibrahim!'

And then, almost beyond belief, a shout sounded faintly from
a great distance: 'Here . . . I am here!'

Now it was my reason's turn to stand still: how had we become so widely separated?

'Ibrahim!'

'Here . . . here!' – and following the sound, leading my horse
by the reins and testing every inch of ground with my feet, I
walked very slowly, very carefully toward the distant voice: and
there was Ibrahim, sitting calmly in his saddle.

'What has happened to you, Ibrahim? Didn't you also blun-
der into the swamp?'

'Swamp . . . ? No – I simply stood still when you suddenly, I
don't know why, galloped away.'

Galloped away . . . The riddle was solved. The struggle against
the swamp had been only a fruit of my imagination. My horse
must have simply stepped into a muddy rut and I, thinking that
we were being drawn into the morass, had whipped it into a fren-
zied gallop; cheated by the darkness, I had mistaken the animal's forward movement for a desperate struggle against the
swamp, and had been racing blindly through the night, unaware
of the many gnarled trees that dotted the plain. . . . These trees,
and not the swamp, had been the immediate, real danger: the
small twig that had struck my hand could as well have been a larger branch, which might have broken my skull and thus brought
my journey to a decisive end in an unmarked grave in southern
Iran. . .

I was furious with myself, doubly furious because now we had lost all orientation and could no longer find a trace of the path. Now we would never find the caravanserai...

But once again I was mistaken.

Ibrahim dismounted to feel the terrain with his hands and so perhaps to rediscover the path; and while he was crawling thus on all fours, his head suddenly struck a wall – the dark wall of the caravanserai of Khan-i-Khet!

But for my imaginery blundering into the swamp we would have gone on, missed the caravanserai and truly lost ourselves in the swamps which, as we subsequently learned, began less than two hundred yards ahead...

The caravanserai was one of the many decayed remnants of the epoch of Shah Abbas the Great – mighty blocks of masonry with vaulted passageways, gaping doorways and crumbling fire-places. Here and there you could discern traces of old carving over the lintels and cracked majolica tiles; the few inhabitable rooms were littered with old straw and horse dung. When Ibra-him and I entered the main hall, we found the overseer of the caravanserai seated by an open fire on the bare ground. At his side was a bare-footed man of diminutive size draped in a tat-tered cloak. Both rose to their feet at our appearance, and the lit-tle stranger bowed solemnly with an exquisite, almost theatrical gesture, the right hand placed over the heart. His cloak was covered with innumerable multicoloured patches; he was dirty, entirely unkempt; but his eyes were shining and his face serene.

The overseer left the room to attend to our horses. I threw off my soaked tunic, while Ibrahim immediately set himself to mak-ing tea over the open fire. With the condescension of a great lord who forfeits none of his dignity by being courteous to his in-feriors, the odd little man graciously accepted the cup of tea which Ibrahim held out toward him.

Without any show of undue curiosity, as if opening a drawing-room conversation, he turned to me: 'You are English, *janab-i-ali?*'

'No, I am a *Namsawi*' (Austrian).

'Would it be improper to ask if it is business that brings you to these parts?'

'I am a writer for newspapers,' I replied. 'I am travelling through your country to describe it to the people of my own. They love to know how others live and what they think.'

He nodded with an approving smile and lapsed into silence. After a while he drew a small clay waterpipe and a bamboo rod from the folds of his cloak; he attached the rod to the clay vessel; then he rubbed something that looked like tobacco between his palms and placed it carefully, as if it were more precious than gold, in the bowl of the pipe, covering it with live coals. With a visible effort, he drew in the smoke through the bamboo rod, violently coughing and clearing his throat in the process. The water in the clay pipe bubbled and a biting odour began to fill the room. And then I recognized it: it was Indian hemp, hashish – and now I understood also the man's strange mannerisms: he was a *hashshashi*, an addict. His eyes were not veiled like those of opium smokers; they shone with a kind of detached, impersonal intensity, staring into a distance that was immeasurably removed from the real world around them.

I looked on in silence. When he finished his pipe at last, he asked me:

'Will you not try it?'

I refused with thanks; I had tried opium once or twice (without any particular enjoyment), but this hashish business seemed too strenuous and unappetizing even to try. The *hashshashi* laughed soundlessly; his squinting eyes glided over me with a friendly irony:

'I know what you are thinking, O my respected friend: you are thinking that hashish is the work of the devil and are afraid of it. Nonsense. Hashish is a gift from God. Very good – especially for the mind. Look here, *hazrat*, let me explain it to you. Opium is bad – there can be no doubt about it – for it awakens in man a craving for unattainable things; it makes his dreams greedy, like those of an animal. But hashish silences all greed and makes one indifferent to all things of the world. That's it: it makes one contented. You could place a mound of gold before a *hashshashi* – not just while he is smoking, but at any time – and he would not even stretch out his little finger for it. Opium makes people weak and cowardly, but hashish kills all fear and makes a man brave as a lion. If you were to ask a *hashshashi* to dive into an icy stream in the middle of winter, he would simply dive into it and laugh... For he has learned that to be without greed is to be without fear – and that if man goes beyond fear he goes beyond danger as well, knowing that whatever happens to him is but his share in all that is happening...'

And he laughed again, with that short, shaking, soundless laughter between mockery and benevolence; then he stopped laughing and only grinned behind his cloud of smoke, his shining eyes fixed on an immovable distance.

.   .   .   .

'MY SHARE IN ALL that is happening . . .' I think to myself as I lie under the friendly Arabian stars. 'I – this bundle of flesh and bone, of sensations and perceptions – have been placed within the orbit of Being, and am within all that is happening . . . "Danger" is only an illusion: never can it "overcome" me: for all that happens to me is part of the all-embracing stream of which I myself am a part. Could it be, perhaps, that danger and safety, death and joy, destiny and fulfilment, are but different aspects of this tiny, majestic bundle that is I? What endless freedom, O God, hast Thou granted to man . . .'

I have to close my eyes, so sharp is the pain of happiness at this thought; and wings of freedom brush me silently from afar in the breath of the wind that passes over my face.

— 6 —

I FEEL STRONG ENOUGH to sit up now, and Zayd brings me one of our camel-saddles to lean upon. 'Make thyself comfortable, O my uncle. It gladdens my heart to see thee well after I had mourned thee for dead.'

'Thou hast been a good friend to me, Zayd. What would I have done without thee all these years if thou hadst not followed my call and come to me?'

'I have never regretted these years with thee, O my uncle. I still remember the day when I got thy letter, more than five years ago, calling me to Mecca. . . The thought of seeing thee again was dear to me, especially as in the meantime thou hadst been blessed with the blessing of Islam. But just then I had married a Muntafiq girl, a virgin, and her love pleased me exceedingly. Those Iraqi girls, they have narrow waists and hard breasts, like this' – and, smiling with remembrance, he presses his forefinger against the hard pommel of the saddle on which I am leaning – 'and it is difficult to let their embraces go. . . So I told myself, "I will go, but not just now: let me wait for a few weeks." But the weeks passed, and the months, and although I soon divorced that woman – the daughter of a dog, she had been making eyes at her cousin – I could not make up my mind to forsake my job with the Iraqi *agayl*, and my friends, and the joys of Baghdad and Basra, and always told myself, "Not just now; after a little while. . . " But one day I was riding away from our camp, where I had collected my monthly pay, and was thinking of spending the night in a friend's quarters, when suddenly thou camest to my mind and I remembered what thou hadst told me in thy letter of thy dear *rafiqa's** death – may God have mercy on her – and I thought of how lonely thou must be without her, and all at once I knew I had to go to thee. And there and then I pulled off the Iraqi star from my *igal* and threw it away; then, without even going to my house to collect my clothes, I turned my drome-dary's head toward the Nufud, toward Najd, and started out, stopping only at the next village to buy a waterskin and some provisions, and rode on and on until I met thee at Mecca, four weeks later. . .'

'And dost thou remember, Zayd, our first journey together in-to the interior of Arabia, southward to the palm orchards and wheat fields of Wadi Bisha, and thence into the sands of Ranya which had never before been trodden by a non-Arab?'

'And how well I remember it, O my uncle! Thou wert so keen on seeing the Empty Quarter,† where the jinns make the sands sing under the sun . . . And what about those *badu* living on its rim, who had never yet seen glass in their lives and thought that thy eyeglasses were made of frozen water? They were like jinns themselves, reading tracks in the sand as other people read a book, and reading from the skies and from the air the coming of a sandstorm hours before it came. . . And dost thou recall, O my uncle, that guide we hired at Ranya – that devil of a *badawi* whom thou wantedst to shoot down when he was about to aban-don us in the midst of the desert? How furious he was about the machine with which thou makest pictures!'

We both laugh at that adventure which lies so far behind us. But at the time we did not feel at all like laughing. We were about six or seven days' journey south of Riyadh when that guide, a fanatical beduin from the *Ikhwan* settlement of Ar-Rayn,

---

* 'Companion'—*i.e.*, wife.

† Rub' al-Khali, the vast, uninhabited sand desert which covers about one quarter of the Arabian Peninsular.

fell into a paroxysm of rage when I explained to him what my camera was for. He wanted to leave us there and then because such heathenish picture-making endangered his soul. I would not have minded getting rid of him had it not been that we were just then in a region with which neither Zayd nor I was familiar and where, left to ourselves, we would certainly have lost our way. At first I tried to reason with our 'devil of a beduin', but to no avail; he remained adamant and turned back his camel toward Ranya. I made it clear to him that it would cost him his life to leave us to almost certain death from thirst. When in spite of this warning he set his dromedary in motion, I aimed my rifle at him and threatened to fire – with every intention of doing so: and this, at last, seemed to outweigh our friend's concern about his soul. After some grumbling, he agreed to lead us to the next large settlement, about three days ahead, where we could place our dispute before the *qadi* for decision. Zayd and I disarmed him and took turns standing guard during the night to prevent him from slipping away. The *qadi* at Quwa'iyya, to whom we appealed a few days later, at first gave judgment in favour of our guide, 'for,' he said, 'it is shameful to make pictures of living beings' (basing it on a wrong interpretation of a saying of the Prophet: for despite the belief – so prevalent among many Muslims to this day – that the depicting of living beings is forbidden, Islamic Law contains no injunction to this effect). Thereupon I showed the *qadi* the open letter from the King 'to all *amirs* of the land and everyone who may read this' – and the *qadi's* face grew longer and longer as he read: 'Muhammad Asad is our guest and friend and dear unto us, and everyone who shows him friendliness shows it to us, and everyone who is hostile to him will be deemed hostile to us. . .' Ibn Saud's words and seal had a magic effect on the severe *qadi*, and he ultimately decided that 'under certain circumstances' it might be permissible to make pictures. . . . Nevertheless, we let our guide go and hired another to lead us to Riyadh.

'And dost thou remember those days in Riyadh, O my uncle, when we were guests of the King and thou wert so unhappy to see the old stables of the palace filled with shiny new motorcars. . . . And the King's graciousness toward thee. . .'

'And dost thou remember, Zayd, how he sent us out to explore the secrets behind the beduin rebellion, and how we journeyed through many nights, and stole into Kuwayt, and at last found out the truth about the cases of glittering new *riyals* and rifles that were coming to the rebels from across the sea. . . ?'

'And that other mission, O my uncle, when Sayyid Ahmad, may God lengthen his life, sent thee to Cyrenaica – and how we secretly crossed the sea to Egypt in a *dhow* – and how we made our way into the Jabal Akhdar, eluding the vigilance of those Italians, may God's curse be upon them, and joined the *mujahidin* under Umar al-Mukhtar? Those were exciting days!'

And so we continue to remind each other of the many days, the innumerable days we have been together, and our 'Dost thou remember? Dost thou remember?' carries us far into the night, until the campfire flickers lower and lower, and only a few pieces of wood remain glowing, and Zayd's face gradually recedes into the shadows and itself becomes like a memory to my heavy eyes.

In the starlit silence of the desert, with a tender, lukewarm wind rippling the sands, the images of past and present intertwine, separate again and call to one another with wondrous sounds of evocation, backward through the years, back to the beginning of my Arabian years, to my first pilgrimage to Mecca and the darkness that overshadowed those early days: to the death of the woman whom I loved as I have loved no woman since and who now lies buried under the soil of Mecca, under a simple stone without inscription that marks the end of her road and the beginning of a new one for me: an end and a beginning, a call and an echo, strangely intertwined in the rocky valley of Mecca. . .

.   .   .   .

'ZAYD, IS THERE some coffee left?'

'At thy command, O my uncle,' answers Zayd. He rises without haste, the tall, narrow brass coffeepot in his left hand and two minute, handleless cups clinking in his right – one for me and one for himself – pours a little coffee into the first cup and hands it to me. From under the shadow of the red-and-white-checked *kufiyya* his eyes regard me with solemn intentness, as if this were a much more serious matter than a mere cup of coffee. These eyes – deepset and long-lashed, austere and sad in repose but ever ready to flash in sudden gaiety – speak of a hundred generations of life in steppes and freedom: the eyes of a man whose ancestors have never been exploited and have never exploited others. But the most beautiful in him are his movements: serene, aware of their own rhythm, never hurried and never hesitant: a precision and economy that reminds you of the interplay of instruments in a well-ordered symphony orchestra. You see such movements often among beduins; the sparseness of the desert is reflected in them. For, apart from the few towns and villages, life in Arabia has been so little moulded by human hands that nature in her austerity has forced man to avoid all diffusion in behaviour and to reduce all doing dictated by his will or by outward necessity to a few, very definite, basic forms, which have remained the same for countless generations and have in time acquired the smooth sharpness of crystals: and this inherited simplicity of action is now apparent in the true Arab's gestures as well as in his attitude toward life.

'Tell me, Zayd, where are we going tomorrow?'

Zayd looks at me with a smile: 'Why, O my uncle, toward Tayma, of course. . . ?'

'No, brother, I wanted to go to Tayma, but now I do not want it any more. We are going to Mecca. . .'

II

BEGINNING OF THE ROAD

— 1 —

IT IS NEARLY EVENING, a few days after my encounter with thirst, when Zayd and I arrive at a forlorn little oasis where we intend to stop for the night. Under the rays of the setting sun the sand hills in the east shine like iridescent masses of agate with ever-changing pastel shadows and subdued light reflexes, so delicate in colour that even the eye seems to do violence to them as it follows the barely perceptible flow of shadows toward the greyness of growing dusk. You can still see clearly the feathery crowns of the palms and, half hidden behind them, the lowly, mud-grey houses and garden walls; and the wooden wheels over the well are still singing.

We make the camels lie down at some distance from the village, below the palm orchards, unload our heavy saddlebags and remove the saddles from the animals' hot backs. A few urchins assemble around the strangers and one of them, a big-eyed little boy in a tattered tunic, offers to show Zayd a place where firewood is to be found; and while the two set out on their errand, I take the camels to the well. As I lower my leather bucket and draw it up filled, some women come from the village to fetch water in copper basins and earthenware pitchers, which they carry free on their heads with both arms outstretched sidewise and bent upward – so as to balance their loads better – holding the corners of their veils in uplifted hands like fluttering wings.

'Peace be with thee, O wayfarer,' they say.

And I answer: 'And with you be peace and the grace of God.'

Their garments are black, and their faces – as almost always with beduin and village women in this part of Arabia – uncovered, so that one can see their large black eyes. Although they have been settled in an oasis for many generations, they have not yet lost the earnest mien of their forefathers' nomad days. Their movements are clear and definite, and their reserve free of all shyness as they wordlessly take the bucket rope from my hands

42

and draw water for my camels – just as, four thousand years ago, that woman at the well did to Abraham's servant when he came from Canaan to find for his master's son Isaac a wife from among their kinsfolk in Padan-Aram.

He made his camels kneel down without the city by a well of water at the time of the evening, the time that women go out to draw water.

And he said, 'O Lord God of my master Abraham, I pray Thee, send me good speed this day, and show kindness unto my master Abraham. Behold, I stand here by the well of water; and the daughters of the men of the city come out to draw water. Let it come to pass that the damsel to whom I shall say, "Let down thy pitcher, I pray thee, that I may drink," – and she shall say, "Drink, and I will give thy camels drink also"; let the same be she that Thou hast appointed for Thy servant Isaac; and thereby shall I know that Thou hast showed kindness unto my master.'

And it came to pass, before he had done speaking, that, behold, Rebecca came out . . . with her pitcher upon her shoulder. And the damsel was very fair to look upon, a virgin, neither had any man known her: and she went down to the well, and filled her pitcher, and came up.

And the servant ran to meet her, and said, 'Let me, I pray thee, drink a little water of thy pitcher.' And she said, 'Drink, my lord'; and she hastened, and let down her pitcher upon her hand, and gave him drink. And when she had done giving him drink, she said; 'I will draw water for thy camels also, until they have done drinking.' And she hastened, and emptied her pitcher into the trough, and ran again unto the well to draw water, and drew for all his camels. . .

This Biblical story floats through my mind as I stand with my two camels before the well of a little oasis amidst the sands of the Great Nufud and gaze at the women who have taken the bucket rope from my hands and now draw water for my animals.

Far away is the country of Padan-Aram and Abraham's time: but these women here, with the power of remembrance their stately gestures have evoked, obliterate all distance of space and make four thousand years appear as of no account in time.

'May God bless your hands, my sisters, and keep you secure.'

'And thou, too, remain under God's protection, O wayfarer,' they reply, and turn to their pitchers and basins to fill them with water for their homes.

. . . .

ON MY RETURN to our camping place, I make the camels kneel down and hobble their forelegs to prevent them from straying at night. Zayd has already lit a fire and is busy making coffee. Water boils in a tall brass coffeepot with a long, curved spout; a smaller pot of a similar shape stands ready at Zayd's elbow. In his left hand he holds a huge, flat iron spoon with a handle two feet long, on which he is roasting a handful of coffee beans over the slow fire, for in Arabia coffee is freshly roasted for every pot. As soon as the beans are lightly tanned, he places them in a brass mortar and pounds them. Thereupon he pours some of the boiling water from the larger pot into the smaller, empties the ground coffee into it and places the pot near the fire to let it slowly simmer. When the brew is almost ready, he adds a few cardamon seeds to make it more bitter, for, as the saying goes in Arabia, coffee, in order to be good, must be 'bitter like death and hot like love'.

But I am not yet ready to enjoy my coffee at leisure. Tired and sweaty after the long, hot hours in the saddle, with clothes clinging dirtily to my skin, I am longing for a bath; and so I stroll back to the well under the palms.

It is already dark. The palm orchards are deserted; only far away, where the houses stand, a dog barks. I throw off my clothes and climb down into the well, holding on with hands and feet to the ledges and clefts in the masonry and supporting myself by the ropes on which the waterskins hang: down to the dark water and into it. It is cold and reaches to my chest. In the darkness by my side stand the drawing-ropes, vertically tautened by the weight of the large, now submerged, skins which in daytime are used to water the plantation. Under the soles of my feet I can feel the thin trickle of water seep upward from the underground spring that feeds the well in a slow, unceasing stream of eternal renewal.

Above me the wind hums over the rim of the well and makes its interior resound faintly like the inside of a sea shell held against the ear – a big, humming sea shell such as I loved to listen to in my father's house many, many years ago, a child just big enough to look over the table top. I pressed the shell against my ear and wondered whether the sound was always there or only when I held it to my ear. Was it something independent of me or did only my listening call it forth? Many times did I try to outsmart the shell by holding it away from me, so that the humming ceased, and then suddenly clapping it back to my ear: but there it was again – and I never found out whether it was going on when I did not listen.

I did not know then, of course, that I was being puzzled by a question that had puzzled much wiser heads than mine for countless ages: the question of whether there is such a thing as 'reality' apart from our minds, or whether our perception creates it. I did not know it then; but, looking back, it seems to me that this great riddle haunted me not only in my childhood but also in later years – as it probably has haunted at one time or another, consciously or unconsciously, every thinking human being: for, whatever the objective truth, to every one of us the world manifests itself only in the shape, and to the extent, of its reflection in our minds: and so each of us can perceive of 'reality' only in conjunction with his own existence. Herein perhaps may be found a valid explanation for man's persistent belief, since the earliest stirrings of his consciousness, in individual survival after death – a belief too deep, too widely spread through all races and times to be easily dismissed as 'wishful thinking'. It would probably not be too much to say that it has been unavoidably necessitated by the very structure of the human mind. To think in abstract, theoretical terms of one's own death as ultimate extinction may not be difficult; but to visualize it, impossible: for this would mean no less than to be able to visualize the extinction of all reality as such – in other words, to imagine nothingness: something that no man's mind is able to do.

It was not the philosophers and prophets who taught us to believe in life after death; all they did was to give form and spiritual content to an instinctive perception as old as man himself.

.   .   .   .

I SMILE INWARDLY at the incongruity of speculating about such profound problems while engaged in the mundane process of washing away the grime and sweat of a long day's journey.

But, after all, is there always a clearly discernible borderline between the mundane and the abstruse in life? Could there have
been, for instance, anything more mundane than setting out in
search of a lost camel, and anything more abstruse, more difficult of comprehension, than almost dying of thirst?

Perhaps it was the shock of that experience that has sharpened
my senses and brought forth the need to render some sort of account to myself: the need to comprehend, more fully than I have
ever done before, the course of my own life. But, then, I remind
myself, can anyone really comprehend the meaning of his own
life as long as he is alive? We do know, of course, what has happened to us at this or that period of our lives; and we do sometimes understand why it happened; but our destination – our
destiny – is not so easily espied: for destiny is the sum of all that
has moved in us and moved us, past and present, and all that
will move us and within us in the future -- and so it can unfold itself only at the end of the way, and must always remain mis-
understood or only half understood as long as we are treading
the way.

How can I say, at the age of thirty-two, what my destiny was
or is?

Sometimes it seems to me that I can almost see the lives of two
men when I look back at my life. But, come to think of it, are
those two parts of my life really so different from one another –
or was there perhaps, beneath all the outward differences of
form and direction, always a unity of feeling and a purpose common to both?

I lift my head and see the round piece of sky over the rim of
the well, and stars. As I stand very still, for a very long time, I
seem to see how they slowly shift their positions, moving on and
on, so that they might complete the rows upon rows of millions
of years which never come to a close. And then, without willing
it, I have to think of the little rows of years that have happened
to me – all those dim years spent in the warm safety of childhood's rooms in a town where every nook and street was familiar to me; thereafter in other cities full of excitements and yearn-
ings and hopes such as only early youth can know; then in a new
world among people whose mien and bearing were outlandish at
first but in time brought forth a new familiarity and a new feeling
of being at home; then in stranger and ever stranger landscapes,

in cities as old as the mind of man, in steppes without horizon, in mountains whose wildness reminded you of the wildness of the human heart, and in hot desert solitudes; and the slow growth of new truths – truths new to me – and that day in the snows of the Hindu-Kush when, after a long conversation, an Afghan friend exclaimed in astonishment: 'But you are a Muslim, only you do not know it yourself . . .!' And that other day, months later, when I did come to know it myself; and my first pilgrimage to Mecca; the death of my wife, and the despair that followed it; and these timeless times among the Arabs ever since: years of deep friendship with a royal man who with his sword had carved for himself a state out of nothingness and stopped only one step short of real greatness; years of wandering through deserts and steppes; risky excursions amidst Arabian beduin warfare and into the Libyan fight for independence; long sojourns in Medina where I endeavoured to round off my knowledge of Islam in the Prophet's Mosque; repeated pilgrimages to Mecca; marriages with beduin girls, and subsequent divorces; warm human relationships, and desolate days of loneliness; sophisticated discourses with cultured Muslims from all parts of the world, and journeys through unexplored regions: all these years of submergence in a world far removed from the thoughts and aims of Western existence.

What a long row of years . . .

All these sunken years now come up to the surface, uncover their faces once again and call me with many voices: and suddenly, in the startled jerk of my heart, I perceive how long, how endless my way has been. 'You have always been only going and going,' I say to myself. 'You have never yet built your life into something that one could grasp with his hands, and never has there been an answer to the question "Whereto?" . . . You have been going on and on, a wanderer through many lands, a guest at many hearths, but the longing has never been stilled, and although you are a stranger no more, you have struck no root.'

Why is it that, even after finding my place among the people who believe in the things I myself have come to believe, I have struck no root?

Two years ago, when I took an Arab wife in Medina, I wanted her to give me a son. Through this son, Talal, who was born to us a few months ago, I have begun to feel that the Arabs are my kin as well as my brethren in faith. I want him to have his roots deep in this land and to grow up in the consciousness of his great heritage of blood as well as culture. This, one might think, should be enough to make a man desirous of settling down for good, of building for himself and his family a lasting home. Why is it, then, that my wanderings are not yet over and that I have still to continue on my way? Why is it that the life which I myself have chosen does not fully satisfy me? What is it that I find lacking in this environment? Certainly not the intellectual interests of Europe. I have left them behind me. I do not miss them. Indeed, I am so remote from them that it has become increasingly difficult for me to write for the European newspapers which provide me with my livelihood; every time I send off an article, it seems as if I were throwing a stone into a bottomless well: the stone disappears into the dark void and not even an echo comes up to tell me that is has reached its goal . . .

While I thus cogitate in disquiet and perplexity, half submerged in the dark waters of a well in an Arabian oasis, I suddenly hear a voice from the background of my memory, the voice of an old Kurdish nomad: *If water stands motionless in a pool it grows stale and muddy, but when it moves and flows it becomes clear: so, too, man in his wanderings.* Whereupon, as if by magic, all disquiet leaves me. I begin to look upon myself with distant eyes, as you might look at the pages of a book to read a story from them; and I begin to understand that my life could not have taken a different course. For when I ask myself, 'What is the sum total of my life?' something in me seems to answer, 'You have set out to exchange one world for another – to gain a new world for yourself in exchange for an old one which you never really possessed.' And I know with startling clarity that such an undertaking might indeed take an entire lifetime.

.   .   .   .

I CLIMB OUT of the well, put on the clean, long tunic which I brought with me, and go back to the fire and to Zayd and the camels; I drink the bitter coffee which Zayd offers me and then lie down, refreshed and warm, near the fire on the ground.

— 2 —

MY ARMS ARE CROSSED under my neck and I am looking into this Arabian night which curves over me, black and starry. A shooting star flies in a tremendous arc, and there another, and yet another: arcs of light piercing the darkness. Are they only bits of broken-up planets, fragments of some cosmic disaster, now aimlessly flying through the vastness of the universe? Oh, no: if you ask Zayd, he will tell you that these are the fiery javelins with which angels drive away the devils that on certain nights stealthily ascend toward heaven to spy upon God's secrets ... Was it perhaps Iblis himself, the king of all devils, who has just received that mighty throw of flame there in the east ... ?

The legends connected with this sky and its stars are more familiar to me than the home of my childhood ...

How could it be otherwise? Ever since I came to Arabia I have lived like an Arab, worn only Arab dress, spoken only Arabic, dreamed my dreams in Arabic; Arabian customs and imageries have almost imperceptibly shaped my thoughts; I have not been hampered by the many mental reservations which usually make it impossible for a foreigner – be he ever so well versed in the manners and the language of the country – to find a true approach to the feelings of its people and to make their world his own.

And suddenly I have to laugh aloud with the laughter of happiness and freedom – so loud that Zayd looks up in astonishment and my dromedary turns its head toward me with a slow, faintly supercilious movement: for now I see how simple and straight, in spite of all its length, my road has been – my road from a world which I did not possess to a world truly my own.

My coming to this land: was it not, in truth, a home-coming? Home-coming of the heart that has espied its old home backward over a curve of thousands of years and now recognizes this sky, my sky, with painful rejoicing? For this Arabian sky – so much darker, higher, more festive with its stars than any other sky – vaulted over the long trek of my ancestors, those wandering herdsmen-warriors, when, thousands of years ago, they set out in the power of their morning, obsessed by greed for land and booty, toward the fertile country of Chaldea and an unknown future: that small beduin tribe of Hebrews, forefathers of that man who was to be born in Ur of the Chaldees.

That man, Abraham, did not really belong in Ur. His was but one among many Arabian tribes which at one time or another had wound their way from the hungry deserts of the Peninsula

toward the northern dreamlands that were said to be flowing
with milk and honey – the settled lands of the Fertile Crescent,
Syria and Mesopotamia. Sometimes such tribes succeeded in
overcoming the settlers they found there and established themselves as rulers in their place, gradually intermingling with the
vanquished people and evolving, together with them, into a new
nation – like the Assyrians and Babylonians, who erected their
kingdoms on the ruins of the earlier Sumerian civilization, or
the Chaldeans, who grew to power in Babylon, or the Amorites,
who later came to be known as Canaanites in Palestine and as
Phoenicians on the coasts of Syria. At other times the oncoming
nomads were too weak to vanquish those who had arrived earlier and were absorbed by them; or, alternatively, the settlers
pushed the nomads back into the desert, forcing them to find
other pastures and perhaps other lands to conquer. The clan of
Abraham – whose original name, according to the Book of
Genesis, was *Ab-Ram*, which in ancient Arabic means 'He of the
High Desire' – was evidently one of those weaker tribes; the
Biblical story of their sojourn at Ur on the fringe of the desert
relates to the time when they found that they could not win for
themselves new homes in the land of the Twin Rivers and were
about to move northwest along the Euphrates toward Haran and
thence to Syria.

'He of the High Desire,' that early ancestor of mine whom
God had driven toward unknown spaces and so to a discovery
of his own self, would have well understood why I am here – for
he also had to wander through many lands before he could build
his life into something that you might grasp with your hands,
and had to be guest at many strange hearths before he was allowed to strike root. To his awe-commanding experience my puny
perplexity would have been no riddle. He would have known – as
I know it now – that the meaning of all my wanderings lay in a
hidden desire to meet myself by meeting a world whose approach
to the innermost questions of life, to reality itself, was different
from all I had been accustomed to in my childhood and youth.

— 3 —

WHAT A LONG WAY, from my childhood and youth in Central Europe to my present in Arabia; but what a pleasant way
for rememberance to travel backward . . .

Amir (now King) Faysal, 1927

There were those early childhood years in the Polish city of
Lwów – then in Austrian possession – in a house that was as
quiet and dignified as the street on which it stood: a long street
of somewhat dusty elegance, bordered with chestnut trees and
paved with wood blocks that muffled the beat of the horses'
hooves and converted every hour of the day into a lazy afternoon. I loved that lovely street with a consciousness far beyond
my childish years, and not merely because it was the street of my
home: I loved it, I think, because of the air of noble self-possession
with which it flowed from the gay centre of that gayest of cities
toward the stillness of the woods on the city's margin and the
great cemetery that lay hidden in those woods. Beautiful carriages would sometimes fly past on silent wheels to the accompaniment of the brisk, rhythmic *trap-trap* of prancing hooves,
or, if it happened to be winter and the street was blanketed with
foot-deep snow, sledges would glide over it and steam would
come in clouds from the horses' nostrils and their bells would
tinkle through the frosty air: and if you yourself sat in the sledge
and felt the frost rush by and bite your cheeks, your childish
heart knew that the galloping horses were carrying you into a
happiness that had neither beginning nor end.

And there were the summer months in the country, where my
mother's father, a wealthy banker, maintained a large estate for
his large family's pleasure. A sluggish little stream with willow
trees along its banks; barns full of placid cows, a chiaroscuro
mysteriously pregnant with the scent of animals and hay and the
laughter of the Ruthenian peasant girls who were busy in the
evenings with milking; you would drink the foaming warm milk
straight from the pails – not because you were thirsty, but because it was exciting to drink something that was still so close to
its animal source . . . Those hot August days spent in the fields
with the farmhands who were cutting the wheat, and with the
women who gathered and bound it in sheaves: young women,
good to look at – heavy of body, full of breast, with hard, warm
arms, the strength of which you could feel when they rolled you
over playfully at noontime among the wheat stacks: but, of
course, you were much too young then to draw further conclusions from those laughing embraces . . .

And there were journeys with my parents to Vienna and Berlin and the Alps and the Bohemian forests and the North Sea

and the Baltic: places so distant that they almost seemed to be new worlds. Every time one set out on such a journey, the first whistle of the train engine and the first jolt of the wheels made one's heart stop beating in anticipation of the wonders that were now to unfold themselves ... And there were playmates, boys and girls, a brother and a sister and many cousins; and glorious Sundays of freedom after the dullness – but not too oppressive a dullness – of weekdays in school: hikes through the countryside, and the first surreptitious meetings with lovely girls of one's own age, and the blush of a strange excitement from which one recovered only after hours and hours ...

It was a happy childhood, satisfying even in retrospect. My parents lived in comfortable circumstances; and they lived mostly for their children. My mother's placidity and unruffled quiet may have had something to do with the ease with which in later years I was able to adapt myself to unfamiliar and, on occasion, most adverse conditions; while my father's inner restlessness is probably mirrored in my own.

·   ·   ·   ·   ·   ·   ·   ·

IF I HAD to describe my father, I would say that this lovely, slim, middle-sized man of dark complexion and dark, passionate eyes was not quite in tune with his surroundings. In his early youth he had dreamed of devoting himself to science, especially physics, but had never been able to realize this dream and had to content himself with being a barrister. Although quite successful in this profession, in which his keen mind must have found a welcome challenge, he never reconciled himself to it fully; and the air of loneliness that surrounded him may have been caused by an ever-present awareness that his true calling had eluded him.

His father had been an orthodox rabbi in Czernowitz, capital of the then Austrian province of Bukovina. I still remember him as a graceful old man with very delicate hands and a sensitive face framed in a long, white beard. Side by side with his deep interest in mathematics and astronomy – which he studied in his spare time throughout his life – he was one of the best chess players of the district. This was probably the basis of his longstanding friendship with the Greek-Orthodox archbishop, himself a chess player of note. The two would spend many an evening together over the chessboard and would round off their sessions by discussing the metaphysical propositions of their respective religions. One might have presumed that, with such a bent of mind, my grandfather would have welcomed his son's – my father's – inclination toward science. But apparently he had made up his mind from the very first that his eldest son would continue the rabbinical tradition which went back in the family for several generations, and refused even to consider any other career for my father. In this resolve he may have been strengthened by a disreputable skeleton in the family cupboard: the memory of an uncle of his – that is, a great-great-uncle of mine – who had in the most unusual way 'betrayed' the family tradition and even turned away from the religion of his forefathers.

That almost mythical great-great-uncle, whose name was never mentioned aloud, seems to have been brought up in the same strict family tradition. At a very young age he had become a full-fledged rabbi and been married off to a woman whom he apparently did not love. As the rabbinical profession did not bring sufficient remuneration in those days, he supplemented his income by trading in furs, which every year necessitated a journey to Europe's central fur market, Leipzig. One day, when he was about twenty-five years old, he set out by horse cart – it was in the first half of the nineteenth century – on one of these long journeys. In Leipzig he sold his furs as usual; but instead of returning to his home town as usual, he sold the cart and the horse as well, shaved off his beard and sidelocks and, forgetting his unloved wife, went to England. For a time he earned his living by menial work, studying astronomy and mathematics in the evening. Some patron seems to have recognized his mental gifts and enabled him to pursue his studies at Oxford, from where he emerged after a few years as a promising scholar and a convert to Christianity. Shortly after sending a letter of divorce to his Jewish wife, he married a girl from among the 'gentiles'. Not much was known to our family about his later life, except that he achieved considerable distinction as an astronomer and university teacher and ended his days as a knight.

This horrifying example seems to have persuaded my grandfather to take a very stern attitude regarding my father's inclination toward the study of 'gentile' sciences; he had to become a rabbi, and that was that. My father, however, was not prepared to give in so easily. While he studied the Talmud in daytime, he spent part of his nights in studying secretly, without the help of a teacher, the curriculum of a humanistic *gymnasium*. In time he confided in his mother. Although her son's surreptitious studies may have burdened her conscience, her generous nature made her realize that it would be cruel to deprive him of a chance to follow his heart's desire. At the age of twenty-two, after completing the eight years' course of a *gymnasium* within four years, my father presented himself for the baccalaureate examination and passed it with distinction. With the diploma in hand, he and his mother now dared to break the terrible news to my grandfather. I can imagine the dramatic scene that ensued; but the upshot of it was that my grandfather ultimately relented and agreed that my father should give up his rabbinical studies and attend the university instead. The financial circumstances of the family did not, however, allow him to go in for his beloved study of physics; he had to turn to a more lucrative profession – that of law – and in time became a barrister. Some years later he settled in the city of Lwów in eastern Galicia and married my mother, one of the four daughters of a rich local banker. There, in the summer of 1900, I was born as the second of three children.

My father's frustrated desire expressed itself in his wide reading on scientific subjects and perhaps also in his peculiar, though extremely reserved, predilection for his second son – myself – who also seemed to be more interested in things not immediately connected with the making of money and a successful 'career'. Nevertheless, his hopes to make a scientist of me were destined to remain unfulfilled. Although not stupid, I was a very indifferent student. Mathematics and natural sciences were particularly boring to me; I found infinitely more pleasure in reading the stirring historical romances of Sienkiewicz, the fantasies of Jules Verne, Red Indian stories by James Fenimore Cooper and Karl May and, later, the verses of Rilke and the sonorous cadences of *Also sprach Zarathustra*. The mysteries of gravity and electricity, no less than Latin and Greek grammar, left me entirely cold – with the result that I always got my promotions only by the skin of my teeth. This must have been a keen disappointment to my father, but he may have found some consolation in the fact that my teachers seemed to be very satisfied with my inclination toward literature – both Polish and German – as well as history.

In accordance with our family's tradition, I received, through private tutors at home, a thorough grounding in Hebrew religious lore. This was not due to any pronounced religiosity in my parents. They belonged to a generation which, while paying lip service to one or another of the religious faiths that had shaped the lives of its ancestors, never made the slightest endeavour to conform its practical life or even its ethical thought to those teachings. In such a society the very concept of religion had been degraded to one of two things: the wooden ritual of those who clung by habit – and only by habit – to their religious heritage, or the cynical insouciance of the more 'liberal' ones, who considered religion as an outmoded superstition to which one might, on occasion, outwardly conform but of which one was secretly ashamed, as of something intellectually indefensible. To all appearances, my own parents belonged to the former category; but at times I have a faint suspicion that my father, at least, inclined toward the latter. Nevertheless, in deference to both his father and his father-in-law, he insisted on my spending long hours over the sacred scriptures. Thus, by the age of thirteen, I not only could read Hebrew with great fluency but also spoke it freely and had, in addition, a fair acquaintance with Aramaic (which may possibly account for the ease with which I picked up Arabic in later years). I studied the Old Testament in the original; the *Mishna* and *Gemara* – that is, the text and the commentaries of the Talmud – became familiar to me; I could discuss with a good deal of self-assurance the differences between the Babylonian and Jerusalem Talmuds; and I immersed myself in the intricacies of Biblical exegesis, called *Targum*, just as if I had been destined for a rabbinical career.

In spite of all this budding religious wisdom, or maybe because of it, I soon developed a supercilious feeling toward many of the premises of the Jewish faith. To be sure, I did not disagree with the teaching of moral righteousness so strongly emphasized throughout the Jewish scriptures, nor with the sublime God-consciousness of the Hebrew Prophets – but it seemed to me that the God of the Old Testament and the Talmud was unduly concerned with the ritual by means of which His worshippers were supposed to worship Him. It also occurred to me that this God was strangely preoccupied with the destinies of one particular nation, the Hebrews. The very build-up of the Old Testament as a history of the descendants of Abraham tended to make God appear not as the creator and sustainer of all mankind but, rather, as a tribal deity adjusting all creation to the requirements of a 'chosen people': rewarding them with conquests if they were righteous, and making them suffer at the hands of nonbelievers whenever they strayed from the prescribed path. Viewed against these fundamental shortcomings, even the ethical fervour of the later Prophets, like Isaiah and Jeremiah, seemed to be barren of a universal message.

But although the effect of those early studies of mine was the opposite of what had been intended – leading me away from, rather than closer to, the religion of my forefathers – I often think that in later years they helped me to understand the fundamental purpose of religion as such, whatever its form. At that time, however, my disappointment with Judaism did not lead me to a search for spiritual truths in other directions. Under the influence of an agnostic environment, I drifted, like so many boys of my age, into a matter-of-fact rejection of all institutional religion; and since my religion had never meant much more to me than a series of restrictive regulations, I felt none the worse for having drifted away from it. Theological and philosophical ideas did not yet really concern me; what I was looking forward to was not much different from the expectations of most other boys: action, adventure, excitement.

Toward the end of 1914, when the Great War was already raging, the first big chance to fulfil my boyish dreams seemed to come within grasp. At the age of fourteen I made my escape from school and joined the Austrian army under a false name. I was very tall for my years and easily passed for eighteen, the minimum age for recruitment. But apparently I did not carry a marshal's baton in my knapsack. After a week or so, my poor father succeeded in tracing me with the help of the police, and I was ignominiously escorted back to Vienna, where my family had settled some time earlier. Nearly four years later I was actually, and legitimately, drafted into the Austrian army; but by then I had ceased to dream of military glory and was searching for other avenues to self-fulfillment. In any case, a few weeks after my induction the revolution broke out, the Austrian Empire collapsed, and the war was over.

. . . .

FOR ABOUT TWO YEARS after the end of the Great War I studied, in a somewhat desultory fashion, history of art and philosophy at the University of Vienna. My heart was not in those studies. A quiet academic career did not attract me. I felt a yearning to come into more intimate grips with life, to enter it without any of those carefully contrived, artificial defences which security-minded people love to build up around themselves; and I wanted to find by myself an approach to the spiritual order of things which, I knew, must exist but which I could not yet discern.

It is not easy to explain in so many words what I meant in those days by a 'spiritual order'; it certainly did not occur to me to conceive of the problem in conventional religious terms or, for that matter, in any precise terms whatsoever. My vagueness, to be fair to myself, was not of my own making. It was the vagueness of an entire generation.

The opening decades of the twentieth century stood in the sign of a spiritual vacuum. All the ethical valuations to which Europe have been accustomed for so many centuries had become amorphous under the terrible impact of what had happened between 1914 and 1918, and no new set of values was yet anywhere in sight. A feeling of brittleness and insecurity was in the air – a presentiment of social and intellectual upheavals that made one doubt whether there could ever again be any permanency in man's thoughts and endeavours. Everything seemed to be flowing in a formless flood, and the spiritual restlessness of youth could nowhere find a foothold. In the absence of any reliable standards of morality, nobody could give us young people satisfactory answers to the many questions that perplexed us. Science said, 'Cognition is everything' – and forgot that cognition without an ethical goal can lead only to chaos. The social reformers, the revolutionaries, the communists – all of whom undoubtedly wanted to build a better, happier world – were thinking only in terms of outward, social and economic, circumstances; and to bridge that defect, they had raised their 'materialistic conception of history' to a kind of new, anti-metaphysical metaphysics. The traditionally religious people, on the other hand, knew nothing better than to attribute to their God qualities derived from their own habits of thought, which had long since become rigid and meaningless: and when we young people saw that these alleged divine qualities often stood in sharp contrast with what was happening in the world around us, we told ourselves: 'The moving forces of destiny are evidently different from the qualities which are ascribed to God; therefore – there is no God.' And it occurred to only very few of us that the cause of all this confusion might lie perhaps in the arbitrariness of the self-righteous guardians of faith who claimed to have the right to 'define' God and, by clothing Him with their own garments, separated Him from man and his destiny.

In the individual, this ethical lability could lead either to complete moral chaos and cynicism or, alternatively, to a search for a creative, personal approach to what might constitute the good life.

This instinctive realization may have been, indirectly, the reason for my choice of history of art as my main subject at the university. It was the true function of art, I suspected, to evoke a vision of the coherent, unifying pattern that must underlie the fragmentary picture of happenings which our consciousness reveals to us and which, it seemed to me, could be only inadequately formulated through conceptual thought. However, the courses which I attended did not satisfy me. My professors – some of them, like Strzygowski and Dvorak, outstanding in their particular fields of study – appeared to be more concerned with discovering the aesthetic laws that govern artistic creation than with baring its innermost spiritual impulses: in other words, their approach to art was, to my mind, too narrowly confined to the question of the *forms* in which it expressed itself.

The conclusions of psychoanalysis, to which I was introduced in those days of youthful perplexity, left me equally, if for somewhat different reasons, unsatisfied. No doubt, psychoanalysis was at that time an intellectual revolution of the first magnitude, and one felt in one's bones that this flinging-open of new, hitherto barred doors of cognition was bound to affect deeply – and perhaps change entirely – man's thinking about himself and his society. The discovery of the role which unconscious urges play in the formation of the human personality opened, beyond any question, avenues to a more penetrating self-understanding than had been offered to us by the psychological theories of earlier times. All this I was ready to concede. Indeed, the stimulus of Freudian ideas was as intoxicating to my young mind as potent wine, and many were the evenings I spent in Vienna's cafés listening to exciting discussions between some of the early pioneers of psychoanalysis, such as Alfred Adler, Hermann Steckl and Otto Gross. But while I certainly did not dispute the validity of its analytical principles, I was disturbed by the intellectual arrogance of the new science, which tried to reduce all mysteries of man's Self to a series of neurogenetic reactions. The philosophical 'conclusions' arrived at by its founder and its devotees somehow appeared to me too pat, too cocksure and over-simplified to come anywhere within the neighbourhood of ultimate truths; and they certainly did not point any new way to the good life.

But although such problems often occupied my mind, they did not really trouble me. I was never given much to metaphysical speculation or to a conscious quest for abstract 'truths'. My interests lay more in the direction of things seen and felt: people, activities and relationships. And it was just then that I was beginning to discover relationships with women.

In the general process of dissolution of established social mores that followed the Great War, many restraints between the sexes had been loosened. What happened was, I think, not so much a revolt against the strait-lacedness of the nineteenth century as, rather, a passive rebound from a state of affairs in which certain moral standards had been deemed eternal and unquestionable to a social condition in which everything was questionable: a swinging of the pendulum from yesterday's comforting belief in the continuity of man's upward progress to the bitter disillusionment of Spengler, to Nietzsche's moral relativism, and to the spiritual nihilism fostered by psychoanalysis. Looking backward on those early postwar years, I feel that the young men and women who spoke and wrote with so much enthusiasm about 'the body's freedom' were very far indeed from the ebullient spirit of Pan they so often invoked: their raptures were too self-conscious to be exuberant, and too easy-going to be revolutionary. Their sexual relations had, as a rule, something casual about them – a certain matter-of-fact blandness which often led to promiscuity.

Even if I had felt myself bound by the remnants of conventional morality, it would have been extremely difficult to avoid being drawn into a trend that had become so widespread; as it was, I rather gloried, like so many others of my generation, in what was considered a 'rebellion against the hollow conventions.' Flirtations grew easily into affairs, and some of the affairs into passions. I do not think, however, that I was a libertine; for in all those youthful loves of mine, however flimsy and short-lived, there was always the lilt of a hope, vague but insistent, that the frightful isolation which so obviously separated man from man might be broken by the coalescence of one man and one woman.

.　　　.　　　.　　　.　　　　.　　　.　　　.　　　.

MY RESTLESSNESS GREW and made it increasingly difficult for me to pursue my university studies. At last I decided to give them up for good and to try my hand at journalism. My father, with probably more justification than I was then willing to concede, strongly objected to such a course, maintaining that before I decided to make writing my career I should at least prove to myself that I could write; 'and, in any case,' he concluded after one of our stormy discussions, 'a Ph.D. degree has never yet prevented a man from becoming a successful writer.' His reasoning was sound; but I was very young, very hopeful and very restless. When I realized that he would not change his mind, there seemed nothing left but to start life on my own. Without telling anyone of my intentions, I said good-bye to Vienna one summer day in 1920 and boarded a train for Prague.

All I possessed, apart from my personal belongings, was a diamond ring which my mother, who had died a year earlier, had left me. This I sold through the good offices of a waiter in Prague's main literary café. Most probably I was thoroughly gypped in the transaction, but the sum of money which I received appeared like a fortune. With this fortune in my pocket I proceeded to Berlin, where some Viennese friends introduced me to the magic circle of littérateurs and artists at the old Café des Westens.

I knew that henceforth I would have to make my way unaided; I would never again expect or accept financial help from my family. Some weeks later, when my father's anger had abated he wrote to me: 'I can already see you ending one day as a tramp in a roadside ditch'; to which I replied: 'No roadside ditch for me – I will come out on top.' How I would come out on top was not in the least clear to me; but I knew that I wanted to write and was, of course, convinced that the world of letters was waiting for me with arms wide open.

After a few months my cash ran out and I began to cast about for a job. To a young man with journalistic aspirations, one of the great dailies was the obvious choice; but I found out that I was no 'choice' to them. I did not find it out all at once. It took me weeks of tiresome tramping over the pavements of Berlin – for even a subway or streetcar fare had by then become a problem – and an endless number of humiliating interviews with editors-in-chief and news editors and sub-editors, to realize that, barring a miracle, a fledgling without a single printed line to his credit had not the slightest chance of being admitted to the sacred precincts of a newspaper. No miracle came my way. Instead, I became acquainted with hunger and spent several weeks subsisting almost entirely on the tea and the two rolls which my landlady served me in the morning. My literary friends at the Café des Westens could not do much for a raw and inexperienced 'would-be'; moreover, most of them lived in circumstances not much different from my own, hovering from day to day on the brink of nothingness and struggling hard to keep their chins above water. Sometimes, in the flush of affluence produced by a luckily placed article or a picture sold, one or another of them would throw a party with beer and frankfurters and would ask me to partake of the sudden bounty; or a rich snob would invite a group of us strange intellectual gypsies to supper in his flat, and would gaze at us with awe while we gorged our empty stomachs with caviar canapés and champagne, repaying our host's munificence with clever talk and an 'insight into bohemian life.' But such treats were only exceptions. The rule of my days was stark hunger – and in the nights my sleep was filled with dreams of steaks and sausages and thick slices of buttered bread. Several times I was tempted to write to my father and beg him for help, which he surely would not have refused; but every time my pride stepped in and I wrote to him instead of the wonderful job and the good salary I had . . .

At last a lucky break came. I was introduced to F. W. Murnau, who just then was rising to fame as a film director (this was a few years before Hollywood drew him to still greater fame and to an untimely, tragic death); and Murnau, with that whimsical impulsiveness which endeared him to all his friends, at once took a fancy to the young man who was looking so eagerly, and with so much hope in the face of adversity, toward the future. He asked me if I would not like to work under him on a new film he was about to begin: and although the job was to be only temporary, I saw the gates of heaven opening before me as I stammered, 'Yes, I would . . . '

For two glorious months, free of all financial worries and entirely absorbed by a host of glittering experiences unlike anything I had ever known, I worked as Murnau's assistant. My self-confidence grew tremendously; and it was certainly not diminished by the fact that the leading lady of the film – a well-known and very beautiful actress – did not prove averse to a flirtation with the director's young assistant. When the film was finished and Murnau had to go abroad for a new assignment, I took leave of him with the conviction that my worst days were over.

Shortly afterward, my good friend Anton Kuh – a Viennese journalist who had recently come to prominence in Berlin as a theatre critic – invited me to collaborate with him on a film scenario which he had been commissioned to write. I accepted the idea with enthusiasm and put, I believe, much work into the script; at any rate, the producer who had commissioned it gladly paid the sum agreed upon, which Anton and I divided fifty-fifty. In order to celebrate our 'entry into the world of films,' we gave a party in one of the most fashionable restaurants in Berlin; and when we received the bill, we found that practically our entire earnings had gone up in lobster, caviar and French wines. But our luck held out. We immediately sat down to writing another scenario – a fantasy woven around the figure of Balzac and a bizarre, entirely imaginary experience of his – and found a buyer on the very day it was completed. This time, however, I refused to 'celebrate' our success, and went instead on a several weeks' holiday to the Bavarian lakes.

After another year full of adventurous ups and downs in various cities of Central Europe, involving all manner of short-lived jobs, I succeeded at last in breaking into the world of journalism.

.   .   .   .

THIS BREAK-THROUGH took place in the autumn of 1921, after another period of financial low. One afternoon, while I was sitting in the Café des Westens, tired and disconsolate, a friend of mine sat down at my table. When I recounted my troubles to him, he suggested:

'There might be a chance for you. Dammert is starting a news agency of his own in co-operation with the United Press of America. It will be called the United Telegraph. I am sure that he will need a large number of sub-editors. I'll introduce you to him, if you like.'

Dr. Dammert was a well-known figure in the political circles of Berlin in the twenties. Prominent in the ranks of the Catholic Centre Party, and a wealthy man in his own right, he enjoyed an excellent reputation; and the idea of working under him appealed to me.

Next day my friend took me to Dr. Dammert's office. The elegant, middle-aged man was suave and friendly as he invited us to be seated.

'Mr. Fingal' (that was my friend's name) 'has spoken to me about you. Have you ever worked before as a journalist?'

'No, sir,' I replied, 'but I have had plenty of other experience. I am something of an expert on Eastern European countries and know several of the languages.' (In fact, the only Eastern European language I could speak was Polish, and I had only the vaguest idea of what was going on in that part of the world; but I was resolved not to let my chance be spoiled by undue modesty.)

'Oh, that is interesting,' remarked Dr. Dammert with a half-smile. 'I have a penchant for experts. But, unfortunately, I can't use an expert on Eastern European affairs just now.'

He must have seen the disappointment in my face, for he quickly continued: 'Still, I may have an opening for you – although it may be somewhat beneath your standing, I wonder . . .'

'What is the opening, sir?' I enquired eagerly, thinking of my unpaid rent.

'Well . . . I need several more telephonists. . . Oh, no, no, don't worry, not at a switchboard: I mean telephonists to transmit news to the provincial newspapers . . .'

This was indeed a comedown from my high expectations. I looked at Dr. Dammert and he looked at me; and when I saw the tightening of the humorous creases around his eyes, I knew that my boastful game was up.

'I accept, sir,' I answered with a sigh and a laugh.

The following week I started my new job. It was a boring job and a far cry from the journalistic 'career' I had been dreaming of. I had nothing to do but transmit by telephone, several times daily, news from a mimeographed sheet to the many provincial newspapers that subscribed to the service; but I was a good telephonist and the pay was good, too.

This went on for about a month. At the end of the month an unforeseen opportunity offered itself to me.

In that year of 1921 Soviet Russia was stricken by a famine of unprecedented dimensions. Millions of people were starving and hundreds of thousands dying. The entire European press was buzzing with gruesome descriptions of the situation; several foreign relief operations were being planned, among them one by Herbert Hoover, who had done so much for Central Europe after the Great War. A large-scale action within Russia was headed by Maxim Gorky; his dramatic appeals for aid were stirring the entire world; and it was rumoured that his wife would shortly visit the capitals of Central and Western Europe in an attempt to mobilize public opinion for more effective help.

Being only a telephonist, I did not participate directly in the coverage of this sensational episode until a chance remark from one of my chance acquaintances (I had many of them in the strangest places) suddenly drew me into its midst. The acquaintance was the night doorman at the Hotel Esplanade, one of Berlin's swankiest, and the remark had been: 'This Madame Gorky is a very pleasant lady; one would never guess that she is a Bolshie . . .'

'Madame Gorky? Where the hell did you see *her*?'

My informant lowered his voice to a whisper: 'She is staying at our hotel. Came yesterday, but is registered under an assumed name. Only the manager knows who she really is. She doesn't want to be pestered by reporters.'

'And how do *you* know it?'

'We doormen know everything that goes on in the hotel,' he replied with a grin. 'Do you think we could keep our jobs for long if we didn't?'

What a story it would make to get an exclusive interview with Madame Gorky – the more so as not a word of her presence in

Berlin had so far penetrated to the press. . . I was all at once on fire.

'Could you,' I asked my friend, 'somehow make it possible for me to see her?'

'Well, I don't know. She is obviously dead-set on keeping herself to herself. . . But I could do one thing: if you sit in the lobby in the evening, I might be able to point her out to you.'

That was a deal. I rushed back to my office at the United Telegraph; almost everyone had gone home by that time, but fortunately the news editor was still at his desk. I buttonholed him.

'Will you give me a press card if I promise to bring back a sensational story?'

'What kind of story?' he enquired suspiciously.

'You give me the press card and I'll give you the story. If I don't, you can always have the card back.'

Finally the old news-hound agreed, and I emerged from the office the proud possessor of a card which designated me as a representative of the United Telegraph.

The next few hours were spent in the lobby of the Esplanade. At nine o'clock my friend arrived on duty. From the doorway he winked at me, disappeared behind the reception desk and reappeared a few minutes later with the information that Madame Gorky was out.

'If you sit here long enough, you're sure to see her when she returns.'

At about eleven o'clock I caught my friend's signal. He was pointing surreptitiously to a lady who had just entered the revolving door: a small, delicate woman in her middle forties, dressed in an extremely well-cut black gown, with a long black silk cape trailing on the ground behind her. She was so genuinely aristocratic in her bearing that it was indeed difficult to imagine her as the wife of the 'working-man's poet,' and still more difficult as a citizen of the Soviet Union. Blocking her way, I bowed and proceeded to address her in my most engaging tones: 'Madame Gorky . . .?'

For an instant she appeared startled, but then a soft smile lighted her beautiful, black eyes and she answered in a German that bore only a faint trace of Slav accent: 'I am not Madame Gorky. . . You are mistaken – my name is so-and-so' (giving a Russian-sounding name which I have forgotten).

'No, Madame Gorky,' I persisted, 'I know that I am not mistaken. I also know that you do not want to be bothered by us reporters – but it would mean a great deal, a very great deal to me to be allowed to speak to you for a few minutes. This is my first chance to establish myself. I am sure you would not like to destroy that chance. . . ?' I showed her my press card. 'I got it only today, and I will have to return it unless I produce the story of my interview with Madame Gorky.'

The aristocratic lady continued to smile. 'And if I were to tell you on my word of honour that I am not Madame Gorky, would you believe me then?'

'If you were to tell me anything on your word of honour, I would believe it.'

She burst out laughing. 'You seem to be a nice little boy.' (Her graceful head reached hardly to my shoulder.) 'I am not going to tell you any more lies. You win. But we can't spend the rest of the evening here in the lobby. Would you give me the pleasure of having tea with me in my rooms?'

And so I had the pleasure of having tea with Madame Gorky in her rooms. For nearly an hour she vividly described the horrors of the famine; and when I left her after midnight, I had a thick sheaf of notes with me.

The sub-editors on night duty at the United Telegraph opened their eyes wide on seeing me at that unusual hour. But I did not bother to explain, for I had urgent work to do. Writing down my interview as quickly as I could, I booked, without waiting for editorial clearance, urgent press calls to all the newspapers we served.

Next morning the bomb burst. While none of the great Berlin dailies had a single word about Madame Gorky's presence in town, all the provincial papers served by our agency carried on their front pages the United Telegraph Special Representative's exclusive interview with Madame Gorky. The telephonist had made a first-class scoop.

In the afternoon a conference of editors took place in Dr. Dammert's office. I was called in and, after a preliminary lecture in which it was explained to me that no news item of importance ought ever to go out without first being cleared by the news editor, I was informed that I had been promoted to reporter.

At last I was a journalist.

— 4 —

SOFT STEPS in the sand: it is Zayd, returning from the well with a filled waterskin. He lets it fall with a plop on the ground near the fire and resumes cooking our dinner: rice and the meat of a little lamb that he bought in the village earlier in the evening. After a final stir with his ladle and a burst of steam from the pot, he turns to me:

'Wilt thou eat now, O my uncle?' – and without waiting for my reply, which, he knows, cannot be anything but Yes, he heaps the contents of the pot on to a large platter, sets it before me, and lifts one of our brass cans, filled with water, for me to wash my hands:

'*Bismillah*, and may God grant us life.'

And we fall to, sitting cross-legged opposite each other and eating with the fingers of the right hand.

We eat in silence. Neither of us has ever been a great talker. Besides, I have somehow been thrown into a mood of remembrance, thinking of the times that passed before I came to Arabia, before I even met Zayd; and so I cannot speak aloud, and speak only silently within myself and to myself, savouring the mood of my present through the many moods of my past.

After our meal, as I lean against my saddle, my fingers playing with the sand, and gaze at the silent Arabian stars, I think how good it would be to have by my side someone to whom I could speak of all that has happened to me in those distant years. But there is nobody with me except Zayd. He is a good and faithful man and was my companion in many a day of loneliness; he is shrewd, delicate in perception and well versed in the ways of man. But as I look sidewise at his face – this clear-cut face framed in long tresses, now bent with serious absorption over the coffeepot, now turning toward the dromedaries which rest on the ground nearby and placidly chew their cud – I know that I need quite another listener: one who not only has had no part in that early past of mine but would also be far away from the sight and smell and sound of the present days and nights: one before whom I could unwrap the pinpoints of my remembrance one by one, so that his eyes might see them and my eyes might see them again, and who would thus help me to catch my own life within the net of my words.

But there is nobody here but Zayd. And Zayd is the present.

III

WINDS

— 1 —

WE RIDE, RIDE, two men on two dromedaries, and the morning glides past us.

'It is strange, very strange,' Zayd's voice breaks through the silence.

'What is strange, Zayd?'

'Is it not strange, O my uncle, that only a few days ago we were going to Tayma and now our camels' heads point toward Mecca? I am sure thou didst not know it thyself before that night. Thou art wayward like a *badawi* . . . like myself. Was it a jinn, O my uncle, who gave me that sudden decision, four years ago, to go to thee at Mecca – and gave thee now thy decision to go to Mecca? Are we letting ourselves be thus blown around by the winds because we do not know what we want?'

'No, Zayd – thou and I, we allow ourselves to be blown by the winds because we do know what we want: our hearts know it, even if our thoughts are sometimes slow to follow – but in the end they do catch up with our hearts and then we think we have made a decision . . .'

.   .   .   .

PERHAPS MY HEART knew it even on that day ten years ago, when I stood on the planks of the ship that was bearing me on my first journey to the Near East, southward through the Black Sea, through the opaqueness of a white, rimless, foggy night, through a foggy morning, toward the Bosporus. The sea was leaden; sometimes foam sprayed over the deck; the pounding of the engines was like the beat of a heart.

I stood at the rail, looking out into the pale opaqueness. If you had asked me what I was thinking then, or what expectations I was carrying with me into this first venture to the East, I would hardly have been able to give a clear answer. Curiosity – perhaps: but it was a curiosity which did not take itself very seriously because it seemed to aim at things of no great importance. The fog of my uneasiness, which seemed to find something related in the welling fog over the sea, was not directed toward foreign lands and the people of coming days. The images of a near future, the strange cities and appearances, the foreign clothes and manners which were to reveal themselves so soon to my eyes hardly occupied my thoughts. I regarded this journey as something accidental and took it, as it were, in my stride, as a pleasing but nevertheless not too important interlude. At that moment my thoughts were perturbed and distracted by what I took to be a preoccupation with my past.

The past? Did I have any? I was twenty-two years old . . . But my generation – the generation of those who had been born at the turn of the century – had lived perhaps more quickly than any other before it, and to me it seemed as if I were looking back into a long expanse of time. All the difficulties and adventures of those years stood before my eyes, all those longings and attempts and disappointments – and the women – and my first assaults on life . . . Those endless nights under stars, when one did not quite know what one wanted and walked with a friend through the empty streets, speaking of ultimate things, quite forgetting how empty the pockets were and how insecure the coming day . . . A happy discontent which only youth can feel, and the desire to change the world and to build it anew . . . How should community be shaped so that men could live rightly and in fullness? How should their relationships be arranged so that they might break through the loneliness which surrounded every man, and truly live in communion? What is good – and what evil? What is destiny? Or, to put it differently: what should one do to become really, and not merely in pretensions, identical with one's own life so that one could say, 'I and my destiny are one'? Discussions which never came to an end . . . The literary cafés of Vienna and Berlin, with their interminable arguments about 'form,' 'style' and 'expression,' about the meaning of political freedom, about the meeting of man and woman . . . Hunger for understanding, and sometimes for food as well . . . And the nights spent in passions without restraint: a dishevelled bed at dawn, when the excitement of the night was ebbing, and slowly became grey and rigid and desolate: but when the morning came one had forgotten the ashes of the dawn and walked again with swinging steps and felt the earth tremble joyfully under one's feet . . . The excitement of a new book or a new face; searching, and finding half-replies; and those very rare moments when the world seemed suddenly, for seconds, to stand still, illumined by the flash of an understanding that promised to reveal something that had never been touched before: an answer to all the questions . . .

. . . .

THEY HAD BEEN strange years, those early Twenties in Central Europe. The general atmosphere of social and moral insecurity had given rise to a desperate hopefulness which expressed itself in daring experiments in music, painting and the theatre, as well as in groping, often revolutionary enquiries into the morphology of culture; but hand-in-hand with this forced optimism went a spiritual emptiness, a vague, cynical relativism born out of increasing hopelessness with regard to the future of man.

In spite of my youth, it had not remained hidden from me that after the catastrophe of the Great War things were no longer right in the broken-up, discontented, emotionally tense and high-pitched European world. Its real deity, I saw, was no longer of a spiritual kind: it was Comfort. No doubt there were still many individuals who felt and thought in religious terms and made the most desperate efforts to reconcile their moral beliefs with the spirit of their civilization, but they were only exceptions. The average European – whether democrat or communist, manual worker or intellectual – seemed to know only one positive faith: the worship of material progress, the belief that there could be no other goal in life than to make that very life continually easier or, as the current expression went, 'independent of nature'. The temples of that faith were the gigantic factories, cinemas, chemical laboratories, dance-halls, hydroelectric works; and its priests were the bankers, engineers, politicians, film stars, statisticians, captains of industry, record airmen, and commissars. Ethical frustration was evident in the all-round lack of agreement about the meaning of Good and Evil and in the submission of all social and economic issues to the rule of 'expediency' – that painted lady of the streets, willing to give herself to anybody, at any time, whenever she is invoked . . . The insatiable craving after power and pleasure had, of necessity, led to the break-up of Western society into hostile groups armed to the teeth and determined to destroy each other whenever and wherever their respective interests clashed. And on the cultural side, the outcome was the creation of a human type whose morality appeared to be confined to the question of practical utility alone, and whose highest criterion of right and wrong was material success.

I saw how confused and unhappy our life had become; how little there was of real communion between man and man despite all the strident, almost hysterical, insistence on 'community' and 'nation'; how far we had strayed from our instincts; and how narrow, how musty our souls had become. I saw all this: but somehow it never seriously occurred to me – as it never seems to have occurred to any of the people around me – that an answer, or at least partial answers, to these perplexities might perhaps be gained from other than Europe's own cultural experiences. Europe was the beginning and the end of all our thinking: and even my discovery of Lao-tse – at the age of seventeen or so – had not altered my outlook in this respect.

.   .   .   .

IT WAS A REAL discovery; I had never before heard of Lao-tse and had not the slightest inkling of his philosophy when one day I chanced upon a German translation of the *Tao-te-king* lying on the counter of a Viennese bookshop. The strange name and title made me mildly curious. Opening the book at random, I glanced at one of its short, aphoristic sections – and felt a sudden thrill, like a stab of happiness, which made me forget my surroundings and kept me rooted where I stood, spellbound, with the book in my hands: for in it I saw human life in all its serenity, free of all cleavages and conflicts, rising up in that quiet gladness which is always open to the human heart whenever it cares to avail itself of its own freedom . . . This was truth, I knew it: a truth that had always been true, although we had forgotten it: and now I recognized it with the joy with which one returns to one's long-lost home . . .

From that time onward, for several years, Lao-tse was to me a window through which I could look out into the glass-clear regions of a life that was far away from all narrowness and all self-created fears, free of the childish obsession which was forcing us, from moment to moment, always to secure our existence anew by means of 'material improvement' at any price. Not that material improvement seemed to be wrong or even unnecessary to me: on the contrary, I continued to regard it as good and necessary: but at the same time I was convinced that it could never achieve its end – to increase the sum total of human happiness – unless it were accompanied by a reorientation of our spiritual attitude and a new faith in absolute values. But how such a reorientation could be brought about and of what kind the new valuations were to be was not quite clear to me. It would certainly have been idle to expect that men would change their aims – and thus the direction of their endeavours – as soon as someone started preaching to them, as Lao-tse did, that one should open oneself up to life instead of trying to grab it to himself and thus to do violence to it. Preaching alone, intellectual realization alone could obviously not produce a change in the spiritual attitude of European society; a new faith of the heart was needed, a burning surrender to values which tolerated no Ifs and Buts: but whence to gain such a faith . . . ?

It somehow did not enter my mind that Lao-tse's mighty challenge was aimed not merely at a passing and therefore changeable intellectual attitude, but at some of the most fundamental concepts out of which that attitude springs. Had I known this, I would have been forced to conclude that Europe could not possibly attain to that weightless serenity of soul of which Lao-tse spoke, unless it summoned the courage to question its own spiritual and ethical roots. I was, of course, too young to arrive consciously at such a conclusion: too young to grasp the challenge of the Chinese sage in all its implications and its entire grandeur. True, his message shook me to my innermost; it revealed to me the vista of a life in which man could become one with his destiny and so with himself: but as I did not clearly see how such a philosophy could transcend mere contemplation and be translated into reality in the context of the European way of life, I gradually began to doubt whether it was realizable at all. I had not yet reached the point where I would even *ask* myself whether the European way of life was, in its fundamentals, the only possible way. In other words, like all the other people around me, I was entirely wrapped up in Europe's egocentric cultural outlook.

And so, although his voice was never quite silenced, Lao-tse receded, step by step, into the background of comtemplative fantasies, and in time ceased to be more than the bearer of lovely poetry. One continued to read him off and on and felt each time the stab of a happy vision; but each time one put the book away with a wistful regret that this was only a dream call to some ivory tower. And although I felt very much at odds with the discordant bitter, greedy world of which I was a part, I did not wish to live in an ivory tower.

Still, there was no warmth in me for any of the aims and endeavours which at that time flowed through Europe's intellectual atmosphere and filled its literature, art and politics with a buzz of animated controversies – for, however contradictory to one another most of those aims and endeavours may have been, they all had obviously one thing in common: the naïve assumption that life could be lifted out of its present confusion and 'bettered' if only its outward – economic or political – conditions were bettered. I strongly felt even then that material progress, by itself, could not provide a solution; and although I did not quite know where a solution might be found, I was never able to evince within myself that enthusiasm which my contemporaries had for 'progress'.

Not that I was unhappy. I had never been an introvert, and just then I was enjoying a more than usual measure of success in my practical affairs. While I was hardly inclined to give much weight to a 'career' as such, work at the United Telegraph – where owing to my knowledge of languages, I was now sub-editor in charge of the news service for the Scandinavian press – seemed to open many avenues into the broader world. The Café des Westens and its spiritual successor, the Romanisches Café – meeting places of the most outstanding writers, artists, journalists, actors, producers of the day – represented something like an intellectual home to me. I stood on friendly and sometimes even familiar terms with people who bore famous names, and regarded myself – at least in outlook if not in fame – as one of them. Deep friendships and fleeting loves came my way. Life was exciting, full of promise and colourful in the variety of its impressions. No, I was certainly not unhappy – only deeply dissatisfied, unsatisfied, not knowing what I was really after, and at the same time convinced, with the absurd arrogance of youth, that one day I would know it. And so I swung along on the pendulum of my heart's content and discontent in exactly the same way as many other young people were doing in those strange years: for, while none of us was really unhappy, only a very few seemed to be consciously happy.

I was not unhappy: but my inability to share the diverse social, economic and political hopes of those around me – of any group among them – grew in time into a vague sense of not quite belonging to them, accompanied, vaguely again, by a desire to belong – to whom? – to be a part of something – of what?

.   .   .   .

AND THEN ONE DAY, in the spring of 1922, I received a letter from my uncle Dorian.

Dorian was my mother's youngest brother. Our relationship had always been rather that of friends than of uncle and nephew. He was a psychiatrist – one of the early pupils of Freud – and at that time headed a mental hospital in Jerusalem. As he was not a Zionist himself and did not particularly sympathize with the aims of Zionism – nor, for that matter, was attracted to the Arabs – he felt lonely and isolated in a world which had nothing to offer him but work and income. Being unmarried, he thought of his nephew as a likely companion in his solitude. In his letter he referred to those exciting days in Vienna when he had guided me into the new world of psychoanalysis; and he concluded: 'Why don't you come and stay some months with me here? I will pay for your journey coming and going; you will be free to return to Berlin whenever you like. And while you are here, you will be living in a delightful old Arab stone house which is cool in summer (and damned cold in winter). We shall spend our time well together. I have plenty of books here, and when you get tired of observing the quaint scenery around you, you can read as much as you want . . .'

I made up my mind with the promptness that has always characterized my major decisions. Next morning I informed Dr. Dammert at the United Telegraph that 'important business considerations' forced me to go to the Near East, and that I would therefore have to quit the agency within a week . . .

If anyone had told me at that time that my first acquaintance with the world of Islam would go far beyond a holiday experience and indeed become a turning point in my life, I would have laughed off the idea as utterly preposterous. Not that I was impervious to the allure of countries associated in my mind – as in the minds of most Europeans – with the romantic atmosphere of the *Arabian Nights:* I did anticipate colour, exotic customs, picturesque encounters; but it never occured to me to anticipate adventures in the realm of the spirit as well, and the new journey did not seem to hold out any special promise of a personal nature. All the ideas and impressions that had previously come my way I had instinctively related to the Western world-view, hoping to attain to a broader reach of feeling and perception within the only cultural environment known to me. And, if you come to think of it, how could I have felt differently? I was only a very, very young European, brought up in the belief that Islam and all it stood for was no more than a romantic by-path of man's history, not even quite 'respectable' from the spiritual and ethical points of view, and therefore not to be mentioned in the same breath, still less to be compared, with the only two faiths which the West considers fit to be taken seriously: Christianity and Judaism.

It was with this hazy, European bias against things Islamic (though not, of course, against the romanticized outward appearances of Muslim life) that I set out in the summer of 1922 on my journey. If, in fairness to myself, I cannot say that I was self-absorbed in an individual sense, I was none the less, without knowing it, deeply enmeshed in that self-absorbed, culturally egocentric mentality so characteristic of the West at all times.

.   .   .   .

AND NOW I STOOD on the planks of a ship on my way to the East. A leisurely journey had brought me to Constanza and thence into this foggy morning.

A red sail emerged out of the veils of fog and slipped by close to the ship; and because it had become visible, one knew that the sun was about to break through the fog. A few pale rays, thin as threads, fell on the mist over the sea. Their paleness had something of the hardness of metal. Under their pressure the milky masses of fog settled slowly and heavily over the water, then bent apart, and finally rose to the right and left of the sun rays in widespread, drifting arcs, like wings.

'Good morning,' said a deep, full voice. I turned around and recognized the black cassock of my companion of the previous evening, and the friendly smile on a face which I had grown to like during the few hours of our acquaintance. The Jesuit *padre* was half Polish and half French and taught history at a college in Alexandria; he was now returning there from a vacation. We had spent the evening after embarkation in lively talk. Although it soon became apparent that we differed widely on many issues, we had, nevertheless, many points of interest in common; and I was already mature enough to recognize that here was a brilliant, serious and at the same time humorous mind at work.

'Good morning, Father Felix; look at the sea. . .'

Daylight and colour had come up with the sun. We stood in the bow of the ship under the morning wind. Tempted by the impossibility, I tried to determine for myself the movement of colour in the breaking waves. Blue? Green? Grey? It could have been blue – but already a shimmer of amaranth red, reflecting the sun, glided over the concave slope of the wave, while the crest broke up into snowy foam and steel-grey, crinkly rags raced over it. What a moment ago had been a wave-hill was now a trembling movement – the breaking-open of a thousand minute, independent eddies in whose shaded cavities the amaranth red changed into deep, satiated green; then the green rose up, changing into oscillating violet, which at first fell back into wine red, but immediately after shot up as turquoise blue and became the crest of the wave, only to break up again; and again the white foam spread its net domineeringly over the writhing water-hills . . . And on and on went the unending play. . .

It gave me an almost physical sensation of disquiet never to be able to grasp this play of colours and its eternally changing rhythm. When I looked at it quite superficially, only from the corner of my eye, as it were, I felt, for seconds, that it might be possible to catch all this within an integrated image; but deliberate concentration, the habit of connecting one isolated concept with another, led to nothing but a series of broken-up, separate pictures. But out of this difficulty, this strangely irritating confusion, an idea came to me with great clarity – or so it seemed to me at the time – and I said, almost involuntarily:

'Whoever could grasp all this with his senses would be able to master destiny.'

'I know what you mean,' replied Father Felix, 'But why should one desire to master destiny? To escape from suffering? Would it not be better to become free of destiny?'

'You are speaking almost like a Buddhist, Father Felix. Do you, too, regard Nirvana as the goal of all being?'

'Oh no, certainly not. . . We Christians do not aim at the extinction of life and feeling – we desire only to lift life out of the region of the material and sensual into the realm of the spirit.'

'But is this not renunciation?'

'It is no renunciation, my young friend. It is the only way to true life, to peace. . .'

The Bosporus opened itself to us, a broad waterway framed on both sides by rocky hills. Here and there one could see pillared, airy palaces, terraced gardens, cypresses rising up in all their dark height, and old janissary castles, heavy masses of stone hanging over the water like the nests of birds of prey. As if from a great distance, I heard the voice of Father Felix continue:

'You see, the deepest symbol of longing – all people's longing – is the symbol of Paradise; you find it in all religions, always in different imageries, but the meaning is always the same – namely the desire to be free from destiny. The people of Paradise had no destiny; they acquired it only after they succumbed to the temptation of the flesh and thus fell into what we call Original Sin: the stumbling of the spirit over the hindering urges of the body, which are indeed only the animal remnants within man's nature. The essential, the human, the humanly-divine part of man is his soul alone. The soul strives toward light, which is spirit: but because of the Original Sin its way is hampered by obstacles arising from the material, non-divine composition of the body and its urges. What the Christian teaching aims at is, therefore, man's freeing himself from the non-essential, ephemeral, carnal aspects of his life and returning to his spiritual heritage.'

The ancient, twin-towered fortress of Rumili Hissar appeared; one of its crenellated walls sloped down almost to the water's edge; on the shore, within the semicircle formed by the fortress walls, lay dreaming a little Turkish cemetery with broken-down tombstones.

'It may be so, Father Felix. But I feel – and this is the feeling of many people of my generation – I feel that there is something wrong in making a distinction between the "essential" and the "non-essential" in the structure of man, and in separating spirit and flesh . . . in short, I cannot agree with your denying all righteousness to physical urges, to the flesh, to earthbound destiny. My desire goes elsewhere: I dream of a form of life – though I must confess I do not see it clearly as yet – in which the entire man, spirit and flesh, would strive after a deeper and deeper fulfilment of his Self – in which the spirit and the senses would not be enemies to one another, and in which man could achieve unity within himself and with the meaning of his destiny, so that on the summit of his days he could say, "*I* am my destiny." '

'That was the Hellenic dream,' replied Father Felix, 'and where did it lead? First to the Orphic and Dionysian mysteries, then to Plato and Plotinus, and so, again, to the inevitable realization that spirit and flesh are opposed to one another . . . To make the spirit free from the domination of the flesh: this is the meaning of Christian salvation, the meaning of our belief in the Lord's self-sacrifice on the Cross. . .' Here he interrupted himself and turned to me with a twinkle: 'Oh, I am not always a missionary . . . pardon me if I speak to you of my faith, which is not yours . . .'

'But I have none,' I assured him.

'Yes,' said Father Felix, 'I know; the lack of faith, or rather the inability to believe, is the central illness of our time. You, like so many others, are living in an illusion which is thousands of years old: the illusion that intellect alone can give a direction to man's striving. But the intellect cannot reach spritual knowledge by itself because it is too much absorbed in the achievement of material goals; it is faith, and faith alone, that can release us from such an absorption.'

'Faith . . . ?' I asked. 'You again bring in this word. There is one thing I can't understand: you say it is impossible to attain through intellect alone to knowledge and to a righteous life; faith is needed, you say. I agree with you entirely. But how does one achieve faith if one has none? Is there a way to it – I mean, a way open to our will?'

'My dear friend – will alone is not enough. The way is only opened by God's grace. But it is always opened to him who prays from the innermost of his heart for enlightenment.'

'To pray! But when one is able to do this, Father Felix, one already *has* faith. You choose to lead me around in a circle – for if a man prays, he must already be convinced of the existence of Him to whom he prays. How did he come to this conviction? Through his intellect? Would not this amount to admitting that faith can be found through the intellect? And apart from that, can "grace" mean anything to somebody who has never had an experience of this kind?'

The priest shrugged his shoulders, regretfully, it seemed to me: 'If one has not been able to experience God by himself, one should allow himself to be guided by the experiences of others who have experienced Him . . .'

. . . .

A FEW DAYS LATER we landed at Alexandria and the same afternoon I went on to Palestine.

The train swept straight as an arrow through the afternoon and the soft, humid Delta landscape. Nile canals, shaded by the sails of many barges, crossed our path. Small towns, dust-grey clusters of houses and lighter minarets, came and went. Villages consisting of box-shaped mud huts swept past. Harvested cotton fields; sprouting sugar-cane fields; abundantly overgrown palms over a village mosque; water buffaloes, black, heavy-limbed, now going home without guide from the muddy pools in which they had been wallowing during the day. In the distance, men in long garments: they seemed to float, so light and clear was the air under the high, blue sky of glass. On the banks of the canals reeds swayed in the wind; women in black tulle cloaks were scooping water into earthenware jars: wonderful women, slender, long-limbed; in their walk they reminded me of long-stemmed plants that sway tenderly and yet full of strength in the wind. Young girls and matrons had the same floating walk.

The dusk grew and flowed like the breath of some great, resting, living being. As the slim men were walking homeward from the fields, their movements appeared lengthened and at the same time lifted out of the slowly disappearing day: each step seemed to have an existence of its own, rounded in itself: between eternity and eternity always that one step. This appearance of lightness and smoothness was perhaps due to the exhilarating evening light of the Nile Delta – perhaps also to my own restlessness at seeing so many new things – but whatever the cause, I suddenly felt in myself all the weight of Europe: the weight of deliberate purpose in all our actions. I thought to myself, 'How difficult it is for us to attain to reality. . . We always try to grab it: but it does not like to be grabbed. Only where it overwhelms man does it surrender itself to him.'

The step of the Egyptian field labourers, already lost in distance and darkness, continued to swing in my mind like a hymn of all high things.

We reached the Suez Canal, made a turn at a right angle, and glided for a while toward the north along the grey-black bank. It was like a drawn-out melody, this long line of the canal at night. The moonlight turned the waterway into something like a real but dream-broad way, a dark band of shining metal. The satiated earth of the Nile valley had with astonishing rapidity made room for chains of sand dunes which enclosed the canal on both sides with a paleness and sharpness rarely to be seen in any other night landscape. In the listening silence stood, here and there, the skeleton of a dredge. Beyond, on the other bank, a camel-rider rushed by, rushed by – hardly seen and already swallowed by the night. . . What a great, simple stream: from the Red Sea, through the Bitter Lakes, to the Mediterranean Sea – right across a desert – so that the Indian Ocean might beat on the quays of Europe . . .

At Kantara the train journey was interrupted for a while and a lazy ferry carried the travellers across the silent water. There was almost an hour before the departure of the Palestinian train. I sat down before the station building. The air was warm and dry. There was the desert: to the right and to the left. Shimmering grey, smudged over, broken through by isolated barking – perhaps it was jackals, perhaps dogs. A beduin, heavily loaded with saddlebags made of bright carpet cloth, came from the ferry and walked toward a group in the distance, which only now I recognized as motionless men and crouching camels, ready-saddled for the march. It seemed that the new arrival had been expected. He threw his saddlebags over one of the animals, a few words were exchanged, all the men mounted and, at the same moment, the camels rose, first on their hind legs, then on their forelegs – the riders rocked forward and backward – then they rode away with soft, swishing sounds, and for a while you could follow the light-coloured, swaying bodies of the animals and the wide, brown-and-white-striped beduin cloaks.

A railway workman strolled toward me. He wore a blue overall and seemed to be lame. He lit his cigarette from mine, then asked me, in broken French:

'You are going to Jerusalem?' And when I said Yes, he continued: 'For the first time?'

I nodded. He was about to go on, then turned back and said: 'Did you see over there the big caravan from the Sinai Desert? No? Then come along, let us visit them. You have time.'

The soles of our shoes crunched in the sand as we walked through the silent emptiness up a narrow, well-trodden path which led into the dunes. A dog barked in the darkness. As we went on, stumbling over low thornbushes, voices reached my ears – confused, muffled, as of many people – and the sharp and nevertheless soft smell of many resting animal bodies mingled with the dry desert air. Suddenly – just as you might see in a city, during a foggy night, the shimmer of an as yet invisible lamp grow up from behind a street corner and make only the fog shine – a narrow streak of light appeared from down below, as if from under ground, and climbed steeply into the dark air. It was the shine of a fire, coming from a deep gorge between two sand dunes, so thickly covered with thornbushes that one could not see its bottom. I could now clearly hear men's voices, but the speakers were still invisible. I heard the breathing of camels, and how they rubbed against one another in the narrow space. A big, black human shadow fell over the light, ran up the opposite slope and down again. After a few more steps I could see it all – a great circle of crouching camels with heaps of pack-saddles and bags here and there, and among them the figures of men. The animal smell was sweet and heavy like wine. Sometimes one of the camels moved its body, which was smudged out of its shape by the darkness around it, lifted its neck and drew in the night air with a snorting sound, as if sighing: and thus I heard for the first time the sighing of camels. A sheep bleated softly; a dog growled; and everywhere outside the gorge the night was black and starless.

It was already late; I had to get back to the station. But I walked very slowly, down the path by which we had come, dazed and strangely shaken, as if by a mysterious experience which had caught hold of a corner of my heart and would not let me go.

.   .   .   .

THE TRAIN CARRIED ME through the Sinai Desert. I was exhausted, sleepless from the cold of the desert night and the rocking of the train over rails resting on loose sand. Opposite me sat a beduin in a voluminous brown *abaya*. He also was freezing and had wrapped his face in his headcloth. He sat crosslegged on the bench, and on his knees lay a curved sword in a scabbard ornamented with silver. It was nearly morning. You could almost recognize the outlines of the dunes outside, and the cactus bushes.

I can still remember how the dawn broke – grey-black, painting shapes, slowly drawing outlines – and how it gradually lifted the sand dunes out of the darkness and built them into harmonious masses. In the growing half-light, a group of tents appeared and rushed by, and near them, silver-grey, like fog curtains in the wind, fishing nets spread vertically between poles for drying: fishing nets in the desert – blowing in the morning wind – dream veils, transparent, unreal, between night and day.

To the right was the desert; to the left the sea. On the shore a lonely camel-rider; perhaps he had been riding all night; now he seemed to be asleep, slumped in the saddle, and they both rocked, man and camel, in a common rhythm. Again black beduin tents. Already there were women outside with earthenware jars on their heads, ready to go to the well. Out of the half-light that grew into light a diaphanous world was emerging, moved by invisible pulses, a wonder of all that is simple and can never end.

The sun struck out over the sand with broader and broader rays and the greyness of dawn burst into an orange-golden firework. We sped on through the oasis of Al-Arish, through colonnaded cathedrals of palms with a thousand pointed arches of palm fronds and a brown-green latticework of light and shade. I saw a woman with a filled jar on her head coming from the well and going slowly up a path under the palms. She wore a red-and-blue dress with a long train and was like a high lady from a legend.

The palm orchards of Al-Arish disappeared as suddenly as they had come. We were now travelling through shell-coloured light. Outside, behind the shaking windowpanes, a stillness such

King Abd al-Aziz ibn Saud

as I never had thought possible. All forms and movements were devoid of a yesterday and a tomorrow – they were simply there, in a heady uniqueness. Delicate sand, built up by the wind into soft hillocks that glowed pale orange under the sun, like very old parchment, only softer, less brittle in their breaks and curves, swinging in sharp, decisive violin strokes on the summits, infinitely tender in the flanks, with translucent water-colour shadows – purple and lilac and rusty pink – in the shallow dips and hollows. Opalescent clouds, cactus bushes here and there and sometimes long-stemmed, hard grasses. Once or twice I saw spare, barefooted beduins and a camel caravan loaded with palm fronds which they were carrying from somewhere to somewhere. I felt enwrapped by the great landscape.

Several times we stopped at small stations, usually no more than a few barracks of timber and tin. Brown, tattered boys ran around with baskets and offered figs, hard-boiled eggs and fresh, flat loaves of bread for sale. The beduin opposite me rose slowly, unwound his headcloth and opened the window. His face was thin, brown, sharply drawn, one of those hawk faces which always look intently ahead. He bought a piece of cake, turned around and was about to sit down, when his eye fell on me; and, without a word, he broke his cake in two and offered me half. When he saw my hesitation and astonishment, he smiled – and I saw that the tender smile fitted his face as well as the intentness of a moment ago – and said a word which I could not understand then but now know was *tafaddal* – 'grant me the favour.' I took the cake and thanked him with a nod. Another traveller – he wore, with the exception of his red fez, European clothes and may have been a small trader – intervened as translator. In halting English he said:

'He say, you traveller, he traveller; your way and his way is together.'

When I now think of this little occurrence, it seems to me that all my later love for the Arab character must have been influenced by it. For in the gesture of this beduin, who, over all barriers of strangeness, sensed a friend in an accidental travelling companion and broke bread with him, I must already have felt the breath and the step of a humanity free of burden.

After a short while came old Gaza, like a castle of mud, living its forgotten life on a sand hill between cactus walls. My beduin collected his saddlebags, saluted me with a grave smile and a nod and left the carriage, sweeping the dust behind him with the long train of his cloak. Two other beduins stood outside on the platform and greeted him with a handshake and a kiss on both cheeks.

The English-speaking trader put his hand on my arm: 'Come along, still quarter-hour time.'

Beyond the sation building a caravan was encamped; they were, my companion informed me, beduins from northern Hijaz. They had brown, dusty, wild-warm faces. Our friend was among them. He appeared to be a person of some account, for they stood in a loose semicircle around him and answered his questions. The trader spoke to them and they turned toward us, friendly – and, I thought, somewhat superciliously – considering our urban existence. An atmosphere of freedom surrounded them, and I felt a strong desire to understand their lives. The air was dry, vibrating, and seemed to penetrate the body. It loosened all stiffness, disentangled all thoughts and made them lazy and still. There was a quality of timelessness in it which made all things seen and heard and smelled assume distinct values in their own right. It began to dawn on me that people who come from the environment of the desert must sense life in a way quite different from that of people in all other regions; they must be free from many obsessions – perhaps also from many dreams – peculiar to inhabitants of colder, richer lands, and certainly from many of their limitations; and because they have to rely more intimately on their own perceptions, these desert dwellers must set a quite different scale of values to the things of the world.

Perhaps it was a presentiment of coming upheavals in my own life that gripped me on that first day in an Arab country at the sight of the beduins: the presentiment of a world which lacks all defining limits but is, none the less, never formless; which is fully rounded in itself – and nevertheless open on all sides: a world that was soon to become my own. Not that I was then conscious of what the future held in store for me; of course not. It was, rather, as when you enter a strange house for the first time and an indefinable smell in the hallway gives you dimly a hint of things which will happen in this house, and will happen to you: and if they are to be joyful things, you feel a stab of rapture in your heart – and you will remember it much later, when all those happenings have long since taken place, and you will tell yourself: 'All this I have sensed long ago, thus and in no other way, in that first moment in the hall.'

— 2 —

A STRONG WIND blows through the desert, and for a while Zayd thinks we are going to have another sandstorm. But although no sandstorm comes, the wind does not leave us. It follows us in steady gusts, and the gusts flow together into a single, unbroken sough as we descend into a sandy valley. The palm village in its centre, consisting of several separate settlements – each surrounded by a mud wall – is veiled in a mist of whirling sand dust.

This area is a kind of wind hole: every day from dawn to sunset the wind beats here with strong wings, settling down during the night, only to rise again the next morning with renewed force; and the palm trees, eternally pressed down by its blows cannot grow to their full height but remain stunted, close to the ground, with broad-spread fronds, always in danger from the encroaching dunes. The village would have long ago been buried in the sands had not the inhabitants planted rows of tamarisks around every orchard. These tall trees, more resistant than palms, form with their strong trunks and ever-green, rustling branches a living wall around the plantations, offering them a doubtful security.

We alight before the mud house of the village *amir*, intending to rest here during the noon heat. The *qahwa* set aside for the reception of guests is bare and poverty-stricken and displays only one small straw mat before the stone coffee hearth. But, as usual, Arabian hospitality overcomes all poverty: for hardly have we taken our places on the mat when a friendly fire of twigs crackles on the hearth; the ringing sound of the brass mortar in which freshly-roasted coffee beans are being pounded gives a livable character to the room; and a mighty platter piled with light-brown dates meets the hunger of the travellers.

Our host – a small, lean old man with rheumy, squinting eyes, clad only in a cotton tunic and a headcloth – invites us to partake of this fare:

'May God give you life; this house is your house, eat in the name of God. This is all we have' – and he makes an apologetic

gesture with his hand, a single movement in which the whole
weight of his fate is expressed with that artless power of evocation so peculiar to people who live close to their instincts – 'but
the dates are not bad. Eat, O wayfarers, of what we can offer
you . . .'

The dates are really among the best I have ever eaten; and the
host is obviously pleased by our hunger which he can satisfy.
And he goes on:

'The wind, the wind, it makes our life hard; but that is God's
will. The wind destroys our plantations. We must always struggle to keep them from being covered by sand. It has not always
been thus. In earlier times there was not so much wind here, and
the village was big and rich. Now it has grown small; many of
our young men are going away, for not everyone can bear such a
life. The sands are closing in on us day by day. Soon there will be
no room left for the palms. This wind . . . But we do not
complain. . . As you know, the Prophet – may God bless
him – told us: "God says, *Revile not destiny, for, behold – I am
destiny . . .*" '

I must have started, for the old man stops speaking and looks
at me attentively; and, as if comprehending why I started, he
smiles with almost a woman's smile, strange to see in that tired,
worn-out face, and repeats softly, as if to himself:

'. . . behold, *I* am destiny' – and in the nod with which he ac-
companies his words lies a proud, silent acceptance of his own
place in life; and never have I seen, even in happy people, a Yes
to reality expressed with so much quiet and sureness. With a
wide, vague, almost sensual turn of his arm he describes a circle
in the air – a circle which encompasses everything that belongs
to this life: the poor, dusky room, the wind and its eternal roar,
the relentless advance of the sands; longing for happiness, and
resignation to what cannot be changed; the platter full of dates;
the struggling orchards behind their shield of tamarisks; the fire
on the hearth; a young woman's laughter somewhere in the
courtyard beyond: and in all these things and in the gesture that
has brought them out and together I seem to hear the song of a
strong spirit which knows no barriers of circumstance and is at
peace with itself.

I am carried back to a time long past, to that autumn day in
Jerusalem ten years ago, when another poor old man spoke to

me of surrender to God, which alone can cause one to be at
peace with Him and so with one's own destiny.

.   .   .   .

DURING THAT AUTUMN I was living in my uncle Dorian's
house just inside the Old City of Jerusalem. It rained almost
every day and, not being able to go out much, I often sat at the
window which overlooked a large yard behind the house. This
yard belonged to an old Arab who was called *hajji* because he
had performed the pilgrimage to Mecca; he rented out donkeys
for riding and carrying and thus made the yard a kind of caravanserai.

Every morning, shortly before dawn, loads of vegetables and
fruits were brought there on camels from the surrounding villages and sent out on donkeys into the narrow bazaar streets of
the town. In daytime the heavy bodies of the camels could be
seen resting on the ground; men were always noisily attending to
them and to the donkeys, unless they were forced to take refuge
in the stables from the streaming rain. They were poor, ragged
men, those camel and donkey drivers, but they behaved like
great lords. When they sat together at meals on the ground and
ate flat loaves of wheat bread with a little bit of cheese or a few
olives, I could not but admire the nobility and ease of their bearing and their inner quiet: you could see that they had respect for
themselves and the everyday things of their lives. The *hajji*, hob-
bling around on a stick – for he suffered from arthritis and had
swollen knees – was a kind of chieftain among them; they appeared to obey him without question. Several times a day he assembled them for prayer and, if it was not raining too hard, they
prayed in the open: all the men in a single, long row and he as
their *imam* in front of them. They were like soldiers in the precision of their movements – they would bow together in the
direction of Mecca, rise again, and then kneel down and touch
the ground with their foreheads; they seemed to follow the in-
audible words of their leader, who between the prostrations
stood barefoot on his prayer carpet, eyes closed, arms folded
over his chest, soundlessly moving his lips and obviously lost in
deep absorption: you could see that he was praying with his
whole soul.

It somehow disturbed me to see so real a prayer combined

with almost mechanical body movements, and one day I asked the *hajji*, who understood a little English:

'Do you really believe that God expects you to show Him your respect by repeated bowing and kneeling and prostration? Might it not be better only to look into oneself and to pray to Him in the stillness of one's heart? Why all these movements of your body?'

As soon as I had uttered these words I felt remorse, for I had not intended to injure the old man's religious feelings. But the *hajji* did not appear in the least offended. He smiled with his toothless mouth and replied:

'How else then should we worship God? Did He not create both, soul and body, together? And this being so, should man not pray with his body as well as with his soul? Listen, I will tell you why we Muslims pray as we pray. We turn toward the Kaaba, God's holy temple in Mecca, knowing that the faces of all Muslims, wherever they may be, are turned to it in prayer, and that we are like one body, with Him as the centre of our thoughts. First we stand upright and recite from the Holy Koran, remembering that it is His Word, given to man that he may be upright and steadfast in life. Then we say, "God is the Greatest," reminding ourselves that no one deserves to be worshipped but Him; and bow down deep because we honour Him above all, and praise His power and glory. Thereafter we prostrate ourselves on our foreheads because we feel that we are but dust and nothingness before Him, and that He is our Creator and Sustainer on high. Then we lift our faces from the ground and remain sitting, praying that He forgive us our sins and bestow His grace upon us, and guide us aright, and give us health and sustenance. Then we again prostrate ourselves on the ground and touch the dust with our foreheads before the might and the glory of the One. After that, we remain sitting and pray that He bless the Prophet Muhammad who brought His message to us, just as He blessed the earlier Prophets; and that He bless us as well, and all those who follow the right guidance; and we ask Him to give us of the good of this world and of the good of the world to come. In the end we turn our heads to the right and to the left, saying, "Peace and the grace of God be upon you" – and thus greet all who are righteous, wherever they may be.

'It was thus that our Prophet used to pray and taught his followers to pray for all times, so that they might willingly surrender themselves to God – which is what *Islam* means – and so be at peace with Him and with their own destiny.'

The old man did not, of course, use exactly these words, but this was their meaning, and this is how I remember them. Years later I realized that with his simple explanation the *hajji* had opened to me the first door to Islam; but even then, long before any thought that Islam might become my own faith entered my mind, I began to feel an unwonted humility whenever I saw, as I often did, a man standing barefoot on his prayer rug, or on a straw mat, or on the bare earth, with his arms folded over his chest and his head lowered, entirely submerged within himself, oblivious of what was going on around him, whether it was in a mosque or on the sidewalk of a busy street: a man at peace with himself.

. . . .

THE 'ARAB STONE HOUSE' of which Dorian had written was really delightful. It stood on the fringe of the Old City near the Jaffa Gate. Its wide, high-ceilinged rooms seemed to be saturated with memories of the patrician life that had passed through them in earlier generations and the walls reverberated with the living present surging into them from the bazaar nearby – sights and sounds and smells that were unlike anything I had experienced before.

From the roof terrace I could see the sharply outlined area of the Old City with its network of irregular streets and alleys carved in stone. At the other end, seemingly near in its mighty expanse, was the site of Solomon's Temple; the Al-Aqsa Mosque – the most sacred after those of Mecca and Medina – stood on its farthest rim, and the Dome of the Rock in the centre. Beyond it, the Old City walls fell off toward the Valley of Kidron; and beyond the valley grew softly rounded, barren hills, their slopes thinly spotted with olive trees. Toward the east there was a little more fertility, and you could see there a garden sloping down toward the road, dark-green, hedged in by walls: the Garden of Gethsemane. From its midst shone between olive trees and cypresses the golden, onion-shaped domes of the Russian Church.

Like an oscillating brew from an alchemist's retort, clear and nevertheless full of a thousand undefinable colours, beyond words, beyond even the grasp of thought: thus you could see from the Mount of Olives the valley of the Jordan and the Dead Sea. Wavy hills and wavy hills, outlined, breath-like, against an opalescent air, with the deep-blue streak of the Jordan and the rounding of the Dead Sea beyond – and still farther beyond, another world in itself, the dusky hills of Moab: a landscape of such an incredible, multiform beauty that your heart trembled with excitement.

Jerusalem was an entirely new world to me. There were historic memories seeping from every corner of the ancient city: streets that had heard Isaiah preach, cobblestones over which Christ had walked, walls that had been old when the heavy step of Roman legionaries echoed from them, arches over doorways that bore inscriptions of Saladin's time. There was the deep blue of the skies, which might not have been unfamiliar to someone who knew other Mediterranean countries: but to me, who had grown up in a far less friendly climate, this blueness was like a call and a promise. The houses and streets seemed to be covered with a tender, oscillating glaze; the people were full of spontaneous movement and grand of gesture. The people – that is, the Arabs: for it was they who from the very beginning impressed themselves on my consciousness as the people of the land, people who had grown out of its soil and its history and were one with the surrounding air. Their garments were colourful and of a Biblical sweep of drapery, and each of them, *fellah* or beduin (for you could often see beduins who came to town to buy or sell their goods), wore them in a manner quite his own, ever so slightly different from the others, as if he had invented a personal fashion on the spur of the moment.

In front of Dorian's house, at a distance of perhaps forty yards, rose the steep, time-worn walls of David's Castle, which was part of the ramparts of the Old City – a typical medieval Arab citadel, probably erected on Herodian foundations, with a slim watchtower like a minaret. (Although it has no direct connection with King David, the Jews have always called it after him because here, on Mount Zion, the old royal palace is said to have stood.) On the Old City side there was a low, broad tower, through which the gateway went, and a bridge of stone arched across the old moat to the gate. That arched bridge was apparently a customary place of rendezvous for beduins when they had occasion to come into the city. One day I noticed a tall beduin standing there without motion, silhouetted against the silver-grey sky like a figure from an old legend. His face, with sharp cheekbones framed in a short, red-brown beard, bore an expression of deep gravity; it was sombre, as if he expected something and yet did not feel expectant. His wide, brown-and-white-striped cloak was worn and tattered – and the fanciful idea came to me, I do not know why, that it had been worn out in many months of danger and flight. Was he, perhaps, one of that handful of warriors who had accompanied young David on his flight from the dark jealousy of Saul, his king? Perhaps David was asleep just now, hiding somewhere in a cave in the Judean hills, and this man here, this faithful and brave friend, had stealthily come with a companion into the royal city to find out how Saul felt about their leader and whether it was safe for him to return. And now this friend of David was waiting here for his comrade, full of dark forebodings: it was not good news that they would bring David . . .

Suddenly the beduin moved, started walking down the ramp, and my dream-fantasy broke. And then I remembered with a start: this man was an Arab, while those others, those figures of the Bible – were Hebrews! But my astonishment was only of a moment's duration; for all at once I knew, with that clarity which sometimes bursts within us like lightning and lights up the world for the length of a heartbeat, that David and David's time, like Abraham and Abraham's time, were closer to their Arabian roots – and so to the beduin of to-day – than to the Jew of today, who claims to be their descendant . . .

I often sat on the stone balustrade below the Jaffa Gate and watched the throng of people going into or coming out of the Old City. Here they rubbed against each other, jostled one another, Arab and Jew, all possible variations of both. There were the strong-boned *fellahin* with their white or brown headcloths or orange-coloured turbans. There were beduins with sharp, clear-cut and, almost without exception, lean faces, wearing their cloaks in a strangely self-confident manner, frequently with hands on hips and elbows wide apart, as if they took it for granted that everyone would make way for them. There were peasant women in black or blue calico dresses embroidered in white across the bosom, often carrying baskets on their heads and moving with a supple, easy grace. Seen from behind, many a woman of sixty could be taken for a young girl. Their eyes also seemed to remain clear and untouched by age – unless they happened to be affected by trachoma, that evil 'Egyptian' eye disease which is the curse of all countries east of the Mediterranean.

And there were the Jews: indigenous Jews, wearing a *tarbush* and a wide, voluminous cloak, in their facial type strongly resembling the Arabs; Jews from Poland and Russia, who seemed to carry with them so much of the smallness and narrowness of their past lives in Europe that it was surprising to think they claimed to be of the same stock as the proud Jew from Morocco or Tunisia in his white *burnus*. But although the European Jews were so obviously out of all harmony with the picture that surrounded them, it was they who set the tone of Jewish life and politics and thus seemed to be responsible for the almost visible friction between Jews and Arabs.

What did the average European know of the Arabs in those days? Practically nothing. When he came to the Near East he brought with him some romantic and erroneous notions; and if he was well-intentioned and intellectually honest, he had to admit that he had no idea at all about the Arabs. I, too, before I came to Palestine, had never thought of it as an Arab land. I had, of course, vaguely known that 'some' Arabs lived there, but I imagined them to be only nomads in desert tents and idyllic oasis dwellers. Because most of what I had read about Palestine in earlier days had been written by Zionists – who naturally had only their own problems in view – I had not realized that the towns also were full of Arabs – that, in fact, in 1922 there lived in Palestine nearly five Arabs to every Jew, and that, therefore, it was an Arab country to a far higher degree than a country of Jews.

When I remarked on this to Mr. Ussyshkin, chairman of the Zionist Committee of Action, whom I met during that time, I had the impression that the Zionists were not inclined to give much consideration to the fact of Arab majority; nor did they seem to attribute any real importance to the Arabs' opposition to Zionism. Mr. Ussyshkin's response showed nothing but contempt for the Arabs:

'There is no real Arab movement here against us; that is, no movement with roots in the people. All that you regard as opposition is in reality nothing but the shouting of a few disgruntled agitators. It will collapse of itself within a few months or at most a few years.'

This argument was far from satisfactory to me. From the very beginning I had a feeling that the whole idea of Jewish settlement in Palestine was artificial, and, what was worse, that it threatened to transfer all the complications and insoluble problems of European life into a country which might have remained happier without them. The Jews were not really coming to it as one returns to one's homeland; they were rather bent on *making* it into a homeland conceived on European patterns and with European aims. In short, they were strangers within the gates. And so I did not find anything wrong in the Arabs' determined resistance to the idea of a Jewish homeland in their midst; on the contrary, I immediately realized that it was the Arabs who were being imposed upon and were rightly defending themsleves against such an imposition.

In the Balfour Declaration of 1917, which promised the Jews a 'national home' in Palestine, I saw a cruel political manoeuvre designed to foster the old principle, common to all colonial powers, of 'divide and rule'. In the case of Palestine, this principle was the more flagrant as in 1916 the British had promised the then ruler of Mecca, Sharif Husayn, as a price for his help against the Turks, an independent Arab state which was to comprise all countries between the Mediterranean Sea and the Persian Gulf. They not only broke their promise a year later by concluding with France the secret Sykes-Picot Agreement (which established French Dominion over Syria and the Lebanon), but also, by implication, excluded Palestine from the obligations they had assumed with regard to the Arabs.

Although of Jewish origin myself, I conceived from the outset a strong objection to Zionism. Apart from my personal sympathy for the Arabs, I considered it immoral that immigrants, assisted by a foreign Great Power, should come from abroad with the avowed intention of attaining to majority in the country and thus to dispossess the people whose country it had been since time immemorial. Consequently, I was inclined to take the side of the Arabs whenever the Jewish-Arab question was brought up – which, of course, happened very often. This attitude of mine was beyond the comprehension of practically all the Jews with whom I came in contact during those months. They could not understand what I saw in the Arabs who, according to them, were no more than a mass of backward people whom they looked upon with a feeling not much different from that of the European settlers in Central Africa. They were not in the least interested in what the Arabs thought; almost none of them took pains to learn Arabic; and everyone accepted without question the dictum that Palestine was the rightful heritage of the Jews.

I still remember a brief discussion I had on this score with Dr. Chaim Weizmann, the undisputed leader of the Zionist movement. He had come on one of his periodic visits to Palestine (his permanent residence was, I believe, in London), and I met him in the house of a Jewish friend. One could not but be impressed by the boundless energy of this man – an energy that manifested itself even in his bodily movements, in the long, springy stride with which he paced up and down the room – and by the power of intellect revealed in the broad forehead and the penetrating glance of his eyes.

He was talking of the financial difficulties which were besetting the dream of a Jewish National Home, and the insufficient response to this dream among people abroad; and I had the disturbing impression that even he, like most of the other Zionists, was inclined to transfer the moral responsibility for all that was happening in Palestine to the 'outside world'. This impelled me to break through the deferential hush with which all the other people present were listening to him, and to ask:

'And what about the Arabs?'

I must have committed a *faux pas* by thus bringing a jarring note into the conversation, for Dr. Weizmann turned his face slowly toward me, put down the cup he had been holding in his hand, and repeated my question:

'What about the Arabs . . .?'

'Well – how can you ever hope to make Palestine your homeland in the face of the vehement opposition of the Arabs who, after all, are in the majority in this country?'

The Zionist leader shrugged his shoulders and answered drily: 'We expect they won't be in a majority after a few years.'

'Perhaps so. You have been dealing with this problem for years and must know the situation better than I do. But quite apart from the political difficulties which Arab opposition may or may not put in your way – does not the moral aspect of the question ever bother you? Don't you think that it is wrong on your part to displace the people who have always lived in this country?'

'But it is *our* country,' replied Dr. Weizmann, raising his eyebrows. 'We are doing no more than taking back what we have been wrongly deprived of.'

'But you have been away from Palestine for nearly two thousand years! Before that you had ruled this country, and hardly ever the whole of it, for less than five hundred years. Don't you think that the Arabs could, with equal justification, demand Spain for themselves – for, after all, they held sway in Spain for nearly seven hundred years and lost it entirely only five hundred years ago?'

Dr. Weizmann had become visibly impatient: 'Nonsense. The Arabs had only *conquered* Spain; it had never been their original homeland, and so it was only right that in the end they were driven out by the Spaniards.'

'Forgive me,' I retorted, 'but it seems to me that there is some historical oversight here. After all, the Hebrews also came as conquerors to Palestine. Long before them were many other Semitic and non-Semitic tribes settled here – the Amorites, the Edomites, the Philistines, the Moabites, the Hittites. Those tribes continued living here even in the days of the kingdoms of Israel and Judah. They continued living here after the Romans drove our ancestors away. They are living here today. The Arabs who settled in Syria and Palestine after their conquest in the seventh century were always only a small minority of the population; the rest of what we describe today as Palestinian or Syrian "Arabs" are in reality only the Arabianized, original inhabitants of the country. Some of them became Muslims in the course of centuries, others remained Christians; the Muslims naturally inter-married with their co-religionists from Arabia. But can you deny that the bulk of those people in Palestine, who speak Arabic, whether Muslims or Christians, are direct-line descendants of the original inhabitants: original in the sense of having lived in this country centuries before the Hebrews came to it?'

Dr. Weizmann smiled politely at my outburst and turned the conversation to other topics.

I did not feel happy about the outcome of my intervention. I had of course not expected any of those present – least of all Dr. Weizmann himself – to subscribe to my conviction that the Zionist idea was highly vulnerable on the moral plane: but I had hoped that my defence of the Arab cause would at least give rise to some sort of uneasiness on the part of the Zionist leadership – an uneasiness which might bring about more introspection and thus, perhaps, a greater readiness to admit the existence of a possible moral right in the opposition of the Arabs. . . None of this had come about. Instead, I found myself facing a blank wall of staring eyes: a censorious disapproval of my temerity, which dared question the unquestionable right of the Jews to the land of their forefathers . . .

How was it possible, I wondered, for people endowed with so much creative intelligence as the Jews to think of the Zionist-Arab conflict in Jewish terms alone? Did they not realize that the problem of the Jews in Palestine could, in the long run, be solved only through friendly co-operation with the Arabs? Were they so hopelessly blind to the painful future which their policy must bring? – to the struggles, the bitterness and the hatred to which the Jewish island, even if temporarily successful, would forever remain exposed in the midst of a hostile Arab sea?

And how strange, I thought, that a nation which had suffered so many wrongs in the course of its long and sorrowful diaspora was now, in single-minded pursuit of its own goal, ready to inflict a grievous wrong on another nation – and a nation, too, that was innocent of all that past Jewish suffering. Such a phenomenon, I knew, was not unknown to history; but it made me, none the less, very sad to see it enacted before my eyes.

.   .   .   .

BY THAT TIME my absorption in the political scene in Palestine was grounded not merely in my sympathy for the Arabs and my worry about the Zionist experiment, but also in a revival of my journalistic interests: for I had become a special correspondent of the *Frankfurter Zeitung*, then one of the most outstanding newspapers in Europe. This connection had come about almost by accident.

One evening, while sorting out old papers which were cluttering up one of my suitcases, I found the press card issued to me a year before in Berlin as a representative of the United Telegraph.

I was about to tear it up when Dorian grabbed my hand and jokingly exclaimed:

'Don't! If you present this card at the office of the High Commissioner, you will receive a few days later an invitation to lunch at Government House . . . Journalists are very desirable creatures in this country.'

Although I did tear up the useless card, Dorian's joke struck a response in my mind. I was, of course, not interested in a luncheon invitation from Government House – but why should I not utilize the rare opportunity of being in the Near East at a time when so few journalists from Central Europe could travel there? Why should I not resume my journalistic work – and not with the United Telegraph but with one of the great dailies? And as suddenly as I had always been wont to make important decisions, I now decided to break into *real* journalism.

Despite my year's work at the United Telegraph, I had no direct connection with any important newspaper, and as I had never yet published anything in my own name, it was entirely unknown to the daily press. This, however, did not discourage me. I wrote an article on some of my impressions in Palestine and sent copies of it to no less than ten German newspapers with a proposal to write a series of articles on the Near East.

This was in the last months of 1922 – a time of the most catastrophic inflation in Germany. The German press was hard-put to survive, and only a very few newspapers could afford to pay foreign correspondents in hard currency. And so it was not in the least surprising that one after another of the ten newspapers to which I had sent the sample article replied in more or less polite terms of refusal. Only one of the ten accepted my suggestion and, apparently impressed by what I had written, appointed me its roving special correspondent in the Near East, enclosing, in addition, a contract for a book to be written on my return. That one newspaper was the *Frankfurter Zeitung*. I was almost bowled over when I saw that I had not merely succeeded in establishing a connection with a newspaper – and what a newspaper! – but had at the first stroke achieved a status that might be envied by many an old journalist.

There was, of course, a snag in it. Owing to the inflation, the *Frankfurter Zeitung* could not pay me in hard currency. The remuneration which they apologetically offered me was in terms of

German marks; and I knew as well as they did that it would hardly suffice to pay for the stamps on the envelopes which would contain my articles. But to be special correspondent of the *Frankfurter Zeitung* was a distinction that by far outweighed the temporary handicap of not being paid for it. I began to write articles on Palestine, hoping that sooner or later some lucky twist of fortune would enable me to travel all over the Near East.

.   .   .   .

I NOW HAD many friends in Palestine, both Jews and Arabs. The Zionists, it is true, looked upon me with some sort of puzzled suspicion because of the sympathy for the Arabs which was so apparent in my dispatches to the *Frankfurter Zeitung*. Evidently they could not make up their minds whether I had been 'bought' by the Arabs (for in Zionist Palestine people had become accustomed to explain almost every happening in terms of money) or whether I was simply a freakish intellectual in love with the exotic. But not all Jews living in Palestine at that time were Zionists. Some of them had come there not in pursuit of a political aim, but out of a religious longing for the Holy Land and its Biblical associations.

To this group belonged my Dutch friend Jacob de Haan, a small, plump, blond-bearded man in his early forties, who had formerly taught law at one of the leading universities in Holland and was now special correspondent of the Amsterdam *Handelsblad* and the London *Daily Express*. A man of deep religious convictions – as 'orthodox' as any Jew of Eastern Europe – he did not approve of the idea of Zionism, for he believed that the return of his people to the Promised Land had to await the coming of the Messiah.

'We Jews,' he said to me on more than one occasion, 'were driven away from the Holy Land and scattered all over the world because we had fallen short of the task God had conferred upon us. We had been chosen by Him to preach His Word, but in our stubborn pride we began to believe that He had made us a "chosen nation" for our own sakes – and thus we betrayed Him. Now nothing remains for us but to repent and to cleanse our hearts; and when we become worthy once again to be the hearers of His Message, He will send a Messiah to lead His servants back to the Promised Land . . .'

'But,' I asked, 'does not this Messianic idea underlie the Zionist movement as well? You know that I do not approve of it: but is it not a natural desire of every people to have a national home of its own?'

Dr. de Haan looked at me quizzically: 'Do you think that history is but a series of accidents? I don't. It was not without a purpose that God made us lose our land and dispersed us; but the Zionists do not want to admit this to themselves. They suffer from the same spiritual blindness that caused our downfall. The two thousand years of Jewish exile and unhappiness have taught them nothing. Instead of making an attempt to understand the innermost causes of our unhappiness, they now try to circumvent it, as it were, by building a "national home" on foundations provided by Western power politics; and in the process of building a national home, they are committing the crime of depriving another people of its home.'

Jacob de Haan's political views naturally made him most unpopular with the Zionists (indeed, a short time after I left Palestine, I was shocked to learn that he had been shot down one night by terrorists). When I knew him, his social intercourse was limited to a very few Jews of his own way of thought, some Europeans, and Arabs. For the Arabs he seemed to have a great affection, and they, on their part, thought highly of him and frequently invited him to their houses. As a matter of fact, at that period they were not yet universally prejudiced against Jews as such. It was only subsequent to the Balfour Declaration – that is, after centuries of good-neighbourly relations and a consciousness of racial kinship – that the Arabs had begun to look upon the Jews as political enemies; but even in the changed circumstances of the early Twenties, they still clearly differentiated between Zionists and Jews who were friendly toward them like Dr. de Haan.

.   .   .   .

THOSE FATEFUL MONTHS of my first sojourn among the Arabs set in motion a whole train of impressions and reflections; some inarticulate hopes of a personal nature demanded to be admitted to my consciousness.

I had come face to face with a life-sense that was entirely new to me. A warm, human breath seemed to flow out of these people's blood into their thoughts and gestures, with none of those painful cleavages of the spirit, those phantoms of fear, greed and inhibition that made European life so ugly and of so little promise. In the Arabs I began to find something I had always unwittingly been looking for: an emotional lightness of approach to all questions of life – a supreme common sense of feeling, if one might call it so.

In time it became most important to me to grasp the spirit of these Muslim people: not because their religion attracted me (for at that time I knew very little about it), but because I recognized in them that organic coherence of the mind and the senses which we Europeans had lost. Might it not be possible, perhaps, by better understanding the life of the Arabs to discover the hidden link between our Western suffering – the corroding lack of inner integration – and the roots of that suffering? To find out, perhaps, what it was that had made us Westerners run away from that solemn freedom of life which the Arabs seemed to possess, even in their social and political decay, and which we also must have possessed at some earlier time? – or else how could we have produced the great art of our past, the Gothic cathedrals of the Middle Ages, the exuberant joy of the Renaissance, Rembrandt's chiaroscuro, the fugues of Bach and the serene dreams of Mozart, the pride of the peacock's tail in the art of our peasants, and Beethoven's roaring, longing ascent toward the misty, hardly perceptible peaks on which man could say, 'I and my destiny are one . . .'

Being unaware of their true nature, we could no longer rightly use our spiritual powers; never again would a Beethoven or a Rembrandt arise among us. Instead, we now knew only that desperate groping after 'new forms of expression' in art, sociology, politics, and that bitter struggle between opposing slogans and meticulously devised principles; and all our machines and skyscrapers could do nothing to restore the broken wholeness of our souls . . . And yet – was that lost spiritual glory of Europe's past really lost forever? Was it not possible to recover something of it by finding out what was wrong with us?

And what at first had been hardly more than a sympathy for the political aims of the Arabs, the outward appearance of Arabian life and the emotional security I perceived in its people, imperceptibly changed into something resembling a personal quest.

I became increasingly aware of an absorbing desire to know what it was that lay at the root of this emotional security and made Arab life so different from the European: and that desire seemed to be mysteriously bound up with my own innermost problems. I began to look for openings that would give me a better insight into the character of the Arabs, into the ideas that had shaped them and made them spiritually so different from the Europeans. I began to read intensively about their history, culture and religion. And in the urge I felt to discover what it was that moved their hearts and filled their minds and gave them direction, I seemed to sense an urge to discover some hidden forces that moved myself, and filled me, and promised to give me direction . . .

IV

VOICES

— 1 —

WE RIDE, AND ZAYD SINGS. The dunes are lower now and wider spaced. Here and there the sand gives way to stretches of gravel and splintery basalt, and in front of us, far to the south, rise the shadowy outlines of hill ranges: the mountains of Jabal Shammar.

The verses of Zayd's song penetrate in a blurred way into my sleepiness, but precisely in the measure that the words escape me, they seem to gain a wider, deeper significance quite unrelated to their outward meaning.

It is one of those camel-rider songs you so often hear in Arabia – chants which men sing to keep their animals to a regular, quick pace and not to fall asleep themselves – chants of desert men accustomed to spaces that know neither limits nor echoes: always sounded in the major key at only one tone level, loose and somewhat husky, coming from high up in the throat, tenderly fading in the dry air: breath of the desert caught in a human voice. None who has travelled through desert lands will ever forget this voice. It is always the same where the earth is barren, the air hot and wide open, and life hard.

We ride, and Zayd sings, as his father must have sung before him, and all the other men of his tribe and of many other tribes over thousands of years: for thousands of years were needed to mould these intensive, monotonous melodies and to bring them to their final form. Unlike the polyphonous Western music, which almost always tends to express individual feeling, these Arabian melodies, with their eternally repeated tone-sequence, seem to be only tonal symbols for an emotional knowledge shared by many people – not meant to evoke moods but to remind you of your own spiritual experiences. They were born very long ago out of the atmosphere of the desert, the rhythms of the wind and of nomad life, the feel of wide expanses, the con-

102

templation of an eternal present: and just as the basic things of human life always remain the same, these melodies are timeless and changeless.

Such melodies are hardly thinkable in the West, where polyphony is an aspect not only of music but of man's feelings and desires. Cool climate, running waters, the sequence of four seasons: these elements give to life so multiform a significance and so many directions that Western man must needs have many longings and, thus, a strong urge to do things for the sake of doing. He must always create, build and overcome in order to see himself again and again reaffirmed in the complexity of his life-forms; and this ever-changing complexity is reflected in his music as well. Out of the sonorous Western singing, with the voice coming from the chest and always playing in several levels, speaks that 'Faustian' nature which causes Western man to dream much, to desire much, to strive after much with a will to conquer – but perhaps also to miss much, and miss it painfully. For, the world of the Westerner is a world of history: eternal becoming, happening, passing away. It lacks the restfulness of staying still; time is an enemy, always to be viewed with suspicion; and never does the Now carry a sound of eternity . . .

To the Arab of the desert and steppe, on the other hand, his landscape is no enticement to dreams: it is hard like the day and knows no twilight of feelings. The Outer and the Inner, the I and the World, are to him not opposite – and mutually opposed – entities, but only different aspects of an unchanging present; his life is not dominated by secret fears; and whenever he does things, he does them because outward necessity and not a desire for inner security demands action. In result, he has not progressed in material achievement as rapidly as the Westerner – but he has kept his soul together.

. . . .

FOR HOW LONG, I ask myself with almost a physical start, will Zayd, and Zayd's people, be able to keep their souls together in the face of the danger that is so insidiously, so relentlessly closing in on them? We are living in a time in which the East can no longer remain passive in the face of the advancing West. A thousand forces – political, social and economic – are hammering at the doors of the Muslim world. Will this world succumb to the pressure of the Western twentieth century and in the process lose not only its own traditional forms but its spiritual roots as well?

— 2 —

THROUGHOUT THE YEARS I have spent in the Middle East – as a sympathetic outsider from 1922 to 1926, and as a Muslim sharing the aims and hopes of the Islamic community ever since – I have witnessed the steady European encroachment on Muslim cultural life and political independence; and wherever Muslim peoples try to defend themselves against this encroachment, European public opinion invariably labels their resistance, with an air of hurt innocence, as 'xenophobia'.

Europe has long been accustomed to simplify in this crude way all that is happening in the Middle East and to view its current history under the aspect of Western 'spheres of interest' alone. While everywhere in the West (outside of Britain) public opinion has shown much sympathy for the Irish struggle for independence or (outside of Russia and Germany) for Poland's dream of national resurrection, no such sympathy is ever extended to similar aspirations among the Muslims. The West's main argument is always the political disruption and economic backwardness of the Middle East, and every active Western intervention is sanctimoniously described by its authors as aiming not merely at a protection of 'legitimate' Western interests but also at securing progress for the indigenous peoples themselves.

Forgetting that every direct, and even benevolent, intervention from outside cannot but disturb a nation's development, Western students of Middle Eastern affairs have always been ready to swallow such claims. They see only the new railroads built by colonial powers, and not the destruction of a country's social fabric; they count the kilowatts of new electricity, but not the blows to a nation's pride. The same people who would never have accepted Imperial Austria's 'civilizing mission' as a valid excuse for her interventions in the Balkans indulgently accept a similar plea in the case of the British in Egypt, the Russians in Central Asia, the French in Morocco or the Italians in Libya. And it never even crosses their minds that many of the social and economic ills from which the Middle East is suffering are a direct outcome of that very Western 'interest'; and that, in addition,

Western intervention invariably seeks to perpetuate and to widen the already existing inner disruptions and so to make it impossible for the peoples concerned to come into their own.

. . . .

I FIRST BEGAN TO realize this in Palestine, in 1922, when I observed the equivocal role of the British administration with regard to the conflict between the Arabs and the Zionists; and it became fully obvious to me early in 1923, when after months of wandering all over Palestine I came to Egypt, which at that time was in almost continual upheaval against the British 'protectorate'. Bombs were often being thrown at public places frequented by British soldiers, to be answered by various repressive measures – martial law, political arrests, deportations of leaders, prohibitions of newspapers. But none of these measures, however severe, could deaden the people's desire for freedom. Through the entire Egyptian nation went something like a wave of passionate sobbing. Not in despair: it was rather the sobbing of enthusiasm at having discovered the roots of its own potential strength.

Only the rich pashas, owners of the tremendous landed estates, were in those days conciliatory toward British rule. The innumerable others – including the miserable *fellahin*, to whom one acre of land appeared to be a bountiful possession for an entire family – supported the freedom movement. One day the itinerant newspaper vendors would cry in the streets, 'All leaders of the Wafd arrested by order of the Military Governor' – but the next day new leaders had taken their places, the gaps were filled again and again: the hunger for freedom and the hatred grew. And Europe had only one word for it: 'xenophobia'.

My coming to Egypt in those days had been due to my wish to extend the scope of my work for the *Frankfurter Zeitung* to other countries besides Palestine. Dorian's circumstances did not permit him to finance such a tour; but when he saw how strongly I desired it, he advanced me a small sum sufficient for the railway journey from Jerusalem to Cairo and a fortnight's stay there.

In Cairo I found lodgings in a narrow alley in a quarter inhabited mainly by Arab artisans and small Greek shopkeepers. The landlady was an old Triestine, tall, thickset, cumbrous, grey; she drank from morning till evening heavy Greek wine and floundered from one mood into another. Hers was a violent, passionate temperament that never seemed to have found itself; but she was friendly toward me and made me feel well in her presence.

After a week or so, my cash was approaching its end. As I did not want to return so soon to Palestine and the safety of my uncle's house, I began to look around for some other means of subsistence.

My Jerusalem friend, Dr. de Haan, had given me a letter of introduction to a business man in Cairo; and to him I went in search of advice. He proved to be a large, genial Hollander with intellectual interests far exceeding his own sphere of activities. From Jacob de Haan's letter he learned that I was a correspondent of the *Frankfurter Zeitung;* and when, at his request, I showed him some of my recent articles, he raised his eyebrows in astonishment:

'Tell me, how old are you?'

'Twenty-two.'

'Then tell me something else, please: who has helped you with these articles – de Haan?'

I laughed. 'Of course not. I wrote them myself. I always do my work myself. But why do you doubt it?'

He shook his head, as if puzzled: 'But it's astonishing . . . Where did you get the maturity to write such stuff? How do you manage to convey in a half-sentence an almost mystical significance to things that are apparently so commonplace?'

I was flattered beyond words at the implied compliment, and my self-esteem rose accordingly. In the course of our conversation, it transpired that my new found acquaintance had no opening in his own business, but he thought he might be able to place me in an Egyptian firm with which he had dealings.

The office to which he directed me lay in one of the older quarters of Cairo, not far from my lodgings: a dingy, narrow lane bordered by once-patrician houses now converted into offices and cheap apartments. My prospective employer, an elderly, bald-headed Egyptian with the face of a time-mellowed vulture, happened to be in need of a part-time clerk to take charge of his French correspondence; and I was able to satisfy him that I could fill the role in spite of my utter lack of business experience. We quickly struck a bargain. I would have to work only three hours a day; the salary was correspondingly low, but it would be enough to pay for my rent and to keep me indefinitely in bread, milk and olives.

Between my lodgings and my office lay Cairo's red-light district – a tangled maze of lanes in which the great and little courtesans spent their days and nights. In the afternoon, on my way to work, the lanes were empty and silent. In the shadow of a bay window a woman's body would stretch itself languorously; at little tables before one or another of the houses girls were sedately drinking coffee in the company of grave, bearded men and conversing, with every appearance of seriousness, about things that seemed to lie far beyond all excitement and physical abandon.

But in the evening, when I was returning home, the quarter was more wide-awake than any other, humming with the tender accords of Arabian lutes and drums and the laughter of women. When you walked under the shine of the many electric lamps and coloured lanterns, at every step a soft arm would wind itself around your neck; the arm might be brown or white – but it always jingled with gold and silver chains and bangles and always smelled of musk, frankincense and warm animal skin. You had to be very determined to keep yourself free of all these laughing embraces and from the calls of *ya habibi* ('O darling') and *saadatak* ('thy happiness'). You had to thread your way between shimmering limbs that were mostly luscious and fair to look upon and intoxicated you with their suggestive convolutions. All Egypt broke over you, Morocco, Algeria, also the Sudan and Nubia, also Arabia, Armenia, Syria, Iran . . . Men in long silken garments sat side by side on benches along the house walls, pleasantly excited, laughing, calling out to girls or silently smoking their *nargiles*. Not all of them were 'customers': many had come simply to spend a pleasant hour or two in the exhilarating, unconventional atmosphere of the quarter . . . Sometimes you had to step back before a ragged dervish from the Sudan, who sang his begging songs with an entranced face and stiffly outstretched arms. Clouds of incense from the swinging censer of an itinerant perfume vendor brushed your face. Off and on you heard singing in chorus, and you began to understand the meaning of some of the whirring, tender Arabic sounds . . . And again and again you heard the soft, rippling voices of pleasure – the animal pleasure of these girls (for they undoubtedly were enjoying themselves) in their light-blue, yellow, red, green, white, gold-glittering garments of flimsy silk, tulle, voile or damask – and their laughter seemed to run with little cat-steps over the cobbled pavement, rising, ebbing down, and then growing up again from other lips . . .

How they could laugh, these Egyptians! How cheerfully they walked day in, day out over the streets of Cairo, striding with swinging steps in their long, shirtlike *gallabiyyas* that were striped in every colour of the rainbow – lightheartedly, free-mindedly – so that one might have thought that all the grinding poverty and dissatisfaction and political turmoil were taken seriously only in a relative sense. The violent, explosive excitement of these people always seemed to be ready to make room, without any visible transition, for perfect serenity and even indolence, as if nothing had ever happened and nothing were amiss. Because of this, most Europeans regarded (and probably do even now) the Arabs as superficial; but even in those early days I realized that this contempt for the Arabs had grown out of the West's tendency to overestimate emotions that appear to be 'deep', and to denounce as 'superficial' everything that is light, airy, un-weighted. The Arabs, I felt, had remained free of those inner tensions and stresses so peculiar to the West: how could we, then, apply our own standards to them? If they seemed to be super-ficial, it was perhaps because their emotions flowed without fric-tion into their behaviour. Perhaps, under the impact of 'Wester-nization', they also would gradually lose the blessed immediacy of their contact with reality: for although that Western influence acted in many ways as a stimulus and fertilizing agent on con-temporary Arab thought, it inevitably tended to produce in the Arabs the same grievous problems that dominated the spiritual and social scene in the West.

. . . .

OPPOSITE MY HOUSE, so close that you could almost touch it, stood a little mosque with a tiny minaret from which five times a day the call to prayer was sounded. A white-turbaned man would appear on the gallery, raise his hands, and begin to chant: '*Allahu akbar* – God is the Greatest! And I bear witness that Muhammad is God's Messenger . . . ' As he slowly turned toward the four points of the compass, the ring of his voice climbed upward, grew into the clear air, rocking on the deep, throaty sounds of the Arabic language, swaying, advancing and retreating. The voice was a dark baritone, soft and strong, capable of a great range; but you could perceive that it was fervour and not art that made it so beautiful.

This chant of the *mu'azzin* was the theme song of my days and evenings in Cairo – just as it had been the theme song in the Old City of Jerusalem and was destined to remain in all my later wanderings through Muslim lands. It sounded the same everywhere in spite of the differences of dialect and intonation which might be evident in the people's daily speech: a unity of sound which made me realize in those days at Cairo how deep was the inner unity of all Muslims, and how artificial and insignificant were the dividing lines between them. They were one in their way of thinking and judging between right and wrong, and one in their perception of what constitutes the good life.

It seemed to me that for the first time I had come across a community in which kinship between man and man was not due to accidents of common racial or economic interests but to something far deeper and far more stable: a kinship of common outlook which lifted all barriers of loneliness between man and man.

.   .   .   .

IN THE SUMMER OF 1923, enriched by a better understanding of Middle Eastern life and politics, I returned to Jerusalem.

Through my good friend Jacob de Haan I became acquainted with Amir Abdullah of neighbouring Transjordan, who invited me to visit his country. There I saw for the first time a true beduin land. The capital, Amman – built on the ruins of Philadelphia, the Greek colony of Ptolemaeus Philadelphus – was at that time a little town of hardly more than six thousand inhabitants. Its streets were filled with beduins, the real beduins of the open steppe whom one rarely saw in Palestine, free warriors and camel breeders. Wonderful horses galloped through the streets; every man was armed, carried a dagger in his sash and a rifle on his back. Circassian oxcarts (for the town had been originally settled by Circassians who had migrated there after the Russian conquest of their homeland in the nineteenth century) plodded heavily through the bazaar, which in spite of its smallness was full of a bustle and commotion worthy of a much larger city.

As there were no adequate buildings in the town, Amir Abdullah lived in those days in a tent camp on a hill overlooking Amman. His own tent was somewhat larger than the others and consisted of several rooms formed by canvas partitions and distinguished by utmost simplicity. In one of them, a black bearskin made a bed on the ground in a corner; in the reception room, a couple of beautiful camel-saddles with silver-inlaid pommels served as armrests when one sat on the carpet.

Except for a Negro servant richly dressed in brocade, with a golden dagger in his belt, there was nobody in the tent when I entered it in the company of Dr. Riza Tawfiq Bey, the *amir's* chief adviser. He was a Turk, formerly a university professor, and had been for three years, before Kemal Ataturk, Minister of Education in the Turkish cabinet. Amir Abdullah, he told me, would be back in a few minutes; just now he was conferring with some beduin chieftains about the latest Najdi raid into southern Transjordan. Those Najdi 'Wahhabis', Dr. Riza explained to me, played within Islam a role not unlike that of the Puritan reformers in the Christian world, inasmuch as they were bitterly opposed to all saint worship and the many mystical superstitions that had crept into Islam over the centuries; they were also irreconcilable enemies of the Sharifian family, whose head was the *amir's* father, King Husayn of the Hijaz. According to Riza Tawfiq Bey, the religious views of the Wahhabis could not be rejected out of hand; they did, in fact, come closer to the spirit of the Koran than the views prevalent among the masses in most of the other Muslim countries, and might thus in time exert a beneficial influence on the cultural development of Islam. The extreme fanaticism of these people, however, made it somewhat difficult for other Muslims to appreciate the Wahhabi movement fully; and this drawback, he suggested, might not be unwelcome to 'certain quarters', to whom a possible reunification of the Arab peoples was a dreadful prospect.

A little later the *amir* came in – a man of about forty years, of middle size, with a short, blond beard – stepping softly on small, black patent-leather slippers, clad in loose Arab garments of swishing white silk with an almost transparent white woollen *abaya* over them. He said:

'*Ahlan wa-sahlan*' – 'Family and plain' – and that was the first time I heard this graceful Arabian greeting.

There was something attractive and almost captivating in the personality of Amir Abdullah, a strong sense of humour, a warmth of expression and a ready wit. It was not difficult to see why he was so popular in those days with his people. Although many Arabs were not happy about the role he had played in the British-inspired Sharifian revolt against the Turks and regarded it as a betrayal of Muslims by Muslims, he had gained a certain prestige by his championship of the Arab cause against Zionism; and the day was yet to come when the twists and turns of his politics would make his name odious throughout the Arab world.

Sipping coffee from minute cups that were handed round by the black retainer, we talked – occasionally assisted by Dr. Riza, who spoke fluent French – of the administrative difficulties in this new country of Transjordan, where everyone was accustomed to carry arms and to obey only the laws of his own clan –

' – but,' said the *amir*, 'the Arabs have plenty of common sense; even the beduins are now beginning to realise that they must abandon their old lawless ways if they want to be free from foreign domination. The intertribal feuds of which thou must have heard so often are now gradually subsiding.'

And he went on describing the unruly, uneasy beduin tribes which used to fight with one another on the slightest pretext. Their blood feuds often lasted for generations and sometimes, handed down from father to son, even for centuries, leading to ever new bloodshed and new bitterness after the original cause had almost been forgotten. There was only one way to bring about a peaceful end: if a young man from the tribe and clan of the last victim abducted a virgin of the tribe and clan of the culprit and made her his wife, the blood of the bridal night – blood of the killer's tribe – symbolically, and finally, avenged the blood that had been spilled in homicide. Occasionally it happened that two tribes had grown weary of a vendetta which had been going on for generations, sapping the strength of both parties; and in such a case, an 'abduction' was not infrequently arranged through a middleman from a third tribe.

'I have done even better than that,' Amir Abdullah told me. 'I have established proper "blood feud commissions" composed of trustworthy men who travel around the country and arrange the symbolic kidnappings and marriages between hostile tribes. But' – and here his eyes twinkled – 'I always impress upon the members of these commissions to be very careful in the choice of the virgins, for I would not like to see *internal* family feuds arise on the grounds of the bridegroom's possible disappointment. . .'

A boy of perhaps twelve years appeared from behind a partition, swept across the dusky tent-room with quick, noiseless steps and jumped without stirrup on to the prancing horse outside the tent which a servant had been holding in readiness for him: the *amir's* eldest son, Talal. In his slim body, in his rapid vault on to the horse, in his shining eyes I saw it again: that dreamless contact with his own life which set the Arab so far apart from all that I had known in Europe.

Observing my obvious admiration of his son, the *amir* said: 'He, like every other Arab child, is growing up with but one thought in mind: freedom. We Arabs do not believe ourselves to be faultless or free from error; but we want to commit our errors ourselves and so learn how to avoid them – just as a tree learns how to grow right by growing, or as running water finds its proper course by flowing. We do not want to be guided to wisdom by people who have no wisdom themselves – who have only power, and guns, and money, and only know how to lose friends whom they could so easily keep as friends . . .'*

.   .   .   .

I DID NOT INTEND to remain indefinitely in Palestine; and it was again Jacob de Haan who helped me. Himself a journalist of established reputation, he had many connections all over Europe. His recommendation secured for me contracts with two small newspapers, one in Holland and the other in Switzerland, for a series of articles to be paid in Dutch guilders and Swiss francs. As these were provincial newspapers of no great standing, they could not afford to pay a large remuneration; but to me, whose habits were simple, the money I received from them appeared ample to finance my planned journey through the Near East.

* At that time (1923) nobody could have foreseen the bitter antagonism which in later years would mar the relations between Amir Abdullah and his son Talal – the son hating his father's complaisance with regard to British policies in the Arab world, and the father resenting his son's passionate outspokenness. Nor could I see on that or on later occasions any sign of the 'mental disturbance' in Talal that led to his enforced abdication from the throne of Jordan in 1952.

I wanted to go to Syria first; but the French authorities, so recently established there in the midst of a hostile population, were unwilling to give a visa to an Austrian 'ex-enemy alien'. This was a bitter blow, but there was nothing I could do about it; and so I decided to go to Haifa and there to board a ship for Istanbul, which in any case was included in my programme.

On the train journey from Jerusalem to Haifa a calamity befell me: I lost a coat containing my wallet and passport. All that I had left were the few silver coins in my trousers pocket. A voyage to Istanbul was, for the time being, out of the question: no passport, no money. Nothing remained but to return by bus to Jerusalem; the fare would have to be paid on arrival with money borrowed, as usual, from Dorian. In Jerusalem I would have to wait for weeks for another passport from the Austrian consulate in Cairo (for at that time there was none in Palestine) and for further driblets of money from Holland and Switzerland.

And so it came about that on the next morning I found myself before a bus office on the outskirts of Haifa. The negotiations about the fare were completed. There was one hour until the departure of the bus, and to while away the time I paced up and down the road, deeply disgusted with myself and with the fate that had forced me into so ignominious a retreat. Waiting is always an evil thing; and the thought of returning to Jerusalem defeated, with my tail between my legs, was most galling – the more so as Dorian had always been sceptical about my ability to realize my plans on the basis of such meagre funds. Moreover, I would not see Syria now, and God alone knew if I would ever come back to this part of the world. It was, of course, always possible that at some later date the *Frankfurter Zeitung* would finance another journey to the Middle East, and that one day the French might lift the embargo on ex-enemy aliens; but that was not certain, and in the meantime I would not see Damascus ... Why, I asked myself bitterly, was Damascus denied to me?

But – was it really? Of course – no passport, no money. But was it absolutely neceassry to have a passport and money .. ?

And, having come so far in my thoughts, I suddenly stopped in my tracks. One could, if one had grit enough, travel on foot, availing oneself of the hospitality of Arab villagers; and one could, perhaps, somehow smuggle oneself across the frontier without bothering about passports and visas ...

And before I was quite aware of it, my mind was made up: I was going to Damascus.

A couple of minutes sufficed to explain to the bus people that I had changed my mind and was not going to Jerusalem after all. It took me a few more to change into a pair of blue overalls and an Arab *kufiyya* (the best possible protection against the Arabian sun); to stuff a few necessities into a knapsack, and to arrange for my suitcase to be despatched to Dorian, C.O.D. And then I set out on my long trek to Damascus.

The overwhelming sense of freedom that filled me was indistinguishable from happiness. I had only a few coins in my pocket; I was embarking on an illegal deed that might land me in prison; the problem of crossing the frontier lay ahead in a vague uncertainty; I was staking everything on my wits alone: but the consciousness of having placed all on a single stake made me happy.

.   .   .   .

I WALKED ON THE ROAD to Galilee. In the afternoon the Plain of Esdrelon lay on the right below me, flecked with rags of light and shadow. I passed through Nazareth and before nightfall reached an Arab village shaded by pepper trees and cypresses. At the door of the first house sat three or four men and women. I stopped, asked whether this was Ar-Rayna, and after a Yes was about to move on – when one of the women called after me:

'*Ya sidi*, wilt thou not refresh thyself?' – and, as if divining my thirst, stretched a pitcher of cold water toward me. When I had drunk my fill, one of the men – obviously her husband – asked me:

'Wilt thou not eat bread with us, and remain in our house overnight?'

They did not ask me who I was, where I was going or what my business was. And I stayed overnight as their guest.

To be a guest of an Arab: even schoolchildren hear about it in Europe. To be a guest of an Arab means to enter for a few hours, for a time, truly and fully, into the lives of people who want to be your brothers and sisters. It is not a mere noble tradition which enables the Arabs to be hospitable in so effusive a way: it is their inner freedom. They are so free of distrust of themselves that

Amir (later King) Abdullah of Jordan

they can easily open their lives to another man. They need none of the specious security of the walls which in the West each person builds between himself and his neighbour.

We supped together, men and women, sitting cross-legged on a mat around a huge dish filled with a porridge of coarsely crushed wheat and milk. My hosts tore small pieces from large, paper-thin loaves of bread with which they deftly scooped up the porridge without ever touching it with their fingers. To me they had given a spoon; but I refused it and attempted, not without success, and to the evident pleasure of my friends, to emulate their simple and nevertheless dainty manner of eating.

When we lay down to sleep – about a dozen people in one and the same room – I gazed at the wooden beams above me from which strings of dried peppers and eggplant were hanging, at the many niches in the walls filled with brass and stoneware utensils, at the bodies of sleeping men and women, and asked myself whether at home I could ever have felt more at home.

In the days that followed, the rust-brown of the Judean hills with their bluish-grey and violet shadows gradually gave way to the more gay and mellow hills of Galilee. Springs and little streams unexpectedly made their appearance. Vegetation became more luxuriant. In groups stood thickly leafed olive trees and tall, dark cypresses; the last summer flowers could still be seen on the hill-sides.

Sometimes I walked part of the way with camel drivers and enjoyed for a while their simple warmth; we drank water from my canteen, smoked a cigarette together; then I walked on alone. I spent the nights in Arab houses and ate their bread with them. I tramped for days through the hot depression along the Lake of Galilee and through the soft coolness around Lake Hule, which was like a mirror of metal, with silvery mists, slightly reddened by the last rays of the evening sun that hovered over the water. Near the shore lived Arab fishermen in huts built of straw mats loosely slung around a framework of branches. They were very poor – but they did not seem to need more than these airy huts, the few faded garments on their backs, a handful of wheat to make bread and the fish they caught themselves: and always they seemed to have enough to ask the wanderer to step in and eat with them.

. . . .

THE NORTHERNMOST POINT in Palestine was the Jewish colony of Metulla, which, I had learned earlier, was a kind of gap between British-administered Palestine and French Syria. On the basis of an agreement between the two governments, this and two neighbouring colonies were shortly to be incorporated into Palestine. During those few weeks of transition Metulla was not effectively supervised by either of the two governments, and thus appeared to be an ideal place from which to slip into Syria. It was, I understood, only later, on the highways, that identification papers would be demanded of the traveller. The Syrian control was said to be very strict; it was practically impossible to go far without being stopped by gendarmes. As Metulla was offici- ally still considered part of Syria, every one of its adult inhabi- tants held, like elsewhere in the country, an identity certificate issued by the French authorities. To secure such a paper for my- self became my most pressing task.

I made some discreet enquiries and was finally guided to the house of a man who might be prepared to part with his certifi- cate for a consideration. He was a large person in his late thirties and was described as such in the crumpled and greasy document which he pulled out of his breast pocket; but as the paper bore no photograph, the problem was not insoluble.

'How much do you want for it?' I asked.

'Three pounds.'

I took from my pocket all the coins I possessed and counted them: they came to fifty-five piasters, that is, a little over half a pound.

'This is all I have,' I said, 'As I must keep something for the rest of my journey, I can give you no more than twenty piasters' (which was exactly one-fifteenth of what he had demanded).

After some minutes of haggling we settled on thirty-five pias- ters, and the document was mine. It consisted of a printed sheet with two columns – one French and the other Arabic – the rele- vant data having been inserted in ink on the dotted lines. The 'personal description' did not bother me much, for, as is usual with such descriptions, it was wonderfully vague. But the age mentioned was thirty-nine – while I was twenty-three, and looked twenty. Even a very careless police officer would im- mediately notice the discrepancy; and so it became necessary to change the age entry. Now if it had been mentioned in one place only, the change would not have been so difficult, but unfortunately it was given in French as well as in Arabic. Despite my careful penning, I achieved what could only be described as an unconvincing forgery; to anybody with eyes in his head it would be obvious that the figures had been altered in both columns. But that could not be helped. I would have to rely on my luck and the negligence of the gendarmes.

Early in the morning my business friend led me to a gully behind the village, pointed to some rocks about half a mile beyond, and said, 'There is Syria.'

I made my way across the gulley. Although the hour was early, it was very hot. It must also have been hot to the old Arab woman who sat under a tree near the rocks beyond which was Syria; for she called out to me in a husky, brittle voice:

'Wouldst thou give a drink of water to an old woman, son?'

I unslung my freshly filled canteen and gave it to her. She drank avidly and then handed it back to me, saying:

'May God bless thee, may He keep thee secure and lead thee to thy heart's goal.'

'Thanks, mother, I do not want more than that.'

And when I turned around and looked back at her, I saw the old woman's lips move as if in prayer and felt a strange elation.

I reached the rocks and passed them: and now I was in Syria. A wide, barren plain lay before me; far away on the horizon I saw the outlines of trees and something that looked like houses; it must be the town of Baniyas. I did not like the look of this plain that offered no tree or bush behind which to take cover – which, so near the frontier, might well become necessary. But there was no other way. I felt as one sometimes feels in a dream in which one has to walk naked down a crowded street . . .

It was nearly noon when I reached a small streamlet bisecting the plain. As I sat down to take off my shoes and socks, I saw in the distance four horsemen moving in my direction. With their rifles held across the saddle, they looked ominously like gendarmes. They *were* gendarmes. There would have been no sense in my trying to run away; and so I comforted myself that whatever was to happen would happen. If I were caught now, I would probably receive no more than a few blows with a rifle butt and be escorted back to Metulla.

I waded through the stream, sat down on the opposite bank

and started leisurely to dry my feet, waiting for the gendarmes to come closer. They came, and stared down at me with suspicion: for although I was wearing Arab headress, I was obviously a European.

'From where?' one of them asked me sharply in Arabic.

'From Metulla.'

'And where to?'

'To Damascus.'

'What for?'

'Oh, well, just a pleasure trip.'

'Any papers?'

'Of course . . .'

And out came 'my' identity certificate and up came my heart to my mouth. The gendarme unfolded the paper and looked at it – and my heart slipped back to its proper place and started to beat again: for I saw that he held the document upside-down, obviously unable to read . . . The two or three big government seals apparently satisfied him, for he ponderously folded and handed it back to me:

'Yes, it is in order. Go.'

For a second I had the impulse to shake his hand, but then thought it better to let our relations remain strictly official. The four men wheeled their horses around and trotted away, while I continued on my march.

Near Baniyas I lost my way. What had been described on my map as a 'road fit for wheeled traffic' proved to be a hardly visible path which meandered over steppe land, swampy ground and across little streams, and in the end petered out entirely near some boulder-strewn hillocks. I wandered over these hills for several hours, up and down, until, in the afternoon, I came upon two Arabs with donkeys that were carrying grapes and cheese to Baniyas. We walked the last stretch together; they gave me grapes to eat; and we separated on reaching the gardens before the town. A clear, narrow, rapidly flowing stream was bubbling by the roadside. I lay down on my belly, thrust my head up to the ears in the icy water and drank and drank . . .

Although I was very tired, I had no intention of staying at Baniyas, which, being the first town on the Syrian side, was bound to have a police post. My encounter with the gendarmes had set me at rest as regards ordinary Syrian troopers, for most of them could be presumed to be illiterate and therefore not in a position to detect my forgery: but a police post, with an officer in it, would be a different story. I therefore set out at a quick pace through narrow lanes and byways, avoiding the main bazaar street where such a post would most likely be located. In one of the lanes I heard the sound of a lute and a man's voice singing to the accompaniment of clapping. Drawn to it, I rounded the corner – and stood quite still: for just opposite me, at a distance of perhaps ten paces, was a door inscribed *Poste de Police*, with several Syrian policemen, an officer among them, sitting on stools in the afternoon sun and enjoying the music of one of their comrades. It was too late to retreat, for they had already seen me, and the officer – apparently also a Syrian – called out to me:

'Hey, come here!'

There was nothing to it but to obey. I advanced slowly – and then a brain-wave struck me. Taking out my camera, I politely greeted the officer in French and continued, without waiting for his questions:

'I am coming from Metulla on a short visit to this town, but would not like to go back without taking a photo of you and your friend here, whose song has so enchanted me.'

Arabs like to be flattered, and in addition they delight in being photographed; and so the officer consented with a smile and requested me to send him the photograph after it was developed and printed (which I later did, with my compliments). It no longer occurred to him to ask me for my identification papers. Instead, he treated me to a cup of sweet tea and wished me *bon voyage* when I finally rose to 'go back to Metulla'. I retreated the way I had come, made a circuit around the town, and proceeded on my way to Damascus.

. . . .

EXACTLY TWO WEEKS AFTER I had left Haifa I arrived at the big village – almost a town – of Majdal ash-Shams, which was inhabited mainly by Druzes and a few Christians. I chose a house which looked fairly prosperous and told the young man who opened the door to my knock that I would be grateful for shelter for the night. With the usual *ahlan wa-sahlan* the door was opened wide, and within a few minutes I found myself accepted into the small household.

As I was now deep in Syria, with several possible ways leading to Damascus, I decided to take my Druze host into my confidence and ask his advice. Knowing that no Arab would ever betray his guest, I placed all the facts squarely before him, including the fact that I was travelling on a false identity certificate. I was told that it would be extremely risky for me to travel on the highway because from here onward it was patrolled by French gendarmes, who would not let me pass as easily as the Syrians had done.

'I think I will send my son with thee,' said my host, pointing toward the young man who had opened the door to me, 'and he will guide thee across the mountains and help thee to avoid the roads.'

After the evening meal we sat down on the open terrace before the house and discussed the route we should take next morning. On my knees was spread the small-scale German map of Palestine and Syria which I had brought with me from Jerusalem, and I was trying to follow on it the course indicated by my Druze friend. While we were thus occupied, a man in the uniform of a police officer – evidently a Syrian – came strolling along the village street. He had appeared so suddenly from around a corner that I had hardly time enough to fold the map, let alone hide it from his view. The officer seemed to recognize a stranger in me, for after passing our terrace with a nod to my host, he turned back at the next corner and slowly walked toward us.

'Who are you?' he asked in French in a not unkind voice.

I repeated my usual rigmarole about being a colonist from Metulla on a pleasure trip; and when he demanded to see my identity certificate, I had to give it to him. He looked at the paper attentively, and his lips twisted in a grin.

'And what is it that you have in your hand?' he continued, pointing to the folded German map. I said that it was nothing of importance; but he insisted on seeing it, unfolded it with the deft fingers of a man accustomed to handling maps, looked at it for a few seconds, folded it carefully and handed it back to me with a smile. Then he said in broken German:

'During the war I served in the Turkish army side by side with the Germans.' And he saluted in the military fashion, grinned once again and walked away.

'He has understood that thou art an *Alemani*. He likes them, and hates the French. He won't bother thee.'

Next morning, accompanied by the young Druze, I set out on what must have been the hardest march of my life. We walked for over eleven hours, with only one break at noon for about twenty minutes, over rocky hills, down deep gorges, through dry river beds, up hills again, between boulders, over sharp pebbles, uphill, downhill, uphill, downhill, until I felt that I could walk no more. When in the afternoon we reached the town of Al-Katana in the plains of Damascus, I was entirely worn out, my shoes were torn and my feet swollen. I wanted to stop overnight at the place, but my young friend advised strongly against it: there were too many French police around, and as it was a town and not a village, I would not so easily find shelter without attracting attention. The only alternative was to secure a ride in one of the automobiles that plied for hire between here and Damascus. I had still my twenty piasters (during the entire journey from Haifa I had had no need to spend a single penny): and twenty piasters happened to be the fare for a car ride to Damascus.

In the ramshackle office of the transport contractor, in the main square of the town, I was informed that I would have to wait for about half an hour until the next car left. I parted from my friendly guide, who embraced me like a brother and set out immediately on the first stage of his way home. Sitting with my knapsack by my side near the door of the booking office, I dozed off under the rays of the late afternoon sun – only to be rudely awakened by someone shaking me by the shoulder: a Syrian gendarme. The usual questions came, followed by the usual answers. But the man was apparently not quite satisfied and told me:

'Come with me to the police station and talk there to the officer in charge.'

I was so tired that it no longer mattered to me whether I was discovered or not.

The 'officer' in the station room proved to be a big, burly French sergeant, his tunic unbuttoned, behind a desk on which stood an almost empty bottle of arrack and a dirty glass. He was completely, angrily, drunk and glared with bloodshot eyes at the policeman who had brought me in.

'What is it now?'

The policeman explained in Arabic that he had seen me, a

stranger, sitting in the main square; and I explained in French that I was not a stranger, but a law-abiding citizen.

'Law-abiding citizen!' the sergeant shouted. 'You people are scamps, vagabonds who walk up and down the country only to annoy us. Where are your papers?'

As I was fumbling with stiff fingers for the identity certificate in my pocket, he banged his fist on the table, and bellowed:

'Never mind, get out of here!' – and as I was closing the door behind me I saw him reach for his glass and bottle.

After the long, long march, what a relief, what an ease to ride – no, almost glide,—in a car from Al-Katana over the broad highway into the orchard-covered plain of Damascus! on the horizon lay my goal: an endless sea of treetops, with a few shining domes and minarets faintly visible against the sky. Far away, somewhat to the right, stood a solitary naked hill, its crest still lighted by the sun, while soft shadows were already creeping up its base. Above the hill, a single cloud, narrow, long, glittering dusk; steep, distant pale blue sky; over the plain, a dove grey golden against the mountains to our right and to our left; a light air.

Then: tall fruit gardens enclosed by mud walls; riders, carts, carriages, soldiers (French soldiers). The dusk became green like water. An officer roared by on a motorcycle, withhis huge goggles resembling a deep-sea fish. Then: the first house. Then: Damascus, a surf of noise after the silence of the open plain. The first lights were leaping up in windows and streets. I felt a gladness such as I could not remember.

But my gladness came to an abrupt end as the car stopped beyond the *poste de police* on the outskirts of the city.

'What is the matter?' I asked the driver by my side.

'Oh, nothing. All cars coming from outside must report to the police on arrival . . .'

A Syrian policeman emerged from the station and asked: 'From where are you coming?'

'Only from Al-Katana,' replied the driver.

'Oh, well, in that case go on' (for this was obviously only local traffic). The driver let in his clutch with a grind. We moved on and I breathed freely once more. But at that moment someone called out from the street, 'The top is loose!' – and a few paces beyond the *poste de police* the driver stopped the aged car to attend to the open top that had flopped down on one side. While he was thus engaged, the policeman approached us idly once again, apparently interested in no more than the driver's mechanical problem. Then, however, his glance alighted on me and I saw, with a stiffening of my whole body, that his eyes became alert. He was looking me up and down, came closer, and squinted at the floor of the car where my knapsack lay.

'Who art thou?' he asked suspiciously.

I began, 'From Metulla ..,' but the policeman was shaking his head unbelievingly. Then he whispered something to the driver; I could make out the words, 'English soldier, deserter.' And for the first time it dawned upon me that my blue overalls, my brown *kufiyya* with its gold-threaded *igal* and my military-type knapsack (which I had bought in a junk shop in Jerusalem) closely resembled the outfit of the Irish constabulary employed in those days by the government of Palestine; and I also remembered that there was an agreement between the French and British authorities to extradite their respective deserters. . .

In my broken Arabic I tried to explain to the policeman that I was no deserter; but he waved aside my explanations:

'Explain all this to the inspector.'

And so I was obliged to go into the police station, while the driver, with a muttered apology for not being able to wait for me started the car and disappeared from view. . . The inspector was out for the time being but, I was told, would be back any moment. I had to wait in a room which contained only a bench and, apart from the main entry, two other doors. Over one of them was inscribed *Gardien de Prison* and over the other simply *Prison*. Amid these very unpropitious surroundings I waited for over half an hour, each minute more and more convinced that this was my journey's end: for 'inspector' sounded much more ominous than simply 'officer'. If I were now discovered, I would have to spend some time, perhaps weeks, in gaol as under-trial prisoner; then I would receive the customary sentence of three months; after serving it I would have to march on foot – accompanied by a mounted gendarme – back to the frontier of Palestine; and, to top it all, I might expect an eviction from Palestine as well for breaking passport regulations. The gloom in the waiting room was nothing compared with the gloom within me.

Suddenly I heard the whirr of a motor car. It stopped before the station gate. A moment later a man in civilian dress with a red *tarbush* on his head entered the room with a quick step, followed by the policeman who was excitedly trying to report something to him. The inspector was quite obviously in a great hurry.

I do not know exactly how it happened, but I presume that what I did at that crucial moment was the outcome of one of those rare flashes of genius which in different circumstances – and perhaps in different men – produce events that change history. With a single bound, I came close to the inspector and, without waiting for his questions, hurled at him a torrent of complaints in French against the insulting clumsiness of the policeman who had taken me, an innocent citizen, for a deserter and caused me to lose my ride into the city. The inspector tried several times to interrupt me, but I never gave him a chance and engulfed him in a flow of words of which, I suppose, he was hardly able to gather one-tenth – probably only the names 'Metulla' and 'Damascus,' which I repeated an endless number of times. He was evidently distressed at being kept away from something he had to do in a hurry; but I did not let him speak and continued, without stopping for breath, with my wordy barrage. Ultimately he threw up his hands in despair and cried:

'Stop, for God's sake! Have you any papers?'

My hand went automatically into my breast pocket and, still pouring out sentence after sentence in an unceasing stream, I thrust the false identity certificate into his hands. The poor man must have felt as if he were drowning, for he only quickly turned over a corner of the folded sheet, saw the government stamp, and threw it back at me:

'All right, all right, go, only go!' – and I did not wait for him to repeat his request.

.   .   .   .

A FEW MONTHS EARLIER, in Jerusalem, I had met a Damascene teacher who had invited me to be his guest whenever I came to Damascus, and it was after his house that I now enquired. A little boy offered himself as my guide and took me by the hand.

Deep evening. The Old City. Narrow lanes which the overhanging oriel windows made more nightly than the night itself could make them. Here and there I could see, in the yellow light of a kerosene lantern, a fruiterer's shop with a mound of watermelons and baskets of grapes outside it. People like shadows. Sometimes behind the latticed windows a woman's shrill voice. And then the little boy said, 'Here'. I knocked at a door. Somebody answered from inside and I lifted the latch and entered a paved courtyard. In the darkness I could discern grapefruit trees heavy with green fruit and a stone basin with a fountain. Someone called out from above:

'*Taffadal, ya sidi*' – and I ascended a narrow staircase along one of the outer walls and walked through an open loggia and into the arms of my friend.

I was dead-tired, entirely exhausted, and let myself fall unresistingly on to the bed that was offered me. The wind rustled in the trees of the courtyard in front and in the trees of the garden behind the house. From the distance came many muffled sounds: the voice of a great Arabian city going to sleep.

.   .   .   .

IT WAS WITH THE excitement of a new understanding, with my eyes opened to things I had not suspected before, that I wandered in those summer days through the alleys of the old bazaar of Damascus and recognized the spiritual restfulness in the life of its people. Their inner security could be observed in the way they behaved toward one another: in the warm dignity with which they met or parted; in the manner in which two men would walk together, holding each other by the hand like children – simply because they felt friendly toward each other; in the manner in which the shopkeepers dealt with one another. Those traders in the little shops, those inexorable callers to passersby, seemed to have no grasping fear and no envy in them: so much so that the owner of a shop would leave it in the custody of his neighbour and competitor whenever it became necessary for him to be away for a while. I often saw a potential customer stop before an untended stall, obviously debating within himself whether to wait for the return of the vendor or to move on to the adjoining stall – and invariably the neighbouring trader, the competitor, would step in to enquire after the customer's wants and sell him the required goods – not his own goods, but those of his absent neighbour – and would leave the purchase price on the neighbour's bench. Where in Europe could one have witnessed a like transaction?

Some of the bazaar streets were thronged with the hardy figures of beduins in their wide, flowing garments: men who always seemed to carry their lives with themselves, and always walked in their own tracks. Tall men with grave, burning eyes were standing and sitting in groups before the shops. They did not talk much to one another – one word, one short sentence, attentively spoken and as attentively received, sufficed for long conversations. These beduins, I felt, did not know chatter, that talking about nothing, with nothing at stake, the hall-mark of worn-out souls; and I was reminded of the words of the Koran which described life in Paradise: '. . . and thou hearest no chatter there . . .' Silence seemed to be a beduin virtue. They wrapped themselves in their wide, brown-and-white or black cloaks and kept silent; they passed you by with a silent child's glance, proud, modest and sensible. When you addressed them in their tongue, their black eyes lit up in a sudden smile: for they were not self-absorbed and liked to be sensed by the stranger. They were *grands seigneurs*, entirely reserved and nevertheless open to all things of life . . .

On a Friday – the Muslim Sabbath – you could perceive a change of rhythm in the life of Damascus – a little whirlwind of happy excitement and, at the same time, solemnity. I thought of our Sundays in Europe; of the silent city streets and closed shops; I remembered all those empty days and the oppression which that emptiness brought forth. Why should it be so? Now I began to understand it: because to most people in the West their everyday life is a heavy load from which only Sundays can release them, Sunday is no longer a day of rest but has become an escape into the unreal, a deceptive forgetfulness behind which, doubly heavy and threatening, the 'weekday' lurks.

To the Arabs, on the other hand, Friday did not seem to be an opportunity to forget their workdays. Not that the fruits of life fell easily and without effort into the laps of these people, but simply because their labours, even the heaviest, did not seem to conflict with their personal desires. Routine, for the sake of routine, was absent; instead, there was an inner contact between a working-man and his work: and so respite became necessary only if one got tired. Such a consonance between man and his work must have been envisaged by Islam as the natural state of affairs and, therefore, no obligatory rest had been prescribed for Friday. The artisans and small shopkeepers in the Damascus bazaars worked for a few hours, abandoned their shops for a few hours during which they went away to the mosque for their noon prayers and afterward met with some friends in a café; then they would come back to their shops and work again for a few hours in glad relaxation, everyone just as he pleased. Only a few shops were closed, and except during the time of prayer, when the people assembled in the mosques, all the streets were as full of bustle as on other days.

One Friday I went with my friend and host into the Umayyad Mosque. The many marble columns which supported the domed ceiling shone under the sun rays that fell through the lintel windows. There was a scent of musk in the air, red and blue carpets covered the floor. In long, even rows stood many hundreds of men behind the *imam* who led the prayer; they bowed, knelt, touched the ground with their foreheads, and rose again: all in disciplined unison, like soldiers. It was very quiet; while the congregation was standing, one could hear the voice of the old *imam* from the distant depths of the huge hall, reciting verses from the Koran; and when he bowed or prostrated himself, the entire congregation followed him as one man, bowing and prostrating themselves before God as if He were present before their eyes. . .

It was at this moment that I became aware how near their God and their faith were to these people. Their prayer did not seem to be divorced from their working day; it was part of it – not meant to help them forget life, but to remember it better by remembering God.

'How strange and wonderful,' I said to my friend as we were leaving the mosque, 'that you people feel God to be so close to you. I wish I could feel so myself.'

'How else could it be, O my brother? Is not God, as our Holy Book says, *nearer to thee than the vein in thy neck?*'

.   .   .   .

SPURRED BY MY NEW AWARENESS, I spent much of my time at Damascus reading all manner of books on Islam on which I could lay my hands. My Arabic, although sufficient for the purposes of conversation, was as yet too weak for reading the Koran in the original, and so I had to take recourse to two translations – one French and the other German – which I borrowed from a library. For the rest, I had to rely on European orientalist works and on my friend's explanations.

However fragmentary, these studies and talks were like the lifting of a curtain. I began to discern a world of ideas of which hitherto I had been entirely ignorant.

Islam did not seem to be so much a religion in the popular sense of the word as, rather, a way of life; not so much a system of theology as a programme of personal and social behaviour based on the consciousness of God. Nowhere in the Koran could I find any reference to a need for 'salvation'. No original, inherited sin stood between the individual and his destiny – for, *nothing shall be attributed to man but what he himself has striven for*. No asceticism was required to open a hidden gate to purity: for purity was man's birthright, and sin meant no more than a lapse from the innate, positive qualities with which God was said to have endowed every human being. There was no trace of any dualism in the consideration of man's nature: body and soul seemed to be taken as one integral whole.

At first I was somewhat startled by the Koran's concern not only with matters spiritual but also with many seemingly trivial, mundane aspects of life; but in time I began to understand that if man were indeed an integral unity of body and soul – as Islam insisted he was – no aspect of his life could be too 'trivial' to come within the purview of religion. With all this, the Koran never let its followers forget that the life of this world was only one stage of man's way to a higher existence, and that his ultimate goal was of a spiritual nature. Material prosperity, it said, is desirable but not an end in itself: and therefore man's appetites, though justified in themselves, must be restrained and controlled by moral consciousness. This consciousness ought to relate not merely to man's relation with God but also to his relations with men; not only to the spiritual perfection of the individual but also to the creation of such social conditions as might be conducive to the spiritual development of all, so that all might live in fullness . . .

All this was intellectually and ethically far more 'respectable' than anything I had previously heard or read about Islam. Its approach to the problems of the spirit seemed to be deeper than that of the Old Testament and had, moreover, none of the latter's predilection for one particular nation; and its approach to the problems of the flesh was, unlike the New Testament, strongly affirmative. Spirit and flesh stood, each in its own right, as the twin aspects of man's God-created life.

Was not perhaps this teaching, I asked myself, responsible for the emotional security I had so long sensed in the Arabs?

.   .   .   .

ONE EVENING MY HOST invited me to accompany him to a party in the house of a rich Damascene friend who was celebrating the birth of a son.

We walked through the winding lanes of the inner city, which were so narrow that the projecting bay windows and lattice-encased balconies almost touched one another from opposite sides of the street. Deep shadows and peaceful silence dozed between the old houses of stone; sometimes a few black-veiled women passed you by with swift little steps, or a bearded man, dressed in a long *kaftan*, appeared from around a corner and slowly disappeared behind another. Always the same corners and irregular angles, always the same narrow lanes which cut across one another in all directions, always promising to lead to astounding revelations and always opening into another, similar lane.

But the revelation did come in the end. My friend and guide stopped before a nondescript wooden door set in a blank, mud-plastered wall and said:

'Here we are,' knocking with his fist against the door.

It opened with a squeak, a very old man bade us welcome with a toothlessly mumbled, '*Ahlan, ahlan wa-sahlan*,' and through a short corridor with two right-angle turns we entered the courtyard of the house that from outside had resembled nothing so much as a mud-coloured barn.

The courtyard was wide and airy, paved like a huge chessboard with white and black marble slabs. In a low, octagonal basin in the centre a fountain was playing and splashing. Lemon trees and oleander bushes, set in small openings in the marble pavement, spread their blossom- and fruit-laden branches all over the courtyard and along the inner house walls, which were covered from base to roof with alabaster reliefs of the most delicate workmanship, displaying intricate, geometrical patterns and leafy arabesques, interrupted only by windows framed in broad, lacelike openwork of marble. On one side of the yard the walls were recessed to form, about three feet above ground level, a deep niche the size of a large room, accessible by broad marble steps. Along the three walled sides of this niche – called *liwan* – ran low, brocaded divans, while on the floor a costly carpet was spread. The niche walls were lined with huge mirrors up to a height of perhaps fifteen feet – and the entire courtyard with its trees, its black-and-white pavement, its alabaster reliefs, marble window embrasures and carved doors which led to the interior of the house, and the many-coloured throng of guests who sat on the divans and strolled around the water basin – all this was duplicated in the mirrors of the *liwan:* and when you looked into them, you discovered that the opposite wall of the courtyard was covered with similar mirrors in its entire width, so that the whole spectacle was being reflected twice, four times, a hundred times, and thus transformed into a magic, endless ribbon of marble, alabaster, fountains, myriads of people, forests of lemon trees, oleander groves – an endless dreamland glistening under an evening sky still rosy from the rays of the setting sun . . .

Such a house – bare and unadorned on the street side, rich and delightful within – was altogether new to me; but in time I came to know that it was typical of the traditional dwellings of the well-to-do not only in Syria and Iraq but also in Iran. Neither the Arabs nor the Persians cared in earlier days for façades: a house was meant to be lived in and its function was limited to its interior. This was something quite different from the forced 'functionalism' so much sought after in modern Western achitecture. The Westerners, entangled in a kind of inverted romanticism, unsure of their own feelings, nowadays build problems; the Arabs and Persians build – or built until yesterday – houses.

The host seated me to his right on the divan, and a barefooted servant offered coffee on a small brass tray. Smoke from bubbling *nargiles* mingled with the rosewater-scented air of the *liwan* and floated in wisps toward the glass-shaded candles which were being lighted, one after another, along the walls and between the darkening green of the trees.

The company – all men – was most varied: men in *kaftans* of striped, rustling Damascus silk or ivory-coloured Chinese raw silk, voluminous *jubbas* of pastel-shaded fine wool, gold-embroidered white turbans over red *tarbushes;* men in European clothes, but obviously completely at ease in their cross-legged position on the divans. Some beduin chieftains from the steppes, with their retinues, were there: eyes black and gloriously alive, and small black beards around lean, brown faces. Their new clothes swished with every movement, and all of them carried silver-sheathed swords. They were indolently and completely at ease: true aristocrats – only that their ease, in distinction from that of European aristocrats, was not a soft shine bred through generations of loving care and good living, but like a warm fire coming out of the sureness of their perceptions. A good air surrounded them, a dry and clear atmosphere -- the same air which I had once sensed in reality on the borders of the desert: embracing in its chastity but not intruding. They were like distant friends, like passing visitors in this place: their free, aimless life awaited them elsewhere.

A dancing-girl came out of one of the doors and ran lightly up the steps to the *liwan*. She was very young, certainly no more than twenty, and very beautiful. Dressed in billowing trousers of some crackling, iridescent silk material, a pair of golden slippers and a pearl-embroidered bodice which not so much covered as accentuated her high, upstanding breasts, she moved with the sensuous grace of one accustomed to be admired and desired: and you could almost hear the ripple of delight that ran through this assembly of men at the sight of her soft-limbed body and her taut ivory skin.

She danced, to the accompaniment of a hand drum wielded by the middle-aged man who had entered the *liwan* immediately behind her, one of those traditional, lascivious dances so beloved in the East – dances meant to evoke slumbering desires and to give promise of a breathless fulfilment.

'O thou wonderful, O thou strange,' murmured my host. Then he slapped my knee lightly and said: 'Is she not like soothing balm on a wound . . . ?'

As quickly as she had come, the dancer disappeared; and nothing remained of her but the hazy shimmer in the eyes of most of the men. Her place on the carpet in the *liwan* was taken by four musicians – some of the best in all Syria, I was told by one of the guests. One of them held a long-necked lute, another a flat, single-headed drum – like a timbrel without jingles – the third an instrument that resembled a zither, and the fourth an Egyptian *tambour* – something like a very wide brass bottle with a bottom of drum-skin.

They began to twang and drum delicately, playfully at first, without any discernible accord, seemingly each man for himself, as if tuning their instruments in preparation for a common upward beat. He with the zither drew his fingertips lightly several times over the strings from high to low with a subdued, harplike effect; the *tambour* player drummed softly, stopped, and drummed again; the man with the lute struck, as if absent-mindedly, a few low, sharp chords in quick succession, chords that seemed only by accident to coincide with the dry, monotonously repeated beat of the timbrel and to draw the *tambour* into a hesitant response to the strumming of the strings, now of the lute, now of the zither – and before you became quite aware of it, a common rhythm had bound the four instruments together and a melody took shape. A melody? I could not say. It rather seemed to me that I was not so much listening to a musical performance as witnessing an exciting happening. Out of the chirping tones of the string instruments there grew up a new rhythm, rising in a tense spiral and then, suddenly, falling down – like the rhythmic rising and falling of a metallic object, faster and slower, softer and stronger: in dispassionate persistence, in endless variations, this one uninterrupted happening, this acoustic phenomenon which trembled in a restrained intoxication, grew up, spread out powerfully, went to the head: and when it suddenly broke off in the midst of a crescendo (how early, much too early!) I knew: I was imprisoned. The tension of this music had imperceptibly enwrapped me; I had been drawn into these tones which in their apparent monotony recalled the eternal recurrence of all things existing and knocked at the doors of your own feelings and called forth, step by step, all that had been moving in you without your knowledge . . . laid bare something that had always been there and now became obvious to you with a vividness that made your heart pound . . .

I had been accustomed to Western music, in which the entire emotional background of the composer is drawn into each individual composition, reflecting in every one of its moods all the other, possible moods: but this Arabian music seemed to flow from a single level of consciousness, from a single tension that was nothing but tension and could therefore assume personal modes of feeling in every listener . . .

After a few seconds of silence the *tambour* rumbled again, and the other instruments followed. A softer sway, a more feminine rhythm than before; the individual voices adjusted themselves more closely to each other, warmly enfolded one another, and, as if bound together in a spell, became more and more excited; they stroked each other, flowed around each other in soft, wavy lines which at first collided, several times, with the roll of the *tambour* as if with a hard obstacle, but gradually grew in aggressiveness, overcame the *tambour* and enslaved it, dragging it along in a common, spiral ascent: and the *tambour*, unwilling at first, soon fell prey to the common rapture and joined, intoxicated, the others; the wavy line lost its feminine softness and raced on with rising violence, quicker, higher, shriller, into a cold furioso of conscious passion that had given up all restraint and now became a dithyrambic climb to some unseen peaks of power and sovereignty; out of the erstwhile circling flow of tones around each other emerged a tremendous rotation in unison – a rushing of wheels out of eternity into eternity, without measure or limit or goal, a breathless, reckless tightrope-walker's run over knife-edge precipices, through one eternal present, toward an awareness that was freedom, and power, and beyond all thought. And, suddenly, in the midst of an upsurging sweep: a stop and a deadly silence. Brutal. Honest. Clean.

Like a rustling of tree leaves, breath returned to the listeners, and the long-drawn murmur '*Ya Allah, ya Allah*' went through them. They were like wise children who play their long-understood and ever-tempting games. They were smiling in happiness . . .

— 3 —

WE RIDE and Zayd sings: always the same rhythm, always the same monotonous melody. For the soul of the Arab is monotonous – but not in sense of poverty of imagination; he has plenty of that; but his instinct does not go, like that of Western man after width, three-dimensional space and the simultaneity of many shades of emotion. Through Arabian music speaks a desire to carry, each time, a single emotional experience to the utmost end of its reach. To this pure monotony, this almost sensual desire to see feeling intensified in a continuous, ascending line, the Arabian character owes its strength and its faults. Its faults: for the world wants to be experienced, emotionally, in space as well. And its strength: for the faith in the possibility of an endless linear ascent of emotional knowledge can in the sphere of the mind lead nowhere but to God. Only on the basis of this inborn drive, so peculiar to people of the desert, could grow the monotheism of the early Hebrews and its triumphant fulfilment, the faith of Muhammad. Behind both stood the motherly desert.

V

SPIRIT AND FLESH

— 1 —

THE DAYS PASS, and the nights are short, and we ride southward at a brisk pace. Our dromedaries are in excellent shape – they have recently been watered, and the last two days have provided them with abundant pasture. There are still fourteen days between here and Mecca, and even more if, as is probable, we spend some time in the towns of Haïl and Medina, both of which lie on our route.

An unusual impatience has taken hold of me: an urgency for which I know no explanation. Hitherto I have been wont to enjoy travelling at leisure, with no particular urge to reach my destination quickly; the days and weeks spent in journey had each of them a fulfilment of its own, and the goal always seemed to be incidental. But now I have begun to feel what I have never felt before in my years in Arabia: an impatience to reach the end of the road. What end? To see Mecca? I have been to the Holy City so often, and know its life so thoroughly, that it no longer holds out any promise of new discoveries. Or is it perhaps a new kind of discovery that I am anticipating? It must be so – for I am being drawn to Mecca by a strange, personal expectancy, as if this spiritual centre of the Muslim world, with its multi-national congregation of people from all corners of the earth, were a kind of promise, a gateway to a wider world than the one in which I am now living. Not that I have grown tired of Arabia; no, I love its deserts, its towns, the ways of its people as I have always loved them: that first hint of Arabian life in the Sinai Desert some ten years ago has never been disappointed, and the succeeding years have only confirmed my original expectation: but since my night at the well two days ago, the conviction has grown within me that Arabia has given me all that it had to give.

I am strong, young, healthy. I can ride for many hours at a stretch without being unduly tired. I can travel – and have been doing so for years – like a beduin, without a tent and without

135

any of the small comforts which the townspeople of Najd often regard as indispensable on long desert journeys. I am at home in all the little crafts of beduin life, and have adopted, almost imperceptibly, the manners and habits of a Najdi Arab. But is this all there is to be? Have I lived so long in Arabia only to become an Arab? – or was it perhaps a preparation for something that is yet to come?

.   .   .   .   .   .

THE IMPATIENCE WHICH I now feel is somehow akin to the turbulent impatience I experienced when I returned to Europe after my first journey to the Near East: the feeling of having been forced to stop short of a tremendous revelation that could have revealed itself to me if only there had been more time . . .

The initial impact of crossing from the Arabian world back into Europe had been somewhat softened by the months spent in Turkey after I had left Syria in the autumn of 1923. Mustafa Kemal's Turkey had in those days not yet entered into its 'reformist', imitative phrase; it was still genuinely Turkish in its life and traditions and thus, because of the unifying bond of its Islamic faith, was still related to the general tenor of Arabian life: but Turkey's inner rhythm seemed somehow heavier, less transparent, less airy – and more Occidental. When I travelled overland from Istanbul to Sofia and Belgrade there was no abrupt transition from East to West; the images changed gradually, one element receding and another imperceptibly taking its place – the minarets growing fewer and farther between, the long *kaftans* of the men giving way to belted peasant blouses, the scattered trees and groves of Anatolia merging into Serbian fir forests – until suddenly, at the Italian frontier, I found myself back in Europe.

As I sat in the train that was taking me from Trieste to Vienna, my recent impressions of Turkey began to lose all their vividness and the only reality that remained was the eighteen months I had spent in Arab countries. It almost gave me a shock to realize that I was looking upon the once so familiar European scenery with the eyes of a stranger. The people seemed so ugly, their movements angular and clumsy, with no direct relationship to what they really felt and wanted: and all at once I knew that in spite of the outward appearance of purpose in all they did, they were living, without being aware of it, in a world of make-believe . . . Obviously, my contact with the Arabs had utterly, irretrievably changed my approach to what I considered essential in life; and it was with something like astonishment that I remembered that other Europeans had experienced Arabian life before me; how was it possible, then, that they had not experienced this same shock of discovery? Or – had they? Had perhaps one or another of them been as shaken to his depths as I was now . . . ?

(It was years later, in Arabia, that I received an answer to this question: it came from Dr. Van der Meulen, then Dutch Minister at Jidda. A man of wide and many-sided culture, he clung to his Christian faith with a fervour nowadays rare among Westerners and was thus, understandably, not a friend of Islam as a religion. None the less, he confessed to me, he loved Arabia more than any other country he had known, not excepting his own. When his service in the Hijaz was approaching its end, he once said to me: 'I believe no sensitive person can ever remain immune to the enchantment of Arabian life, or pull it out of his heart after living among the Arabs for a time. When one goes away, one will forever carry within oneself the atmosphere of this desert land, and will always look back to it with longing – even if one's home is in richer, more beautiful regions . . .')

I stopped for a few weeks in Vienna and celebrated a reconciliation with my father. By now he had got over his anger at my abandonment of my university studies and the unceremonious manner in which I had left his roof. After all, I was now a correspondent of the *Frankfurter Zeitung* – a name that people in Central Europe used to pronounce almost with awe in those days – and had thus justified my boastful claim that I would 'come out on top'.

From Vienna I proceeded straight to Frankfurt to present myself in person to the newspaper for which I had been writing for well over a year. I did this with a great deal of self-assurance, for the letters from Frankfurt had made it evident that my work was appreciated; and it was with a feeling of having definitely 'arrived' that I entered the sombre, old-fashioned edifice of the *Frankfurter Zeitung* and sent up my card to the editor-in-chief, the internationally famous Dr. Heinrich Simon.

When I came in, he looked at me for a moment in speechless

astonishment, almost forgetting to get up from his chair; but soon he regained his composure, rose and shook hands with me:

'Sit down, sit down. I have been expecting you.' But he continued to stare at me in silence until I began to feel uncomfortable.

'Is there anything wrong, Dr. Simon?'

'No, no, nothing is wrong – or, rather, everything is wrong...' And then he laughed and went on: 'I somehow had expected to meet a man of middle age with gold-rimmed spectacles – and now I find a boy... oh, I beg your pardon; how old are you, anyway?'

I suddenly recalled the jovial Dutch merchant in Cairo who had asked me the same question the year before; and I burst out laughing:

'I am over twenty-three, sir – nearly twenty-four.' And then I added: 'Do you find it too young for the *Frankfurter Zeitung*?'

'No...' replied Simon slowly, 'not for the *Frankfurter Zeitung*, but for your articles. I somehow took it for granted that only a much older man would be able to overcome his natural desire for self-assertion and leave his own personality, as you have been doing, entirely in the background of his writings. That, as you know, is the secret of mature journalism: to write objectively about what you see and hear and think without relating those experiences directly to your own, *personal* experiences... On the other hand, now that I think of it, only a very young man could have written with so much enthusiasm, so much – how shall I say – so much thrill...' Then he sighed: 'I do hope that it doesn't wear off and you don't become as smug and jaded as the rest of them...'

The discovery of my extreme youth seemed to have strengthened Dr. Simon's conviction that he had found in me a highly promising correspondent; and he fully agreed that I should return to the Middle East as soon as possible – the sooner the better. Financially, there was no longer any obstacle to such a plan, for the German inflation had at last been overcome and the stabilization of currency had brought almost immediately a wave of prosperity in its wake. The *Frankfurter Zeitung* was once again in a position to finance the journeys of its special correspondents. Before I could go out again, however, I was expected to produce the book for which the newspaper had originally contracted me;

and it was decided that during this time I should be attached to the editorial office in order to acquire a thorough knowledge of the workings of a great newspaper.

Despite my impatience to go abroad again, those months in Frankfurt were tremendously stimulating. The *Frankfurter Zeitung* was not just a large newspaper; it was almost a research institute. It employed about forty-five full-fledged editors, not counting the many sub-editors and assistants in the newsrooms. The editorial work was highly specialized, with every area of the world and every major political or ecomonic subject entrusted to an outstanding expert in his field: and this in pursuance of an old tradition that the articles and dispatches of the *Frankfurter Zeitung* should be not merely ephemeral reflections of passing events but, rather, a kind of documentary evidence which politicians and historians might draw upon. It was common knowledge that in the Foreign Office in Berlin the editorials and political analyses of the *Frankfurter Zeitung* were filed with the same reverence that was accorded the *notes verbales* of foreign governments. (In fact, Bismarck is quoted to have once said of the then chief of the newspaper's Berlin bureau, 'Dr. Stein is the Ambassador of the *Frankfurter Zeitung* to the Court of Berlin.') To be a member of such an organization was very gratifying indeed to a man of my age; the more so as my hesitant views about the Middle East were met with serious attention by the editors and often became the subject of the daily editorial conferences; and the final triumph came on the day when I was asked to write an editorial on a current Middle Eastern problem.

.   .   .   .

MY WORK AT THE *Frankfurter Zeitung* gave a strong impetus to my conscious thinking. With greater clarity than ever before, I began to relate my Eastern experiences to the Western world of which I was once again a part. Just as some months earlier I had discovered a connection between the emotional security of the Arabs and the faith they professed, it now began to dawn upon me that Europe's lack of inner integration and the chaotic state of its ethics might be an outcome of its loss of contact with the religious faith that had shaped Western civilization.

Here, I saw, was a society in search of a new spiritual orientation after it had abandoned God: but apparently very few Westerners realized what it was all about. The majority seemed to think, consciously or subconsciously, more or less along these lines: 'Since our reason, our scientific experiments and our calculations do not reveal anything definite about the origin of human life and its destinies after bodily death, we ought to concentrate all our energies on the development of our material and intellectual potential and not allow ourselves to be hampered by transcendental ethics and moral postulates based on assumptions which defy scientific proof.' Thus, while Western society did not expressly deny God, it simply no longer had room for Him in its intellectual system.

In earlier years, after I had become disappointed with the religion of my ancestors, I had given some thought to Christianity. In my eyes, the Christian concept of God was infinitely superior to that of the Old Testament in that it did not restrict God's concern to any one group of people but postulated His Fatherhood of all mankind. There was, however, an element in the Christian religious view that detracted from the universality of its approach: the distinction it made between the soul and the body, the world of faith and the world of practical affairs.

Owing to its early divorce from all tendencies aiming at an affirmation of life and of worldly endeavours, Christianity, I felt, had long ceased to provide a moral impetus to Western civilization. Its adherents had grown accustomed to the idea that it was not the business of religion to 'interfere' with practical life; they were content to regard religious faith as a soothing convention, meant to foster no more than a vague sense of personal morality – especially sexual morality – in individual men and women. In this they were assisted by the age-old attitude of a Church which, in pursuance of the principle of a division between 'that which is God's and that which is Caesar's', had left the entire field of social and economic activities almost untouched – with the result that Christian politics and business had developed in a direction entirely different from all that Christ had envisaged. In not providing its followers with a concrete guidance in worldly affairs, the religion which the Western world professed had failed in what, to me, appeared to have been the true mission of Christ and, indeed, the cardinal task of every religion: to show man not merely how to *feel* but also how to *live* rightly. With an instinctive feeling of having been somehow let down by his religion, Western man had, over the centuries, lost all his real faith in Christianity; with the loss of this faith, he had lost the conviction that the universe was an expression of one Planning Mind and thus formed one organic whole; and because he had lost that conviction, he was now living in a spiritual and moral vacuum.

In the West's gradual falling away from Christianity I saw a revolt against the Pauline life-contempt that had so early, and so completely, obscured the teachings of Christ. How, then, could Western society still claim to be a Christian society? And how could it hope, without a concrete faith, to overcome its present moral chaos?

A world in upheaval and convulsion: that was our Western world. Bloodshed, destruction, violence on an unprecedented scale; the breakdown of so many social conventions, a clash of ideologies, an embittered, all-round fight for new ways of life: these were the signs of our time. Out of the smoke and the shambles of a world war, innumerable smaller wars and a host of revolutions and counter-revolutions, out of economic disasters that transcended anything until then recorded: out of all these tremendous happenings emerged the truth that the present-day Western concentration on material, technical progress could never by itself resolve the existing chaos into something resembling order. My instinctive, youthful conviction that 'man does not live by bread alone' crystallized into the intellectual conviction that the current adoration of 'progress' was no more than a weak, shadowy substitute for an earlier faith in absolute values – a pseudo-faith devised by people who had lost all inner strength to believe in absolute values and were now deluding themselves with the belief that somehow, by mere evolutionary impulse, man would outgrow his present difficulties . . . I did not see how any of the new economic systems that stemmed from this illusory faith could possibly constitute more than a palliative for Western society's misery: they could, at best, cure some of its symptoms, but never the cause.

* * * * * * * *

WHILE I WORKED ON the editorial staff of the *Frankfurter Zeitung*, I paid frequent visits to Berlin, where most of my friends resided; and it was on one of those trips that I met the woman who was later to become my wife.

From the moment I was introduced to Elsa amidst the bustle of the Romanisches Café, I was strongly attracted, not only by the delicate beauty of her appearance – her narrow, fine-boned face with its serious, deep-blue eyes and the sensitive mouth that bespoke humour and kindness – but even more by the inward, sensually intuitive quality of her approach to people and things. She was a painter. Her work, which I later came to know, may not have been outstanding, but it bore the same imprint of serene intensity that expressed itself in all her words and gestures. Although she was some fifteen years older than I – that is, in her late thirties – her smooth face and slender, flexible body gave her a much younger appearance. She was probably the finest representative of the pure 'Nordic' type I have ever encountered, having all its clearness and sharpness of outline with none of the angularity and stolidity that so often goes with it. She descended from one of those old Holstein families which might be described as the North German equivalent of the English 'yeomanry'; but the unconventional freedom of her manner had caused the yeoman earthiness to give way to a quite un-Nordic warmth and flair. She was a widow and had a six-year-old son, to whom she was greatly devoted.

The attraction must have been mutual from the very outset, for after that first meeting we saw each other very often. Filled as I was with my recent impressions of the Arab world, I naturally communicated them to Elsa; and she, unlike most of my other friends, displayed an extraordinary understanding and sympathy for the strong but as yet inchoate feelings and ideas which these impressions had produced in me: so much so that when I wrote a kind of introduction to the book in which I was describing my Near Eastern travels, I felt as if I were addressing myself to her:

When a European travels in any country of Europe which he has never seen before, he continues to move within his own, though perhaps somewhat widened, environment and can easily grasp the difference between the things that habit has made familiar to him and the newness that now comes his way. For, whether we are Germans or Englishmen, and whether we travel through France, Italy or Hungary, the spirit of Europe unifies us all. Living as we do within a well-defined orbit of associations, we are able to under-

stand one another and to make ourselves understood through those associations as if through a common language. We call this phenomenon 'community of culture'. Its existence is undoubtedly an advantage; but like all advantages that stem from habit, this one is occasionally a disadvantage as well: for sometimes we find that we are wrapped up in that universal spirit as if in cotton wool; that we are lulled by it into a laziness of the heart; that it has made us forget the tightrope-walk of our earlier, more creative times – that reaching out after intangible realities. In those earlier times they would perhaps have been called 'intangible possibilities', and the men who went out in search of them – whether discoverers or adventurers or creative artists – were always seeking only the innermost springs of their own lives. We late-comers are also seeking our own lives – but we are obsessed by the desire to secure our own life before it unfolds itself. And we dimly suspect the sin that lies hidden in such endeavour. Many Europeans begin to feel it today: the terrible danger of avoiding dangers.

In this book I am describing a journey into a region whose 'difference' from Europe is too great to be easily bridged: and difference is, in a way, akin to danger. We are leaving the security of our too uniform environment, in which there is little that is unfamiliar and nothing that is surprising, and entering into the tremendous strangenesses of 'another' world.

Let us not deceive ourselves: in that other world we may perhaps comprehend this or that of the many colourful impressions that come our way, but we can never – as we might in the case of a Western country – consciously grasp the total picture. It is more than space that separates us from the people of that 'other' world. How to communicate with them? It is not enough to speak their language; in order to comprehend their feel of life one would have to enter into their environment fully and begin to live within their associations. Is this possible?

And – would it be desirable? It might be, after all, a bad bargain to exchange our old, familiar habits of thought for strange, unfamiliar ones.

But are we really excluded from that world? I do not think so. Our feeling of exclusion rests mainly on an error peculiar to our Western way of thinking: we are wont to underestimate the creative value of the unfamiliar and are always tempted to do violence to it, to appropriate it, to take it over, on our own terms, into our *own intellectual environment. It seems to me, however, that our age of disquiet no longer permits such cavalier attempts; many of us are beginning to realize that cultural distance can, and should, be overcome by means other than intellectual rape: it might perhaps be overcome by surrendering our senses to it.*

Because this unfamiliar world is so entirely different from all that you have known at home; because it offers so much that is strikingly strange in image and sound, it brushes you sometimes, if you permit yourself to be attentive, with a momentary remembrance of things long known and long forgotten: those intangible realities of your own life. And when this breath of remembrance reaches you from beyond the abyss that separates your world from that other, that unfamiliar one, you ask yourself whether it is not perhaps herein – and only herein – that the meaning of all wandering lies: to become aware of the strangeness of the world around you and thereby to reawaken your own, personal, forgotten reality . . .

And because Elsa intuitively understood what I tried so inadequately, like one who gropes in darkness, to convey in these stammering words, I strongly felt that she, and she alone, could understand what I was after and could help me in my search . . .

— 2 —

ANOTHER DAY of wandering is over. There is silence within me, and the night is silent around me. The wind glides softly over the dunes and ripples the sand on their slopes. In the narrow circle of the firelight I can see Zayd's figure busy over his pots and pans, our saddlebags lying nearby where we tossed them when we made camp for the night, and our saddles with their high wooden pommels. A little beyond, already melting into the darkness, the crouching bodies of the two dromedaries, tired after the long march, their necks stretched on the sand; and still farther beyond, only faintly visible under the starlight, but as near to you as your own heartbeat, the empty desert.

There are many more beautiful landscapes in the world, but none, I think, that can shape man's spirit in so sovereign a way. In its hardness and sparseness, the desert strips our desire to comprehend life of all subterfuges, of all the manifold delusions with which a more bountiful nature may entrap man's mind and cause him to project his own imageries into the world around him. The desert is bare and clean and knows no compromise. It sweeps out of the heart of man all the lovely fantasies that could be used as a masquerade for wishful thinking, and thus makes him free to surrender himself to an Absolute that has no image: the farthest of all that is far and yet the nearest of all that is near.

Ever since man began to think, the desert has been the cradle of all his beliefs in One God. True, even in softer environments and more favourable climes have men had, time and again, an inkling of His existence and oneness, as, for instance, in the ancient Greek concept of *Moira*, the indefinable Power behind and above the Olympian gods: but such concepts were never more than the outcome of a vague feeling, a divining rather than certain knowledge – until the knowledge broke forth with dazzling certainty to men of the desert and from out of the desert. It was from a burning thornbush in the desert of Midian that the voice of God rang out to Moses; it was in the wilderness of the Judean desert that Jesus received the message of the Kingdom of God; and it was in the cave of Hira, in the desert hills near Mecca, that the first call came to Muhammad of Arabia.

It came to him in that narrow, dry gorge between rocky hills, that naked valley burnt by the desert sun – an all-embracing Yes to life, both of the spirit and of the flesh: the call that was destined to give form and purpose to a formless nation of tribes and, through it, to spread within a few decades, like a flame and a promise, westward as far as the Atlantic Ocean and eastward to the Great Wall of China: destined to remain a great spiritual power to this day, more than thirteen centuries later, outliving all political decay, outlasting even the great civilization which it brought into being: the call that came to the Prophet of Arabia . . .

.　　.　　.　　.　　.　　.　　.　　.

I SLEEP AND I AWAKE. I think of the days that have passed and yet are not dead; and sleep again and dream; and awake again and sit up, dream and remembrance flowing gently together in the half-light of my awakening.

The night is near to morning. The fire has died down entirely. Rolled in his blanket sleeps Zayd; our dromedaries lie motionless, like two mounds of earth. The stars are still visible, and you might think there is still time to sleep: but low on the eastern sky there appears, palely born out of the darkness, a faint streak of light above another, darker streak that lies over the horizon: twin heralds of dawn, time of the morning prayer.

Obliquely over me I see the morning star, which the Arabs call *Az-Zuhra*, 'The Shining One'. If you ask them about it, they will tell you that The Shining One was once a woman . . .

There were once two angels, Harut and Marut, who forgot to be humble, as it behoves angels to be, and boasted of their invincible purity: 'We are made of light; we are above all sin and desire, unlike the weak sons of man, sons of a mother's dark womb.' But they forgot that their purity had not come from their own strength, for they were pure only because they knew no desire and had never been called upon to resist it. Their arrogance displeased the Lord, and He said to them: 'Go down to earth and stand your test there.' The proud angels went down to earth and wandered, clothed in human bodies, among the sons of man. And on the very first night they came upon a woman whose beauty was so great that people called her The Shining One. When the two angels looked at her with the human eyes and feelings they now had, they became confused and, just as if they had been sons of man, the desire to possess her arose in them. Each of them said to her: 'Be willing unto me'; but The Shining One answered: 'There is a man to whom I belong; if you want me, you must free me of him.' And they slew the man; and with the unjustly spilt blood still on their hands, they satisfied their burning lust with the woman. But as soon as the desire left them, the two erstwhile angels became aware that on their first night on earth they had sinned twofold – in murder and fornication – and that there had been no sense in their pride . . . And the Lord said: 'Choose between punishment in this world and punishment in the Hereafter.' In their bitter remorse, the fallen angels chose punishment in this world: and the Lord ordained that they be suspended on chains between heaven and earth and remain thus suspended until the Day of Judgment as a warning to angels and men that all virtue destroys itself if it loses humility. But as no human eye can see angels, God changed The Shining One into a star in the heavens so that people might always see her and, remembering her story remember the fate of Harut and Marut.

The outline of this legend is much older than Islam; it seems

Author and North-Arabian Amir

to have originated in one of the many myths which the ancient Semites wove around their goddess Ishtar, the Grecian Aphrodite of later days, both of whom were identified with the planet we now call Venus. But in the form in which I heard it, the story of Harut and Marut is a typical creation of the Muslim mind, an illustration of the idea that abstract purity, or freedom from sin, can have no moral meaning so long as it is based on a mere absence of urges and desires: for is not the recurrent necessity of choosing between right and wrong the premise of all morality?

Poor Harut and Marut did not know this. Because as angels they had never been exposed to temptation, they had considered themselves pure and morally far above man – not realizing that the denial of the 'legitimacy' of bodily urges would indirectly imply a denial of all moral value in human endeavours: for it is only the presence of urges, temptations and conflicts – the possibility of *choice* – which makes man, and him alone, into a moral being: a being endowed with a soul.

It is on the basis of this conception that Islam, alone among all higher religions, regards the soul of man as one aspect of his 'personality' and not as an independent phenomenon in its own right. Consequently, to the Muslim, man's spiritual growth is inextricably bound up with all the other aspects of his nature. Physical urges are an integral part of this nature: not the result of an 'original sin' – a concept foreign to the ethics of Islam – but positive, God-given forces, to be accepted and sensibly used as such: hence, the problem for man is not how to suppress the demands of his body but, rather, how to co-ordinate them with the demands of his spirit in such a way that life might become full and righteous.

The root of this almost monistic life-assertion is to be found in the Islamic view that man's original nature is essentially good. Contrary to the Christian idea that man is born sinful, or the teaching of Hinduism that he is originally low and impure and must painfully stagger through a long chain of incarnations toward the ultimate goal of perfection, the Koran says: *Verily, We create man in a perfect state* – a state of purity that may be destroyed only by subsequent wrong behaviour – *and thereupon We reduce him to the lowest of low, with the exception of those who have faith in God and do good works.*

— 3 —

THE PALM ORCHARDS of Haïl lie before us.

We halt by the side of an old, ruined watchtower to prepare ourselves for our entry into the town; for old Arabian custom, always concerned with personal aesthetics, demands of the traveller that he enter a town in his best attire, fresh and clean as if he had just mounted his dromedary. And so we utilize our remaining water for washing our hands and faces, clip our neglected beards and pull our whitest tunics from the saddlebags. We brush the weeks of desert dust from our *abayas* and from the gaily-coloured tassels of our saddlebags, and dress our camels in their best finery; and now we are ready to present ourselves in Haïl.

This town is far more Arabian than, say, Baghdad or Medina; it does not contain any elements from non-Arab countries and peoples; it is pure and unadulterated like a bowl of freshly drawn milk. No foreign dress is visible in the bazaar, only loose Arabian *abayas*, *kufiyyas* and *igals*. The streets are much cleaner than those in any other city of the Middle East – cleaner, even, than any other town in Najd, which is noted for its un-Eastern cleanliness (probably because the people of this land, having always been free, have retained a greater measure of self-respect than elsewhere in the East). The houses, built of horizontal layers of packed mud, are in good repair – with the exception of the demolished city walls which bear witness to the last war between Ibn Saud and the House of Ibn Rashid and of Ibn Saud's conquest of the town in 1921.

The hammers of the coppersmiths pound into shape all manner of vessels, the saws of the carpenters bite shriekingly into wood, shoemakers tap the soles of sandals. Camels loaded with fuel and skins full of butter make their way through the crowds; other camels, brought in by beduins for sale, fill the air with their bellowing. Gaudy saddlebags from Al-Hasa are being fingered by experienced hands. The auctioneers, an ever-recurring fixture in any Arabian town, move up and down the bazaar and, with loud cries, offer their goods for sale. Here and there you can see hunting falcons jumping up and down on their wooden perches, tethered by thin leather thongs. Honey-coloured *saluqi* hounds stretch their graceful limbs lazily in the sun. Thin beduins in worn *abayas*, well-dressed servants and bodyguards of the *amir* – almost all of them from the southern provinces – mingle with traders from Baghdad, Basra and Kuwayt and the natives of Haïl. These natives – that is, the men, for of the women you see hardly more than the black *abaya* which conceals head and body – belong to one of the most handsome races in the world. All the grace of appearance and movement to which the Arab nation has ever attained seems to be embodied in this tribe of Shammar, of which the pre-Islamic poets sang: 'In the highlands live the men of steel and the proud, chaste women.'

When we arrive before the *amir's* castle, where we intend to spend the next two days, we find our host holding court in the open outside the castle gates. Amir Ibn Musaad belongs to the Jiluwi branch of the House of Ibn Saud and is a brother-in-law of the King. One of the most powerful of the King's governors, he is called 'Amir of the North' because he holds sway not only over the Jabal Shammar province but over the whole of northern Najd up to the confines of Syria and Iraq – an area almost as large as France.

The *amir* (who is an old friend of mine) and a few beduin *shaykhs* from the steppes are sitting on the long, narrow brick bench built along the castle wall. In a long row at their feet crouch Ibn Musaad's *rajajil*, the men-at-arms with rifles and silver-sheathed scimitars who never leave him throughout the day, not so much for protection as for prestige; next to them, the falconers with their birds perched on gloved fists, lower servants, beduins, a throng of retainers, great and small, down to the stable boys – all feeling equal to one another as men in spite of the differences in their stations. And how could it be otherwise in this land where you never address anyone as 'my lord,' except God in prayer? Facing them in a large semicircle squat the many beduins and townspeople who are bringing their complaints and quarrels before the *amir* for settlement.

We make our camels lie down outside the circle, hand them over to the care of a couple of retainers who have rushed over to us and proceed toward the *amir*. He rises; and all who have been sitting by his side on the bench and on the ground before him rise with him. He stretches his hand toward us:

'*Ahlan wa-sahlan* – and may God grant you life!'

I kiss the *amir* on the tip of his nose and his forehead, and he kisses me on both cheeks and pulls me to the bench by his side. Zayd finds a place among the *rajajil*.

Ibn Musaad introduces me to his other guests; some of the faces are new to me and some are familiar from previous years. Among these is Ghadhban ibn Rimal, supreme *shaykh* of the Sinjara Shammar – that delightful old warrior whom I always call 'uncle'. Nobody would guess from his almost tattered appearance that he is one of the mightiest chieftains of the North, and has so loaded his young wife with gold and jewels that, according to popular belief, two slave maidens have to support her when she wants to leave her huge tent which rests on sixteen poles. His eyes twinkle as he embraces me and whispers into my ear:

'No new wife yet?' – to which I can only reply with a smile and a shrug.

Amir Ibn Musaad must have overheard this quip, for he laughs aloud and says:

'It is coffee and not wives that a tired traveller needs' – and calls out, '*Qahwa!*'

'*Qahwa!*' repeats the servant nearest the *amir;* and the one at the farthest end of the row takes up the call, '*Qahwa!*' – and so on until the ceremonious command reaches the castle gate and re-echoes from within. In no time a servant appears bearing the traditional brass coffeepot in his left hand and several small cups in his right hand, pours out the first for the *amir*, the second for me, and then serves the other guests in the order of their rank. The cup is refilled once or twice, and when a guest indicates he has had enough, it is filled again and passed on to the next man.

The *amir* is apparently curious to know the results of my journey to the frontier of Iraq, but he betrays his interest only in brief questions as to what befell me on the way, reserving a fuller enquiry until we are alone. Then he resumes the judicial hearing which my arrival has interrupted.

Such an informal court of justice would be inconceivable in the West. The *amir*, as ruler and judge, is of course assured of all respect – but there is no trace of subservience in the respect which the beduins show him. Each of the plaintiffs and defendants proudly rests in the consciousness of his free humanity; their gestures are not hesitant, their voices are often loud and assertive and everyone speaks to the *amir* as to an elder brother, calling him – as is beduin custom with the King himself – by his first name and not by his title. There is no trace of haughtiness in Ibn Musaad's bearing. His handsome face with its short, black beard, his middle-sized, somewhat stocky figure speak of that unstudied self-restraint and easy dignity which in Arabia so often goes hand-in-hand with great power. He is grave and curt. With authoritative words he immediately decides the simpler cases and refers the more complicated ones, which require learned jurisprudence, to the *qadi* of the district.

It is not easy to be the supreme authority in a great beduin region. An intimate knowledge of the various tribes, family relationships, leading personalities, tribal grazing areas, past history and present idiosyncrasies is needed to hit upon the correct solution in the excited complexity of a beduin plaint. Tact of heart is as important here as sharpness of intellect, and both must work together with needle-point precision in order to avoid a mistake: for in the same way as beduins never forget a favour done to them, they never forget a judicial decision which they consider unjust. On the other hand, a just decision is almost always accepted with good grace even by those against whom it has gone. Ibn Musaad measures up to these requirements probably better than any other of Ibn Saud's *amirs;* he is so rounded, so quiet and so without inner contradictions that his instinct almost always shows him the right way whenever his reason reaches a dead end. He is a swimmer in life; he lets himself be borne by the waters and masters them by adapting himself to them.

Two ragged beduins are now presenting their quarrel before him with excited words and gestures. Beduins are, as a rule, difficult to deal with; there is always something unpredictable in them, a sensitive excitability which knows no compromise – always heaven and hell close to each other. But now I can see how Ibn Musaad parts their seething passions and smoothes them with his quiet words. One might think he would order the one to be silent while the other pleads for what he claims to be his right: but no – he lets them talk both at the same time, outshout each other, and only occasionally steps in with a little word here and a question there – to be immediately submerged in their passionate arguments; he gives in, and seemingly retreats, only to cut in

again a little later with an appropriate remark. It is an entranc-
ing spectacle, this adaptation of the judge's own mind to a reality so conflictingly interpreted by two angry men: not so much a
search for truth in a juridical sense as the slow unveiling of a hidden, objective reality. The *amir* approaches this goal by fits and
starts, draws out the truth, as if by a thin string, slowly and
patiently, almost imperceptibly to both plaintiff and defendant –
until they suddenly stop, look at each other in puzzlement, and
realize: judgment has been delivered – a judgment so obviously
just that it requires no further explanation ... Whereupon one
of the two stands up hesitantly, straightens his *abaya* and tugs
his erstwhile opponent by the sleeve in an almost friendly manner: 'Come' – and both retreat, still somewhat bewildered and
at the same time relieved, mumbling the blessing of peace over
the *amir*.

The scene is wonderful, a real piece of art: a prototype, it
seems to me, of that fruitful collaboration between jurisprudence
and justice which in Western courts and parliaments is still in its
infancy – but stands here in all its perfection in the dusty market
square before the castle of an Arab *amir* ...

Ibn Musaad, reclining indolently against the mud wall, takes
up the next case. His face, strong, furrowed, looking out of deep-
set eyes which warm and pierce, is the face of a real leader of
men, a masterly representative of the greatest quality of his race:
common sense of the heart.

Some of the others present obviously feel a similar admiration.
A man sitting on the ground before me – he is a beduin of the
tribe of Harb and one of the *amir's* men-at-arms – cranes his
neck up toward me with a smile on his face:

'Is he not like that sultan of whom Mutannabi says,

> *I met him when his gleaming sword was sheathed,*
> *I saw him when it streamed with blood,*
> *And always found him best of all mankind:*
> *But best of all in him was still his noble mind ... ?'*

It does not strike me as incongruous to hear an unlettered beduin quote verses of a great Arabian poet who lived in the tenth
century – certainly not as incongruous as it would have been to
hear a Bavarian peasant quote Goethe or an English stevedore

William Blake or Shelley. For, despite the more general spread
of education in the West, the highlights of Western culture are
not really shared by the average European or American – while,
on the other hand, very wide segments of uneducated and sometimes even illiterate Muslims do share consciously, daily, in the
cultural achievements of their past. Just as this beduin here has
been able to call to mind an appropriate verse from Mutannabi
to illustrate a situation of which he was a witness, many a ragged
Persian without schooling – a water carrier, a porter in a bazaar,
a soldier in an outlying frontier post – carries in his memory innumerable verses of Hafiz or Jami or Firdawsi and weaves them
with evident enjoyment into his everyday conversation. Although they have largely lost that creativeness which made their
cultural heritage so great, these Muslim people have even now a
direct, living contact with its summits.

. . . .

I STILL REMEMBER THE DAY when I made this discovery in
the bazaar of Damascus. I was holding in my hands a vessel, a
large bowl of baked clay. It had a strangely solemn shape: big
and round, like a somewhat flattened sphere of almost musical
proportions; out of the roundness of its wall, which had in it the
tenderness of a woman's cheek, two handles bent outward in
perfect curves that would have done honour to a Greek amphora.
They had been kneaded by hand; I could still discern the finger-
prints of a humble potter in the clay. Around the vessel's inward-
turned rim he had etched with swift, sure strokes of his stylus a
delicate arabesque like the hint of a rose garden in bloom. He
had been working quickly, almost negligently when he created
this splendid simplicity which bought to mind all the glories of
Saljuk and Persian pottery one so admires in the museums of
Europe: for he had not intended to create a work of art. All that
he was making was a cooking-pot – nothing but a cooking-pot,
such as a *fellah* or beduin can buy any day in any bazaar for a
few copper coins . . .

I knew the Greeks had created similar or even greater perfection, probably in cooking-pots as well: for they, too – water carrier and market porter, soldier and potter – had truly shared in a
culture that did not rest merely on the creative excitement of a
few select individuals, on a few peaks which only men of genius

could reach, but was common to all. Their pride in things beautiful, the things which were part of that culture, was part of their
day-by-day doings as well: a continuous partaking in a joint,
living possession.

As I held that vessel in my hands, I knew: blessed are people
who cook in such pots their daily meals; blessed are they whose
claim to a cultural heritage is more than an empty boast . . .

— 4 —

'WILT THOU NOT grant me the pleasure of dining with me
now, O Muhammad?' Amir Ibn Musaad's voice breaks through
my reverie. I look up – and Damascus recedes into the past,
where it belongs, and I am sitting once again on the bench by the
side of the 'Amir of the North'. The judicial session is apparently
over; one by one the litigants depart. Ibn Musaad rises, and his
guests and men-at-arms rise with him. The throng of the *rajajil*
parts to make way for us. As we pass under the gateway they
close their ranks and follow us into the castle yard.

A little later, the *amir*, Ghadhban ibn Rimal and myself sit
down together at a meal consisting of a huge platter of rice with
a whole roasted sheep on it. Besides us there are only two of the
amir's attendants and a pair of golden *saluqi* hounds in the room.

Old Ghadhban lays his hand on my shoulder and says: 'Thou
hast not yet answered my question – no new wife yet?'

I laugh at his persistence: 'I have a wife at Medina, as thou
knowest. Why should I take another?'

'Why? May God protect me! *One* wife – and thou still a
young man! Why, when I was thy age . . .'

'I am told,' interjects Amir Ibn Musaad, 'that thou dost not
do so badly even now, O Shaykh Ghadhban.'

'I am an old wreck, O Amir, may God lengthen thy life; but
sometimes I need a young body to warm my old bones . . .
But tell me,' turning again to me, 'what about that Mutayri
girl thou didst marry two years ago? What didst thou do with
her?'

'Why – nothing: and that's just the point,' I reply.

'Nothing . . . ?' repeats the old man, his eyes wide open. 'Was
she so ugly?'

'No, on the contrary, she was very beautiful . . .'

'What is it all about?' asks Ibn Musaad. 'What Mutayri girl

are you two talking about? Enlighten me, O Muhammad.'

And so I proceed to enlighten him about that marriage that led to nothing.

I was then living at Medina, wifeless and lonely. A beduin from the tribe of Mutayr, Fahad was his name, used to spend hours every day in my *qahwa* entertaining me with fantastic tales of his exploits under Lawrence during the Great War. One day he said to me: 'It is not good for a man to live alone as thou dost, for thy blood will clot in thy veins: thou shouldst marry.' And when I jokingly asked him to produce a prospective bride, he replied: 'That's easy. The daughter of my brother-in-law, Mutriq, is now of marriageable age, and I, as her mother's brother, can tell thee that she is exceedingly beautiful.' Still in a joking mood, I asked him to find out whether the father would be willing. And lo, next day Mutriq himself came to me, visibly embarrassed. After a few cups of coffee and some hemming and hawing, he finally told me that Fahad had spoken to him of my alleged desire to marry his daughter. 'I would be honoured to have thee for my son-in-law, but Ruqayya is still a child – she is only eleven years old . . .'

Fahad was furious when he heard of Mutriq's visit. 'The rascal! The lying rascal! The girl is fifteen years old. He does not like the idea of marrying her to a non-Arab but, on the other hand, he knows how close thou art to Ibn Saud and does not want to offend thee by an outright refusal; and so he pretends that she is still a child. But I can tell thee: her breasts are like this' – and he described with his hands a bosom of alluring proportions – 'just like pomegranates ready to be plucked.'

Old Ghadhban's eyes shimmer at this description: 'Fifteen years old, beautiful, and a virgin . . . and then, he says, nothing! What more couldst thou want than that?'

'Well, wait until I tell the rest of the story . . . I must admit that I was becoming more and more interested, and perhaps also a little bit spurred by Mutriq's resistance. I presented Fahad with ten golden sovereigns and he did his best to persuade the girl's parents to give her to me in marriage; a similar gift went to her mother, Fahad's sister. What exactly happened in their house I do not know; all I know is that the two ultimately prevailed upon Mutriq to consent to the marriage . . .'

'This Fahad,' says Ibn Musaad, 'seems to have been a sly fellow. He and his sister were obviously expecting still greater bounty from thee. And what happened then?'

I go on telling them how the marriage was duly solemnized a few days later in the absence of the bride who, according to custom, was represented by her father as her legal guardian and bearer of her consent – the latter being testified to by two witnesses. A sumptuous wedding feast followed, with the usual gifts to the bride (whom I had never yet seen), her parents, and several other close relatives – among whom, naturally, Fahad figured most prominently. The same evening my bride was brought to my house by her mother and some other veiled females, while from the roofs of the neighbouring houses women sang wedding songs to the accompaniment of hand drums.

At the appointed hour I entered the room in which my bride and her mother were awaiting me. I was unable to distinguish the one from the other, for both were heavily covered in black: but when I uttered the words demanded by custom, 'Thou mayest now retire,' one of the two veiled ladies rose and silently left the room; and thus I knew that the one who had remained was my wife.

'And then, my son, what happened then?' prompts Ibn Rimal as I pause at this stage of my narrative; and the *amir* looks at me quizzically.

'Then . . . There she sat, the poor girl, obviously most terrified at having thus been delivered to an unknown man. And when I asked her, as gently as I knew how, to unveil her face, she only drew her *abaya* tighter about herself.'

'They always do that!' exclaims Ibn Rimal. 'They are always terrified at the beginning of the bridal night; and, moreover, it is becoming for a young girl to be modest. But afterward they are usually glad – wasn't thine?'

'Well, not quite. I had to remove her face-veil myself, and when I had done so I beheld a girl of great beauty with an oval, wheat-coloured face, very large eyes and long tresses which hung down to the cushions on which she was sitting; but it was indeed the face of a child – she could not have been more than eleven years old, just as her father had claimed . . . Fahad's and his sister's greed had made them represent her to me as being of marriageable age, while poor Mutriq had been innocent of any lie.'

'So what?' asks Ibn Rimal, obviously not understanding what

I am driving at. 'What is wrong with eleven years? A girl grows
up, doesn't she? And she grows up more quickly in a husband's
bed . . .'

But Amir Ibn Musaad says, 'No, Shaykh Ghadhban; he is not
a Najdi like thee. He has more brains in his head.' And, grinning
at me, he continues: 'Don't listen to Ghadhban, O Muhammad.
He is a Najdi, and most of us Najdis have our brains not here' –
indicating his head – 'but here' – and he points to quite another
portion of his own anatomy.

We all laugh, and Ghadhban mutters into his beard: 'Then I
certainly have more brains than thou hast, O Amir.'

At their urging, I go on with the story and tell them that, whatever old Ghadhban's views on the matter, the extreme youth of
my child-bride did not represent an extra bonus to me. I could
feel no more than pity for the girl who had been made a victim of
her uncle's mean stratagem. I treated her as one would treat a
child, assuring her that she had nothing to fear from me; but she
did not speak a word and her trembling betrayed her panic. Rum-
maging through a shelf, I found a piece of chocolate, which I offered her: but she, never having seen chocolate in her life, refused it with a violent shake of her head. I tried to put her at ease
by telling her an amusing story from the *Arabian Nights,* but she
did not even seem to grasp it, let alone find it funny. Finally she
uttered her first words: 'My head is aching . . . ' I got hold of
some aspirin tablets and thrust them into her hand with a glass
of water. But this caused only a still more violent outbreak of
terror (only later did I learn that some of her women friends had
told her that those strange people from foreign lands sometimes
drug their wives on their bridal night in order to rape them the
more easily). After a couple of hours or so, I succeeded in convincing her that I had no aggressive designs. In the end she fell
asleep like the child she was, while I made a bed for myself on
the carpet in a corner of the room.

In the morning I sent for her mother and demanded that she
take the girl home. The woman was stupefied. She had never
heard of a man who refused so choice a morsel – an eleven-year-
old virgin – and must have thought that there was something
radically wrong with me.

'And then?' asks Ghadhban.

'Nothing – I divorced the girl, having left her in the same state as she had come to me. It was not a bad deal for the family, who kept both the girl and the dower which I had paid, together with the many presents. As for myself, a rumour went around that there was no manhood in me and several well-wishers tried to persuade me that someone, perhaps a former wife, had cast a spell over me, from which I could only free myself by a counter-spell.'

'When I think of thy subsequent marriage in Medina, O Muhammad, and thy son,' says the *amir* with a laugh, 'I am sure thou hast wrought a strong counterspell . . .'

— 5 —

LATER AT NIGHT, as I am about to go to bed in the room put at my disposal, I find Zayd more silent than usual. He stands near the doorway, visibly lost in some distant thoughts, his chin resting on his breast and his eyes fixed on the blue and moss-green medallion of the Khorasan carpet that covers the floor.

'How does it feel, Zayd, to be back in the town of thy youth after all these years? – for in the past he has always refused to enter Haïl whenever I had occasion to visit it.

'I am not sure, O my uncle,' he replies slowly. 'Eleven years . . . It is eleven years since I was here last. Thou knowest that my heart would not let me come here earlier and behold the People of the South ruling in the palace of Ibn Rashid. But of late I have been telling myself, in the words of the Book, *O God, Lord of Sovereignty! Thou givest sovereignty to whom Thou pleasest and takest away sovereignty from whom Thou pleasest. Thou exaltest whom Thou pleasest and abasest whom Thou pleasest. In Thy hand is all the good, and Thou hast power over all things.* No doubt, God gave sovereignty to the House of Ibn Rashid, but they did not know how to use it rightly. They were bountiful to their people but hard on their own kin and reckless in their pride; they spilled blood, brother killing brother; and so God took away their rule and handed it back to Ibn Saud. I think I should not grieve any longer – for is it not written in the Book, *Sometimes you love a thing, and it may be the worst for you – and sometimes you hate a thing, and it may be the best for you?*'

There is a sweet resignation in Zayd's voice, a resignation im-plying no more than the acceptance of something that has al-ready happened and cannot therefore be undone. It is this acquiescence of the Muslim spirit to the immutability of the past – the recognition that whatever has happened had to happen in this particular way and could have happened in no other – that is so often mistaken by Westerners for a 'fatalism' inherent in the Islamic outlook. But a Muslim's acquiescence to fate relates to the past and not to the future: it is not a refusal to act, to hope and to improve, but a refusal to consider past reality as anything but an act of God.

'And beyond that,' continues Zayd, 'Ibn Saud has not behaved badly toward the Shammar. They know it, for did they not support him with their swords three years ago when that dog Ad-Dawish rose against him?'

They did indeed, with the magnanimity of the vanquished so characteristic of true Arabs at their best. In that fateful year, 1929, when Ibn Saud's kingdom shook to its very foundations under the blows of the great beduin revolt led by Faysal ad-Dawish, all the Shammar tribes living in Najd put aside their one-time animosity toward the King, rallied around him and contributed largely to his subsequent victory over the rebels. This reconciliation was truly remarkable, for it had been only a few years earlier that Ibn Saud had conquered Haïl by force of arms and thus re-established the hegemony of the South over the North; and the more remarkable in view of the age-old mutual dislike – which goes deeper than any dynastic struggle for power – between the tribe of Shammar and the people of southern Najd, of whom Ibn Saud is one. To a large extent, this antipathy (which even the recent reconciliation has not entirely eradicated) is an expression of the traditional rivalry between North and South that goes through the entire history of the Arabs and has its counterpart in many other nations as well: for it often happens that a small difference in the inner rhythm of life produces more hostility between closely related tribes than racial strangeness could cause between entirely different neighbouring nations.

Apart from political rivalry, another factor plays a considerable role in the emotional divergencies between the Arabian North and South. It was in the south of Najd, in the vicinity of Riyadh, that nearly two hundred years ago the puritan reformer, Muhammad ibn Abd al-Wahhab, rose and stirred the tribes – then Muslims in name only – to a new religious enthusiasm. It was in the then insignificant House of Ibn Saud, chieftains of the small township of Dar'iyya, that the reformer gained the iron arm which gave the force of action to his inspiring word, and within a few decades, gathered 'a large part of the Peninsula within that glowing, uncompromising movement of faith known as 'Wahhabism'. In all the Wahhabi wars and conquests of the last one hundred and fifty years, it was always the people of the South who carried aloft the banners of puritanism, while the North only halfheartedly went along with them: for although the Shammar share the Wahhabi tenets in theory, their hearts have remained remote from the fiery, unyielding religious persuasion of the South. Living close to the 'borderlands', Syria and Iraq, and always connected with them by trade, the Shammar have in the course of ages acquired a suave laxity of outlook and a readiness for compromise quite unknown to the more isolated Southerners. The men of the South know only extremes: and for the last century and a half they have known nothing but dreams of *jihad* – proud, haughty men who regard themselves as the only true respresentatives of Islam and all other Muslim peoples as heretics.

With all this, the Wahhabis are certainly not a separate sect. A 'sect' would presuppose the existence of certain separate doctrines which would distinguish its followers from the great mass of all the other followers of the same faith. In Wahhabism, however, there are no separate doctrines – on the contrary: this movement has made an attempt to do away with all the accretions and superimposed doctrines which in the course of many centuries have grown up around the original teachings of Islam, and to return to the pristine message of the Prophet. In its uncompromising clarity, this was certainly a great attempt, which in time could have led to a complete freeing of Islam from all the superstitions that have obscured its message. Indeed, all the renaissance movements in modern Islam – the *Ahl-i-Hadith* movement in India, the Sanusi movement in North Africa, the work of Jamal ad-Din al-Afghani and the Egyptian Muhammad Abduh – can be directly traced back to the spiritual impetus set in motion in the eighteenth century by Muhammad ibn Abd al-Wahhab. But the Najdi development of his teachings suffers from two defects which have prevented it from becoming a force of spiritual destiny. One of these defects is the narrowness with which it seeks to confine almost all religious endeavours to a literal observation of injunctions, overlooking the need for penetrating to their spiritual content. The other defect is rooted in the Arab character itself – in that zealotic, self-righteous orientation of feeling which concedes to no one the right to differ: an attitude as peculiar to the true Semite as its diametrical opposite – complete laxity in matters of faith. It is a tragic quality of the Arabs that they must always swing between two poles and never can find a middle way. Once upon a time – hardly two centuries ago – the Arabs of Najd were innerly more distant from Islam than any other group in the Muslim world; while ever since the advent of Muhammad ibn Abd al-Wahhab they have regarded themselves not merely as champions of the Faith but almost as its sole owners.

The spiritual meaning of Wahhabism – the striving after an inner renewal of Muslim society – was corrupted almost at the same moment when its outer goal – the attainment of social and political power – was realized with the establishment of the Saudi Kingdom at the end of the eighteenth century and its expansion over the larger part of Arabia early in the nineteenth. As soon as the followers of Muhammad ibn Abd al-Wahhab achieved power, his idea became a mummy: for the spirit cannot be a servant of power – and power does not want to be a servant of the spirit.

The history of Wahhab Najd is the history of a religious idea which first rose on the wings of enthusiasm and longing and then sank down into the lowlands of pharisaic self-righteousness. For all virtue destroys itself as soon as it ceases to be longing and humility: Harut! Marut!

VI

DREAMS

— 1 —

TO BE FRIEND AND GUEST of a great Arabian *amir* means to be regarded and treated as friend and guest by all his officials, by his *rajajil*, by the shopkeepers in his capital, and even by the beduins of the steppe under his authority. The guest can scarcely mention a wish without its being fulfilled at once, whenever it can be fulfilled; from hour to hour he is overwhelmed by the warm, unquestioning graciousness which envelops him in the market place of the town no less than in the wide halls and corridors of the castle.

As so often before, this happens to me during the two days I stop at Haïl. When I wish to drink coffee, the melodious sound of the brass mortar immediately rings out in my private reception room. When, in the morning, I casually mention to Zayd within the hearing of one of the *amir's* servants a beautiful camel-saddle I have just seen in the bazaar, it is brought to me in the afternoon and placed at my feet. Several times a day a gift arrives: a long robe of mango-patterned Kashmir wool, or an embroidered *kufiyya*, or a white Baghdad sheepskin for the saddle, or a curved Najdi dagger with a silver handle ... And I, travelling very lightly, am unable to offer Ibn Musaad anything in return except a large-scale English map of Arabia which, to his great delight, I have painstakingly marked with Arabic place names.

Ibn Musaad's generosity bears a strong resemblance to the ways of King Ibn Saud: which, after all, is not so surprising when one considers their close relationship. Not only are they cousins but they have also shared — ever since Ibn Saud was a young man and Ibn Musaad still a boy — most of the difficulties, vicissitudes and dreams of the King's early reign. And beyond that, their personal ties were cemented years ago by Ibn Saud's

162

marriage to Jawhara, the sister of Ibn Musaad – the woman who meant more to the King than any he married before or after her.

. . . .

ALTHOUGH MANY PEOPLE have been admitted to his friendship, not many have been privileged to observe the most intimate, and perhaps the most significant, aspect of Ibn Saud's nature: his great capacity for love, which, had it been allowed to unfold and endure, might have led him to far greater heights than he has achieved. So much stress has been laid on the immense number of women he has married and divorced that many outsiders have come to regard him as something of a libertine engrossed in endless pursuit of physical pleasure; and few, if any, are aware that almost every one of Ibn Saud's marriages – apart from those alliances dictated by political considerations – was the outcome of a dim, insatiable desire to recapture the ghost of a lost love.

Jawhara, the mother of his sons Muhammad and Khalid, was Ibn Saud's great love; and even now, after she has been dead for some thirteen years, the King never speaks of her without a catch in his throat.

She must have been an extraordinary woman – not merely beautiful (for Ibn Saud has known and possessed many beautiful women in his extremely exuberant marital career) but also endowed with that instinctive feminine wisdom which joins the rapture of the spirit to the rapture of the body. Ibn Saud does not often allow his emotions to become deeply involved in his relations with women, and this accounts perhaps for the ease with which he marries and divorces his wives. But with Jawhara he seems to have found a fulfilment that has never been repeated. Although even in her lifetime he had other wives, his real love was reserved to her as exclusively as if she had been his only wife. He used to write love poems to her; and once, in one of his more expansive moments, he told me: 'Whenever the world was dark around me and I could not see my way out of the dangers and difficulties that beset me, I would sit down and compose an ode to Jawhara; and when it was finished, the world was suddenly lighted, and I knew what I had to do.'

But Jawhara died during the great influenza epidemic of 1919, which also claimed Ibn Saud's first-born and most beloved son,

Turki; and this double loss left a never-healed scar on his life.

It was not only to a wife and a son that he could give his heart so fully: he loved his father as few men love theirs. The father – Abd ar-Rahman – whom I knew in my early years in Riyadh, was, though a kind and pious man, certainly not an outstanding personality like his son, and had not played a particularly spectacular role during his long life. Nevertheless, even after Ibn Saud had acquired a kingdom by his own effort and was undisputed ruler of the land, he behaved toward his father with such humility that he would never even consent to set foot in a room of the castle if Abd ar-Rahman was in the room below – 'for,' he would say, 'how can I allow myself to walk over my father's head?' He would never sit down in the old man's presence without being expressly invited to do so. I still remember the discomfiture this kingly humility caused me one day at Riyadh (I think it was in December, 1927). I was paying one of my customary visits to the King's father in his apartments in the royal castle; we were sitting on the ground on cushions, the old gentleman expatiating on one of his favourite religious themes. Suddenly an attendant entered the room and announced, 'The *Shuyukh* is coming.' In the next moment Ibn Saud stood in the doorway. Naturally, I wanted to rise, but old Abd ar-Rahman gripped me by the wrist and pulled me down, as if to say, 'Thou art *my* guest.' I was embarrassed beyond words at thus having to remain seated while the King, after greeting his father from afar, was left standing in the doorway, obviously awaiting permission to enter the room, but he must have been accustomed to similar whimsies on his father's part, for he winked at me with a half-smile to put me at ease. Meanwhile, old Abd ar-Rahman went on with his discourse, as if no interruption had occurred. After a few minutes he looked up, nodded to his son and said: 'Step closer, O my boy, and sit down.' The King was at that time forty-seven or forty-eight years old.

Some months later – we were at Mecca at the time – news was brought to the King that his father had died at Riyadh. I shall never forget the uncomprehending stare with which he looked for several seconds at the messenger, and the despair which slowly and visibly engulfed the features that were normally so serene and composed; and how he jumped up with a terrible roar, 'My father is dead!' and, with great strides, ran out of the room, his *abaya* trailing on the ground behind him; and how he bounded up the stairway, past the awe-struck faces of his men-at-arms, not knowing himself where he was going or why, shouting, shouting, 'My father is dead! My father is dead!' For two days afterward he refused to see anyone, took neither food nor drink and spent day and night in prayer.

How many sons of middle age, how many kings who had won themselves a kingdom through their own strength, would have thus mourned the passing of a father who had died the peaceful death of old age?

— 2 —

FOR IT WAS ENTIRELY by his own efforts that Abd al-Aziz ibn Saud won his vast kingdom. When he was a child, his dynasty had already lost the last remnants of its power in Central Arabia and had been superseded by its one-time vassals, the dynasty of Ibn Rashid of Haïl. Those were bitter days for Abd al-Aziz. The proud and reserved boy had to watch a foreign *amir* governing his paternal city of Riyadh in the name of Ibn Rashid: for now the family of Ibn Saud – once the rulers of almost all Arabia – were only pensioners of Ibn Rashid, tolerated and no longer feared by him. In the end, this became too much even for his peace-loving father, Abd ar-Rahman, and he left Riyadh with his entire family, hoping to spend his remaining days in the house of his old friend, the ruler of Kuwayt. But he did not know what the future held in store; for he did not know what was in his son's heart.

Among all the members of the family there was only one who had any inkling of what was happening in this passionate heart: a younger sister of his father. I do not know much about her; I only know that whenever he dwells on the days of his youth, the King always mentions her with great reverence.

'She loved me, I think, even more than her own children. When we were alone, she would take me on her lap and tell me of the great things which I was to do when I grew up: "Thou must revive the glory of the House of Ibn Saud," she would tell me again and again, and her words were like a caress. "But I want thee to know, O Azayyiz,"* she would say, "that even the glory of the House of Ibn Saud must not be the end of thy endeavours.

* Affectionate diminutive of Abd al-Aziz.

Thou must strive for the glory of Islam. Thy people sorely need a leader who will guide them on to the path of the Holy Prophet – and thou shalt be that leader." These words have always remained alive in my heart.'

Have they, really?

Throughout his life Ibn Saud has loved to speak of Islam as a mission that had been entrusted to him; and even in later days, when it had long since become obvious that kingly power weighed more with him than his erstwhile championship of an ideal, his great eloquence has often succeeded in convincing many people – perhaps even himself – that this ideal was still his goal.

Such childhood reminiscences were often brought up in the course of the intimate gatherings at Riyadh which usually took place after the *isha* prayer (about two hours after sunset). As soon as the prayer in the castle mosque was over, we would assemble around the King in one of the smaller rooms and listen to one hour's reading from the Prophet's Traditions or from a commentary on the Koran. Afterward the King would invite two or three of us to accompany him to an inner chamber in his private quarters. One evening, I remember, while leaving the assembly in the wake of the King, I was once again struck by the majestic height with which he towered far above those who surrounded him. He must have caught my admiring glance, for he smiled briefly with that indescribable charm of his, took me by the hand and asked:

'Why dost thou look at me like this, O Muhammad?'

'I was thinking, O Long-of-Age, that nobody could fail to recognize the king in thee when he sees thy head so far above the heads of the crowd.'

Ibn Saud laughed and, still leading me by the hand on his slow procession through the corridor, he said: 'Yes, it is pleasant to be so tall. But there was a time when my tallness gave me nothing but heartache. That was years ago, when I was a boy and was living in the castle of Shaykh Mubarak at Kuwayt. I was thin and extremely tall, much taller than my years would warrant, and the other boys in the castle – those of the *shaykh's* family and even of my own – made me a target of their jokes, as if I were a freak. This caused me great distress, and sometimes I myself thought that I was truly a freak. I was so ashamed of my

height that I would draw in my head and shoulders to make myself smaller when I walked through the rooms of the palace or
over the streets of Kuwayt.'

By then we had reached the King's apartments. His eldest son,
Crown Prince Saud, was already waiting there for his father. He
was about my own age and, though not as tall as his father, quite
imposing in appearance. His features were far more rugged than
the King's and had none of the latter's mobility and vivacity.
But he was a kind man and well thought of by the people.

The King sat down on the cushions that were spread along the
walls and motioned us all to follow suit. Then he commanded:
'*Qahwa!*' The armed slave at the door immediately called out into the corridor, '*Qahwa!*' – whereupon this traditional call was
taken up and repeated in rapid succession by other attendants
down the entire length of the corridor, one after the other:
'*Qahwa!*' – '*Qahwa!*' – in a delightful ceremony of repetition, until it reached the King's coffee-kitchen a few rooms away: and in
a trice a golden-daggered attendant appeared with the brass
coffeepot in one hand and tiny cups in the other. The King received the first cup and the other cups were handed round to the
guests in the order in which they were seated. On such informal
occasions, Ibn Saud would talk freely of anything that occurred
to him – about what was happening in distant parts of the world,
about a strange new invention that had been brought to his
notice, about people and customs and institutions; but above all,
he liked to talk about his own experiences and would encourage
others to participate in the conversation. On that particular
evening, Amir Saud started the ball rolling when he laughingly
turned to me:

'Someone expressed a doubt to me today about thee, O Muhammad. He said that he was not at all sure whether thou art not
an English spy in the guise of a Muslim . . . But don't worry: I
was able to assure him that thou art indeed a Muslim.'

Unable to hold back a grin, I replied: 'That was very kind of
thee, O Amir, may God lengthen thy life. But how couldst thou
be so certain about this? Is it not that God alone knows what is
in a man's heart?'

'That is true,' retorted Amir Saud, 'but in this case I have been
given a special insight. A dream last week has given me this insight . . . I saw myself standing before a mosque and looking up

at the minaret. Suddenly a man appeared on the gallery of the minaret, cupped his hands before his mouth and started the call to prayer, *God is the Greatest, God alone is Great,* and continued it to the end, *There is no God but God:* – and when I looked closely, I saw that the man was thou. When I awoke I knew with certainty, although I had never doubted it, that thou art truly a Muslim: for a dream in which God's name was extolled could not have been a deception.'

I was strongly moved by this unsolicited assertion of my sincerity by the King's son and by the earnest nod with which the King affirmed, as it were, Amir Saud's surprising narration. Taking up the thread, Ibn Saud remarked:

'It does often happen that God enlightens our hearts through dreams which sometimes foretell the future and sometimes make clear the present. Hast thou thyself never experienced such a dream, O Muhammad?'

'Indeed I have, O Imam, a long time ago, long before I ever thought of becoming a Muslim – before I even had set foot in a Muslim country. I must have been nineteen years old or so at the time, and lived in my father's house in Vienna. I was deeply interested in the science of man's inner life' (which was the closest definition of psychoanalysis I could give the King), 'and was in the practice of keeping by my bedside paper and pencil in order to jot down my dreams at the moment of awakening. By doing so, I found, I was able to remember those dreams indefinitely, even if I did not keep them constantly in mind. In that particular dream, I found myself in Berlin, travelling in that underground railway they have there – with the train going sometimes through a tunnel below ground and sometimes over bridges high above the streets. The compartment was filled with a great throng of people – so many that there was no room to sit down and all stood tightly packed without being able to move; and there was only a dim light from a single electric bulb. After a while the train came out of the tunnel; it did not come on to one of those high bridges, but emerged instead on to a wide, desolate plain of clay, and the wheels of the train got stuck in the clay and the train stopped, unable to move foreward or backward.

'All the travellers, and I among them, left the carriages and started looking about. The plain around us was endless and empty and barren – there was no bush on it, no house, not even

a stone – and a great perplexity fell over the people's hearts:
Now that we have been stranded here, how shall we find our way
back to where other humans live? A grey twilight lay over the
immense plain, as at the time of early dawn.

'But somehow I did not quite share the perplexity of the others.
I made my way out of the throng and beheld, at a distance of
perhaps ten paces, a dromedary crouched on the ground. It was
fully saddled – in exactly the way I later saw camels saddled in
thy country, O Imam – and in the saddle sat a man dressed in a
white-and-brown-striped *abaya* with short sleeves. His *kufiyya*
was drawn over his face so that I could not discern his features.
In my heart I knew at once that the dromedary was waiting for
me, and that the motionless rider was to be my guide; and so,
without a word, I swung myself on to the camel's back behind
the saddle in the way a *radif*, a pillion rider, rides in Arab lands.
In the next instant, the dromedary rose and started forward in a
long-drawn, easy gait, and I felt a nameless happiness rise within
me. In that fast, smooth gait we travelled for what at first
seemed to be hours, and then days, and then months, until I lost
all count of time; and with every step of the dromedary my happiness rose higher, until I felt as if I were swimming through air.
In the end, the horizon to our right began to redden under the
rays of the sun that was about to rise. But on the horizon far
ahead of us I saw another light: it came from behind a huge,
open gateway resting on two pillars – a blinding-white light, not
red like the light of the rising sun to our right – a cool light that
steadily grew in brightness as we approached and made the happiness within me grow beyond anything that words could describe. And as we came nearer and nearer to the gateway and its
light, I heard a voice from somewhere announce, "This is the
westernmost city!" – and I awoke.'

'Glory be unto God!' exclaimed Ibn Saud, when I had finished.
'And did not this dream tell thee that thou wert destined for Islam?'

I shook my head: 'No, O Long-of-Age, how could I have
known it? I had never thought of Islam and had never even
known a Muslim . . . It was seven years later, long after I had
forgotten that dream, that I embraced Islam. I recalled it only
recently when I found it among my papers, exactly as I had jot-
ted it down that night upon awaking.'

'But it was truly thy fortune which God showed thee in that dream, O my son! Dost thou not recognize it clearly? The coming of the crowd of people, and thou with them, into a pathless waste, and their perplexity: is not that the condition of those whom the opening *sura* of the Koran describes as "those who have gone astray"? And the dromedary which, with its rider, was waiting for thee: was not this the "right guidance" of which the Koran speaks so often? And the rider who did not speak to thee and whose face thou couldst not see: who else could he have been but the Holy Prophet, upon whom be God's blessing and peace? He loved to wear a cloak with short sleeves . . . and do not many of our books tell us whenever he appears in dreams to non-Muslims or to those who are not yet Muslims, his face is always covered? And that white, cool light on the horizon ahead: what else could it have been but a promise of the light of faith which lights without burning? Thou didst not reach it in thy dream because, as thou hast told us, it was only years later that thou camest to know Islam for the truth itself . . . '

'Thou mayest be right, O Long-of-Age . . . But what about that "westernmost city" to which the gateway on the horizon was to lead me? – for, after all, my acceptance of Islam did not lead me to the West: it led me, rather, away from the West.'

Ibn Saud was silent and thoughtful for a moment; then he raised his head and, with that sweet smile which I had come to love, said: 'Could it not have meant, O Muhammad, that thy reaching Islam would be the "westernmost" point in thy life – and that after that, the life of the West would cease to be thine . . . ?'

After a while the King spoke again: 'Nobody knows the future but God. But sometimes He chooses to give us, through a dream, a glimpse of what is to befall us in the future. I myself have had such dreams twice or thrice, and they have always come true. One of them, indeed, has made me what I am . . . I was at that time seventeen years old. We were living as exiles in Kuwayt, but I could not bear the thought of the Ibn Rashids ruling over my homeland. Often would I beg my father, may God bestow His mercy upon him, "Fight, O my father, and drive the Ibn Rashids out! Nobody has a better claim to the throne of Riyadh than thou!" But my father would brush aside my stormy demands as fantasies, and would remind me that Muhammad ibn Rashid was the most powerful ruler in the lands of the

Arabs, and that he held sway over a kingdom that stretched from the Syrian Desert in the north to the sands of the Empty Quarter in the south, and that all beduin tribes trembled before his iron fist. One night, however, I had a strange dream. I saw myself on horseback on a lonely steppe at night, and in front of me, also on horseback, was old Muhammad ibn Rashid, the usurper of my family's kingdom. We were both unarmed, but Ibn Rashid held aloft in his hand a great, shining lantern. When he saw me approach, he recognized the enemy in me and turned and spurred his horse to flight; but I raced after him, got hold of a corner of his cloak, and then of his arm, and then of the lantern – and I blew out the lantern. When I awoke, I knew with certainty that I was destined to wrest the rule from the House of Ibn Rashid . . .'

.   .   .   .

IN THE YEAR OF THAT DREAM, 1897, Muhammad ibn Rashid died. This seemed to Abd al-Aziz ibn Saud an opportune moment to strike; but Abd ar-Rahman, his father, was not inclined to risk the peaceful life at Kuwayt in so dubious an undertaking. But the son's passion was more stubborn than the father's inertia; and in the end the father gave in. With the assistance of his friend, Shaykh Mubarak of Kuwayt, he raised a few beduin tribes that had remained faithful to his family, took the field against the Ibn Rashids in the old Arabian manner, with dromedaries and horses and tribal banners, was quickly routed by superior enemy forces and – in his innermost probably more relieved than disappointed – returned to Kuwayt, resolved never again to disturb the evening of his life by warlike adventures.

But the son did not give up so easily. He always remembered his dream of victory over Muhammad ibn Rashid; and when his father renounced all claims to kingship over Najd, it was that dream which prompted young Abd al-Aziz to undertake his reckless bid for power. He got hold of a few friends – among them his cousins Abdullah ibn Jiluwi and Ibn Musaad – drummed together some venturesome beduins, until the whole company came to forty men. They rode out of Kuwayt like robbers, stealthily, without banners or drums or songs; and, avoiding the much-frequented caravan routes and hiding in daytime, they reached the vicinity of Riyadh and made camp in a secluded valley. On the same day, Abd al-Aziz selected five companions out of the forty and thus addressed the rest:

'We six have now placed our destinies in the hands of God. We are going to Riyadh – to conquer or to lose it for good. If you should hear sounds of fighting from the town, come to our assistance; but if you do not hear anything by sunset tomorrow, then you shall know that we are dead, and may God receive our souls. Should this happen, you others return secretly, as fast as you can, to Kuwayt.'

And the six men set out on foot. At nightfall they reached the town and entered it through one of the breaches which years ago Muhammad ibn Rashid had made in the walls of the conquered city to humiliate its inhabitants. They went, their weapons hidden under their cloaks, straight to the house of the Rashidi *amir*. It was locked, for the *amir*, fearing the hostile populace, was accustomed to spend his nights in the citadel opposite. Abd al-Aziz and his companions knocked on the door; a slave opened it, only to be immediately overpowered, bound and gagged; the same happened to the other inmates of the house – at that hour only a few slaves and women. The six adventurers helped themselves to some dates from the *amir's* larder and passed the night reciting, by turns, from the Koran.

In the morning the doors of the citadel were opened and the *amir* stepped out, surrounded by armed bodyguards and slaves. Crying, 'O God, in Thy hands is Ibn Saud!' Abd al-Aziz and his five companions hurled themselves with their naked swords upon the surprised enemy. Abdullah ibn Jiluwi threw his javelin at the *amir;* but he ducked in time and the javelin stuck with quivering shaft in the mud wall of the citadel – there to be seen to this day. The *amir* retreated in panic into the gateway; while Abdullah pursued him single-handedly into the interior of the citadel, Abd al-Aziz and his four remaining companions attacked the bodyguards, who, despite their numerical superiority, were too confused to defend themselves effectively. An instant later there appeared on the flat roof the *amir*, hard-pressed by Abdullah ibn Jiluwi, begging for mercy, which was not granted; and when he fell down on the rampart of the roof and received the fatal swordstroke, Abd al-Aziz cried out from below, 'Come, O men of Riyadh! Here am I, Abd al-Aziz, son of Abd ar-Rahman of the House of Ibn Saud, your rightful ruler!' And the men

of Riyadh, who hated their northern oppressors, came running
with their arms to the aid of their Prince; and on their dromedaries galloped his thirty-five companions through the city gates,
sweeping all opposition before them like a stormwind. Within
one hour Abd al-Aziz ibn Saud was uncontested ruler of the city.

That was in the year 1901. He was twenty-one years old. His
youth came to a close, and he entered upon the second phase of
his life, that of mature man and ruler.

Step by step, province by province, Ibn Saud wrested Najd
from the House of Ibn Rashid pushing them back to their homeland, the Jabal Shammar, and its capital Haïl. This expansion
was as calculated as if it had been devised by a general staff
working with maps, logistics and geopolitical notions – although
Ibn Saud had no general staff and had probably never laid eyes
on a map. His conquests proceeded spirally, with Riyadh as their
fixed centre, and no forward step was ever taken until the previously conquered territory had been thoroughly subdued and
consolidated. At first he acquired the districts to the east and
north of Riyadh, then he extended his realm over the western
deserts. His northward progress was slow, for the Ibn Rashids
still possessed considerable power and were, in addition, supported by the Turks, with whom they had formed a close alliance in the past decades. Ibn Saud was also hampered by his
poverty: the southern regions of Najd could not provide him
with sufficient revenue for supplying large groups of fighting men
for any length of time.

'At one time,' he once told me, 'I was so poor that I had to pawn
the jewel-encrusted sword which Shaykh Mubarak had given
me with a Jewish moneylender at Kuwayt. I could not even afford a carpet for my saddle – but the empty sacks that were
placed under the sheepskin did as well.'

There was yet another problem which made Ibn Saud's early
career a very hard one: the attitude of the beduin tribes.

In spite of all its towns and villages, Central Arabia is primarily a land of beduins. It was their support or antagonism
that decided the issues in the warfare between Ibn Saud and Ibn
Rashid at almost every stage. They were fickle and changeable
and usually joined whichever party seemed to be in the ascen-
dant at the moment or offered the hope of greater spoils. A past-
master of such double-dealing was Faysal ad-Dawish, supreme

chieftain of the powerful Mutayr tribe, whose allegiance could always tip the scales in favour of one or the other of the two rival dynasties. He would come to Haïl to be loaded with gifts by Ibn Rashid; he would abandon Ibn Rashid and come to Riyadh to swear fealty to Ibn Saud – only to betray him a month later; he was faithless to all, brave and shrewd and obsessed by a tremendous greed for power; and many were the sleepless nights which he caused Ibn Saud.

Beset by such difficulties, Ibn Saud conceived a plan – at first probably intended to be no more than a political manoeuvre, but destined to develop into a grand idea capable of altering the face of the entire Peninsula: the plan of settling the nomad tribes. It was obvious that, once having settled down, the beduins would have to give up their double game between the warring parties. Living as nomads, it was easy for them to fold their tents at a moment's notice and to move with their herds hither and thither, from one side to the other; but a settled mode of life would make this impossible, for a shifting of their allegiance to the enemy would bring with it the danger of losing their houses and plantations: and nothing is as dear to a beduin as his possessions.

Ibn Saud made the settlement of beduins the most important point in his programme. In this he was greatly assisted by the teachings of Islam, which always stressed the superiority of the settled over the nomadic way of life. The King sent out religious teachers who instructed the tribesmen in the faith and preached the new idea with unexpected success. The organization of the *Ikhwan* ('brethren') – as the settled beduins began to call themselves – took shape. The very first *Ikhwan* settlement was that of Alwa-Mutayr, the clan of Ad-Dawish; their settlement, Artawiyya, grew within a few years into a town of nearly thirty thousand inhabitants. Many other tribes followed suit.

The religious enthusiasm of the *Ikhwan* and their warlike potential became a powerful instrument in the hands of Ibn Saud. From then onward his wars assumed a new aspect: borne by the religious fervour of the *Ikhwan*, they outgrew their erstwhile character of a dynastic struggle for power and became wars of faith. To the *Ikhwan*, at least, this rebirth of faith had more than a personal connotation. In their uncompromising adherence to the teachings of the great eighteenth-century reformer, Muham-

mad ibn Abd al-Wahhab (which aimed at a restoration of Islam
to the austere purity of its beginnings and rejected all later 'innovations'), the *Ikhwan* were, no doubt, often filled with an exag-
gerated sense of personal righteousness; but what most of them
desired above all else was not merely personal righteousness but
the establishment of a new society that could with justice be
called Islamic. True, many of their concepts were primitive and
their ardour frequently bordered on fanaticism; but given proper guidance and education, their deep religious devotion might
have enabled them to broaden their outlook and in time to become the nucleus of a genuine social and spiritual resurgence of
all Arabia. Unfortunately, however, Ibn Saud failed to grasp the
tremendous import of such a development and remained content with imparting to the *Ikhwan* only the barest rudiments of
religious and secular education – in fact, only as much as seemed
necessary to maintain their zealotic fervour. In other words, Ibn
Saud saw in the *Ikhwan* movement only an instrument of power.
In later years, this failure on his part was destined to recoil on
his own policies and at one stage to endanger the very existence of
the kingdom he had created; and it gave perhaps the earliest indication that he lacked that inner greatness which his people had
come to expect of him. But the disillusionment of the *Ikhwan*
with the King and the King's disillusionment with them was a
long time in the making...

In 1913, with the tremendous striking force of the *Ikhwan* at
his disposal, Ibn Saud at last felt strong enough to attempt the
conquest of the province of Al-Hasa on the Persian Gulf, which
had once belonged to Najd but had been occupied by the Turks
fifty years earlier.

Warring against the Turks was no new experience to Ibn Saud;
off and on he had encountered Turkish detachments, especially
field artillery, within the armies of Ibn Rashid. But an attack on
Al-Hasa, which was directly administered by the Turks, was
quite a different affair: it would bring him into head-on collision
with a Great Power. But Ibn Saud had no choice. Unless he
brought Al-Hasa and its ports under his control, he would always remain cut off from the outer world, unable to obtain
sorely needed supplies of arms, ammunition and many necessities of life. The need justified the risk; but the risk was so great
that Ibn Saud hesitated long before undertaking an assault on

Al-Hasa and its capital, Al-Hufuf. To this day he is fond of recounting the circumstances in which the final decision was made:

'We were already in view of Al-Hufuf. From the sand dune on which I was sitting I could clearly see the walls of the powerful citadel overlooking the town. My heart was heavy with indecision as I weighed the advantages and the dangers of this undertaking. I felt tired; I longed for peace and home; and with the thought of home, the face of my wife, Jawhara, came before my eyes. I began to think of verses which I might tell her if she were by my side – and before I realized it, I was busy composing a poem to her, completely forgetting where I was and how grave a decision I had to make. As soon as the poem was ready in my mind I wrote it down, sealed it, called one of my couriers and commanded him: "Take the two fastest dromedaries, ride to Riyadh without stopping and hand this over to Muhammad's mother." And as the courier was disappearing in a cloud of sand dust, I suddenly found that my mind had made a decision regarding the war: I would attack Al-Hufuf, and God would lead me to victory.'

His confidence proved justified. In a daring assault, his warriors stormed the citadel; the Turkish troops surrendered and were permitted to withdraw with their arms and equipment to the coast, whence they embarked for Basra. The Ottoman government, however, was not prepared to yield its possession so easily. A punitive expedition against Ibn Saud was decided upon at Istanbul. But before it could be undertaken, the Great War broke out, forcing the Turks to deploy all their military forces elsewhere; and with the end of the war, the Ottoman Empire ceased to exist.

Deprived of Turkish support and hemmed in to the north by territories which were now administered by Britain and France, Ibn Rashid could no longer put up effective resistance. Led by Faysal ad-Dawish – now one of the most valiant paladins of Ibn Saud – the King's forces took Haïl in 1921, and the House of Ibn Rashid lost its last stronghold.

The climax of Ibn Saud's expansion came in 1924-1925, when he conquered the Hijaz, including Mecca, Medina and Jidda, and expelled the Sharifian dynasty which had come to power there after Sharif Husayn's British-supported revolt against the

Turks in 1916. It was with the conquest of this Holy Land of Islam that Ibn Saud, now forty-five years old, fully emerged into the view of the outer world.

His unprecedented rise to power at a time when most of the Middle East had succumbed to Western penetration filled the Arab world with the hope that here at last was the leader who would lift the entire Arab nation out of its bondage; and many other Muslim groups besides the Arabs began to look to him to bring about a revival of the Islamic idea in its fullest sense by establishing a state in which the spirit of the Koran would reign supreme.

A good and just man in his personal affairs, loyal to his friends and supporters, generous towards his enemies and implacable towards hypocrites, graced by intellectual gifts far above the level of most of his followers, Ibn Saud has established a condition of public security in his vast domains unequalled in Arab lands since the time of the early Caliphate a thousand years ago. His personal authority is tremendous, but it does not rest so much on actual power as on the suggestive strength of his character. He is utterly unassuming in words and demeanor. His truly democratic spirit enables him to converse with the beduins who come to him in dirty, tattered garments as if he were one of them, and to allow them to call him by his first name, Abd al-Aziz. On the other hand, he can be haughty and contemptuous towards highly-placed officials whenever he discerns servility in them. He despises all snobbery. I remember an incident in Mecca when, during a dinner at the royal palace, the head of one of Mecca's noblest families wrinkled his nose at the 'beduin crudity' of some of the Najdis present who were gustily eating their rice in large fistfuls; in order to demonstrate his own refinement, the Meccan aristocrat daintily manipulated his food with his fingertips – when suddenly the voice of the King boomed out: 'You fine people toy with your food so gingerly: is it because you are accustomed to dig with your fingers in dirt? We people of Najd are not afraid of our hands; they are clean – and therefore we eat heartily and by the handful!'

Sometimes, when he is entirely relaxed, a gentle smile plays about Ibn Saud's mouth and gives an almost spiritual quality to the beauty of his face. I am sure that were music not regarded as reprehensible by the strict Wahhabi code which Ibn Saud follows, he would undoubtedly have expressed himself in it; but as it is, he shows his musical bent only in his little poems, his colourful descriptions of experiences, and his songs of war and love which have spread through the whole of Najd and are sung by men as they ride on their dromedaries across the desert and women in the seclusion of their chambers. And it reveals itself in the way his daily life follows a regular, elastic rhythm suited to the demands of his royal office. Like Julius Caesar, he possesses to a high degree the capacity to pursue several trains of thought at one and the same time, without in the least curtailing the intensity with which he attacks each individual problem: and it is this remarkable gift which permits him to direct personally all the affairs of his vast kingdom without falling into confusion or breaking down from overwork.

The acuteness of his perceptions is often uncanny. He has an almost unfailing, instinctive insight into the motives of the people with whom he has to deal. Not infrequently – as I myself have had opportunity to witness – he is able to read men's thoughts before they are spoken, and seems to sense a man's attitude towards him at the very moment of that man's entering the room. It is this ability which has made it possible for Ibn Saud to thwart several exceedingly well-prepared attempts on his life, and to make many a lucky on-the-spot decision in political matters.

And it is such qualities, too, which make Abd al-Aziz ibn Saud the very embodiment of the beduin life-sense and character, as well as of beduin concepts and feelings: concepts and feelings which, in the last resort, were responsible for the spirital phenomenon of monotheism, first manifested among the early Hebrews (who, after all, were but a small beduin tribe that had migrated from Arabia northwards into the lands of the Fertile Crescent) and culminating in the revelation of the Koran to the Arabian Prophet, Muhammad.

For, more than anything else, it was beduin Arabia that became the soil and matrix of a way of life which was destined to express itself, in the course of time, in a great spiritual movement and thereafter in a civilization which extended its influence, directly and indirectly, over almost the whole world: the religion of Islam and the civilization engendered by it. The

Amir (later King) Saud, 1928

human and social prerequisite of this development was what may be described as 'beduin culture' – a way of life which will soon belong to the past and of which history offers no other example.

All in all, the way of life of the beduin was not a mere preamble to a higher civilization: it is a rounded, complete culture in itself. It is a culture no doubt formed and influenced by climate and geography and to a certain extent imbued with what may be described as 'barbaric' notions; but in the last resort it is the outcome of realistic human responses to a human condition reduced to the barest essentials of life and lacking all those incidentals of ease which mould society in softer climes.

The natural environment of the beduin is hard and inclement. Steppes and deserts, sometimes traversed by dry river-beds which carry water only after infrequent rains; the scorching heat of summer days and the biting cold of winter nights; shallow desert wells here and there, yielding scant quantities of mostly brackish water; a vegetation so scarce for most of the year that it allows only for the breeding of camels and small cattle; and a tremendous expanse of skies, pale and burning in daytime like molten metal, and infinitely high and majestic, black and starry, by night: all this has contributed to the emergence of a special human type and of moral and social characteristics not to be found anywhere else.

From his earliest childhood to his death, from generation to generation, and from century to century, the beduin has been accustomed to contemplate infinity and eternity in the sky above him and in the stillness and solitude of the desert around him; and, at the same time, he has learned to observe human life in all its fundamental nakedness, devoid of the garments of security and the rudiments of settled comfort. His instinctive understanding of the frailty and insignificance of human life and his appreciation of human motivations has become acute, sharpened by the awareness of ever-present danger and, hence, the necessity of gauging correctly the reactions of one's fellow-man. Thus, cosmic consciousness and an instinctive directness of perception have become the basic characteristics of the beduin psyche.

Nor is this all. The hardness of his environment has made the beduin realize the intrinsic loneliness of human existence, and thus the need for close cooperation between individuals; and the instinctive desire for cooperation gradually achieved maturity in the conscious concept of tribal solidarity. In its turn, the consciousness of belonging to a definite human group, the tribe, brought with it the desire for enhancing its strength and durability even at the price of personal loss: and so, pride and courage, fervour and enthusiasm for extra-personal goals – all this epitomized in the Arabian concept of *hamasah* – became the natural expression of beduin tribalism, just as the concept of hospitality (*diyafah*) became the hallmark of the individual beduin, man and woman alike. And dominating all these traits, embracing them, as it were, within a single sweep of consciousness is the ideal of *muruwwah* – that untranslatable concept common to man, woman and child, comprising virtues like generosity, sense of honour, directness, valour, chivalry and courtesy. Allied to all this is an exceptional sense of *language* – the ability to express the most complicated perception of reality in a single phrase, or in a *mot juste*, or in poetry: so much so that, next to the Koran, the speech of the beduin has forever remained the standard by which Arab philologists measure the purity of style and diction in all forms of Arabic literature.

In short, beduin life as it has manifested itself throughout known history cannot by any means be characterised as 'primitive'. To be sure, it is an unruly life, full of contradictions, of weird ideas and tribal warfare, of violence as well as of outstanding examples of kindness and generosity, of betrayals as well as of deeds of supreme self-sacrifice: a form of life which has remained stationary throughout countless centuries, lacking what is described as 'progress': but, nevertheless, it is a fully developed, mature culture, possessed of a life-perception all its own and absolutely different from all other cultural formations.

All this must be stressed if one is to understand the 'how' and 'why' of Arabia's spiritual and social history.

The belief in the One God – the faith of the early Hebrews – originated in Arabia. It was the natural faith of the beduin who at some point in history became aware of the insignificance of the individual as faced with the immense grandeur of the creative force perceptibly acting throughout the universe: and there was only one short step from this to the concept of God, the Creator. However hazy and corrupted this concept may have become to the beduin in the course of time, it always remained in the background of his consciousness. Behind all the polytheism of ancient Arabia, behind the worship of stars and trees and moon-goddesses and stones, there was always a dim realization – evidenced in all pre-Islamic poetry and folklore – that there is an inconceivable Supreme Being behind and above all observable reality.

Thus, the human ground was prepared for the revelation of the Koran and its subsequent triumph in Arabia.

The teachings of the Koran found from the very first moment of their enunciation a living echo in the feelings and ethical valuations of the Arab. They attained to the very kernel of the beduin concept of *muruwwah*: they demanded of man that he be truthful, courageous, generous and compassionate; proud towards brutal force and humble before goodness; and, above all, conscious of man's ephemeral insignificance before the Infinite and Eternal.

In no other community could the tenets of Islam have so readily coincided with what the people who were first addressed by the Koran had always instinctively felt and regarded as true. In other words, the Arabs of the Prophet's time – the Arabs who were the embodiment of beduin culture – recognized the ethics of Islam as something that they had always known without being aware that they knew it. To phrase it yet differently, one might say that God's final message to man was revealed through the medium – and in the language – of the one people that was able to grasp its innermost purport all at once and to translate its ideological dynamism into reality by virtue of its own, unique psychological make-up: and this explains why Islam, carried forward by the Arabs, spread so irresistibly, within a few decades, to the shores of the Atlantic and the borders of China.

— 3 —

ON THE MORNING of my departure from Haïl I am awakened by a loud music which flows in through the open window of my castle chamber: a singing, chirping and strumming, like a hundred violins and wind instruments being tuned before the opening of a grand-opera performance: that disjointed polyphony of short, discordant strokes which, because they are so many and so subdued, seems to churn up a mysterious, almost ghostly unity of tone. . . . But this must indeed be a huge orchestra, so mighty are the waves of sound it sends forth. . . .

As I step to the window and look out into the dawning grey of the morning, over and beyond the empty market place, beyond the mud-grey houses of the town, towards the foothills where the tamarisks and the palm orchards grow – I recognize it: it is the music of the draw wells in the orchards which are just beginning their day's work, hundreds of them. In large leather bags the water is being drawn up by camels, the draw ropes run over crudely fashioned wooden pulleys, and each pulley rubs against its wooden axle and sings, pipes, creaks and soughs in a multitude of high and low tones until the rope is fully unrolled and the pulley comes to a standstill; whereupon it gives out a violent sound like a shout, and the shout gradually fades away in sighing chords, now powerfully accompanied by the rush of water into wooden troughs; and then the camel turns round and goes slowly back to the well – and again the pulley makes music while the ropes roll over it and the waterskin sinks down into the well.

Because there are so many wells, the singing does not stop for a single moment; the tones now meet in accords, now separate; some of them begin with new jubilation while others die away from each other – roaring, creaking, piping, singing – what a magnificent orchestra! It is not co-ordinated by human design: and therefore it almost reaches the greatness of nature, whose will is impenetrable.

VII

MIDWAY

— 1 —

WE HAVE LEFT HAÏL and are riding toward Medina: now three riders – for one of Ibn Musaad's men, Mansur al-Assaf, is accompanying us part of the way on an errand of the *amir*.

Mansur is so handsome that if he were to appear on the streets of a Western city all the women would turn to look after him. He is very tall, with a strong, virile face and amazingly even features. His skin is whitish-brown – an infallible mark of good birth among Arabs – and a pair of black eyes survey the world keenly from beneath well-shaped brows. There is nothing in him of Zayd's delicacy or of Zayd's quiet detachment; the lines of his face speak of violent, if controlled, passions and lend to his appearance an aura of sombreness quite unlike the serene gravity of my Shammar friend. But Mansur, like Zayd, has seen a lot of the world and makes a pleasant companion.

In the grey-and-yellow, pebbly soil that has now replaced the sands of the Nufud we can descry the little animal life that fills it: tiny grey lizards zigzag between our camels' feet at an incredible speed, take refuge under a thorny shrub and watch our passing with blazing eyes; little grey field mice with bushy tails, resembling squirrels; and their cousins, the marmots, whose flesh is highly esteemed by the beduins of Najd and is, indeed, one of the tenderest delicacies I have ever tasted. There is also the foot-long edible lizard called *dhab* which thrives on the roots of plants and tastes like a cross between chicken and fish. Black four-legged beetles the size of a small hen's egg can be observed as they roll with touching patience a ball of dry camel-dung; pushing it backward with strong hind legs while the body leans on the forelegs, they roll the precious find painfully toward their homes, fall on their backs if a pebble happens to obstruct their path, turn over with difficulty on their legs again, roll their possession a few inches farther, fall again, get up again and work,

183

tirelessly . . . Sometimes a grey hare jumps away in long leaps from beneath grey bushes. Once we see gazelles, but too distant to shoot; they disappear in the blue-grey shadows between two hills.

'Tell me, O Muhammad,' asks Mansur, 'how did it happen that thou hast come to live among the Arabs? And how didst thou come to embrace Islam?'

'I will tell thee how it happened,' interposes Zayd. 'First he fell in love with the Arabs, and then with their faith. Isn't it true, O my uncle?'

'What Zayd says is true, O Mansur. Many years ago, when I first came to Arab lands, I was attracted by the way you people lived. And when I began to ask myself what you thought and what you believed in, I came to know about Islam.'

'And didst thou, O Muhammad, find all at once that Islam was the True Word of God?'

'Well, no, this did not come about so quickly. For one thing, I did not then believe that God had ever spoken directly to man, or that the books which men claimed to be His word were anything but the works of wise men . . .'

Mansur stares at me with utter incredulity: 'How could that be, O Muhammad? Didst thou not even believe in the Scriptures which Moses brought, or the Gospel of Jesus? But I have always thought that the peoples of the West believe at least in them?'

'Some do, O Mansur, and others do not. I was one of those others . . .'

And I explain to him that many people in the West have long ceased to regard the Scriptures – their own as well as those of others – as true Revelations of God, but see in them rather the history of man's religious aspirations as they have evolved over the ages.

'But this view of mine was shaken as soon as I came to know something of Islam,' I add. 'I came to know about it when I found that the Muslims lived in a way quite different from what the Europeans thought should be man's way; and every time I learned something more about the teachings of Islam, I seemed to discover something that I had always known without knowing it . . .'

And so I go on, telling Mansur of my first journey to the Near East – of how in the Desert of Sinai I had my first impression of

the Arabs; of what I saw and felt in Palestine, Egypt, Transjordan and Syria; of how in Damascus I had my first premonition that a new, hitherto unsuspected way to truth was slowly
unfolding before me; and how, after visiting Turkey, I returned
to Europe and found it difficult to live again in the Western
world: for, on the one hand, I was eager to gain a deeper understanding of the strange uneasiness which my first acquaintance
with the Arabs and their culture had produced in me, hoping
that it would help me better understand what I myself expected
of life; and, on the other hand, I had reached the point where it
was becoming clear to me that never again would I be able to
identify myself with the aims of Western society.

●   ●   ●   ●   ●   ●   ●   ●

IN THE SPRING of 1924 the *Frankfurter Zeitung* sent me out on
my second journey to the Middle East. The book describing my
previous travels had at last been completed. (It was published a
few months after my departure under the title *Unromantisches
Morgenland* – by which I meant to convey that it was not a book
about the romantic, exotic outward picture of the Muslim East
but rather an endeavour to penetrate to its day-by-day realities.
Although its anti-Zionist attitude and unusual predilection for
the Arabs caused something of a flutter in the German press, I
am afraid it did not sell very well.)

Once again I crossed the Mediterranean and saw the coast of
Egypt before me. The railway journey from Port Said to Cairo
was like turning the leaves of a familiar book. Between the Suez
Canal and Lake Manzala the Egyptian afternoon unfolded itself. Wild ducks swam in the water and tamarisks shook their
finely scalloped branches. Villages grew up out of the plain,
which was at first sandy and sparsely covered with vegetation.
Dark water buffaloes, often coupled with camels, were drawing
ploughs with lazy limbs through the spring soil. As we turned
westward from the Suez Canal, Egyptian green enveloped us.
When I saw once again the slim, tall women who were swaying
in indescribable rhythm, striding over the fields and carrying
pitchers free on their heads with arms outstretched, I thought to
myself: Nothing in the whole world – neither the most perfect
automobile nor the proudest bridge nor the most thoughtful
book – can replace this grace which has been lost in the West

and is already threatened in the East – this grace which is nothing but an expression of the magic consonance between a human being's Self and the world that surrounds him . . .

This time I travelled first class. In the compartment there were only two passengers besides me: a Greek businessman from Alexandria who, with the ease so characteristic of all Levantines, soon involved me in an animated conversation and supplied witty observations on all we saw; and an Egyptian *umda*, a village headman, who – judging from his costly silk *kaftan* and the thick, gold watch chain that protruded from his sash – was obviously rich but seemed content to remain entirely uneducated. In fact, almost as soon as he joined our conversation, he readily admitted that he could neither read nor write; nevertheless, he also displayed a sharp common sense and frequently crossed swords with the Greek.

We were talking, I remember, about some of the social principles in Islam which at that time strongly occupied my thoughts. My Greek fellow traveller did not entirely agree with my admiration of the social equity in the Law of Islam.

'It is not as equitable as you seem to think, my dear friend' – and, changing from the French, into which we had lapsed, into Arabic again for the benefit of our Egyptian companion, he now turned to him: 'You people say that your religion is so equitable. Couldst thou perhaps then tell us why it is that Islam allows Muslim men to marry Christian or Jewish girls but does not allow your daughters and sisters to marry a Christian or Jew? Dost thou call this justice, huh?'

'I do, indeed,' replied the portly *umda* without a moment's hesitation, 'and I shall tell thee why our religious law has been thus laid down. We Muslims do not believe that Jesus – may peace and God's blessing be upon him – was God's son, but we do consider him, as we consider Moses and Abraham and all the other Prophets of the Bible, a true Prophet of God, all of them having been sent to mankind in the same way as the Last Prophet, Muhammad – may God bless him and give him peace – was sent: and so, if a Jewish or Christian girl marries a Muslim, she may rest assured that none of the persons who are holy to her will ever be spoken of irreverently among her new family; while, on the other hand, should a Muslim girl marry a non-Muslim, it is certain that he whom she regards as God's Messen-

ger will be abused . . . and perhaps even by her own children:
for do not children usually follow their father's faith? Dost thou
think it would be fair to expose her to such pain and humiliation?'

The Greek had no answer to this except an embarrassed shrug
of his shoulders; but to me it seemed that the simple, illiterate
umda had, with that common sense so peculiar to his race,
touched the kernel of a very important problem. And once again
as with that old *hajji* in Jerusalem, I felt that a new door to Islam
was being opened to me.

.   .   .   .

IN ACCORDANCE WITH MY changed financial circumstances,
I was now able to live in Cairo in a style which would have been
unthinkable a few months earlier. I no longer needed to count
pennies. The days when, during my first stay in this city, I had to
subsist on bread, olives and milk, were forgotten. But in one respect I kept faith with the 'traditions' of my past: instead of putting up in one of the fashionable quarters of Cairo, I rented
rooms in the house of my old friend, the fat woman from Trieste,
who received me with open arms and a motherly kiss on both
cheeks.

On the third day after my arrival, at sunset, I heard the muffled sound of cannon from the Citadel. At the same moment a
circle of lights sprang up on the highest galleries of the two minarets that flanked the Citadel mosque; and all the minarets of all
the mosques in the city took up that illumination and repeated
it: on every minaret a similar circle of lights. Through old Cairo
there went a strange movement; quicker and at the same time
more festive became the step of the people, louder the polyphonous noise in the streets: you could sense and almost hear a new
tension quiver at all corners.

And all this happened because the new crescent moon announced a new month (for the Islamic calendar goes by lunar
months and years), and that month was Ramadan, the most
solemn month of the Islamic year. It commemorates the time,
more than thirteen hundred years ago, when, according to tradition, Muhammad received the first revelation of the Koran.
Strict fasting is expected of every Muslim during this month.
Men and women, save those who are ill, are forbidden to take

food or drink (and even to smoke) from the moment when the first streak of light on the eastern horizon announces the coming dawn, until sunset: for thirty days. During these thirty days the people of Cairo went around with glowing eyes, as if elevated to holy regions. In the thirty nights you heard cannonfire, singing and cries of joy, while all the mosques glowed with light until daybreak.

Twofold, I learned, is the purpose of this month of fasting. One has to abstain from food and drink in order to feel in one's own body what the poor and hungry feel: thus, social responsibility is being hammered into human consciousness as a religious postulate. The other purpose of fasting during Ramadan is self-discipline – an aspect of individual morality strongly accentuated in all Islamic teachings (as, for instance, in the total prohibition of all intoxicants, which Islam regards as too easy an avenue of escape from consciousness and responsibility). In these two elements – brotherhood of man and individual self-discipline – I began to discern the outlines of Islam's ethical outlook.

In my endeavour to gain a fuller picture of what Islam really meant and stood for, I derived great benefit from the explanations which some of my Cairene Muslims friends were able to provide me. Outstanding among them was Shaykh Mustafa al-Maraghi, one of the most prominent Islamic scholars of the time and certainly the most brilliant among the *ulama* of Al-Azhar University (he was destined to become its rector some years later). He must have been in his middle forties at that time, but his stocky, muscular body had the alertness and vivacity of a twenty-year-old. In spite of his erudition and gravity, his sense of humour never left him. A pupil of the great Egyptian reformer Muhammad Abduh, and having associated in his youth with that inspiring firebrand, Jamal ad-Din al-Afghani, Shaykh Al-Maraghi was himself a keen, critical thinker. He never failed to impress upon me that the Muslims of recent times had fallen very short indeed of the ideals of their faith, and that nothing could be more erroneous than to measure the potentialities of Muhammad's message by the yardstick of present-day Muslim life and thought –

' – just as,' he said, 'it would be erroneous to see in the Christians' unloving behaviour toward one another a refutation of Christ's message of love . . .'

With this warning, Shaykh Al-Maraghi introduced me to Al-Azhar.

Out of the crowded bustle of Mousky Street, Cairo's oldest shopping centre, we reached a small, out-of-the-way square, one of its sides occupied by the broad, straight front of the Azhar Mosque. Through a double gate and a shadowy forecourt we entered the courtyard of the mosque proper, a large quadrangle surrounded by ancient arcades. Students dressed in long, dark *jubbas* and white turbans were sitting on straw mats and reading with low voices from their books and manuscripts. The lectures were given in the huge, covered mosque-hall beyond. Several teachers sat, also on straw mats, under the pillars which crossed the hall in long rows, and in a semicircle before each teacher crouched a group of students. The lecturer never raised his voice, so that it obviously required great attention and concentration not to miss any of his words. One should have thought that such absorption would be conducive to real scholarship; but Shaykh Al-Maraghi soon shattered my illusions:

'Dost thou see those "scholars" over there?' he asked me. 'They are like those sacred cows in India which, I am told, eat up all the printed paper they can find in the streets . . . Yes, they gobble up all the printed pages from books that have been written centuries ago, but they do not digest them. They no longer think for themselves; they read and repeat, read and repeat – and the students who listen to them learn only to read and repeat, generation after generation.'

'But, Shaykh Mustafa,' I interposed, 'Al-Azhar is, after all, the central seat of Islamic learning, and the oldest university in the world! One encounters its name on nearly every page of Muslim cultural history. What about all the great thinkers, the theologians, historians, philosophers, mathematicians it has produced over the last ten centuries?'

'It stopped producing them several centuries ago,' he replied ruefully. 'Well, perhaps not quite; here and there an independent thinker has somehow managed to emerge from Al-Azhar even in recent times. But on the whole, Al-Azhar has lapsed into the sterility from which the whole Muslim world is suffering, and its old impetus is all but extinguished. Those ancient Islamic thinkers whom thou hast mentioned would never have dreamed that after so many centuries their thoughts, instead of being continued and developed, would only be repeated over and over again, as if they were ultimate and infallible truths. If there is to be any change for the better, *thinking* must be encouraged instead of the present thought-imitation . . .'

Shaykh Al-Maraghi's trenchant characterization of Al-Azhar helped me to realize one of the deepest causes of the cultural decay that stared one in the face everywhere in the Muslim world. Was not the scholastic petrifaction of this ancient university mirrored, in varying degrees, in the social sterility of the Muslim present? Was not the counterpart of this intellectual stagnation to be found in the passive, almost indolent, acceptance by so many Muslims of the unnecessary poverty in which they lived, of their mute toleration of the many social wrongs to which they were subjected?

And was it any wonder then, I asked myself, that, fortified by such tangible evidences of Muslim decay, so many erroneous views about Islam itself were prevalent throughout the West? These popular, Western views could be summarized thus: The downfall of the Muslims is mainly due to Islam which, far from being a religious ideology comparable to Christianity or Judaism, is a rather unholy mixture of desert fanaticism, gross sensuality, superstition and dumb fatalism that prevents its adherents from participating in mankind's advance toward higher social forms; instead of liberating the human spirit from the shackles of obscurantism, Islam rather tightens them; and, consequently, the sooner the Muslim peoples are freed from their subservience to Islamic beliefs and social practices and induced to adopt the Western way of life, the better for them and for the rest of the world . . .

My own observations had by now convinced me that the mind of the average Westerner held an utterly distorted image of Islam. What I saw in the pages of the Koran was not a 'crudely materialistic' world-view but, on the contrary, an intense God-consciousness that expressed itself in a rational acceptance of all God-created nature: a harmonious side-by-side of intellect and sensual urge, spiritual need and social demand. It was obvious to me that the decline of the Muslims was not due to any shortcomings in Islam but rather to their own failure to live up to it.

For, indeed, it was Islam that had carried the early Muslims to tremendous cultural heights by directing all their energies to-

ward conscious thought as the only means to understanding the
nature of God's creation and, thus, of His will. No demand had
been made of them to believe in dogmas difficult or even impossible of intellectual comprehension; in fact, no dogma whatsoever was to be found in the Prophet's message: and, thus, the
thirst after knowledge which distinguished early Muslim history
had not been forced, as elsewhere in the world, to assert itself in
a painful struggle against the traditional faith. On the contrary,
it had stemmed exclusively from that faith. The Arabian Prophet
had declared that *Striving after knowledge is a most sacred duty
for every Muslim man and woman:* and his followers were led to
understand that only by acquiring knowledge could they fully
worship the Lord. When they pondered the Prophet's saying,
God creates no disease without creating a cure for it as well, they
realized that by searching for unknown cures they would contribute to a fulfilment of God's will on earth: and so medical research became invested with the holiness of a religious duty.
They read the Koran verse, *We create every living thing out of
water* – and in their endeavour to penetrate to the meaning of
these words, they began to study living organisms and the laws
of their development: and thus they established the science of
biology. The Koran pointed to the harmony of the stars and
their movements as witnesses of their Creator's glory: and thereupon the sciences of astronomy and mathematics were taken up
by the Muslims with a fervour which in other religions was reserved for prayer alone. The Copernican system, which established the earth's rotation around its axis and the revolution of
the planets around the sun, was evolved in Europe at the beginning of the sixteenth century (only to be met by the fury of the
ecclesiastics, who read in it a contradiction of the literal teachings of the Bible): but the foundations of this system had actually been laid six hundred years earlier, in Muslim countries –
for already in the ninth and tenth centuries Muslim astronomers
had reached the conclusion that the earth was globular and that
it rotated around its axis, and had made accurate calculations of
latitudes and longitudes; and many of them maintained – without ever being accused of heresy – that the earth rotated around
the sun. And in the same way they took to chemistry and physics
and physiology, and to all the other sciences in which the Muslim
genius was to find its most lasting monument. In building that

monument they did no more than follow the admonition of their Prophet that *If anybody proceeds on his way in search of knowledge, God will make easy for him the way to Paradise;* that *The scientist walks in the path of God;* that *The superiority of the learned over the mere pious is like the superiority of the moon when it is full over all other stars;* and that *The ink of the scholars is more precious than the blood of martyrs.*

Throughout the whole creative period of Muslim history – that is to say, during the first five centuries after the Prophet's time – science and learning had no greater champion than Muslim civilization and no home more secure than the lands in which Islam was supreme.

Social life was similarly affected by the teachings of the Koran. At a time when in Christian Europe an epidemic was regarded as a scourge of God to which man had but to submit meekly – at that time, and long before it, the Muslims followed the injunction of their Prophet which directed them to combat epidemics by segregating the infected towns and areas. And at a time when even the kings and nobles of Christendom regarded bathing as an almost indecent luxury, even the poorest of Muslim houses had at least one bathroom, while elaborate public baths were common in every Muslim city (in the ninth century, for instance, Cordoba had three hundred of them): and all this in response to the Prophet's teaching that *Cleanliness is part of faith.* A Muslim did not come into conflict with the claims of spiritual life if he took pleasure in the beautiful things of material life, for, according to the Prophet, *God loves to see on His servants an evidence of His bounty.*

In short, Islam gave a tremendous incentive to cultural achievements which constitute one of the proudest pages in the history of mankind; and it gave this incentive by saying Yes to the intellect and No to obscurantism, Yes to action and No to quietism, Yes to life and No to asceticism. Little wonder, then, that as soon as it emerged beyond the confines of Arabia, Islam won new adherents by leaps and bounds. Born and nurtured in the world-contempt of Pauline and Augustinian Christianity, the populations of Syria and North Africa, and a little later of Visigothic Spain, saw themselves suddenly confronted with a teaching which denied the dogma of Original Sin and stressed the inborn dignity of earthly life: and so they rallied in ever-increasing numbers to the new creed that gave them to understand that man was God's vicar on earth. This, and not a legendary 'conversion at the point of the sword', was the explanation of Islam's amazing triumph in the glorious morning of its history.

It was not the Muslims that had made Islam great: it was Islam that had made the Muslims great. But as soon as their faith became habit and ceased to be a programme of life, to be consciously pursued, the creative impulse that underlay their civilization waned and gradually gave way to indolence, sterility and cultural decay.

.　　.　　.　　.　　.　　.　　.　　.

THE NEW INSIGHT I had gained, and the progress I was making in the Arabic language (I had arranged for a student of Al-Azhar to give me daily lessons), made me feel that now at last I possessed something like a key to the Muslim mind. No longer was I so certain that a European 'could never consciously grasp the total picture', as I had written in my book only a few months earlier; for now this Muslim world no longer seemed so entirely alien to Western associations. It occurred to me that if one was able to achieve a certain degree of detachment from his own past habits of thought and allow for the possibility that they might not be the only valid ones, the once so strange Muslim world might indeed become graspable . . .

But although I found much in Islam that appealed to my intellect as well as to my instincts, I did not consider it desirable for an intelligent man to conform all his thinking and his entire view of life to a system not devised by himself.

'Tell me, Shaykh Mustafa,' I asked my erudite friend Al-Maraghi on one occasion, 'why should it be necessary to confine oneself to one particular teaching and one particular set of injunctions? Mightn't it be better to leave all ethical inspiration to one's inner voice?'

'What thou art really asking, my young brother, is why should there be any institutional religion. The answer is simple. Only very few people – only prophets – are really able to understand the inner voice that speaks in them. Most of us are trammelled by our personal interests and desires – and if everyone were to follow only what his own heart dictates, we would have complete moral chaos and could never agree on any mode of behaviour.

Thou couldst ask, of course, whether there are no exceptions to the general rule – enlightened people who feel they have no need to be "guided" in what they consider to be right or wrong; but then, I ask thee, would not many, very many people claim that exceptional right for themselves? And what would be the result?'

.   .   .   .

I HAD BEEN IN CAIRO for nearly six weeks when I suffered a recurrence of malaria, which had first attacked me in Palestine the previous year. It began with a headache and dizziness and pains in all my limbs; and by the end of the day I was flat on my back, unable to lift my hand. Signora Vitelli, my landlady, bustled around me almost as if she were enjoying my helplessness; but her concern was genuine. She gave me hot milk to drink and placed cold compresses over my head – but when I suggested that perhaps a doctor should be called in, she bristled indignantly:

'A doctor – pooh! What do those butchers know about malaria! I know more about it than any of them. My sainted second husband died of it in Albania. We had been living in Durazzo for some years and he, poor soul, was often racked with pains worse than yours; but he always had confidence in me . . .'

I was too weak to argue, and let her fill me up with a potent brew of hot Greek wine and quinine – not any of your sugar-coated pills but the real, powdered stuff which shook me with its bitterness almost more than the fever did. But somehow, strange to say, I had full confidence in Mama Vitelli in spite of her ominous reference to her 'sainted second husband'.

That night, while my body was burning with fever, I suddenly heard a tender, intensive music from the street: the sound of a barrel organ. It was not one of those ordinary barrel organs with wheezy bellows and cracked pipes, but rather something that reminded you of the brittle, old clavichords which, because they were too delicate and too limited in nuances, had long ago been discarded in Europe. I had seen such barrel organs earlier in Cairo: a man carried the box on his back, a boy followed him, turning the handle; and the tones fell singly, short and neat, like arrows hitting their mark, like the tinkling of glass, with spaces in-between. And as they were so unmixed and so isolated from one another, these tones did not allow the listener to grasp the whole melody, but dragged him instead, in jerks, through tender, tense moments. They were like a secret which you were trying to unravel, but could not; and they tormented you with their eternal repetition in your head, over and over through the night, like a whirling circle from which there was no escape, like the dance of the whirling dervishes you had seen at Scutari – was it months, was it years ago? – after you had passed through the world's densest cypress forest . . .

It had been a most unusual forest, that Turkish cemetery at Scutari, just across the Bosporus from Istanbul: alleys and paths between innumerable cypresses and, under them, innumerable upright and fallen tombstones with weather-worn Arabic inscriptions. The cemetery had long ago ceased to be used; its dead had been dead for a very long time. Out of their bodies had sprung mighty tree trunks, sixty, eighty feet high, growing into the changing seasons and into the stillness which in that grove was so great that no room was left for melancholy. Nowhere did one feel so strongly as here that the dead might be asleep. They were the dead of a world which had allowed its living to live peacefully; the dead of a humanity without hurry.

After a short wandering through the cemetery, then through the narrow, hilly lanes of Scutari, I came upon a little mosque which revealed itself as such only in the beautiful ornamental arabesques over the door. As the door was half open I entered – and stood in a dusky room, in the centre of which several figures sat on a carpet in a circle around an old, old man. They all wore long cloaks and high, brown, brimless felt hats. The old *imam* was reciting a passage from the Koran in a monotonous voice. Along one wall sat a few musicians: drum-beaters, flutists and *kamanja* players with their long-necked, violinlike instruments.

It struck me that this strange assembly must be the 'whirling dervishes' of whom I had heard so much: a mystic order that aimed at bringing about, by means of certain rhythmically repeated and intensified movements, an ecstatic trance in the adept which was said to enable him to achieve a direct and personal experience of God.

The silence which followed the *imam's* recitation was suddenly broken by the thin, high-pitched sound of a flute; and the music set in monotonously, almost wailingly. As if with one movement the dervishes rose, threw off their cloaks and stood in their white, flowing tunics which reached to the ankles and were belted at the waist with knotted scarves. Then each of them made a half-turn, so that, standing in a circle, they faced one another in pairs; whereupon they crossed their arms over the chest and bowed deeply before one another (and I had to think of the old minuet, and of cavaliers in embroidered coats bowing before their ladies). The next moment all the dervishes stretched their arms sidewise, the right palm turned upward and the left downward. Like a whispered chant, the word *Huwa* – 'He' (that is, God) – came from their lips. With this softly breathed sound on his lips, each man began to turn slowly on his axis, swaying in rhythm with the music that seemed to come from a great distance. They threw back their heads, closed their eyes, and a smooth rigidity spread over their faces. Faster and faster became the circling movement; the voluminous tunics rose and formed wide circles around the spinning figures, making them resemble white, swirling eddies in a sea; deep was the absorption in their faces ... The circling grew into a whirling rotation, an intoxication and ecstasy rose visibly in all the men. In countless repetitions their half-open lips murmured the word, *Huwa ... Huwa ... Huu-wa ...* ; their bodies whirled and whirled, round and round, and the music seemed to draw them into its muffled, swirling, monotonous chords, monotonously ascending – and you felt as if you yourself were being irresistibly drawn into an ascending whirlpool, a steep, spiral, dizzying stairway, higher, higher, always higher, always the same steps, but always higher, in ever-rising spirals, toward some unfathomable, ungraspable end ...

... until the large, friendly hand which Mama Vitelli placed on your forehead brought the whirling to a standstill, and broke the dizzy spell, and brought you back from Scutari to the coolness of a stone-flagged room in Cairo ...

Signora Vitelli had been right, after all. Her ministrations helped me to overcome my malaria bout, if not sooner, at least as soon as any professional doctor could have done. Within two days I was almost free of fever, and on the third day I could exchange my bed for a comfortable chair. Still, I was too exhausted to think of going about, and time hung heavily. Once or twice my teacher-student from Al-Azhar visited me and brought me some books.

My recent fever-borne remembrance of the whirling dervishes of Scutari somehow bothered me. It had unexpectedly acquired a puzzling significance that had not been apparent in the original experience. The esoteric rites of this religious order – one of the many I had encountered in various Muslim countries – did not seem to fit into the picture of Islam that was slowly forming in my mind. I requested my Azhari friend to bring me some orientalist works on the subject; and, through them, my instinctive suspicion that esoterism of this kind had intruded into the Muslim orbit from non-Islamic sources was confirmed. The speculations of the *sufis*, as the Muslim mystics were called, betrayed Gnostic, Indian and occasionally even Christian influences which had brought in ascetic concepts and practices entirely alien to the message of the Arabian Prophet. In his message, *reason* was stressed as the only real way to faith. While the validity of mystical experience was not necessarily precluded in this approach, Islam was primarily an intellectual and not an emotional proposition. Although, naturally enough, it produced a strong emotional attachment in its followers, Muhammad's teaching did not accord to emotion as such any independent role in religious *perceptions:* for emotions, however profound, are far more liable to be swayed by subjective desires and fears than reason, with all its fallibility, ever could be.

.   .   .   .

'IT WAS IN SUCH bits and pieces, Mansur, that Islam revealed itself to me: a glimpse here and a glimpse there, through a conversation, a book, or an observation – slowly, almost without my being aware of it . . .'

— 2 —

WHEN WE MAKE CAMP for the night, Zayd starts to bake our bread. He makes a dough of coarse wheat flour, water and salt and shapes it into a flat, round loaf about an inch thick. Then he clears a hollow in the sand, fills it with dry twigs and sets fire to them; and when the flame, after a sudden burst, has died down, he places the loaf on the glowing embers, covers it with hot ashes and lights a new mound of twigs on top of it. After a while he uncovers the bread, turns it over, covers it as before and lights another fire over it. After another half hour the ready loaf is dug out from the embers and slapped with a stick to remove the remaining sand and ashes. We eat it with clarified butter and dates. There is no bread more delicious than this.

Mansur's hunger, like Zayd's and mine, has been satisfied, but his curiosity has not. As we lie around the fire, he continues to ply me with questions about how I finally became a Muslim – and while I try to explain it to him, it strikes me, with something like astonishment, how difficult it is to put into words my long way to Islam.

'– for, O Mansur, Islam came over me like a robber who enters a house by night, steathily, without noise or much ado: only that, unlike a robber, it entered to remain for good. But it took me years to discover that I was to be a Muslim . . .'

Thinking back to those days of my second Middle East journey – when Islam began to occupy my mind in all earnest – it seems to me that even then I was conscious of pursuing a journey of discovery. Every day new impressions broke over me; every day new questions arose from within and new answers came from without. They awakened an echo of something that had been hidden somewhere in the background of my mind; and as I progressed in my knowledge of Islam I felt, time and time again, that a truth I had always known, without being aware of it, was gradually being uncovered and, as it were, confirmed.

In the early summer of 1924 I started out from Cairo on a long wandering which was to take the better part of two years. For almost two years I trekked through countries old in the wisdom of their traditions but eternally fresh in their effect on my mind. I travelled leisurely, with long halts. I revisited Transjordan and spent some days with Amir Abdullah, revelling in the warm virility of that beduin land which had not yet been forced to adapt its character to the stream of Western influences. As this time a French visa had been arranged for me by the *Frankfurter Zeitung*, I was able to see Syria again. Damascus came and went. The Levantine liveliness of Beirut embraced me for a short while soon to be forgotten in the out-of-the-way sleepiness of Syrian Tripoli with its air of silent happiness. Small, old-fashioned sailing ships were rocking on their moorings in the open port, their Latin masts creaking softly. On low stools before a coffeehouse on the quay sat the burghers of Tripoli, relishing their cup of coffee and their *nargiles* in the afternoon sun. Everywhere peace and contentment and apparently enough to eat; and even the beggars seemed to enjoy themselves in the warm sun, as if saying, 'Oh, how good it is to be a beggar in Tripoli!'

I came to Aleppo. Its streets and buildings reminded me of Jerusalem: old stone houses that appeared to have grown out of the soil, dark, arched passageways, silent squares and court-yards, carved windows. The inner life of Aleppo, however, was entirely different from that of Jerusalem. The dominant mood of Jerusalem had been the strange side-by-side of conflicting na-tional currents, like a painful, complicated cramp; next to a world of contemplation and deep religious emotion there had brooded, like a cloud of poison, an almost mystical hatred over people and things. But Aleppo – although a mixture of Arabian and Levantine, with a hint of nearby Turkey – was harmonious and serene. The houses with their stony façades and wooden bal-conies were alive even in their stillness. The quiet industriousness of the artisans in the ancient bazaar; the courtyards of the many old caravanserais with their arcades and loggias full of bales of goods; frugality together with gay covetousness, and both free from all envy; the absence of all hurry, a restfulness which em-braced the stranger and made him wish that his own life were rooted in restfulness: all this flowed together in a strong, win-ning melody.

From Aleppo I went by car to Dayr az-Zor, a little town in northernmost Syria, whence I intended to proceed to Baghdad on the old caravan route parallel to the Euphrates; and it was on that journey that I first met Zayd.

In distinction from the Damascus-Baghdad route, which had been frequented by cars for some years, the route along the Eu-phrates was then little known; in fact, only one car had travelled it before me some months back. My Armenian driver had him-self never gone beyond Dayr az-Zor, but he was confident that he could somehow find his way. Nevertheless, he felt the need of more tangible information; and so we went together to the bazaar in search of it.

The bazaar street ran the whole length of Dayr az-Zor, which was something of a cross between a Syrian provincial town and a beduin metropolis, with an accent on the latter. Two worlds met there in a strange familiarity. In one of the shops modern, badly printed picture postcards were being sold, while next to it

a few beduins were talking about the rainfalls in the desert and
about the recent feuds between the Syrian tribe of Bishr-Anaza
and the Shammar of Iraq; one of them mentioned the audacious
raid which the Najdi beduin chieftain, Faysal ad-Dawish, had
made a short time ago into southern Iraq; and frequently the
name of the Grand Man of Arabia, Ibn Saud, cropped up. Ancient muzzle-loaders with long barrels and silver-inlaid butts –
guns which nobody was buying any more because the modern
repeating rifles were far more effective – led a dreamy, dusty
existence between secondhand uniform tunics from three continents, Najdi camel-saddles, Goodyear tyres, storm lanterns
from Leipzig and brown beduin cloaks from Al-Jawf. The
Western goods, however, did not appear like intruders among
the old; their utility had given them a natural place of their own.
With their wide-awake sense of reality, the beduins seemed to
take easily to all these new things which but yesterday had been
beyond their ken, and to make them their own without betraying
their old selves. This inner stability, I mused, ought to give them
the strength to bear the onrush of the new era and, perhaps, not
to succumb to it – for now it was coming close to these people
who until recently had been so withdrawn and so hidden: but it
was no hostile knocking on their door; they received all that
newness with innocent curiosity and fingered it, so to speak,
from all sides, contemplating its possible usefulness. How little I
realized then what Western 'newness' could do to the simple, unlettered beduins . . .

As my Armenian driver was making enquiries from a group of
beduins, I felt a tug at my sleeve. I turned around. Before me
stood an austerely handsome Arab in his early thirties.

'With thy permission, O *effendi*,' he said in a slow, husky
voice, 'I hear thou art going by car to Baghdad and art not sure
of thy way. Let me go with thee; I might be of help.'

I liked the man at once and asked him who he was.

'I am Zayd ibn Ghanim,' he replied, 'I serve with the *agayl* in
Iraq.'

It was only then that I observed the khaki colour of his *kaftan*
and the seven-pointed star, emblem of the Iraqi Desert Constabulary, on his black *igal*. This kind of troops, called *agayl* among
Arabs, had already existed in Turkish times: a corps of voluntary levies, recruited almost exclusively from Central Arabia –

men to whom the desert steppe was home and the dromedary a friend. Their adventurous blood drove them from their austere homeland out into a world in which there was more money, more movement, more change between today and tomorrow.

Zayd told me that he had come to Dayr az-Zor with one of his officers on some business connected with the administration of the Syro-Iraqi frontier. While the officer had since returned to Iraq, Zayd had remained behind to attend to a private matter; and now he would prefer to go back with me than to take the more customary but circuitous route via Damascus. He frankly admitted that he had never yet travelled all the way along the Euphrates, and he knew as well as I did that because of its many loops and turns we would not always have the river to guide us – 'but,' he added, 'desert is desert, the sun and the stars are the same, and, *insha-Allah*, we shall find our way.' His grave self-confidence pleased me, and I gladly agreed to have him along.

Next morning we left Dayr az-Zor. The great Hammada Desert opened itself up to the wheels of our Model T Ford: an unending plain of gravel, sometimes smooth and level like asphalt and sometimes stretching in waves from horizon to horizon. At times the Euphrates appeared to our left, muddy, quiet, with low banks: a silent lake, you might think, until a fast-drifting piece of wood or a boat caught your eye and betrayed the powerful current. It was a broad, a royal river; it made no sound; it was not playful; it did not rush; it did not splash. It went, glided, a widespread band, unfettered, choosing its sovereign way in countless turns down the imperceptible incline of the desert, an equal within an equal, a proud within a proud: for the desert was as widespread and mighty and quiet as the river.

Our new companion, Zayd, sat next to the driver with his knees drawn up and one leg dangling over the car door; on his foot glowed a new boot of red morocco leather which he had bought the day before in the bazaar of Dayr az-Zor.

Sometimes we met camel-riders who appeared from nowhere in the midst of the desert, stood still for a moment and gazed after the car, and again set their animals in motion and disappeared. They were obviously herdsmen; the sun had burned their faces a deep bronze. Short halts in lonely, dilapidated caravanserais alternated with endless stretches of desert. The Euphrates had disappeared beyond the horizon. Sand hard-blown by the wind, wide patches of gravel, here and there a few tufts of grass or a thornbush. To our right a range of low hills, naked and fissured, crumbling under the hot sun, grew up suddenly and concealed the endlessness of the desert. 'What could there be, beyond that narrow range of hills?' one asked oneself in wonderment. And although one knew that the same level or hilly desert lay beyond, the same sand and the same hard pebbles offered their virgin rigidity to the sun, a breath of unexplained mystery was in the air: 'What *could* there be?' The atmosphere was without answer or echo, the vibrating quiet of the afternoon knew no sound but the drone of our engine and the swish of tyres over gravel. Did the rim of the world drop there into a primeval abyss? Because I did not know, the unknown was there; and because I would perhaps never come to know, it was the unknowable unknown.

In the afternoon our driver discovered that at the last caravanserai he had forgotten to take in water for his engine. The river was far away; there was no well for many miles around; all about us, up to the wavy horizon, brooded an empty, white-hot, chalky plain; a soft, hot wind played over it, coming from nowhere and going into nowhere, without beginning and without end, a muffled hum out of eternity itself.

The driver, casual like all Levantines (a quality which I used to appreciate in them – but not just then), said: 'Oh, well, even so we shall reach the next caravanserai.'

But it looked as if we might not reach it 'even so'. The sun was blazing, the water bubbled in the radiator as in a tea kettle. Again we met herdsmen. Water? No, none for fifteen camel hours.

'And what do *you* drink?' asked the Armenian in exasperation.

They laughed. 'We drink camels' milk.' They must have wondered in their hearts at these ridiculous people in the fast-moving devil's cart, asking about water – while every beduin child could have told them that there was no water in these parts.

Unpleasant prospect: to remain stuck here in the desert with engine failure, without water and food, and to wait until another car came our way – perhaps tomorrow or the day after tomorrow – or perhaps next month . . .

In time the driver lost his smiling insouciance. He stopped the car and lifted the radiator cap; a white, thick jet of steam hissed into the air. I had some water in my thermos and sacrificed it to the god of the engine. The Armenian added a little oil to it, and the brave Ford carried us for a while.

'I think we might find water there to our right,' said the optimist. 'Those hills look so green – there seems to be fresh grass there: and where grass grows at this time of year, when there are no rains, there must be water. And if there is water there, why shouldn't we drive up and fetch it?'

Logic has always something irresistible about it; and so it was even here, although the Armenian's logic seemed to walk on crutches. We left the path and rattled a few miles toward the hills: no water . . . The slopes were covered not with grass but with greenish stones.

There was a hissing sound in the motor, the pistons beat hoarsely, smoke was escaping in grey wisps from the slits of the hood. A few minutes more, and something would crack: a break in the crankshaft or a similar nicety. But this time we had strayed far from the caravan route; if anything happened now, we would sit hopelessly in this desolation. Almost our entire supply of oil had flowed into the radiator. The Armenian had become hysterical; he was 'looking for water', driving to the left, then to the right, making turns and twists like a performer in a circus arena; but the water refused to materialize, and the bottle of cognac which I yielded with a sigh did not do much good to the hot radiator, apart from enveloping us in a cloud of alcoholic vapour which made Zayd (who, of course, never drank) almost vomit.

This last experiment drove him from the stony lethargy in which he had been lost for so long. With an angry movement he pulled his *kufiyya* lower down over his eyes, leaned out over the hot rim of the car and started looking about the desert plain – looking with the precise, careful concentration so peculiar to people who live much in the open and are accustomed to rely on their senses. We waited anxiously, without much hope – for, as he had told us earlier, he had never before been in this part of the country. But he pointed with his hand toward north and said:

'There.'

The word was like a command; the driver, glad to have somebody to relieve him of responsibility, obeyed at once. With a painful panting of the engine we drove northward. But suddenly

Zayd raised himself a little, put his hand on the driver's arm, and bade him stop. For a while he sat with his head bent foreward, like a scenting retriever; around his compressed lips there quivered a small, hardly perceptible tension.

'No – drive there!' he exclaimed, and pointed to northeast. 'Fast!' And again the driver obeyed without a word. After a couple of minutes, 'Stop!' and Zayd jumped lightly out of the car, gathered his long cloak in both hands and ran straight ahead, stopped, turned around several times as if searching or intently listening – and for long moments I forgot the engine and our plight, so captivated was I by the sight of a man straining all his nerves to orientate himself in nature . . . And all of a sudden he started off with long leaps and disappeared in a hollow between two mounds. A moment later his head reappeared and his hands waved:

'Water!'

We ran to him – and there it was: in a hollow protected from the sun by overhanging rocks glittered a little pool of water, remnant of the last winter rains, yellow-brown, muddy, but nevertheless water, water! Some incomprehensible desert instinct had betrayed its presence to the man from Najd . . .

And while the Armenian and I scooped it into empty gasoline tins and carried it to the much-abused engine, Zayd strolled smilingly, a silent hero, up and down by the side of the car.

．　　．　　．　　　．　　　．　　　．　　　．　　　．

AT NOON OF THE THIRD day we reached the first Iraqi village – Ana on the Euphrates – and rode for hours between its palm orchards and mud walls. Many *agayl* were there, most of them, as Zayd told us, of his own tribe. In the shade of palm trees they strode among sleek horses on which sun and green-filtered light were reflected: kings full of grace and condescension. To some of them Zayd nodded in passing, and his long, black tresses shook on both sides of his face. In spite of his hard life in desert and burning heat, he was so sensitive that during our fast progress over village roads he wound his headcloth around his mouth in order to avoid swallowing dust – the dust which did not bother even us pampered townspeople. When we again rode over pebbles and there was no longer any dust, he swept his *kufiyya* back with a movement of almost girlish grace and began to sing: he suddenly opened his mouth and sang, with the suddenness of a mountain wall precipitously jutting out of a plain. It was a Najdi *qasida*, a kind of ode – a swaying of long-drawn-out tunes in an unchanging rhythm, flowing, like the desert wind, from nowhere into nowhere.

In the next village he requested the driver to stop, jumped out of the car, thanked me for the lift, slung his rifle on his back, and disappeared between the palms; and in the car there remained a scent that had no name – the scent of a humanity entirely rounded in itself, the vibrating remembrance of a long-forgotten, never-forgotten innocence of the spirit.

On that day at Ana I did not think I would ever see Zayd again; but it happened otherwise . . .

.   .   .   .

THE FOLLOWING DAY I arrived at Hit, a little town on the Euphrates, at the point where the old caravan road from Damascus to Baghdad emerges from the desert. Crowning the top of a hill with its walls and bastions, the town resembled an ancient, half-forgotten fortress. No life was visible in or around it. The outer houses seemed to have grown into the walls; there were no windows in them, only a few slits, like loopholes. A minaret rose from the interior of the town.

I stopped for the night in a caravanserai near the river bank. While supper was being prepared for the 'driver and myself, I went to wash my hands and face at the well in the courtyard. As I was crouching on the ground, someone took the long-spouted water can that I had put down, and gently poured water over my hands. I looked up – and saw before me a heavy-boned, dark-visaged man with a fur cap on his head; unasked, he was assisting me in my washing. He was obviously not an Arab. When I asked him who he was, he answered in broken Arabic: 'I am a Tatar, from Azarbaijan.' He had warm, doglike eyes and his one-time military tunic was almost in shreds.

I started conversing with him, partly in Arabic and partly in the odds and bits of Persian which I had managed to pick up from an Iranian student in Cairo. It transpired that the Tatar's name was Ibrahim. Most of his life – he was now nearly forty – had been spent on Iranian roads; for years he had driven freight wagons from Tabriz to Tehran, from Meshhed to Birjand, from

Tehran to Isfahan and Shiraz, and at one time had called a team
of horses his own; he had served as a trooper in the mounted
Iranian gendarmerie, as a personal bodyguard to a Turkoman
chieftain, and as a stable boy in the caravanserais of Isfahan;
and now, having come to Iraq as a mule driver in a caravan of
Iranian pilgrims bound for Karbala, he had lost his job after a
quarrel with the leader of the caravan and was stranded in a
foreign country.

Later that night I lay down to sleep on a wooden bench in the
palm-studded courtyard of the caravanserai. Sultry heat and
clouds of mosquitoes, heavy and thick from sucking human
blood. A few lanterns threw their sad, dim light into the darkness. Some horses, belonging perhaps to the landlord, were
tethered to one of the walls. Ibrahim, the Tatar, was brushing
one of them; from the way he handled it one could see that he
not only knew horses but loved them; his fingers stroked the
shaggy mane as a lover might stroke his mistress.

An idea came suddenly to my mind. I was on my way to Iran,
and long months of travel on horseback lay ahead of me. Why
not take this man along? He seemed to be a good and quiet man;
and I would surely need somebody like him, who knew almost
every road in Iran and was at home in every caravanserai.

When I suggested next morning that I might engage him as my
servant, he almost wept with gratitude and said to me in Persian:

'*Hazrat*, you will never regret it . . .'

  .   .   .   .

IT WAS NOON OF THE fifth day of the car journey from
Aleppo when I caught my first view of the widespread oasis of
Baghdad. From between the crowns of myriads of palms shone a
gilded mosque cupola and a tall minaret. On both sides of the
road lay a vast, ancient graveyard with crumbling tombstones,
grey and barren and forsaken. Fine, grey dust hovered motionless over it; and in the hard light of the noon this dusty greyness
was like a silver-embroidered gauze veil – a misty partition between the dead world of the past and the living present. So it
should always be, I thought to myself, when one approaches a
city whose past has been so entirely different from its present
that the mind cannot encompass the difference . . .

And then we dived into the midst of the palms – mile after mile of enormous tree trunks and curving fronds – until suddenly the palm groves stopped short at the steep bank of the Tigris. This river was unlike the Euphrates: muddy-green, heavy and gurgling – like an exotic stranger after the silent, royal flow of that other river. And when we crossed it over a swaying boat-bridge, the fiery heat of the Persian Gulf closed over us.

Of its former magnificence and splendour nothing remained in Baghdad. The Mongol invasions of the Middle Ages had destroyed the city so thoroughly that nothing was left to remind one of the old capital of Harun ar-Rashid. What remained was a dreary city of haphazardly built brick dwellings – a temporary arrangement, it would almost seem, in anticipation of a possible change. Indeed, such a change was already under way in the form of a new political reality. The city had begun to stir, new buildings were coming up; out of a sleepy Turkish provincial headquarters an Arabian metropolis was slowly emerging.

The immense heat impressed its sign on every appearance and made all movement sluggish. The people walked slowly through the streets. They seemed to be of heavy blood, without gaiety and without grace. Their faces looked sombre and unfriendly from under black-and-white-checked headcloths; and whenever you saw a handsome Arab face with an expression of proud, self-sufficient dignity, there was almost invariably a red or red-and-white *kufiyya* over it – which meant that the man was not from here but from the north, or from the Syrian Desert, or from Central Arabia.

But a great strength was apparent in these men: the strength of hatred – hatred of the foreign power that denied them their freedom. The people of Baghdad had always been obsessed by longing for freedom as by a demon. Perhaps it was this demon which so sombrely overshadowed their faces. Perhaps these faces wore quite a different look when they met with their own kin in the narrow side lanes and walled courtyards of the town. For, if you looked more closely at them, they were not entirely without charm. They could occasionally laugh as other Arabs did. They would sometimes, like other Arabs, trail the trains of their cloaks with aristocratic nonchalance in the dust behind them, as if they were walking over the tessellated floors of marble palaces. They let their women stroll over the streets in colourful brocade wraps: precious, veiled women in black-and-red, blue-silver and bordeaux-red – groups of brocaded figures gilding slowly by on noiseless feet . . .

.　　.　　.　　.　　.　　.　　.　　.

A FEW WEEKS AFTER my arrival in Baghdad, as I was strolling through the Great Bazaar, a shout reverberated from one of the dusky, barrel-roofed passageways. From around a corner a man raced by; then another, and a third; and the people in the bazaar started to run as if gripped by a terror of which they, but not I, knew the reason. Beat of horses' hooves: a rider with a terrified face galloped into the crowd, which broke before him. More running people, all coming from one direction and carrying the shoppers in the bazaar along with them. In jolts and jerks, the whole throng began to press forward. Shopkeepers placed with frantic hurry wooden planks before their shops. Nobody spoke. No one called out to another. Only off and on you could hear the cries of falling people; a child wailed piercingly . . .

What has happened? No answer. Pale faces everywhere. A heavy wagon, still half loaded with bales, rushed driverless with galloping horses through the narrow lane. Somewhere in the distance a mound of earthenware vessels crashed down, and I could distinctly hear the sherds rolling on the ground. Apart from these isolated sounds and the tramping and panting of the people, there was a deep, tense silence, such as sometimes occurs at the beginning of an earthquake. Only the clattering steps of running feet; sometimes the scream of a woman or child broke out of the pressing, flowing mass. Again some riders. Panic, flight, and silence. A mad confusion at the crossings of the covered streets.

Caught in the throng at one of these crossings, I could not move forward or backward, and indeed did not know where to go. At that moment I felt someone grasp my arm: and there was Zayd, pulling me toward him and behind a barrier of barrels between two shops.

'Don't budge,' he whispered.

Something whizzed by – a rifle bullet? Impossible . . .

From far away, somewhere deep in the bazaar, came the muffled roar of many voices. Again something whizzed and whined, and this time there was no possibility of mistaking it: it *was* a bullet . . . In the distance a faint, rattling sound, as if somebody were scattering dry peas over a hard floor. It slowly approached and grew in volume, that regular, repeated rattling: and then I recognized it: machine guns . . .

Once again, as so many times before, Baghdad had risen in revolt. On the preceding day, the twenty-ninth of May, 1924, the Iraqi parliament had ratified, much against the popular will, a Treaty of Friendship with Great Britain; and now a nation in despair was trying to defend itself against the friendship of a great European power . . .

As I subsequently learned, all entrances to the bazaar had been sealed off by British troops to suppress a demonstration, and many people were killed that day by indiscriminate cross-firing into the bazaar. Had it not been for Zayd, I would probably have run straight into the machine-gun fire.

That was the real beginning of our friendship. Zayd's world-wise, reticent manliness appealed strongly to me; and he, on his part, had quite obviously taken a liking to the young European who had so little prejudice in him against the Arabs and their manner of living. He told me the simple story of his life: how he, as his father before him, had grown up in the service of the rulers of Haïl, the Shammar dynasty of Ibn Rashid; and how, when Haïl was conquered by Ibn Saud in 1921 and the last *amir* of the House of Ibn Rashid became Ibn Saud's prisoner, many men of the Shammar tribe, and Zayd among them, left their homelands, preferring an uncertain future to submission to a new ruler. And there he was, wearing the seven-pointed star of Iraq on his *igal* and pining for the land of his youth.

During the weeks of my sojourn in Iraq we saw a lot of each other, and remained in touch through the years that followed. I wrote to him occasionally, and once or twice a year sent him a small present purchased in one of the Iranian or Afghan bazaars; and every time he would answer in his clumsy, almost illegible scrawl, recalling the days we had spent together riding along the banks of the Euphrates or visiting the winged lions in the ruins of Babylon. Finally, when I came to Arabia in 1927, I asked him to join me; which he did in the following year. And ever since he has been my companion, more a comrade than a servant.

IN THE EARLY TWENTIES automobiles were still compar-
atively rare in Iran, and only a few cars plied for hire between
the main centres. If one wanted to leave the three or four trunk
roads, one had to depend on horse-driven vehicles; and even
these could not go everywhere, for there were many parts of Iran
where no roads existed at all. For someone like me, avid to meet
the people of the land on their own terms, travel on horseback
was clearly indicated. And so, during my last week in Baghdad,
assisted by Ibrahim, I attended every morning the horse market
outside the city. After days of negotiations, I purchased a horse
for myself and a mule for Ibrahim. My mount was a beautiful
chestnut stallion of South-Iranian breed, while the mule – a lively, obstinate animal with muscles like steel cables under a grey
velvet skin – had obviously come from Turkey; it would easily
carry, apart from its rider, the large saddlebags in which I was to
keep all my personal necessities.

Riding my horse and leading the mule by the halter, Ibrahim
set out one morning toward Khaniqin, the last Iraqi town on the
Iranian frontier and terminus of a branch line of the Baghdad
Railway; and I followed two days later by train, to meet him
there.

We left Khaniqin and the Arabian world behind us. Before us
stood yellow hills, like sentinels against the higher mountains:
the mountains of the Iranian plateau, a new, waiting world. The
frontier post was a lonely little building topped by a faded, tattered flag in green, white and red with the symbol of the lion with
sword and rising sun. A few customs officers in sloppy uniforms
and white slippers on their feet, black of hair and white of skin,
examined my scanty luggage with something like friendly irony.
Then one of them addressed me:

'Everything is in order, *janab-i-ali*. Your graciousness is above
our deserts. Would you grant us the favour of drinking a glass of
tea with us?'

And while I was still wondering at the bizarre, old-fashioned
courtesy of these phrases, it occurred to me how different, in
spite of its many Arabic words, the Persian language was from
the Arabic. A melodious, cultivated sweetness lay in it, and the
soft, open intonation of its vowels sounded strangely 'Western'
after the hot consonant language of the Arabs.

We were not the only travellers; several heavy canvas wagons,

Mansur

each drawn by four horses, were standing before the customs house, and a mule caravan was encamped nearby. The men were cooking their food over open campfires. They seemed to have given up all thought of going ahead, despite the early hour of the afternoon, and we, I do not remember why, decided to do the same. We spent the night in the open, sleeping on the ground on our blankets.

In the early dawn all the wagons and caravans began to move toward the naked mountains; and we rode with them. As the road mounted steadily, we soon outpaced the slow-moving wagons and rode on alone, deeper and deeper into the mountain land of the Kurds, the land of the tall, blond herdsmen.

I saw the first of them when, at a turn of the road, he stepped out of a rustling hut made of branches and offered us, wordlessly, a wooden bowl brimming with buttermilk. He was a boy of perhaps seventeen years, barefoot, ragged, unwashed, with the remnants of a felt cap on his tousled head. As I drank the thin, lightly salted and wonderfully cool milk, I saw over the rim of the bowl the blue eyes that were fixedly gazing at me. There was something in them of the brittle, damp-sweet fogginess which lies over new-born animals – a primeval sleepiness, not yet quite broken . . .

In the afternoon we reached a Kurdish tent village that lay softly tucked between hilly slopes. The tents resembled those of beduin half-nomads in Syria or Iraq: coarse black cloth of goat hair stretched over several poles, with walls of straw matting. A stream was flowing nearby, its banks shaded by groups of white poplars; on a rock over the water a family of storks excitedly clattered their beaks and beat their wings. A man in an indigo-blue jacket was striding with long, light steps toward the tents; out of his earth-bound but nevertheless very loose movements spoke old nomad blood. A woman wearing an amaranth-red, trailing dress, with a tall earthenware jar on her shoulder, slowly approached the stream; her thighs were clearly outlined against the soft cloth of her dress: they were long and tensed like violin strings. She knelt down by the water's edge and bent over to scoop water into her jar; her turbanlike headdress came loose and touched, like a red stream of blood, the glittering surface of the water – but only for an instant, to be taken up and again wound around the head with a single, gliding gesture that still belonged, as it were, to her kneeling-down and was part of the same movement.

Somewhat later I sat on the bank, in the company of an old man and four young women. All four had the perfect charm and naturalness born of life in freedom: beauty that was aware of itself and yet was chaste; pride which knew no hiding and yet was hardly distinguishable from shyness and humility. The prettiest among them bore the chirping bird-name *Tu-Tu* (with the vowel pronounced as in French). Her entire forehead was covered, down to the delicate brow, by a carmine-red scarf; the eyelids were tinted with antimony; from under the scarf protruded auburn locks with little silver chains braided into them; at every movement of the head they tinkled against the tender, concave cheekline.

We all enjoyed the conversation, although my Persian was still clumsy. (The Kurds have a language of their own, but most of them also understand Persian, which is related to it.) They were shrewd, these little women who had never gone beyond the environment of their tribe and, of course, could neither read nor write; they easily understood my stumbling expressions and often found the word for which I was groping and put it, with a matter-of-fact sureness, into my mouth. I asked them about their doings, and they answered me, enumerating the many little and yet so great things which fill the day of a nomad woman: grinding grain between two flat stones; baking bread in glowing ashes; milking sheep; shaking curds in leather bags until they turn to butter; spinning with hand spindles yarn out of sheep's wool; knotting carpets and weaving *kilims* in patterns almost as old as their race; bearing children; and giving their men restfulness and love . . .

Unchanging life: today, yesterday and tomorrow. For these shepherds no time exists, except the sequence of days, nights and seasons. The night has been made dark for sleep; the day is light for the necessities of life; winter reveals itself in the growing cold and the scarcity of pastures in the mountains: and so they wander with their flocks and tents down into the warm plains, into Mesopotamia and to the Tigris; later, when the summer grows up with its sultriness and hot winds, back into the mountains, either here or to another place within the traditional grounds of the tribe.

'Don't you ever desire to live in houses of stone?' I asked the old man, who had hardly spoken a word and had smilingly listened to our talk. 'Don't you ever desire to have fields of your own?'

The old man shook his head slowly: 'No ... if water stands motionless in pools, it becomes stale, muddy and foul; only when it moves and flows does it remain clear ...'

*   *   *   *   *   *   *   *

IN TIME, KURDISTAN receded into the past. For nearly eighteen months I wandered through the length and breadth of that strangest of all lands, Iran. I came to know a nation that combined in itself the wisdom of thirty centuries of culture and the volatile unpredictability of children; a nation that could look with a lazy irony at itself and all that happened around it – and a moment later could tremble in wild, volcanic passions. I enjoyed the cultured ease of the cities and the sharp, exhilarating steppe winds; I slept in the castles of provincial governors with a score of servants at my disposal, and in half-ruined caravanserais where at night you had to take care to kill the scorpions before you were stung by them. I partook of whole, roasted sheep as guest of Bakhtiari and Kashgai tribesmen, and of turkeys stuffed with apricots in the dining rooms of rich merchants; I watched the abandonment and blood-intoxication of the festival of Muharram, and listened to the tender verses of Hafiz sung to the accompaniment of a lute by the heirs of Iran's ancient glories. I strolled under the poplars of Isfahan and admired the stalactite portals, precious faïence façades and gilded domes of its great mosques. Persian became almost as familiar to me as Arabic. I held converse with educated men in cities, soldiers and nomads, traders in the bazaars, cabinet ministers and religious leaders, wandering dervishes and wise opium smokers in wayside taverns. I stayed in towns and villages and trekked through deserts and perilous salt swamps, and lost myself entirely in the timeless air of that broken-down wonderland. I came to know the Iranian people and their life and their thoughts almost as if I had been born among them: but this land and this life, complex and fascinating like an old jewel that sparkles dimly through multiple facets, never came as close to my heart as the glass-clear world of the Arabs.

For over six months I rode on through the wild mountains and steppes of Afghanistan: six months in a world where the arms which every man carried were not meant for ornament, and where every word and every step had to be watched lest a bullet should come singing through the air. Sometimes Ibrahim and I and our occasional companions had to defend our lives against bandits, of whom Afghanistan was full in those days; but if it happened to be Friday, bandits held out no threat, for they considered it shameful to rob and kill on the day set aside for the worship of the Lord. Once, near Kandahar, I narrowly missed being shot because I had inadvertently looked upon the uncovered face of a pretty village woman working in the field; while among the Mongol villagers in the high gorges of the Hindu-Kush – descendants of the warrior hosts of Jinghiz Khan – it was not regarded as unseemly to let me sleep on the floor of the one-room hut side by side with the host's young wife and sisters. For weeks I was guest of Amanullah Khan, King of Afghanistan, in his capital, Kabul; for long nights I discussed with his learned men the teachings of the Koran; and on other nights I discussed with Pathan *khans* in their black tents how best to circumvent areas engaged in intertribal warfare.

And with every day of those two years in Iran and Afghanistan the certainty grew in me that I was approaching some final answer.

.   .   .   .

'FOR IT SO HAPPENED, Mansur, that the understanding of how Muslims lived brought me daily closer to a better understanding of Islam. Islam was always uppermost in my mind . . .'

'It is time for the *isha* prayer,' says Zayd, glancing at the night sky.

We line up for the last prayer of the day, all three of us facing toward Mecca: Zayd and Mansur stand side by side and I in front of them, leading the congregational prayer (for the Prophet has described every assembly of two or more as a congregation). I raise my hands and begin, *Allahu akbar* – 'God alone is Great' – and then recite, as Muslims always do, the opening *sura* of the Koran:

In the name of God, the Most Gracious, the Dispenser of Grace.
All praise is due to God alone, Sustainer of the Universe,

The Most Gracious, the Dispenser of Grace,
Lord of the Day of Judgment.
Thee alone do we worship,
And Thee alone do we beseech for help.
Lead us the right way,
The way of those upon whom is Thy favour,
Not of those who earn Thy wrath, nor of those who go astray.

And I follow with the hundred and twelfth *sura:*

In the name of God, the Most Gracious, the Dispenser of Grace,
Say: God is One,
The Self-Sufficient on Whom everything depends.
He begets not, nor is He begotten,
And there is naught that could be likened unto Him.

There are few things, if any, which bring men so close to one another as praying together. This, I believe, is true of every religion, but particularly so of Islam, which rests on the belief that no intermediary is necessary, or indeed possible, between man and God. The absence of all priesthood, clergy, and even of an organized 'church' makes every Muslim feel that he is truly sharing in, and not merely attending, a common act of worship when he prays in congregation. Since there are no sacraments in Islam, every adult and sane Muslim may perform any religious function whatsoever, whether it be leading a congregation in prayer, performing a marriage ceremony or conducting a burial service. None need be 'ordained' for the service of God: the religious teachers and leaders of the Muslim community are simple men who enjoy a reputation (sometimes deserved and sometimes not) for erudition in theology and religious law.

— 3 —

I AWAKE AT DAWN: but my eyelids are heavy with sleep. Over my face the wind glides with a soft, humming sound out of the fading night into the rising day.

I get up to wash the sleep from my face. The cold water is like a touch from faraway landscapes – mountains covered with dark trees, and streams that move and flow and always remain clear . . . I sit on my haunches and lean my head back so that my face

might long remain wet; the wind strokes its wetness, strokes it
with the tender memory of all cool days, of long-past wintry
days . . . of mountains and rushing waters . . . of riding through
snow and glistening whiteness . . . the whiteness of that day
many years ago when I rode over snow-covered Iranian mountains without path, pushing slowly forward, every step of the
horse a sinking-down into snow and the next a toilsome clam-
bering out of snow . . .

At noon of that day, I remember, we rested in a village inhabited by strange folk who resembled gypsies. Ten or twelve
holes in the ground, roofed over with low domes of brushwood
and earth, gave the lonely settlement – it was in southeastern
Iran, in the province of Kirman – the appearance of a city of
moles. Like underworld beings from a fairy tale, people crawled
out of the dark openings to wonder at the rare strangers. On top
of one of the earthen domes sat a young woman combing her
long, black, tousled hair; her olive-brown face was turned with
closed eyes toward the pale midday sun, and she sang with a low
voice a song in some outlandish tongue. Metal arm-rings jangled
around her wrists; which were narrow and strong like the fet-
locks of wild animals in a primeval forest.

To warm my numbed limbs, I drank tea and arrack – lots of
it – with the gendarme who accompanied Ibrahim and me. As I
remounted my horse, entirely drunk, and set out at a gallop, the
whole world lay suddenly wide and transparent before my eyes
as never before; I saw its inner pattern and felt the beat of its
pulse in the white loneliness and beheld all that had been hidden
from me but a moment ago; and I knew that all the answers are
but waiting for us while we, poor fools, ask questions and wait
for the secrets of God to open themselves up to us: when they,
all the while, are waiting for us to open ourselves up to them . . .

A tableland opened before us, and I spurred my horse and
flew like a ghost through crystalline light, and the snow whirled
up by the hooves of my horse flew around me like a mantle of
sparks, and the hooves of my horse thundered over the ice of
frozen streams . . .

I think it must have been then that I experienced, not yet fully
understanding it myself, the opening of grace – that grace of
which Father Felix had spoken to me long, long ago, when I was
starting out on the journey that was destined to change my whole

life: the revelation of grace which tells you that *you* are the expected one ... More than a year was to elapse between that mad ride over ice and snow and my conversion to Islam; but even then I rode, without knowing it, straight as an arrow toward Mecca.

. . . .

AND NOW MY FACE is dry, and that Iranian winter day of more than seven years ago falls back into the past. It falls back – but not to disappear: for that past is part of this present.

A cool breeze, breath of the morning that is to come, makes the thornbushes shiver. The stars are beginning to pale. Zayd! Mansur! Get up, get up! Let us rekindle the fire and heat our coffee – and then we shall saddle the dromedaries and ride on, through another day, through the desert that waits for us with open arms.

VIII

JINNS

— 1 —

THE SUN IS ABOUT TO SET when a big, black snake suddenly slithers across our path: it is almost as thick as a child's arm and perhaps a yard long. It stops and rears its head in our direction. With almost a reflex movement, I slide down from the saddle, unsling my carbine, kneel and take aim – and at the same moment I hear Mansur's voice behind me:

'Don't shoot – don't . . . !' – but I have already pressed the trigger; the snake jerks, writhes and is dead.

Mansur's disapproving face appears over me. 'Thou shouldst not have killed it . . . anyhow, not at the time of sunset: for this is the time when the jinns come out from under ground and often assume the shape of a snake . . .'

I laugh and reply: 'O Mansur, thou dost not really believe those old wives' tales about jinns in the shape of snakes?'

'Of course I believe in jinns. Does not the Book of God mention them? As to the shapes in which they sometimes appear to us – I don't know . . . I have heard they can assume the strangest and most unexpected of forms . . .'

You may be right, Mansur, I think to myself, for, indeed, is it so farfetched to assume that, apart from the beings which our senses can perceive, there may be some that elude our perception? Is it not a kind of intellectual arrogance which makes modern man reject the possibility of life-forms other than those which can be observed and measured by him? The existence of jinns, whatever they may be, cannot be proved by scientific means. But neither can science disprove the possible existence of living beings whose biological laws may be so entirely different from our own that our outer senses can establish contact with them only under very exceptional circumstances. Is it not possible that such an occasional crossing of paths between these unknown worlds and ours gives rise to strange manifestations

218

which man's primitive fantasy has interpreted as ghosts, demons
and such other 'supernatural' apparitions?

As I remount my dromedary, playing with these questions
with the half-smiling disbelief of a man whose upbringing has
made him more thick-skinned than are people who have always
lived closer to nature, Zayd turns with a serious countenance
toward me:

'Mansur is right, O my uncle. Thou shouldst not have killed
the snake. Once, many years back – when I left Haïl after Ibn
Saud had taken the town – I shot a snake like that one on my
way to Iraq. It was also at the time when the sun was setting. A
short while afterward, when we stopped to say our sunset prayer,
I suddenly felt a leaden weight in my legs and a burning in my
head, and my head began to roar like the roar of falling waters,
and my limbs became like fire, and I could not stand upright and
fell to the ground like an empty sack, and everything became
dark around me. I do not know how long I remained in that darkness, but I remember that in the end I stood up again. An unknown man stood to my right and another to my left, and they
led me into a great, dusky hall that was full of men who walked
up and down in excitement and talked to each other. After a
while I became aware that these were two distinct parties, as
before a court of justice. An old man of very small size was sitting on a raised dais in the background; he seemed to be a judge
or chieftain, or something like that. And all at once I knew that I
was the accused.

'Someone said: "He has killed him just before sunset by a shot
from his rifle. He is guilty." One of the opposing party retorted:
"But he did not know whom he was killing; and he pronounced
the name of God when he pulled the trigger." But those of the
accusing party shouted: "He did not pronounce it!" – whereupon
the other party repeated, all together, in chorus: "He did, he did
praise the name of God!" – and so it continued for a while, back
and forth, accusation and defence, until in the end the defending
party seemed to gain their point and the judge in the background
decided: "He did not know whom he was killing, and he did
praise the name of God. Lead him back!"

'And the two men who had brought me to the hall of judgment took me under the arms again, led me back the same way
into that great darkness out of which I had come, and laid me on

the ground. I opened my eyes – and saw myself lying between a few sacks of grain which had been piled on both sides of me; and over them was stretched a piece of tent cloth to protect me from the rays of the sun. It seemed to be early forenoon, and my companions had evidently made camp. In the distance I could see our camels grazing on the slope of a hill. I wanted to raise my hand, but my limbs were extremely weary. When one of my companions bent his face over me, I said, "Coffee . . ." – for from nearby I heard the sound of the coffee mortar. My friend jumped up: "He speaks, he speaks! He has come to!" – and they brought me fresh, hot coffee. I asked them, "Was I unconscious the whole night?" And they answered, "The whole night? Full four days thou didst not budge! We always loaded thee like a sack onto one of the camels, and unloaded thee again at night; and we thought that we would have to bury thee here. But praise be to Him who gives and takes life, the Living who never dies . . ."

'So thou seest, O my uncle, one should not kill a snake at sunset.'

And although half of my mind continues to smile at Zayd's narrative, the other half seems to sense the weaving of unseen forces in the gathering dusk, an eerie commotion of sounds so fine that the ear can hardly grasp them, and a breath of hostility in the air: and I have a faint feeling of regret at having shot the snake at sunset . . .

— 2 —

IN THE AFTERNOON of our third day out of Haïl we stop to water our camels at the wells of Arja, in an almost circular valley enclosed between low hills. The two wells, large and full of sweet water, lie in the centre of the valley; each of them is the communal property of the tribe – the western one belongs to the Harb, the eastern to the Mutayr. The ground around them is as bald as the palm of one's hand, for every day around noon hundreds of camels and sheep are driven in from distant pastures to be watered here, and every little blade of grass which grows out of the soil is nibbled away before it can even take breath.

As we arrive, the valley is full of animals, and ever-new flocks and herds appear from between the sun-drenched hills. Around the wells there is a great crowding and commotion, for it is not an easy thing to satisfy the thirst of so many animals. The herdsmen draw up the water in leather buckets on long ropes, accompanying their work with a chant to keep the multiple movements even: for the buckets are very big and, when filled with water, so heavy that many hands are needed to draw them out of the depth. From the well nearest us – the one that belongs to the Mutayr tribe – I can hear the men chant to the camels:

> *Drink, and spare no water,*
> *The well is full of grace and has no bottom!*

Half of the men sing the first verse and the others the second, repeating both several times in quick tempo until the bucket appears over the rim of the well; then the women take over and pour the water into leathern troughs. Scores of camels press forward, bellowing and snorting, quivering with excitement, crowding around the troughs, not visibly pacified by the men's soothing calls, *Hu-oih . . . huu-oih!* One and another pushes its long, flexible neck forward, between or over its companions, so as to still its thirst as quickly as possible; there is a rocking and pushing, a swaying and thronging of light-brown and dark-brown, yellow-white and black-brown and honey-coloured bodies, and the sharp, acrid smell of animal sweat and urine fills the air. In the meantime, the bucket has been filled again, and the herdsmen draw it up to the quick accompaniment of another couplet:

> *Naught can still the camels' thirst*
> *But God's grace and the herdsman's toil!*

– and the spectacle of rushing water, of drinking and slurping and calling and chanting starts all over again.

An old man standing on the rim of the well raises his arm in our direction and calls out:

'May God give you life, O wayfarers! Partake of our bounty!' – whereupon several other men disentangle themselves from the crowd around the well and run toward us. One of them takes hold of my dromedary's halter and makes it kneel down, so that I may dismount in comfort. Quickly a way is made for our animals to the trough, and the women pour out water for them: for we are travellers and therefore have a prior claim.

'Is it not wonderful to behold,' muses Zayd, 'how well these

Harb and Mutayr are keeping their peace now, so soon after they have been warring against each other?' (For it is only three years since the Mutayr were in rebellion against the King, while the Harb were among his most faithful supporters.) 'Dost thou remember, O my uncle, the last time we were here? How we by-passed Arja in a wide circle at night, not daring to approach the wells – not knowing whether friend or foe was here . . . ?'

Zayd is referring to the great beduin rebellion of 1928-1929 – the culmination of a political drama which shook Ibn Saud's kingdom to its foundations and, for a time, involved myself in it.

   .   .   .   .

WHEN THE CURTAIN ROSE in 1927, peace was reigning in the vast realm of Saudi Arabia. King Ibn Saud's struggle for power was over. His rule in Najd was no longer contested by any rival dynsaty. His was Haïl and the Shammar country, and his, too, was the Hijaz after he had ousted the Sharifian dynasty in 1925. Outstanding among the King's warriors was that same re-doutable beduin chieftain, Faysal ad-Dawish, who had caused him so much worry in earlier years. Ad-Dawish had distin-guished himself in the King's service and proved his loyalty time and time again: in 1921 he conquered Haïl for the King; in 1924 he led a daring raid into Iraq, from where the Sharifian family, protected by the British, intrigued against Ibn Saud; in 1925 he took Medina and played a decisive role in the conquest of Jidda. And now, in the summer of 1927, he was resting on his laurels in his *Ikhwan* settlement of Artawiyya, not far from the frontier of Iraq.

For many years that frontier had been the scene of almost continuous beduin raids arising from tribal migrations in search of pastures and water; but in a series of agreements be-tween Ibn Saud and the British – who were responsible for Iraq as the Mandatory Power – it had been decided that no obstacles should be placed in the way of such necessary migrations, and that no fortifications of any kind should be erected on either side of the Najd-Iraq frontier. In the summer of 1927, however, the Iraqi government built and garrisoned a fort in the vicinity of the frontier wells of Bisayya, and officially announced its inten-tion to build other forts along the frontier. A ripple of uneasiness ran through the tribes of northern Najd. They saw themselves threatened in their very existence, cut off from the wells on which they were entirely dependent. Ibn Saud protested against this open breach of aggreements, only to receive – months later – an evasive answer from the British High Commissioner in Iraq.

Faysal ad-Dawish, always a man of action, told himself: 'It may not be convenient for the King to start a quarrel with the British – but I will dare it.' And in the last days of October, 1927, he set out at the head of his *Ikhwan*, attacked and destroyed the fort of Bisayya, giving no quarter to its Iraqi garrison. British aeroplanes appeared over the scene, reconnoitred the situation and withdrew – against their habit – without dropping a single bomb. It would have been easy for them to repel the raid (an action to which they were entitled by virtue of their treaties with Ibn Saud) and then to settle the problem of the forts by diplomatic negotiations. But was the British-Iraqi government really interested in a speedy, peaceful settlement of the dispute?

Deputations from the nothern Najdi tribes appeared before Ibn Saud and pleaded for a campaign against Iraq. Ibn Saud energetically refused all such demands, declared Ad-Dawish a transgressor, and ordered the *amir* of Haïl to keep close watch over the frontier regions. The financial allowances which the King was giving to most of the *Ikhwan* were temporarily cut off from the tribes under Ad-Dawish's control; and he himself was bidden to remain at Artawiyya and there await the King's judgment. The Iraqi government was officially informed of all these measures and notified that Ad-Dawish would be punished severely. At the same time, however, Ibn Saud demanded that in the future the frontier treaties be more strictly observed by Iraq.

This new conflict could thus have been easily ironed out. But when matters had reached this point, the British High Commissioner let Ibn Saud know that he was sending out an air squadron to chastise Ad-Dawish's *Ikhwan* (who had long since returned to their home territory) and to 'force them to obedience toward their King'. Since at the time there was no telegraph at Riyadh, Ibn Saud sent posthaste a courier to Bahrain, from where a telegram was dispatched to Baghdad, protesting against the proposed measure and invoking the treaties which forbade either party to pursue lawbreakers across the frontier. He stressed that he had no need of British 'assistance' in enforcing his authority over Ad-Dawish; and, finally, he warned that a British air action over Najdi territory would have dangerous repercussions among the *Ikhwan*, who were already sufficiently stirred up.

The warning remained unheeded. Toward the end of January, 1928 – three months after the Bisayya incident – a British squadron flew across the frontier and bombed Najdi territory, wreaking havoc among Mutayri beduin encampments and indiscriminately killing men, women, children and cattle. All the northern *Ikhwan* began to prepare for a campaign of vengeance against Iraq; and it was only thanks to Ibn Saud's great prestige among the tribes that the movement was stopped in time and confined to a few minor frontier skirmishes.

In the meantime, the destroyed fort of Bisayya was quietly rebuilt by the British and two new forts were erected on the Iraqi side of the border.

.   .   .   .

FAYSAL AD-DAWISH, summoned to Riyadh, refused to come and justify an action which, in his opinion, had been undertaken in the King's own interest. Personal resentment added to his bitterness. He, Faysal ad-Dawish, who had served the King so faithfully and so well, was only *amir* of Artawiyya – which, in spite of the large number of its inhabitants, was no more than an overgrown village. His leadership had been decisive in the conquest of Haïl – but the King's cousin, Ibn Mussaad, and not he, had been appointed *amir* of Haïl. During the Hijaz campaign it was he, Ad-Dawish, who besieged Medina for months and finally forced its surrender – but not he had been made its *amir*. His passionate, frustrated urge for power gave him no rest. He said to himself: 'Ibn Saud belongs to the tribe of Anaza and I to the tribe of Mutayr. We are equal to another in the nobility of our descent. Why should *I* admit to Ibn Saud's superiority?'

Such reasoning has always been the curse of Arabian history: none will admit that another is better than he.

One by one, other dissatisfied *Ikhwan* chieftains began to forget how much they owed to Ibn Saud. Among them was Sultan ibn Bujad, *shaykh* of the powerful Atayba tribe and *amir* of Ghatghat, one of the largest *Ikhwan* settlements in Najd: victor of the battle of Taraba in 1918 against the forces of Sharif Husayn; conqueror of Taïf and Mecca in 1924. Why had he to be content with being no more than *amir* of Ghatghat? Why had not he, but one of the King's sons, been made *amir* of Mecca? Why had he not at least been appointed *amir* of Taïf? He, like Faysal ad-Dawish, saw himself cheated of what he considered his due; and since he was Ad-Dawish's brother-in-law, it appeared only logical for the two to make common cause against Ibn Saud.

In the autumn of 1928, Ibn Saud called a congress of chieftains and *ulama* to Riyadh with a view to solving all these disputes. Almost all tribal leaders came except Ibn Bujad and Ad-Dawish. Adamant in their opposition, they declared Ibn Saud a heretic – for had he not made treaties with the infidels and introduced into the lands of the Arabs such instruments of the devil as motor-cars, telephones, wireless sets and aeroplanes? The *ulama* assembled at Riyadh unanimously declared that such technical innovations were not only permissible but most desirable from the religious point of view since they increased the knowledge and strength of the Muslims; and that, on the authority of the Prophet of Islam, treaties with non-Muslim powers were equally desirable if they brought peace and freedom to Muslims.

But the two rebellious chieftains continued their denunciations and found a ready echo among many of the simple *Ikhwan*, who did not possess sufficient knowledge to see anything but the influence of Satan in Ibn Saud's actions. His earlier failure to impart education to the *Ikhwan* and turn their religious fervour to positive ends began to bear its tragic fruit . . .

The steppes of Najd were now humming like a beehive. Mysterious emissaries rode on fast dromedaries from tribe to tribe. Clandestine meetings of chieftains took place at remote wells. And, finally, the agitation against the King burst out in open revolt, drawing in many other tribes besides the Mutayr and Atayba. The King was patient. He tried to be understanding. He sent messengers to the recalcitrant tribal leaders and tried to reason with them: but in vain. Central and northern Arabia became the scene of widespread guerilla warfare; the almost proverbial public security of the country vanished and complete chaos reigned in Najd; bands of rebel *Ikhwan* swept across it in all directions, attacking villages and caravans and tribes that had remained loyal to the King.

After innumerable local skirmishes between rebel and loyal

tribes, a decisive battle was fought on the plain of Sibila, in central Najd, in the spring of 1929. On one side was the King with a large force; on the other, the Mutayr and the Atayba, supported by factions from other tribes. The King was victorious. Ibn Bujad surrendered unconditionally and was brought in chains to Riyadh. Ad-Dawish was severely wounded and said to be dying. Ibn Saud, mildest of all Arabian kings, sent his personal physician to attend him – and that doctor, a young Syrian, diagnosed a serious injury to the liver, giving Ad-Dawish a week to live; whereupon the King decided: 'We shall let him die in peace; he has received his punishment from God.' He ordered that the wounded enemy be brought back to his family at Artawiyya.

But Ad-Dawish was far from dying. His injury was not nearly as serious as the young doctor had assumed; and within a few weeks he was sufficiently recovered to slip away from Artawiyya, more than ever bent on revenge.

•   •   •   •   •   •   •

AD-DAWISH'S ESCAPE from Artawiyya gave a new impetus to the rebellion. It was rumoured that he himself was somewhere in the vicinity of the Kuwayt frontier recruiting new tribal allies to his own, still considerable, force of Mutayr. Among the first to join him were the Ajman, a small but valiant tribe living in the province of Al-Hasa near the Persian Gulf; their *shaykh*, Ibn Hadhlayn, was Faysal ad-Dawish's maternal uncle. Apart from this, there was no love lost between Ibn Saud and the Ajman. Years ago they had slain the King's younger brother Saad and, fearing his revenge, had migrated to Kuwayt. Subsequently Ibn Saud had forgiven them and allowed them to return to their ancestral territory, but the old resentment continued to rankle. It flared up into open enmity when, during negotiations for a settlement, the Ajman chieftain and several of his followers were treacherously murdered in the camp of Ibn Saud's relative, the eldest son of the *amir* of Al-Hasa.

The alliance of the Ajman with the Mutayr kindled a new spark among the Atayba tribes in central Najd. After the capture of their *amir*, Ibn Bujad, they had reassembled under a new chieftain; and now they rose once again against the King, forcing him to divert most of his strength from northern to central Najd. The fight was hard, but slowly Ibn Saud got the upper hand. Group after group, he overwhelmed the Atayba until, in the end, they offered to surrender. In a village half way between Riyadh and Mecca their *shaykhs* pledged fealty to the King – and the King again forgave them, hoping that at last he would have a free hand against Ad-Dawish and the rest of the rebels in the north. But hardly had he returned to Riyadh when the Atayba broke their pledge for the second time and renewed their warfare. Now it was a fight to the finish. For a third time the Atayba were defeated and almost decimated – and with the complete destruction of the *Ikhwan* settlement of Ghatghat, a town larger than Riyadh, the King's authority was re-established in central Najd.

Meanwhile, the struggle in the north continued. Faysal ad-Dawish and his allies were now solidly entrenched in the vicinity of the border. Ibn Musaad, the *amir* of Haïl, attacked them time and time again in behalf of the King. Twice it was reported that Ad-Dawish had been killed; and both times the tidings proved false. He lived on, stubbornly and uncompromisingly. His eldest son and seven hundred of his warriors fell in battle; but he fought on. The question cropped up: From where does Ad-Dawish receive the money which even in Arabia is necessary for waging war? From where his arms and ammunition?

Vague reports became current that the rebel, once so bitterly critical of Ibn Saud's treaty relations with the 'infidels', was now himself treating with the British. Rumour had it that he was a frequent visitor in Kuwayt: could he be doing this, people asked themselves, without the knowledge of the British authorities? Was it not possible, rather, that turmoil in the lands of Ibn Saud suited their own purpose only too well?

.　　.　　.　　.　　.　　.　　.　　.

ONE EVENING IN RIYADH, in the summer of 1929, I had gone to bed early and, before falling asleep, was diverting myself with an old book on the dynasties of Oman, when Zayd abruptly came into my room:

'There is a man here from the *Shuyukh*. He wants to see thee at once.'

I hurriedly dressed and went to the castle. Ibn Saud was awaiting me in his private apartments, sitting cross-legged on a divan with heaps of Arabic newspapers around him and one from

Cairo in his hands. He answered my greeting briefly and, without interrupting his reading, motioned me to his side on the divan. After a while he looked up, glanced at the slave who was standing by the door and indicated with a movement of his hand that he wished to be left alone with me. As soon as the slave had closed the door behind him, the King laid down the newspaper and looked at me for a while from behind his glittering glasses, as if he had not seen me for a long time (although I had spent some hours with him that very morning).

'Busy with writing?'

'No, O Long-of-Age, I have not written anything for weeks.'

'Those were interesting articles thou hast written about our frontier problems with Iraq.'

He was evidently referring to a series of dispatches I had written for my Continental newspapers about two months earlier; some of them had also appeared in a newspaper in Cairo where, I flatter myself, they helped to clarify a very involved situation. Knowing the King, I was certain that he was not speaking at random but had something definite in mind; and so I remained silent, waiting for him to continue. He did continue:

'Perhaps thou wouldst like to write something more about what is happening in Najd – about this rebellion and what it portends.' There was a trace of passion in his voice as he went on: 'The Sharifian family hates me. Those sons of Husayn who now rule in Iraq and Transjordan will always hate me, for they cannot forget that I have taken the Hijaz from them. They would like my realm to break up, for then they could return to the Hijaz . . . and their friends, who pretend to be my friends as well, might not dislike it either . . . They did not build those forts for nothing: they *wanted* to cause me trouble and to push me away from their frontiers . . .'

From behind Ibn Saud's words I could hear jumbled, ghostly sounds – the rolling and rushing of railroad trains which, though still imaginary, might easily become real tomorrow: the spectre of a British railroad running from Haifa to Basra. Rumours of such a plan had been rampant for years. It was well known that the British were concerned about securing the 'land route to India': and this, indeed, was the meaning of their mandates over Palestine, Transjordan and Iraq. A railroad from the Mediterranean to the Persian Gulf would not only form a new, valuable

link in Britain's imperial communications but would also afford
greater protection to the oil pipeline that was to be laid from
Iraq across the Syrian Desert to Haifa. On the other hand, a
direct rail connection between Haifa and Basra would have to
cut across Ibn Saud's northeastern provinces – and the King
would never even entertain such a suggestion. Was it not possible that the building of forts along the Iraq-Najd frontier, in
flagrant contravention of all the existing agreements, represented
the first stage of a carefully devised scheme to bring about
enough disturbance within this critical area to 'justify' the establishment of a small, semi-independent buffer state more amen-
able to the British? Faysal ad-Dawish could serve this purpose
as well as, or perhaps even better than, a member of the Sharifian family, for he was a Najdi himself and had a strong following among the *Ikhwan*. That his alleged religious fanaticism was
only a mask was obvious to anyone acquainted with his past;
what he really wanted was power alone. There was no doubt
that, left to himself, he could not have held out for so long
against Ibn Saud. But – had he been left to himself?

After a long pause, the King continued: 'I have been thinking,
as everyone has, about the supplies of arms and ammunition
that Ad-Dawish seems to have at his disposal. He has plenty of
them – and plenty of money, too, it has been reported to me. I
wonder whether thou wouldst not like to write about these
things – I mean, those mysterious sources of Ad-Dawish's supplies. I have my own suspicions about them; perhaps even more
than suspicions – but I would like thee to find out for thyself all
thou canst, for I may be wrong.'

So that was it. Although the King spoke almost casually, in a
conversational tone, it was obvious that he had weighed every
word before he uttered it. I looked hard at him. His face, so
grave a moment before, broke into a broad smile. He placed his
hand on my knee and shook it:

'I want thee, O my son, to find out for thyself – I repeat: for
thyself – from where Ad-Dawish is getting his rifles, his ammunition and the money he is throwing about so lavishly. There is
hardly any doubt in my own mind, but I wish that someone like
thee, who is not directly involved, would tell the world of the
crooked truth behind Ad-Dawish's rebellion ... I think thou
wilt be able to find out the truth.'

Ibn Saud knew what he was doing. He has always known that I love him. Although I often disagree with his policies, and never make a secret of my disagreement, he has never withheld his confidence from me and often asks my advice. He trusts me all the more, I believe, because he is well aware that I do not expect any personal gain from him and would not even accept a post in his government, for I want to remain free. And so, on that memorable evening in the summer of 1929, he calmly suggested to me that I should go out and explore the web of political intrigue behind the *Ikhwan* rebellion – a mission which probably entailed personal risk and certainly could be accomplished only at the cost of strenuous efforts.

But the *Shuyukh* was not disappointed in my reactions. Apart from my affection for him and his country, the task which he now entrusted to me seemed to promise an exciting adventure, not to speak of a possible journalistic 'scoop'.

'Over my eyes and my head be thy command, O Long-of-Age,' I immediately replied. 'I shall certainly do what I can.'

'Of that I have no doubt, O Muhammad; and I expect thee to keep thy mission a secret. There may be danger in it – what about thy wife?'

The wife was a girl from Riyadh whom I had married the previous year; but I was able to assure the King on this point:

'She will not cry, O Imam; it was only today that I was thinking of divorcing her. We do not seem to suit one another.'

Ibn Saud smiled knowingly, for divorcing a wife was a thing not unfamiliar to him. 'But what about other people – thy kinsfolk?'

'There is no one, I believe, who would mourn should anything happen to me – except, of course, Zayd; but he will accompany me in any case, and the things that befall me will befall him as well.'

'That is all to the good,' replied the King. 'And, oh, before I forget: thou wilt require some funds for the undertaking' – and slipping his hand under the cushion behind him, he drew out a purse and thrust if into my hand; from its weight I immediately guessed that it was filled with golden sovereigns. I remember thinking to myself: How certain he must have been, even before he asked me, that I would accept his suggestion . . . !

•   •   •   •   •   •   •   •   •

BACK IN MY QUARTERS, I called Zayd, who had been
awaiting my return.

'If I should ask thee, Zayd, to accompany me on an enterprise
that might prove dangerous – wouldst thou go with me?'

Zayd replied: 'Dost thou think, O my uncle, that I would let
thee go alone, whatever the danger? But where are we going?'

'We are going to find out from where Ad-Dawish is getting
his arms and his money. But the King insists that no one should
know what we are doing until it has been done; so thou must be
on guard.'

Zayd did not even bother to reassure me, but turned instead
to the more practical question:

'We can't very well ask Ad-Dawish or his men; how then do
we set about it?'

On my way back from the castle I had been ruminating over
this problem. It appeared to me that the best starting point
would be one of the cities of central Najd, where there were
many merchants who had intimate connections with Iraq and
Kuwayt. Finally I settled upon Shaqra, the capital of the province of Washm, about three days' journey from Riyadh, where
my friend Abd ar-Rahman as-Siba'i might be able to help me.

The following day was occupied with preparations for our expedition. As I did not want to attract too much attention to my
movements, I cautioned Zayd not to draw provisions, as was
customary with us, from the King's storehouses, but to purchase
everything we needed from the bazaar. By evening Zayd had collected the necessary assortment of foodstuffs: about twenty
pounds of rice, the same amount of flour for bread, a small skin
containing clarified butter, dates, coffee beans and salt. He had
also bought two new waterskins, a leather bucket and a goat-hair
rope long enough for very deep wells. We were already well provided with arms and ammunition. Into our saddlebags we stuffed two changes of clothing per man; and each of us wore a
heavy *abaya* which, together with the blankets over our saddles,
would serve as covering on cool nights. Our dromedaries, which
had spent several weeks at pasture, were in excellent condition;
the one I had recently given to Zayd was an extremely fleet
Omani racer, while I rode the beautiful old 'northern' thorough-
bred which had once belonged to the last Rashidi *amir* of Haïl
and had been presented to me by Ibn Saud.

After nightfall we rode out of Riyadh. By dawn we reached Wadi Hanifa, a deep, barren river bed between steep hills – the site of the decisive battle fought over thirteen hundred years ago between the Muslim forces of Abu Bakr, the Prophet's successor and First Caliph of Islam, and those of the 'false prophet', Musaylima, who for many years had opposed the Muslims. The battle signalled the final victory of Islam in Central Arabia. Many of the original Companions of the Prophet fell in it, and their graves are visible to this day on the rocky slopes of the *wadi*.

During the forenoon we passed the ruined city of Ayayna, once a large, populous settlement, stretching along both banks of Wadi Hanifa. Between rows of tamarisks lay the remnants of the past: broken-down house walls, with the crumbling pillars of a mosque or the ruin of a palatial building rising here and there, all of them speaking of a higher, more gracious style of architecture than that of the simple mud buildings one sees in present-day Najd. It is said that until about one hundred and fifty or two hundred years ago, the entire course of Wadi Hanifa from Dar'iyya (the original capital of the Ibn Saud dynasty) to Ayayna – a distance of over fifteen miles – was one single city; and that when a son was born to the *amir* of Dar'iyya, the news of his birth, passed along from rooftop to rooftop by the women, travelled within minutes to the utmost end of Ayayna. The story of Ayayna's decay is so clouded by legends that it is difficult to discern the historical facts. Most probably the town was destroyed by the first Saudi ruler when it refused to accept the teachings of Muhammad ibn Abd al-Wahhab; but Wahhabi legend has it that, as a sign of God's wrath, all the wells of Ayayna dried up in a single night, forcing the inhabitants to abandon the city.

At noon of the third day we sighted the mud walls and bastions of Shaqra and the high palms which towered above its houses. We rode between empty orchards and through empty streets; and only then we remembered that it was Friday and that everyone must be at the mosque. Off and on we encountered a woman cloaked from head to toe in a black *abaya;* she would start at the sight of the strangers and draw her veil across her face with a quick, shy movement. Here and there children played in the shadow of the houses; a solid warmth was brooding over the crowns of the palms.

We went straight to the house of my good friend Abd ar-

Rahman as-Siba'i, who at that time was in charge of the *bayt al-mal*, or treasury, of the province. We dismounted before the open gate and Zayd called into the courtyard, ' *Ya walad!*' – 'O boy!' – and as a servant boy came running out of the house, Zayd announced: 'Guests are here!'

While Zayd and the boy busied themselves with unsaddling the dromedaries in the courtyard, I made myself at home in Abd ar-Rahman's *qahwa*, where another servant immediately lit a fire under the brass pots on the coffee hearth. Hardly had I drunk the first sip when voices became audible from the courtyard – questions and answers rang out: the master of the house had returned. Already from the staircase, still invisible, he shouted his greeting of welcome to me, and then appeared in the doorway with open arms: a delicate little man with a short, light-brown beard and a pair of deep-set, humorous eyes in a smiling face. In spite of the heat he wore a long fur coat under his *abaya*. This fur coat was one of his most treasured possessions. He never tired of telling everyone who was not already aware of its history that it had once belonged to the former King of the Hijaz, Sharif Husayn, and had fallen into his, Abd ar-Rahman's, hands at the conquest of Mecca in 1924. I cannot remember ever having seen him without that coat.

He embraced me warmly and, standing on his toes, kissed me on both cheeks: '*Ahlan wa-sahlan wa-marhaba!* Welcome to this lowly house, O my brother. Lucky is the hour that brings thee here!'

And then came the usual questions: Whence, and whereto, and how is the King, and was there rain on the way – or didst thou at least hear of rains? – the whole traditional exchange of Arabian news. I told him that Anayza, in central Najd, was my destination – which was not quite true but could well have been.

In earlier years Abd ar-Rahman had been engaged in extensive trade between Najd and Iraq and was thoroughly familiar with both Basra and Kuwayt. It was not difficult to get him to talk of those places and to sound him out about people who might recently have arrived from there (for it seemed to me that with Faysal ad-Dawish being reported so near the border of Kuwayt, either that place or Basra might furnish some indication as to his source of supplies). I learned that a member of the well-known Al-Bassam family of Anayza – an old acquaintance of mine – had recently visited Kuwayt on the way back from Basra, and, not wanting to expose himself to the hazards of a journey through rebel-infested territory, had returned via Bahrain to Najd. He was in Shaqra at present, and if I wanted, Abd ar-Rahman would send for him: for, in accordance with ancient Arabian custom, it is for the new arrival to be visited rather than to pay visits. Soon afterward, Abdullah al-Bassam joined us in Abd ar-Rahman's *qahwa*.

Abdullah, although belonging to perhaps the most important family of businessmen in all Najd, was not himself a rich man. His life had been full of ups and downs – mostly downs – experienced not only in Najd but also in Cairo, Baghdad, Basra, Kuwayt, Bahrain and Bombay. He knew everybody who was anybody in those places, and carried in his shrewd head a store of information about everything that was going on in Arab countries. I told him that I had been asked by a German business firm to explore the possibilities of importing agricultural machinery into Kuwayt and Basra; and since I had been offered a fat commission by the firm, I was anxious to find out which of the local merchants in those two towns were likely to entertain such a proposition. Al-Bassam mentioned several names, and then added:

'I am sure that some of the Kuwayti people will be interested in thy project. They are always importing things from abroad, and nowadays trade seems to be quite lively – so lively that large consignments of silver *riyals* are arriving almost every day directly from the mint at Trieste.'

The mention of the silver *riyals* gave me a jolt. This particular kind of *riyal*, the Maria Theresa thaler, constituted, side by side with the official Arabian currencies, the chief commercial coinage of the entire Peninsula. It was minted at Trieste and sold at its silver value, plus a small minting charge to the various governments and also to a few outstanding merchants with large trade interests among the beduins; for the beduins were averse to accepting paper money and took only gold or silver – preferably Maria Theresa thalers. Large imports of these coins by Kuwayti traders seemed to indicate that a brisk business was going on between them and the beduins.

'Why,' I asked Al-Bassam, 'should Kuwayti merchants import *riyals* just now?'

'I do not know,' he replied, with a trace of perplexity in his voice. 'They talk of buying meat-camels from beduins near Kuwayt for sale in Iraq, where the prices are high nowadays; though I do not quite see how they expect to find many camels in the steppes around Kuwayt in these disturbed times . . . I should rather think,' he added with a laugh, 'that it would be more profitable to buy riding-camels in Iraq and to sell them to Ad-Dawish and his men – but, of course, Ad-Dawish would not have the money to pay for them . . .'

Would he not, indeed?

That night, before going to bed in the room assigned to us by our host, I drew Zayd into a corner and told him:

'We are going to Kuwayt.'

'It will not be easy, O my uncle,' replied Zayd; but the gleam in his eyes spoke more eloquently than his words of his readiness to embark on something that was not only not easy but extremely dangerous. It would, of course, be child's play to travel across territory controlled by forces and tribes loyal to the King; but for at least one hundred miles or so before reaching the borders of Kuwayt we would be entirely on our own in the midst of hostile territory through which the rebellious Mutayr and Ajman tribesmen were roaming. We could, of course, travel to Kuwayt by sea via Bahrain, but that would require a permit from the British authorities and thus expose all our movements to the closest scrutiny. The same objection would apply to travelling via Al-Jawf and the Syrian Desert into Iraq, and thence to Kuwayt; for it would be too optimistic to suppose that we could slip through the many control points in Iraq. There remained, therefore, nothing but the direct overland route to Kuwayt. How to penetrate undetected into the town itself was a question that could not be easily answered at present; and so we left it to the future, trusting in our luck and hoping for unforeseen opportunities.

Abd ar-Rahman as-Siba'i wanted me to stay with him for some days, but when I pleaded urgent business, he let us go the next morning, after augmenting our food supply by a quantity of dried camel-meat – a delicious addition to the rather monotonous fare ahead of us. He also insisted that I should visit him on my return journey, to which, in truth, I could only answer, *Insha-Allah* – 'God willing.'

.   .   .   .

FROM SHAQRA WE TRAVELLED for four days toward north-east without encountering anything unusual. On one occasion we were stopped by a detachment of loyal Awazim beduins who formed part of Amir Ibn Musaad's forces; but my open letter from the King immediately put them at rest and, after the customary exchange of desert tidings, we continued on our way.

Before dawn of the fifth day we approached a region over which Ibn Saud's arm no longer extended. From now on day travel was out of the question; our only safety lay in darkness and stealth.

We made camp in a convenient gulley not far from the main course of the great Wadi ar-Rumma, the ancient, dry river bed that runs across northern Arabia toward the head of the Persian Gulf. The gulley was thickly overhung with *arfaj* bushes, which would afford us some cover as long as we kept close to the al-most vertical bank. We hobbled our camels securely, fed them a mixture of coarse barley flour and date kernels – thus obviating the necessity of letting them out to pasture – and settled down to await the nightfall. We did not dare light a fire, for even in day-time its smoke might betray us; and so we had to content our-selves with a meal of dates and water.

How sound our precautions were became evident in the late af-ternoon, when the strains of a beduin riding-chant suddenly struck our ears. We took hold of our camels' muzzles to prevent them from snorting or bellowing, and pressed ourselves, rifle in hand, flat against the protecting wall of the gulley.

The chanting grew louder as the unknown riders approached; we could already discern the words, *La ilaha ill'Allah, la ilaha ill'Allah* – 'There is no God but God, There is no God but God' – the usual *Ikhwan* substitute for the more worldy travel chants of 'unreformed' beduins. There was no doubt that these were *Ikhwan*, and in this area they could only be hostile *Ikhwan*. After a while they appeared over the crest of a hillock, just above the bank of the gulley – a group of eight or ten camel-riders slowly advancing in single file, sharply outlined against the afternoon sky, each of them wearing the white *Ikhwan* turban over his red-and-white-checked *kufiyya*, two bandoliers across the chest and a rifle slung on the saddle-peg behind him: a sombre and for-bidding cavalcade, swaying forward and backward, forward and backward, in rhythm with the gait of the dromedaries and the great but now so misused words, *La ilaha ill'Allah* ... The sight was impressive and at the same time pathetic. These were men to whom their faith obviously meant more than anything else in life; they thought they were fighting for its purity and for the greater glory of God, not knowing that their fervour and their longing had been harnessed to the ambitions of an unscrupulous leader in quest of personal power ...

They were on they 'right' side of the gulley as far as we were concerned: for had they been riding on the opposite side, they would have seen us as plainly as we could now see them from beneath the protective overhang of the bushes. When, with the lilt of the Creed on their lips, they disappeared from view down the hill, we sighed with relief.

'They are like jinns,' whispered Zayd. 'Yes, like the jinns who know neither joy of life nor fear of death ... They are brave and strong in faith, no one can deny that – but all they dream about is blood and death and Paradise ...'

And, as if in defiance of the *Ikhwan's* gloomy puritanism, he began to sing, *sotto voce*, a very worldly Syrian love song: 'O thou maiden of golden-brown flesh ...'

As soon as it was quite dark, we resumed our surreptitious march in the direction of distant Kuwayt.

.   .   .   .

'LOOK THERE, O MY UNCLE!' Zayd suddenly exclaimed. 'A fire!'

It was too small a fire for a beduin encampment; a lonely herdsman, perhaps? But what herdsman would dare light a fire here unless he were one of the rebels? Still, it would be better to find out. If it was only one man, we could easily take care of him and also, possibly, gather some precious information about enemy movements in the area.

The soil was sandy and the feet of our camels made almost no noise as we cautiously approached the fire. In its light we could now make out the crouching figure of a solitary beduin. He seemed to be peering into the darkness in our direction, and then as if satisfied with what he had seen, he rose without hurry, crossed his arms over his chest – perhaps to indicate that he was unarmed – and calmly, without the least appearance of fright, awaited our coming.

'Who art thou?' Zayd called out sharply, his rifle pointed at the ragged stranger.

The beduin smiled slowly and answered in a deep, sonorous voice: 'I am a Sulubbi . . .'

The reason for his calm now became obvious. The strange, gypsy-like tribe (or rather group of tribes) to which he belonged had never taken part in Arabia's almost unceasing beduin warfare; enemies to none, they were attacked by none.

The Sulubba (sing., Sulubbi) have remained to this day an enigma to all explorers. Nobody really knows their origin. That they are not Arabs is certain: their blue eyes and light-brown hair belie their sunburned skins and carry a memory of northern regions. The ancient Arab historians tell us that they are descendants of crusaders who had been taken prisoner by Saladin and brought to Arabia, where they later became Muslims; and, indeed, the name Sulubba has the same root as the word *salib*, that is, 'cross', and *salibi*, which means 'crusader'. Whether this explanation is correct is difficult to say. In any case, the beduins regard the Sulubba as non-Arabs and treat them with something like tolerant contempt. They explain this contempt, which contrasts sharply with the Arab's otherwise so pronounced sense of human equality, by asserting that these people are not really Muslims by conviction and do not live like Muslims. They point out that the Sulubba do not marry, but are 'promiscuous like dogs', without consideration even of close blood relationship, and that they eat carrion, which Muslims consider unclean. But this may be a *post factum* rationalization. I am rather inclined to think that it was the awareness of the Sulubba's racial strangeness that caused the extremely race-conscious beduin to draw a magic circle of contempt around them – an instinctive defence against blood mixture, which must have been very tempting in the case of the Sulubba: for they are, almost without exception, beautiful people, taller than most of the Arabs and of a great regularity of features; the women, especially, are very lovely, full of an elusive grace of body and movement.

But whatever the cause, the beduin's contempt for the Sulubba has made their life secure: for anyone who attacks or harms them is deemed by his kinsfolk to have forfeited his honour. Apart from this, the Sulubba are highly esteemed by all desert dwellers as veterinarians, saddle-makers, tinkers and smiths.

The beduin, though despising handicraft too much to practise it himself, is nevertheless in need of it, and the Sullubba are there to help him in his need. They are also efficient herdsmen and, above all, unquestioned masters in the art of hunting. Their ability to read tracks is almost legendary, and the only people who can compare with them in this respect are the Al Murra beduins on the northern fringes of the Empty Quarter.

Relieved at finding that our new acquaintance was a Sulubbi, I told him frankly that we were Ibn Saud's men – which was quite safe in view of the respect which these people have for authority – and requested him to extinguish his fire. This done, we settled on the ground for a lengthy conversation.

He could not tell us much about the disposition of Ad-Dawish's forces, 'for,' he said, 'they are always on the move, like jinns, never resting at one place for long'. It transpired, however, that no large concentration of hostile *Ikhwan* happened to be in our immediate vicinity just now, although small parties were constantly crossing the desert in all directions.

An idea suddenly struck me: might we not utilize the Sulubbi's instinct for hunting and pathfinding to lead us to Kuwayt?

'Hast thou ever been to Kuwayt?' I asked him.

The Sulubbi laughed. 'Many times. I have sold gazelle skins there and clarified butter and camel wool. Why, it is only ten days since I returned from there.'

'Then thou couldst perhaps guide us to Kuwayt? – I mean, guide us in such a manner as to avoid meeting *Ikhwan* on the way?'

For a few moments the Sulubbi pondered over this question; then he replied hesitantly: 'I might, but it would be dangerous for me to be caught by the *Ikhwan* in thy company. I might, though, but . . . but it would cost thee a lot.'

'How much?'

'Well . . .' – and I could discern the tremor of greed in his voice – 'well, O my master, if thou wouldst give me one hundred *riyals*, I might guide thee and thy friend to Kuwayt in such a manner that none but the birds of the sky would set eyes on us.'

One hundred *riyals* was equivalent to ten sovereigns – a ridiculously small sum considering what it would mean to us; but the Sulubbi had probably never in his life held so much cash in his hands.

'I shall give thee one hundred *riyals* – twenty now and the rest after we reach Kuwayt.'

Our prospective guide had obviously not expected his demand to be so readily granted. Perhaps he regretted that he had not set his price higher, for, as an afterthought, he added:

'But what about my dromedary? If I ride with you to Kuwayt and then back, the poor beast will be worn out entirely, and I have only one . . .'

Not wishing to prolong the negotiations, I promptly replied: 'I shall buy thy dromedary. Thou shalt ride it to Kuwayt, and there I shall hand it to thee as a gift – but thou must lead us back as well.'

That was more than he could have hoped for. With great alacrity he rose, disappeared into the darkness and reappeared after a few minutes, leading an old but beautiful and obviously hardy animal. After some haggling we settled upon one hundred and fifty *riyals* as its price, on the understanding that I would pay him fifty now and the rest, together with his reward, in Kuwayt. Zayd fetched a purse filled with *riyals* from one of our saddlebags and I started counting the coins into the lap of the Sulubbi. From the depths of his bedraggled tunic he drew out a piece of cloth in which his money was tied; and as he started to add my *riyals* to his hoard, the glitter of a new coin caught my eye.

'Stop!' I exclaimed, placing my hand over his. 'Let me see that shining *riyal* of thine.'

With a hesitant gesture, as if afraid of being robbed, the Sulubbi laid the coin gingerly on the palm of my hand. It felt sharp-edged, like a new coin, but to make sure I lit a match and looked at it closely. It was indeed a new Maria Theresa thaler – as new as if it had just left the mint. And when I held the match over the rest of the Sulubbi's money, I discovered five or six more coins of the same startling newness.

'Where didst thou get these *riyals*?'

'I came by them honestly, O my master, I swear . . . I did not steal them. A Mutayri gave them to me some weeks ago near Kuwayt. He bought a new camel-saddle from me because his was broken . . .'

'A Mutayri? Art thou certain?'

'I am certain, O my master, and may God kill me if I speak a lie . . . He was of Ad-Dawish's men, one of a party that had recently been fighting against the *amir* of Haïl. It surely was not wrong to take money from him for a saddle . . . ? I could not well refuse, and I am sure that the *Shuyukh*, may God lengthen his life, will understand this . . .'

I reassured him that the King would not bear any malice toward him, and his anxiety subsided. On questioning him further, I found that many other Sulubba had received such new *riyals* from various partisans of Ad-Dawish in exchange for goods or small services . . .

. . . .

OUR SULUBBI INDEED PROVED himself an outstanding guide. For three nights he led us a meandering course across rebel territory, over pathless stretches which even Zayd, who knew this country well, had never seen before. The days were spent in hiding; the Sulubbi was a past-master at finding unsuspected places of concealment. On one occasion he led us to a water hole which, he told us, was unknown even to the beduins of the region; its brackish, brown water assuaged the thirst of our camels and enabled us to refill our waterskins. Only twice did we see groups of *Ikhwans* in the distance, but on neither occasion were they allowed to see us.

In the forenoon of the fourth morning after our meeting with the Sulubbi, we came within sight of the town of Kuwayt. We did not approach it from the southwest, as travellers from Najd would have done, but from the west, along the road from Basra, so that anyone who met us would think we were Iraqi traders.

Once in Kuwayt, we made ourselves at home in the compound of a merchant with whom Zayd was acquainted from his days in the Iraqi Constabulary.

A damp, oppressive heat lay over the sandy streets and the houses built of sunbaked mud bricks; and, accustomed to the open steppes of Najd, I was soon drenched with perspiration. But there was no time for rest. Leaving the Sulubbi in charge of the camels – with the strict injunction not to mention to anyone from where we had come – Zayd and I proceeded to the bazaar to make our preliminary investigations.

Not being familiar with Kuwayt myself, and not wishing to make Zayd more conspicuous by my presence, I remained for about an hour alone in a coffee shop, drinking coffee and smoking a *nargile*. When Zayd at last re-appeared, it was obvious from his triumphant expression that he had found out something of importance.

'Let us go outside, O my uncle. It is easier to talk in the market place without being overheard. And here I have brought something for thee – and for me as well' – and from under his *abaya* he produced two Iraqi *igals* of thick, loosely plaited brown wool. 'These will make Iraqis of us.'

Through discreet enquiries Zayd ascertained that a former partner of his – a companion of his old smuggling days in the Persian Gulf – was now living in Kuwayt, apparently still engaged in his accustomed trade.

'If there is anyone who can tell us something about gun-running in this town, it is Bandar. He is a Shammar like myself – one of those stubborn fools who could never fully reconcile themselves to Ibn Saud's rule. We must not let him know that we are working for the *Shuyukh* – and, I think, not even from where we have come; for Bandar is not really a fool. He is a very cunning man – indeed, he has tricked me too often in the past that I should trust him now.'

We finally traced the man to a house in a narrow lane close to the main bazaar. He was tall and thin, perhaps forty years of age, with close-set eyes and a sour, dyspeptic expression; but his features lit up in genuine pleasure when he beheld Zayd. Because of my light skin, I was introduced as a Turk who had settled in Baghdad and had been engaged in exporting Arab horses from Basra to Bombay. 'But it does not pay nowadays to bring horses to Bombay,' added Zayd. 'Those merchants from Anayza and Burayda have completely cornered the market there.'

'I know,' replied Bandar, 'those dirty Southerners of Ibn Saud are not content with having taken away our country; they are bent on taking away our livelihood as well . . .'

'But what about gun-running, Bandar?' asked Zayd. 'There should be a lot of business here, with all these Mutayr and Ajman desirous of twisting Ibn Saud's neck – heh?'

'There *was* a lot of business,' replied Bandar, with a shrug of his shoulders. 'Until a few months ago I was making quite good money buying up rifles in Transjordan and selling them to the people of Ad-Dawish. But now all that is finished, entirely finished. You couldn't sell a single rifle now.'

Riza Khan (later Shah) of Iran

'How is that? I should think Ad-Dawish would need them more than ever before.'

'Yes,' retorted Bandar, 'so he does. But he gets them at a price for which one like thee or me could never afford to sell ... He gets them in cases, from overseas – English rifles, almost new – and he pays ten *riyals* for a rifle with two hundred rounds of ammunition.'

'Praise be unto God!' exclaimed Zayd in genuine astonishment. 'Ten *riyals* for an almost new rifle with two hundred rounds: but that is impossible ... !'

It really did seem impossible, for at that time used Lee-Enfield rifles cost in Najd about thirty to thirty-five *riyals* apiece, without ammunition; and even if one took into consideration that the prices at Kuwayt might be lower than in Najd, the tremendous difference was still unaccountable.

Bandar smiled wryly. 'Well, it seems that Ad-Dawish has powerful friends. Very powerful friends ... Some say that one day he will become an independent *amir* in northern Najd.'

'What thou sayest, O Bandar,' I interposed, 'is all well and good. Perhaps Ad-Dawish will really make himself independent of Ibn Saud. But he has no money, and without money even the great Alexander could not have built a kingdom.'

Bandar broke out into a loud guffaw: 'Money? Ad-Dawish has plenty of that – plenty of new *riyals*, which come to him in cases, like the rifles, from beyond the sea.'

'Cases of *riyals*? But that is very strange. From where could a beduin obtain cases of new *riyals*?'

'That I do not know,' replied Bandar. 'But I do know that almost daily some of his men are taking delivery of new *riyals* that are reaching them through various merchants in the city. Why, only yesterday I saw Farhan ibn Mashhur at the port supervising the unloading of such cases.'

This was indeed news. I knew Farhan well. He was a grandnephew of that famous Syrian beduin prince, Nuri ash-Shaalan, who had once fought together with Lawrence against the Turks. I had first met young Farhan in 1924 in Damascus, where he was notorious for his revels in all the doubtful places of entertainment. Some time afterward he fell out with his great-uncle, migrated with a sub-section of his tribe, the Ruwala, to Najd, where he suddenly became 'pious' and joined the *Ikhwan* movement. I met him again in 1927 in Ibn Musaad's castle at Haïl. By then he had donned the huge, white turban of the *Ikhwan* as a symbol of his new-found faith, and was enjoying the bounty of the King; when I reminded him of our previous meetings in Damascus, he quickly changed the subject. Stupid and ambitious as he was, he had seen in Ad-Dawish's revolt an opportunity to achieve an independent amirate for himself in Al-Jawf, an oasis north of the Great Nufud – for in Arabia, as elsewhere, rebels follow the time-honoured practice of dividing the lion's skin before the lion has been killed.

'So Farhan is here in Kuwayt?' I asked Bandar.

'Of course. He comes here as often as Ad-Dawish, and goes freely in and out of the *shaykh's* palace. The *shaykh*, they say, has a great liking for him.'

'But do not the British object to Ad-Dawish's and Farhan's coming to Kuwayt? I seem to remember that some months ago they announced that they would not allow Ad-Dawish or his people to enter this territory . . . ?'

Bandar guffawed again. 'So they did, so they did. But, I have told thee: Ad-Dawish has very powerful friends . . . I am not sure whether he is in town just now; but Farhan is. He goes every evening to the Great Mosque for the *maghrib* prayer – thou canst see him there with thine own eyes if thou dost not believe me . . .'

And see him we did. When, taking Bandar's hint, Zayd and I strolled in the early evening in the vicinity of the Great Mosque, we almost collided with a group of beduins, unmistakably Najdi in bearing, who emerged from around a street corner. At their head was a man in his middle thirties, somewhat shorter than the tall beduins who surrounded and followed him, his handsome face adorned by a short, black beard. I recognized him at once. I do not know to this day whether he recognized me; his eyes met mine for a moment, swept over me with a puzzled expression, as if he were trying to recall a dim memory, and then turned away; and an instant later he and his retinue were lost in the throng of people moving toward the mosque.

We decided not to extend our clandestine sojourn in Kuwayt unduly by waiting for an opportunity to see Ad-Dawish as well. Bandar's revelations were confirmed by Zayd's adroit enquiries from other acquaintances in the town. Ad-Dawish's mysterious supplies of Lee-Enfield rifles – only superficially disguised as 'purchases' – clearly pointed to a Kuwayti merchant who had always been prominent as an importer of arms; and the large amounts of mint-new Maria Theresa *riyals* that circulated in the bazaars of Kuwayt were in almost every case traceable to Ad-Dawish and the men around him. Short of seeing his actual depots and examining the consignment papers – which was scarcely within the realm of likelihood – we had enough evidence to confirm the suspicions the King had voiced during his talk with me.

My mission was completed; and in the following night we made our way out of Kuwayt as stealthily as we had come. During Zayd's and my investigations in the bazaars, our Sulubbi had found out that there were no rebel groups at the moment to the south of Kuwayt. And so to the south we went – in the direction of Al-Hasa province, which was firmly under the control of the King. After two strenuous night marches, we encountered, not far from the coast, a detachment of Banu Hajar beduins who had been sent out by the *amir* of Al-Hasa to reconnoitre the latest positions of the rebels; and in their company we re-entered loyal territory. Once safely within Ibn Saud's realm, we parted from our Sulubbi guide who, contentedly pocketing his well-earned reward, rode away toward the west on the camel I had 'presented' to him, while we continued southward in the direction of Riyadh.

. . . .

THE SERIES OF ARTICLES which I subsequently wrote made it clear for the first time that the rebels were being supported by a great European power. They pointed out that the basic aim of these intrigues was to push Ibn Saud's frontiers southward and, ultimately, to convert his northernmost province into an 'independent' principality between Saudi Arabia and Iraq, which would allow the British to build a railway line across its territory. Apart from this, Ad-Dawish's rebellion offered a welcome means to bring about so much confusion in Ibn Saud's kingdom that he would be in no position to resist, as he had hitherto done, Britain's demands for two important concessions: one of them being the lease of the Red Sea port of Rabigh, north of Jidda, where the British had long wanted to establish a naval base, and the other, control of that sector of the Damascus-Medina railway which runs through Saudi territory. A defeat of Ibn Saud at the hands of Ad-Dawish would have brought these schemes well within the realm of practical possibility.

A flash of sensation followed the publication of my articles in the European and Arabic (mainly Egyptian) press; and it may well be that the premature disclosure of all that secret planning contributed something to its subsequent frustration. At any rate, the plan of a British railway from Haifa to Basra was allowed to lapse into oblivion in spite of the large sums which appeared to have been spent for preliminary surveys, and was never heard of again.

What happened afterward is a matter of history: that same summer of 1929, Ibn Saud protested to the British against the freedom accorded Ad-Dawish to purchase arms and ammunition at Kuwayt. Since he had no tangible 'proof' that these arms were being supplied by a foreign power, the King could protest only against the sales as such. The British authorities replied that it was the traders in Kuwayt who were supplying arms to the rebels – and that Britain could do nothing to stop this, since in the treaty of Jidda of 1927 they had lifted their embargo on the import of arms to Arabia. If Ibn Saud wanted, they said, he too could import arms via Kuwayt ... When Ibn Saud objected that the very same treaty obliged both Britain and Saudi Arabia to prevent in their territories all activities directed against the security of the other party, he received the answer that Kuwayt could not be termed 'British territory' since it was an independent shaykhdom with which Britain had no more than treaty relations ...

And so the civil war continued. In the late autumn of 1929, Ibn Saud personally took the field, this time determined to pursue Ad-Dawish even into Kuwayt if – as had always been the case in the past – that territory remained open to the rebels as a refuge and base for further operations. In the face of this determined attitude, which Ibn Saud took care to communicate to the British authorities, they apparently realized that it would be too risky to pursue their game further. British aeroplanes and armoured cars were sent out to prevent Ad-Dawish from retreating again into Kuwayti territory. The rebel realized that his cause was lost; never would he be able to withstand the King in open battle; and so he started to negotiate. The King's terms were crisp and clear: the rebel tribes must surrender; their arms, horses and dromedaries would be taken away from them; Ad-Dawish's life would be spared, but he would have to spend the rest of his days in Riyadh.

Ad-Dawish, always so active and full of movement, could not resign himself to inaction and immobility: he refused the offer. Fighting a last-ditch battle against the overwhelming forces of the King, the rebels were completely routed; Ad-Dawish and a few other leaders – among them Farhan ibn Mashhur and Naif abu Kilab, chieftain of the Ajman – fled to Iraq.

Ibn Saud demanded Ad-Dawish's extradition. For a time it seemed that King Faysal of Iraq would refuse his demand by invoking the ancient Arabian law of hospitality and sanctuary; but finally he gave in. Early in 1930, Ad-Dawish, seriously ill, was handed over to the King and brought to Riyadh. When after a few weeks it became obvious that this time he was really dying, Ibn Saud, with his customary generosity, had him brought back to his family at Artawiyya, where his stormy life came to an end.

And once again peace reigned in the realm of Ibn Saud . . .

.   .   .   .

AND ONCE AGAIN PEACE reigns around the wells of Arja.

'May God give you life, O wayfarers! Partake of our bounty!' calls out the old Mutayri beduin, and his men help us to water our camels. All grudges and enmities of the so recent past seem to be forgotten, as if they had never been.

For the beduins are a strange race: quick to flare up in uncontrollable passion at even imaginary provocations, and just as quick to swing back to the steady rhythm of a life in which modesty and kindness prevail: always heaven and hell in close proximity.

And as they draw water for our camels in their huge leather buckets, the Mutayri herdsmen chant in chorus:

> *Drink, and spare no water,*
> *The well is full of grace and has no bottom . . .*

— 3 —

ON THE FIFTH NIGHT after our departure from Hail, we reach the plain of Medina and see the dark outline of Mount Uhud.

The dromedaries move with tired step; we have a long march behind us, from early morning deep into this night. Zayd and Mansur are silent, and I am silent. In the moonlight the city appears before us with its crenellated walls and the slim, straight minarets of the Prophet's Mosque.

We arrive before the gate which, because it faces north, is called the Syrian. The dromedaries shy before the shadows of its heavy bastions, and we have to use our canes to make them enter the gateway.

Now I am again in the City of the Prophet, home after a long wandering: for this city has been my home for several years. A deep, familiar quiet lies over its sleeping, empty streets. Here and there a dog rises lazily before the feet of the camels. A young man walks by singing; his voice sways in a soft rhythm and fades away in a side-lane. The carved balconies and oriel windows of the houses hang black and silent over us. The moonlit air is lukewarm like fresh milk.

And here is my house.

Mansur takes leave to go to some friends, while we two make the camels kneel down before the door. Zayd hobbles them without a word and begins to unload the saddlebags. I knock at the door. After a while I hear voices and footsteps from within. The shine of a lantern appears through the fanlight, the bolts are drawn and my old Sudanese maid servant, Amina, exclaims joyfully:

'Oh, my master has come home!'

IX

PERSIAN LETTER

— 1 —

IT IS AFTERNOON. I am sitting with a friend in his palm garden just outside the southern gate of Medina. The multitude of palm trunks in the orchard weaves a grey-green twilight into its background, making it appear endless. The trees are still young and low; sunlight dances over their trunks and the pointed arches of their fronds. Their green is somewhat dusty because of the sand-storms which occur almost daily at this time of year. Only the thick carpet of lucerne under the palms is of a brilliant, faultless green.

Not far in front of me rise the city walls, old, grey, built of stone and mud bricks, with bastions jutting forward here and there. From behind the wall tower the luxuriant palms of another garden in the interior of the city, and houses with weather-browned window shutters and enclosed balconies; some of them have been built into the city wall and have become part of it. In the distance I can see the five minarets of the Prophet's Mosque, high and tender like the voices of flutes, the great green dome which vaults over and conceals the little house of the Prophet – his home while he lived and his grave after he died – and still farther, beyond the city, the naked, rocky range of Mount Uhud: a brown-red backdrop for the white minarets of the Holy Mosque, the crowns of the palms and the many houses of the town.

The sky, glaringly lighted by the afternoon sun, lies glass-clear over opalescent clouds, and the city is bathed in a blue, gold- and green-streaked light. A high wind plays around the soft clouds, which in Arabia can be so deceptive. Never can you say here, ' Now it is cloudy; soon it will rain ': for even as the clouds mass heavily, as if pregnant with storm, it often happens that a roar of wind comes suddenly from out of the desert and sweeps them apart; and the faces of the people who have been waiting for rain turn away in silent resignation, and they mutter.

249

' There is no power and no strength except in God '– while the sky glares anew in a light-blue clearness without mercy.

I bid good-bye to my friend and walk back toward the outer city gate. A man passes by driving a pair of donkeys loaded with lucerne, himself riding on a third donkey. He lifts his staff in greeting and says, ' Peace be with thee,' and I reply with the same words. Then comes a young beduin woman, her black robe trailing behind her and the lower part of her face covered with a veil. Her shining eyes are so black that iris and pupil merge into one; and her step has something of the hesitant, swinging tension of young steppe animals.

I enter the city and cross the huge, open square of Al-Manakha to the inner city wall; beneath the heavy arch of the Egyptian Gate, under which the money-changers sit clinking their gold and silver coins, I step into the main bazaar – a street hardly twelve feet across, tightly packed with shops around which a small but eager life pulsates.

The vendors praise their goods with cheerful songs. Gay head-cloths, silken shawls and robes of figured Kashmir wool attract the eye of the passerby. Silversmiths crouch behind small glass cases containing beduin jewellery – arm-rings and ankle-rings, necklaces and earrings. Perfume vendors display basins filled with henna, little red bags with antimony for colouring the eye-lashes, multicoloured bottles of oils and essences, and heaps of spices. Traders from Najd are selling beduin garments and camel-saddles and long-tasselled red and blue saddlebags from eastern Arabia. An auctioneer runs through the street, shouting at the top of his voice, with a Persian carpet and a camel-hair *abaya* over his shoulder and a brass samovar under his arm. Floods of people in both directions, people from Medina and the rest of Arabia and – as the time of the pilgrimage has ended only a short while ago – from all the countries between the steppes of Senegal and those of the Kirghiz, between the East Indies and the Atlantic Ocean, between Astrakhan and Zanzibar: but in spite of the multitude of people and the narrowness of the street, there is no hurried frenzy here, no pushing and jostling: for in Medina time does not ride on the wings of pursuit.

But what might appear even more strange is that despite the great variety of human types and costumes that fills them, there is nothing of an 'exotic' medley in the streets of Medina: the variety of appearances reveals itself only to the eye that is determined to analyze. It seems to me that all the people who live in this city, or even sojourn in it temporarily, very soon fall into what one might call a community of mood and thus also of behaviour and, almost, even of facial expression: for all of them have fallen under the spell of the Prophet, whose city it once was and whose guests they now are . . .

Even after thirteen centuries his spiritual presence is almost as alive here as it was then. It was only because of him that the scattered group of villages once called Yathrib became a city and has been loved by all Muslims down to this day as no city anywhere else in the world has ever been loved. It has not even a name of its own: for more than thirteen hundred years it has been called *Madinat an-Nabi*, 'the City of the Prophet'. For more than thirteen hundred years, so much love has converged here that all shapes and movements have acquired a kind of family resemblance, and all differences of appearance find a tonal transition into a common harmony.

This is the happiness one always feels here – this unifying harmony. Although life in Medina today has only a formal, distant relationship with what the Prophet aimed at; although the spritual awareness of Islam has been cheapened here, as in many other parts of the Muslim world: an indescribable emotional link with its great spiritual past has remained alive. Never has any city been so loved for the sake of one single personality; never has any man, dead for over thirteen hundred years, been loved so personally, and by so many, as he who lies buried beneath the great green dome.

And yet he never claimed to be anything but a mortal man, and never have Muslims attributed divinity to him, as so many followers of other Prophets have done after the Prophet's death. Indeed, the Koran itself abounds in statements which stress Muhammad's humanness: *Muhammad is naught but a Prophet; all prophets have passed away before him; if he dies or is slain, will ye then turn back upon your heels?* His utter insignificance before the majesty of God has thus been expressed the Koran: *Say* [O Muhammad]: '*I do not possess any power to grant you evil or good . . . I do not even possess any power to convey benefit or harm to myself, except as God may please; and had I known the Unknowable, I would have acquired much good, and no evil would ever have befallen me. I am nothing but a warner and the giver of glad tidings to those who have faith in God . . .'*

It was precisely because he was only human, because he lived like other men, enjoying the pleasures and suffering the ills of human existence, that those around him could so encompass him with their love.

This love has outlasted his death and lives on in the hearts of his followers like the *leitmotif* of a melody built up of many tones. It lives on in Medina. It speaks to you out of every stone of the ancient city. You can almost touch it with your hands: but you cannot capture it in words . . .

— 2 —

AS I STROLL THROUGH the bazaar in the direction of the Great Mosque, many an old acquaintance hails me in passing. I nod to this and that shopkeeper and finally allow myself to be dragged by my friend Az-Zughaybi down on to the little platform on which he sells cloth to beduins.

'When didst thou return, O Muhammad, and from where? It is months since thou has been here.'

'I am coming from Haïl and from the Nufud.'

'And wilt thou not remain at home for a time?'

'No brother, I am leaving for Mecca the day after tomorrow.'

Az-Zughaybi calls out to the boy in the coffee shop opposite, and soon the tiny cups are clinking before us.

'But why, O Muhammad, art thou going to Mecca now? The season of *hajj* is past . . .'

'It is not a desire for pilgrimage that takes me to Mecca. After all, am I not a *hajji* five times over? But somehow I have a feeling that I will not long remain in Arabia, and want to see once again the city in which my life in this land began . . .' And then I add with a laugh: 'Well, brother – to tell thee the truth, I do not understand myself why I am going to Mecca; but I know I have to . . .'

Az-Zughaybi shakes his head in dismay: 'Thou wouldst leave this land, and thy brethren? How canst thou speak like this?'

A familiar figures passes by with a long, hurried stride: it is Zayd, obviously in search of someone.

'Hey, Zayd, where to?'

He turns abruptly toward me with an eager face:

'It is thee I have been looking for, O my uncle; there was a pack of letters waiting thy return at the post office. Here they are. And peace be upon thee, Shaykh Az-Zughaybi!'

Sitting cross-legged before Az-Zughaybi's shop, I go through the bundle of envelopes: there are several letters from friends in Mecca; one from the editor of the *Neue Zürcher Zeitung* of Switzerland, whose correspondent I have been for the past six years; one from India, urging me to come there and make the acquaintance of the largest single Muslim community in the world; a few letters from various parts of the Near East; and one with a Tehran postmark – from my good friend Ali Agha, from whom I have not heard for more than a year. I open it and glance through the pages covered with Ali Agha's elegant *shiqasta** writing:

To our most beloved friend and brother, the light of our heart, the most respected Asad Agha, may God lengthen his life and protect his steps. Amen.

Peace be upon you and the grace of God, ever and ever. And we pray to God that He may give you health and happiness, knowing that it will please you to hear that we also are in perfect health, God be praised.

We did not write to you for a long time because of the uneven manner in which our life has been progressing in the past months. Our father, may God grant him mercy, has passed away a year ago and we, being the eldest son, had to spend much time and worry on the arrangement of our family affairs. Also, it has been God's will that the affairs of his unworthy servant have prospered beyond expectation, the Government having granted him a promotion to lieutenant colonel. In addition, we hope soon to be joined in matrimony with a gracious and beautiful lady, our second cousin Shirin – and in this way our old, unsettled days are coming to a close. As is well known to your friendly heart, we have not been without sin and error in our past – but did not Hafiz say,

'O God, Thou hast thrown a plank into the midst of a sea – Couldst Thou have desired that it remain dry?'

So old Ali Agha is at last going to settle down and become respectable! He was not so respectable when I first met him, a

* Lit., 'broken' – a Persian variant of the Arabic script, used for rapid writing.

little over seven years ago, in the town of Bam, to which he had been 'exiled'. Although he was only twenty-six then, his past had been full of action and excitement; he had taken part in the political upheavals which preceded the assumption of power by Riza Khan, and could have played a considerable role in Tehran had he not lived a bit too gaily. His presence in out-of-the-way Bam in the southeastern corner of Iran had been brought about by his worried and influential father in the hope that the son might be reformed if he were removed from the pleasures of Tehran. But Ali Agha seemed to have found compensations even in Bam – women, arrack and the sweet poison of opium, to which he was greatly devoted.

At that time, in 1925, he was the district gendarmerie commander with the rank of lieutenant. As I was about to cross the great Dasht-i-Lut desert, I looked him up with a letter of introduction from the governor of Kirman province – which in its turn was based on a letter from Riza Khan, the Prime Minister and dictator. I found Ali Agha in a shady garden of orange trees, oleanders and palms through whose pointed vaults the rays of the sun were filtered. He was in his shirt sleeves. A carpet was spread on the lawn, and on it were dishes with the remnants of a meal and half-empty bottles of arrack. Ali Agha apologized, ' It is impossible to find wine in this damned hole,' and forced me to drink the local arrack – a terrible brew which went to the brain like a blow. With the swimming eyes of a northern Persian he glanced through the letter from Kirman, tossed it aside and said: ' Even if you had come without introduction, I would have accompanied you myself on your journey through the Dasht-i-Lut. You are my guest. I would never let you ride alone into the Baluchi desert.'

Someone who until then had been sitting half concealed in the shadow of a tree rose slowly: a young woman in a knee-length, light-blue silk tunic and wide, white Baluchi trousers. She had a sensual face that seemed to burn from within, large red lips and beautiful but strangely vague eyes; the lids were painted with antimony.

'She is blind,' Ali Agha whispered to me in French, 'and she is a wonderful singer.'

I admired the great tenderness and respect with which he treated the girl who, as a public singer, belonged to a category in

Iran more or less equated with courtesans; he could not have behaved better toward any of the great ladies of Tehran.

We sat down, all three of us, on the carpet, and while Ali Agha
busied himself with brazier and opium pipe, I talked with the
Baluchi girl. In spite of her blindness she could laugh as only
those can laugh who dwell deep in inner gladness; and she made
shrewd and witty remarks such as a lady of the great world need
not have been ashamed of. When Ali Agha finished his pipe, he
took her gently by the hand and said:

'This stranger here, this Austrian, would surely like to hear
one of your songs; he has never yet heard the songs of the
Baluchis.'

Over the sightless face lay a faraway, dreamy happiness as she
took the lute that Ali Agha handed to her and began to strum the
strings. She sang with a deep, husky voice a Baluchi tent song
which sounded like an echo of life from her warm lips . . .

I return to the letter:

*I wonder if you still remember, brother and respected friend,
how we travelled together in those old days through the Dasht-i-
Lut, and how we had to fight for our lives with those Baluchi
bandits . . . ?*

Do I remember? I smile inwardly at Ali Agha's idle question
and see myself and him in the desolate Dasht-i-Lut, the 'Naked
Desert' which spreads its huge emptiness from Baluchistan deep
into the heart of Iran. I was about to cross it in order to reach
Seistan, the easternmost province of Iran, and thence to proceed
to Afghanistan; as I had come from Kirman, there was no other
way but this.

We stopped, together with our escort of Baluchi gendarmes, at
a green oasis on the fringe of the desert in order to hire camels
and buy provisions for the long trek ahead. Our temporary
headquarters were in the station house of the Indo-European
Telegraph. The station-master, a tall, bony, sharp-eyed man,
almost never let me out of sight and seemed to appraise me with
his glances.

'Beware of this man,' Ali Agha whispered to me, 'he is a
bandit. I know him and he knows that I know him. Until a few
years ago he was a real robber, but now he has saved up enough

money and has become respectable – and makes more money from supplying arms to his former colleagues. I am only waiting for an opportune moment to catch him at it. But the fellow is cunning and it is difficult to prove anything. Since he has heard that you are an Austrian he is very excited. During the World War some Austrian and German agents were trying to arouse the tribes in these parts against the British; they had bags of gold coins with them: and our friend thinks that every German or Austrian is similarly equipped.'

But the cunning of the station-master benefited us, for he was able to find for me two of the best riding-camels of the region. The rest of the day was occupied with haggling about waterskins, camel-hair ropes, rice, clarified butter and many other odds and ends necessary for the desert journey.

The afternoon of the following day we started. Ali Agha decided to go ahead with four gendarmes to prepare a camping place for the night, and the drawn-out line of their domedaries soon disappeared beyond the horizon. We others – Ibrahim, myself and the fifth gendarme – followed at a slower pace.

We swayed (how new it was then to me!) with the strange, swinging amble of the slim-limbed dromedaries, at first through sand dunes, yellow, sparsely dotted with clumps of grass, then deeper and deeper into the plain – into an endless, soundless grey plain, flat and empty – so empty that it seemed not to flow but to fall toward the horizon: for your eye could find nothing there on which to rest, no ridge on the gound, no stone, no bush, not even a blade of grass. No animal sound, no chirping of birds or humming of a beetle broke through that vast silence, and even the wind, deprived of all impediment, swept low without voice over the void – no, fell into it, as a stone falls into an abyss . . . This was not a silence of death, but rather of the unborn, of that which had never yet come to life: the silence before the First Word.

And then it happened. The silence broke. A human voice struck gently, chirpingly, into the air and remained suspended, as it were: and to you it seemed as if you could not only hear but see it, so lonely and so undisguised by other sounds it floated over the desert plain. It was our Baluchi soldier. He sang a song of his nomad days, a half-sung and half-spoken rhapsody, a quick succession of hot and tender words which I could not understand. His voice rang in a very few tones, at one single level, with a persistence that gradually grew into something like splendour as it enveloped the brittle melody in a byplay of throaty sounds, and, by sheer repetition and variation of the same theme, unfolded an unsuspected wealth in its flat tones – flat and limitless, like the land in which it had been born . . .

The part of the desert through which we now travelled was called the 'Desert of Ahmad's Bells'. Many years ago, a caravan led by a man named Ahmad lost its way here, and all of them, men and animals, perished from thirst; and to this day, it is said, the bells which Ahmad's camels wore around their necks are sometimes heard by travellers – ghostly, mournful sounds which entice the unwary from their path and lead them to death in the desert.

Shortly after sunset we caught up with Ali Agha and the advance guard and made camp amidst some *kahur* shrubs – the last we would see for days. A fire was made from dry twigs, and the inevitable tea prepared – while Ali Agha smoked his usual opium pipe. The camels were fed coarse barley meal and made to kneel in a circle around us. Three of the gendarmes were posted as sentries on the outlying dunes, for the region in which we found ourselves was in those days a playground of the dreaded demons of the desert, the Baluchi tribal raiders from the south.

Ali Agha had just finished his pipe and tea and was drinking arrack – alone, for I was not in a mood to keep him company – when a rifle shot shattered the silence of the night. A second shot from one of our sentries answered and was followed by an outcry somewhere in the darkness. Ibrahim, with great presence of mind, immediately threw sand on the fire. More rifle shots from all directions. The sentries were now invisible, but one could hear them call out to one another. We did not know how many the attackers were, for they kept uncannily silent. Only off and on a faint stab of light from a rifle muzzle announced their presence; and once or twice I could discern white-clad figures flitting through the blackness. Several low-aimed bullets whizzed over our heads, but none of us were hit. Gradually the commotion died down, a few more shots fell and were sucked in by the night; and the raiders, apparently disconcerted by our watchfulness, vanished as quietly as they had come.

Ali Agha called in the sentries and we held a short council.

Originally we had intended to spend the night here; but as we had no idea how strong the attacking party was, and whether they would not return with reinforcements, we decided to break camp immediately and to move on.

The night was as black as pitch; heavy, low clouds had concealed the moon and the stars. In summertime it is better, as a rule, to travel in the desert at night; but under normal circumstances we would not have risked a march in such darkness for fear of losing our way, for the hard gravel of Dasht-i-Lut does not keep any tracks. In the early times the Iranian kings used to mark the caravan routes in such deserts by guideposts of masonry, but like so many other good things of the old days, these marks had long since disappeared. Indeed, they were no longer necessary: the wire of the Indo-European Telegraph, laid by the British at the beginning of the century from the Indian frontier across the Dasht-i-Lut to Kirman, served equally well, or even better, as a guide; but in a night like this, wire and telegraph posts were invisible.

This we discovered to our dismay when after about half an hour the gendarme who had been riding ahead as our guide suddenly reined in his mount and shamefacedly reported to Ali Agha:

'*Hazrat*, I cannot see the wire any more . . .'

For a moment we all remained silent. There were wells, we knew, only along the route marked by the telegraph line, and and even these were very widely spaced. To lose one's way here would mean to perish like Ahmad's legendary caravan . . .

Thereupon Ali Agha spoke up in a way which was quite unlike his usual manner; and one could safely presume that arrack and opium were responsible. He drew out his pistol and bellowed:

'Where is the wire? Why did you lose the wire, you sons of dogs? Oh, I know – you are in league with those bandits and are trying to lead us astray so that we may perish from thirst and thus be easy plunder!'

This reproach was certainly unjust, for a Baluchi would never betray a man with whom he has eaten bread and salt. Our gendarmes, obviously hurt by their lieutenant's accusation, assured us of their innocence, but Ali Agha broke in:

'Silence! Find the wire immediately or I will shoot down every one of you, you sons of burned fathers!'

I could not see their faces in the darkness but could sense how deeply they, the free Baluchis, were feeling the insult; they no longer even bothered to reply. Then suddenly one of them – our guide of a while ago – detached himself from the group, struck his camel with his whip and disappeared at a gallop into the darkness.

'Where to?' shouted Ali Agha and received a few indistinct words in reply. For a few seconds one could hear the soft padding of the camel's feet, then the sounds dived into the night.

In spite of my conviction, a moment before, of the innocence of the Baluchi gendarme, the hesitant thought crossed my mind: Now he has gone to the bandits; Ali Agha was right, after all ... I heard Ali Agha draw back the safety-catch of his pistol and I did the same. Ibrahim slowly unslung his carbine. We sat motionless in our saddles. One of the dromedaries grunted softly, a gendarme's rifle butt struck against a saddle. Long minutes passed. You could almost hear the breathing of the men. Then, abruptly, a shout came from a great distance. To me it sounded merely like, '*Ooo*,' but the Baluchis seemed to understand it and one of them, cupping his hands to his mouth, excitedly shouted something back in the Brahui tongue. Again that distant shout. One of the gendarmes turned toward Ali Agha and said in Persian:

'The wire, *hazrat!* He has found the wire!'

The tension broke. Relieved, we followed the voice of the invisible scout directing us from time to time. When we reached him, he rose in his saddle and pointed into the darkness:

'There is the wire.'

And rightly, after a few moments we almost struck against a telegraph post.

The first thing Ali Agha did was very characteristic of him. He caught the soldier by his belt, drew him close to himself and, learning over the saddle, kissed him on both cheeks:

'It is I, and not thou, who is a son of a dog, my brother. Forgive me ...'

It subsequently transpired that the Baluchi, this child of the wilderness, had been riding in a zigzag until he heard from a distance of half a mile the wind hum in the wire: a humming that was even now, when I passed directly under it, almost imperceptible to my European ears ...

We proceeded slowly, cautiously, through the black night, from invisible telegraph pole to invisible telegraph pole, one of the gendarmes always riding ahead and calling out each time his hand struck a pole. We had found our way and were determined not to lose it again.

.   .   .   .

I AWAKEN FROM MY REVERIE and return to Ali Agha's letter:

With the promotion to lieutenant colonel, this humble individual has been appointed to the General Staff; and this, O beloved friend and brother, appeals to us more than garrison life in a provincial town . . .

I am sure it does; Ali Agha has always had a flair for life in the capital and its intrigues – especially political intrigues. And, indeed, in his letter he goes on to describe the political atmosphere of Tehran, those endless wranglings under the surface, those intricate manoeuvrings with which foreign powers have for so long managed to keep Iran in a state of restlessness that makes it well-nigh impossible for the strange, gifted nation to come into its own.

Right now we are being harassed by the English oil company; great pressure is being exerted upon our Government to extend the concession and thus to prolong our slavery. The bazaars are buzzing with rumours, and God alone knows where all this will lead to . . .

The bazaar has always played a most important role in the political life of Eastern countries; and this is particularly true of the Tehran bazaar, in which the hidden heart of Iran pulsates with a persistence that defies all national decay and all passing of time. Between the lines of Ali Agha's letter this huge bazaar, almost a city in itself, reappears before my eyes with the vividness of a sight seen only yesterday: a wide-meshed twilight labyrinth of halls and passageways roofed with vaults of pointed arches. In the main street, next to small, dark booths filled with cheap trifles, there are covered patios with skylights, stores in which the

most expensive European and Asiatic silks are being sold; next
to ropemakers' workshops, the glass cases of the silversmiths full
of delicate filigree work; multicoloured textiles from Bokhara
and India mingle with rare Persian carpets – hunting carpets
with figures of knights on horseback, lions, leopards, peacocks
and antelopes; glass-pearl necklaces and automatic lighters next
to sewing machines; black, unhappy umbrellas side by side with
yellow-embroidered sheepskin robes from Khorasan: all assembled in this extremely long hall as if in an immense and not
too carefully arranged shop window.

In the innumerable side-lanes of this tangled maze of handi-
crafts and commerce, the shops are grouped according to trades.
Here you see the long line of saddlers and leatherworkers, with
the red of dyed leather as the dominant colour and the sourish
smell of leather permeating the air. There are the tailors: and
from every niche – for most of the shops consist only of a single
raised niche with about three or four square yards of floor space
– one hears the whirring of industrious sewing machines; long
garments are hung out for sale, always the same garments – so
that when you walk you sometimes think that you are standing
still. You have a similar impression in many other parts of the
bazaar as well; none the less, the abundance of sameness at every
single point has nothing in common with monotony; it intoxi-
cates the stranger and fills him with uneasy satisfaction. Even
though you visit the bazaar for the hundredth time, you find the
mood around you always the same, seemingly unchanged – but
of that inexhaustible, vibrating changelessness of an ocean wave
which always alters its forms but keeps its substance unchanged.

The bazaar of the coppersmiths: a chorus of bronze bells are
the swinging hammers which beat out of copper, bronze and
brass the most varied shapes, transforming formless metal sheets
into bowls and basins and goblets. What an acoustic sureness,
this hammering in altering tempos across the whole length of the
bazaar – every man acquiescing to the rhythm of the others – so
that there should be no dissonance to the ear: a hundred work-
men hammering on different objects in different shops – but in
the whole bazaar street only one melody . . . In this deep, more
than merely musical, almost social desire for harmony appears the
hidden grace of the Iranian soul.

The spice bazaar: silent alleys of white sugar cones, rice bags, mounds of almonds and pistachios, hazelnuts and melon kernels, basins full of dried apricots and ginger, brass plates with cinnamon, curry, pepper, saffron and poppy seeds, the many little bowls of aniseed, vanilla, cummin, cloves and countless odd herbs and roots which exude a heavy, overpowering aroma. Over the shining brass scales crouch the lords of these strangenesses, like buddhas, with crossed legs, from time to time calling out in an undertone to a passerby and asking after his wants. All speech is only whisper here: for one cannot be noisy where sugar flows smoothly from bag into balance scale, and one cannot be noisy where thyme or aniseed is being weighed . . . It is the same adaptation to the mood of the material which enables the Iranian to knot noble carpets out of innumerable coloured wool threads – thread by thread, fraction of an inch by fraction of an inch – until the whole stands there in its playful perfection. It is no accident that Persian carpets have no equal in the world. Where else could one find this deep quiet, this thoughtfulness and absorption in one's own doing? – where else such eyes, dark depths to which time and the passing of time mean so little?

In cavernous niches, somewhat larger than the usual ones, sit silent miniature painters. They are copying old miniatures from hand-written books that have long ago been torn to shreds, depicting in breath-fine lines and colours the great things of life: fights and hunts, love and happiness and sadness. Fine and thin as nerve-threads are their brushes; the colours are not entrusted to lifeless vessels but are mixed on the living palm of the painter and distributed in minute blobs and drops on the fingers of the left hand. On new pages of flawless whiteness the old miniatures experience a rebirth, stroke after stroke, shade after shade. Side by side with the flaking gold backgrounds of the originals emerge the shining ones of the copies. The faded orange trees of a royal park blossom again in a new spring; the tender women in silks and furs repeat once again their loving gestures; anew rises the sun over an old knightly polo game . . . Stroke after stroke, shade after shade, the silent men follow the creative adventures of a dead artist, and there is as much love in them as there was enchantment in him; and this love makes you almost forget the imperfection of the copies . . .

Time passes, and the miniature painters sit bent over their work, strangers unto the day. Time passes; in the bazaar streets nearby Western junk penetrates with stubborn gradualness into the shops; the kerosene lamp from Chicago, the printed cotton cloth from Manchester and the teapot from Czechoslovakia advance victoriously: but the miniature painters sit cross-legged on their worn straw mats, burrowing with tender eyes and fingertips into the blissful old joys, and give to their royal hunts and ecstatic lovers a new awakening, day after day . . .

Numberless are the people in the bazaar: gents with European collar and often trailing Arabian *abaya* over a European or semi-European suit, conservative burghers in long *kaftans* and silken sashes, peasants and artisans in blue or drab jackets. Singing dervishes – Iran's aristocratic beggars – in white, flowing garments, sometimes with a leopard skin over the back, long hair and mostly of fine build. The women of the middle class are, according to their means, dressed in silk or cotton, but always in black, with the traditional short Tehran veil standing stiffly away from their faces; the poorer ones wear a light-coloured flowered cotton wrap. Ancient mullahs ride on magnificently caparisoned asses or mules and turn upon the stranger a fanatical stare that seems to ask: 'What are *you* doing here? Are you one of those who work for our country's ruin?'

Iran's long experience of Western intrigues has made its people suspicious. No Iranian really expects any good to come to his country from the *farangis*. But Ali Agha does not seem to be unduly pessimistic:

Iran is old – but certainly not yet ready to die. We have often been oppressed. Many nations have swept over us, and all of them have passed away: but we remain alive. In poverty and oppression, in ignorance and darkness: but we remain alive. This is because we Iranians always go our own way. How often has the outside world tried to force on us new ways of life – and has always failed. We do not oppose outer forces with violence, and therefore it may sometimes appear as if we had surrendered to them. But we are of the tribe of the muryune – *that little, insignificant ant which lives under walls. You, light of my heart, must have seen sometimes in Iran how well-built houses with strong walls suddenly collapse for no apparent reason. What was the reason? Nothing but those tiny ants which for many years, with unceasing industry, have been burrowing passages and cavities in the foundations, always advancing by a hair's breadth, slowly, patiently, in all directions – until at last the wall loses its balance and topples over. We Iranians are such ants. We do not oppose the powers of the world with noisy and useless violence, but allow them to do their worst, and burrow in silence our passageways and cavities, until one day their building will suddenly collapse . . .*

And have you seen what happens when you throw a stone into water? The stone sinks, a few circles appear on the surface, spread out and gradually fade away, until the water is as placid as before. We Iranians are such water.

The Shah, may God prolong his life, has a heavy burden to bear, with the English on one side and the Russians on the other. But we have no doubt that, by the grace of God, he will find a way to save Iran . . .

Ali Agha's implicit faith in Riza Shah does not, on the surface, appear to be misplaced. He is undoubtedly one of the most dynamic personalities I have ever met in the Muslim world, and of all the kings I have known, only Ibn Saud can compare with him.

The story of Riza Shah's rise to power is like a fantastic fairy tale, possible only in this Eastern world where personal courage and willpower can sometimes lift a man out of utter obscurity to the pinnacle of leadership. When I came to know him during my first stay in Tehran in the summer of 1924, he was Prime Minister and undisputed dictator of Iran; but the people had not yet quite overcome their shock at seeing him appear so suddenly, so unexpectedly, at the helm of the country's affairs. I still remember the wonderment with which an old Iranian clerk in the German Embassy at Tehran once told me: 'Do you know that but ten years ago this Prime Minister of ours stood guard as an ordinary trooper before the gates of this very embassy? And that I myself occasionally gave him a letter to deliver to the Foreign Ministry and admonished him, "Make haste, you son of a dog, and don't dawdle in the bazaar . . . !" '

Yes, it had not been so many years since Riza the trooper stood sentry before the embassies and public buildings of Tehran. I could picture him as he stood there in the shabby uniform of the Iranian cossack brigade, leaning on his rifle and gazing at the activity in the streets around him. He would watch Persian people stroll along like dreamy shadows or sit in the cool of evening along the water channels, as I watched them. And from the English bank behind his back he would hear the rattling of typewriters, the bustle of busy people, the whole rustling stir which distant Europe had brought into that Tehran building with its blue faïence façade. It may have been then, for the first time (nobody told me this, but I somehow think it must have been so), that in the unschooled head of the soldier Riza a wondering, questioning thought arose: 'Must it be like this . . . ? Must it be that people of other nations work and strive, while our life flows past like a dream?'

And it was perhaps at that moment that desire for change – creator of all great deeds, discoveries and revolutions – began to flicker in his brain and mutely call for expression . . .

At other times he may have stood sentry before the garden gateway of one of the great European embassies. The well-tended trees moved with the wind, and the gravelled pathways crunched under the feet of white-garbed servants. In that house in the midst of the park a mysterious power seemed to dwell; it cowed every Iranian who passed through the gate and caused him to straighten his clothes self-consciously and made his hands embarrassed and awkward. Sometimes elegant carriages drew up and Iranian politicians stepped out of them. The soldier Riza knew many of them by sight: this one was the foreign minister, that one the finance minister. Almost always they had tense, apprehensive faces when they entered that gateway, and it was amusing to observe their expressions when they left the embassy: sometimes they were radiant, as if a great favour had been conferred upon them; sometimes pale and depressed, as if a sentence of doom had just been passed over them. Those mysterious people within had pronounced the sentence. The soldier Riza wondered: 'Must it be thus . . . ?'

Occasionally it happened that an Iranian clerk came running from the office building Riza was guarding, thrust a letter into his hand and said: 'Carry this quickly to so and so. But make haste, thou son of a dog, otherwise the Ambassador will be angry!' Riza was accustomed to being thus addressed, for his own officers were not in the least fastidious in their choice of epithets. But possibly – no, almost certainly – the words 'son of a dog' gave him a stab of humiliation, for he knew: he was not a

son of a dog but the son of a great nation that called names like
Rustam, Darius, Nushirwan, Kay Khosru, Shah Abbas, Nadir
Shah its own. But what did 'those within' know of this? What
did they know of the forces which moved like a dark, dumb
stream through the breast of the forty-year-old soldier and sometimes threatened to burst his ribs and make him bite his fists in
powerless despair, 'Oh, if only I could . . .'?

And the desire for self-affirmation that weepingly dwells in
every Iranian sometimes rose up with painful, unexpected
violence in the soldier Riza, and made his mind clear and made
him suddenly understand a strange pattern in all he saw . . .

The Great War was over. After the Bolshevik revolution, the
Russian troops which had previously occupied northern Iran
were withdrawn; but immediately afterward communist upheavals broke out in the Iranian province of Gilan on the
Caspian Sea, led by the influential Kuchuk Khan and supported
by regular Russian units on land and sea. The government sent
out troops against the rebels, but the badly disciplined and
poorly equipped Iranian soldiers suffered defeat after defeat;
and the battalion in which Sergeant Riza, then nearly fifty years
old, was serving proved no exception. But once, when his unit
turned to flight after an unlucky skirmish, Riza could not hold
himself any longer. He stepped from the breaking ranks and
called out, for everyone to hear: 'Why do you run away,
Iranians – you, Iranians!' He must have felt what Charles the
Twelfth of Sweden had felt when he lay wounded on the field of
Poltava and saw his soldiers race by in headless flight and called
out to them with a despairing voice: 'Why do you run away,
Swedes – you Swedes!' But the difference was that King Charles
was bleeding from many wounds and had nothing at his disposal except his voice, while the soldier Riza was unhurt and
had a loaded Mauser pistol in his hand – and his voice was
strong and threatening as he warned his comrades: 'Whoever
flees, I will shoot him down – even if it is my brother!'

Such an outburst was something new to the Iranian troops.
Their confusion gave way to astonishment. They became
curious: what could this man have in mind? Some officers protested and pointed out the hopelessness of their position; and
one of them scoffed: 'Will *you*, perhaps, lead us to victory?' In
that second, Riza may have relived all the disappointments of

his earlier years, and all his dumb hopes were suddenly lighted up. He saw the end of a magic rope before him; and he grasped it. 'Accepted!' he cried, and turned to the soldiers: 'Will you have me as your leader?'

In no nation is the cult of the hero so deeply ingrained as in the Iranian; and this man here seemed to be a hero. The soldiers forgot their terror and their flight and roared with jubilation: '*You* shall be our leader!' – 'So be it,' replied Riza, 'I will lead you; and I will kill whosoever attempts to flee!' But no one thought any longer of flight. They threw away the cumbersome knapsacks, attached their bayonets to their rifles: and under Riza's leadership the whole battalion turned round and captured a Russian battery in a surprise assault, drew other Iranian units with it, overran the enemy – and after a few hours the battle was decided in favour of the Iranians.

Some days later a telegram from Tehran promoted Riza to the rank of captain; and he could now affix the title *khan* to his name.

He had got hold of the end of the rope and climbed up on it. His name had suddenly become famous. In quick succession he became major, colonel, brigadier. In the year 1921 he brought about, in company with the young journalist Zia ad-Din and three other officers, a *coup d'état*, arrested the corrupt cabinet and, with the help of his devoted brigade, forced the weak and insignificant young Shah Ahmad to appoint a new cabinet: Zia ad-Din became Prime Minister, Riza Khan Minister of War. He could neither read nor write. But he was like a demon in his drive for power. And he had become the idol of the army and the people, who now, for the first time in ages, saw a man before them: a leader.

In the political history of Iran scenes change quickly. Zia ad-Din disappeared from the stage and reappeared as an exile in Europe. Riza Khan remained – as Prime Minister. It was rumoured in Tehran in those days that Riza Khan, Zia ad-Din and the Shah's younger brother, the Crown Prince, had conspired to remove the Shah from the throne; and it was whispered – nobody knows to this day whether it is true – that at the last moment Riza Khan had betrayed his friends to the Shah in order not to risk his own future in so dubious an undertaking. But whether true or not, soon afterward the Prime Minister – Riza Khan – advised the young Shah Ahmad to undertake a pleasure trip to Europe. He accompanied him with great pomp on the automobile journey to the border of Iraq and is said to have told him: 'If your Majesty ever returns to Iran, you will be able to say that Riza Khan understands nothing of the world.'

He no longer needed to share his power with anyone; he was, in fact if not in name, the sole overlord of Iran. Like a hungry wolf, he threw himself into work. All Iran was to be reformed from top to bottom. The hitherto loose administration was centralized; the old system of farming out entire provinces to the highest bidder was abolished; the governors ceased to be satraps and became officials. The army, the dictator's pet child, was reorganized on Western patterns. Riza Khan started campaigns against unruly tribal chieftains who had previously regarded themselves as little kings and often refused to obey the Tehran government; he dealt harshly with the bandits who for many decades had terrorized the countryside. Some order was brought into the finances of the country with the assistance of an American adviser; taxes and customs began to flow in regularly. Order was brought out of chaos.

As if echoing the Turkish Kemalist movement, the idea of a republic emerged in Iran, first as a rumour, then as a demand of the more progressive elements of the populace – and finally as the open aim of the dictator himself. But here Riza Khan seems to have committed an error of judgment: a powerful cry of protest arose from the Iranian masses.

This popular opposition to republican tendencies was not due to any love of the reigning house, for nobody in Iran had much affection for the Qajar dynasty which – because of its Turkoman origin – had always been regarded as 'foreign'; nor was it due to any sentimental predilection for the round, boyish face of Shah Ahmad. It was something quite different: it was prompted by the people's fear of losing their religion as the Turks had lost theirs in the wake of Ataturk's revolution. In their ignorance, the Iranians did not understand all at once that a republican form of government would correspond much more closely to the Islamic scheme of life than a monarchial one; guided by the conservatism of their religious leaders – and perhaps justifiably frightened by Riza Khan's obvious admiration of Kemal Ataturk – the Iranians sensed in his proposal only a threat to Islam as the dominant force in the country.

A great excitement took hold of the urban population, especially in Tehran. A furious mob, armed with sticks and stones, assembled before Riza Khan's office building and uttered curses and threats against the dictator who but yesterday had been a demigod. Riza Khan's aides urgently advised him not to go out before the excitement subsided; but he brushed them aside and, accompanied by only one orderly and entirely unarmed, left the office compound in a closed carriage. As soon as the carriage emerged from the gates, the mob seized the horses' reins and brought them to a standstill. Some people tore the carriage door open – 'Drag him out, drag him out into the street!' But already he was getting out himself, his face livid with rage, and began to beat the heads and shoulders of those about him with his riding crop: 'You sons of dogs, away from me, away! How dare you! I am Riza Khan! Away to your women and your beds!' And the raging crowd, which had been threatening death and destruction but a few minutes ago, became silent under the impact of his personal courage; they drew back, melted away, one by one, and disappeared in the side-alleys. Once again a great leader had spoken to his people; he had spoken in anger, and the people were cowed. It may have been at that moment that a feeling of contempt broke through Riza Khan's love for his people, and clouded it forever.

But in spite of Riza Khan's prestige success, the republic did not materialize. The debacle of this plan made it obvious that military power alone could not bring about a 'reform movement' in the face of the people's resistance. Not that the Iranians were opposed to reform as such: but they instinctively realized that an imported, Western political doctrine would mean the end of all hope of ever attaining to a healthy development within the context of their own culture and religion.

Riza Khan did not understand this, then or ever, and thus became estranged from his people. Their love for him vanished and a fearful hatred gradually took its place. They began to ask themselves: What has the hero really done for his country? They enumerated Riza Khan's achievements: the reorganization of the army – but at the price of tremendous costs which placed crushing tax burdens on the already impoverished people; the suppressed tribal rebellions – but also the suppressed patriots: showy building activity in Tehran – but ever-growing misery among the peasants in the countryside. People began to remember that but a few years ago Riza Khan had been a poor soldier – and now he was the richest man in Iran, with innumerable acres of land to his name. Were these the 'reforms' about which so much had been spoken? Did the few glittering office buildings in Tehran and the luxury hotels which had sprung up here and there under the dictator's influence really represent any betterment of the people's lot?

. . . .

IT WAS AT THIS STAGE of his career that I came to know Riza Khan. Whatever the rumours about his personal ambition and alleged selfishness, I could not fail to recognize the man's greatness from the moment he first received me in his office at the War Ministry. It was probably the simplest office occupied anywhere, at any time, by a prime minister: a desk, a sofa covered with black oilcloth, a couple of chairs, a small bookshelf and a bright but modest carpet on the floor were all that the room contained; and the tall, heavy-set man in his middle fifties who rose from behind the desk was attired in a plain khaki uniform without any medals, ribbons or badges of rank.

I had been introduced by the German Ambassador, Count von der Schulenburg (for although I was Austrian myself, I represented a great German newspaper). Even during that first, formal conversation I became aware of the sombre dynamism of Riza Khan's nature. From under grey, bushy brows a pair of sharp, brown eyes regarded me – Persian eyes that were usually veiled by heavy lids: a strange mixture of melancholy and hardness. There were bitter lines around his nose and mouth, but the heavy-boned features betrayed an uncommon power of will which kept the lips compressed and filled the jaw with tension. When you listened to his low and well-modulated voice – the voice of a man accustomed to speak words of importance and to weigh each of them on his tongue before it was permitted to become sound – you thought you were listening to a man with a thirty-year career of staff officer and high dignitary behind him: and you could hardly believe that it was only six years since Riza Khan had been a sergeant, and only three since he had learned to read and write.

He must have sensed my interest in him – and perhaps also

my affection for his people – for he insisted that this interview should not be the last, and asked me, as well as Schulenburg, to tea next week at his summer residence at Shemran, the beautiful garden resort some miles out of Tehran.

I arranged with Schulenburg to come first to him (like most of the other foreign representatives, he also was spending the summer in Shemran) and to go together to the Prime Minister's residence. But as it happened, I was unable to arrive in time. A few days earlier I had purchased a small four-wheeled hunting carriage with two spirited horses. How spirited they were became fully obvious a few miles outside Tehran, when, following some wicked impulse, they obstinately refused to go ahead and insisted on returning home. For about twenty minutes I struggled with them; in the end, I let Ibrahim take horses and carriage home and set out on foot in search of some other means of transportation. A tramp of two miles brought me to a village where I fortunately found a *droshky*, but when I arrived at the German Embassy, it was about an hour and a half after the appointed time. I found Schulenburg pacing up and down his study like an angry tiger, with all his usual suavity gone: for to his Prussian-*cum*-ambassadorial sense of discipline, such an offence against punctuality seemed no less than blasphemy. At my sight he exploded with indignation:

'You can't – you can't do that to a prime minister! Have you forgotten that Riza Khan is a dictator and, like all dictators, extremely touchy?'

'My horses seem to have overlooked this fine point, Count Schulenburg,' was my only reply. 'Even if it had been the Emperor of China, I would not have been able to arrive any earlier.'

At that the Count recovered his sense of humour and broke out into loud laughter:

'By God, such a thing has never happened to me before! Let's go then – and hope that the footman doesn't slam the door in our faces . . .'

He did not. When we arrived at Riza Khan's palace the tea party was long over and all the other guests had departed, but the dictator did not appear in the least offended by my breach of protocol. Upon hearing the reasons for our delay, he exclaimed:

'Well, I would like to see these horses of yours! I think they must belong to the opposition party. I don't know whether it might not be wise to have them placed in police custody!'

If anything, my *contretemps* rather helped than hindered the establishment of an easy, informal relationship between the all-powerful Prime Minister of Iran and the young journalist, which later made it possible for me to move about the country with a freedom greater than that accorded to most other foreigners.

.   .   .   .

BUT ALI AGHA'S LETTER does not refer to the Riza Khan of those early days, the man who lived with a simplicity almost un-believable in display-loving Iran: it refers to Riza Shah Pahlavi, who ascended the Peacock Throne in 1925; it refers to the king who has given up all pretence of humility and now seeks to emulate Kemal Ataturk in building a vainglorious Western façade onto his ancient Eastern land . . .

I come to the end of the letter:

Although you, beloved friend, are now in the blessed City of the Holy Prophet, we trust you have not forgotten nor ever will forget your unworthy friend and his country . . .

O Ali Agha, friend of my younger days –'light of my heart', as you yourself would phrase it – your letter has made me drunk with remembrance: Persia-drunk as I became when I began to know your country, that old, dim jewel set in a setting of ancient gold and cracked marble and dust and shadows – the shadows of all the days and nights of your melancholy country and of the dark, dreaming eyes of your people . . .

I still remember Kirmanshah, the first Iranian town I saw after I left the mountains of Kurdistan. A strange, faded, opaque atmosphere lay about it, muffled, subdued – not to say shabby. No doubt, in every Eastern city poverty lies close to the surface, much more visible than in any European city – but to that I was already accustomed. It was not just poverty in an economic sense which thrust itself upon me, for Kirmanshah was said to be a prosperous town. It was rather a kind of depression that lay over the people, something that was directly connected with them and seemed to have hardly anything to do with economic circumstances.

All these people had large, black eyes under thick, black brows that often met over the bridge of the nose, weighted by heavy lids like veils. Most of the men were slim (I hardly remember having seen a fat man in Iran); they never laughed aloud, and in their silent smiles lurked a faint irony which seemed to conceal more than it revealed. No mobility of features, no gesticulations, only quiet, measured movements: as if they wore masks.

As in all Eastern cities, the life of the town was concentrated in the bazaar. It revealed itself to the stranger as a subdued mixture of brown, gold-brown and carpet-red, with shimmering copper plates and basins here and there and perhaps a blue majolica painting over the door of a caravanserai with figures of black-eyed knights and winged dragons. If you looked more carefully, you could discover in this bazaar all the colours of the world – but none of these variegated colours could ever quite assert itself in the unifying shadows of the vaults that covered the bazaar and drew everything together into a sleepy duskiness. The pointed arches of the vaulted roof were pierced at regular intervals by small openings to let in the daylight. Through these openings the rays of the sun fell in; in the aromatic air of the halls they gained the quality of a substance and resembled opaque, slanted pillars of light; and not the people seemed to go through them but they, the shining pillars, seemed to go through the shadowy people . . .

For the people in this bazaar were gentle and silent like shadows. If a trader called out to the passerby, he did so in a low voice; none of them praised his wares with calls and songs, as is the custom in Arabian bazaars. On soft soles life threaded its way here. The people did not elbow or shove one another. They were polite – with a politeness which seemed to bend forward to you but in reality held you at arm's length. They were obviously shrewd and did not mind starting a conversation with the stranger – but only their lips were talking. Their souls stood somewhere in the background, waiting, weighing, detached . . .

In a teahouse some men of the working class sat on straw mats – perhaps artisans, labourers, caravan drivers – huddled together around an iron basin filled with glowing coals. Two long-stemmed pipes with round porcelain bowls made the round. The sweetish smell of opium was in the air. They smoked wordlessly; each man took only a few deep draughts at a time, passing the pipe on to his neighbour. And then I saw what I had not observed before: many, very many people were smoking opium, some of them more and others less publicly. The shopkeeper in his niche; the loafer under the arched gateway of a caravanserai; the coppersmith in his workshop during a moment of respite: they all were smoking with the same withdrawn, somewhat tired face, gazing with dull eyes into a spaceless void . . .

Fresh, green poppies with thick buds were being sold by vendors all over the bazaar and apparently consumed in this way – another, milder form of taking opium. Even children were eating the seeds in doorways and corners. Two, three of them would divide the delicacy among themselves with an old-age tolerance toward each other, without childish egoism – but also without childish joy or vivacity. But how could they have been otherwise? In their earliest life they were given a heavy brew of poppy seeds to drink whenever they cried and bothered their parents. When they grew up and began to roam the streets, the borderlines of quietude, lassitude and kindness were already blurred in them.

And then I knew what had moved me so strongly when I first beheld the melancholy eyes of the Iranians: the sign of a tragic destiny in them. I felt that the opium belonged to them in the same way as a suffering smile belongs to the face of a sufferer; it belonged to their gentleness, to their inner lassitude – it belonged even to their great poverty and great frugality. It did not seem to be so much vice as expression – and perhaps also help. Help against what? Strange land of questions . . .

．　　　．　　　．　　　．　　　．　　　．　　　．　　　．

MY MIND DWELLS SO LONG on my impressions of Kirmanshah, the first Iranian city I came to know, because those impressions continued, in varying forms but always unchanged in substance, throughout the year and a half that I remained in Iran. A soft, pervasive melancholy was the dominant note everywhere. It was perceptible in villages and towns, in the daily doings of the people and in their many religious festivals. Indeed, their religious feeling itself, so unlike that of the Arabs, bore a strong tinge of sadness and mourning: to weep over the tragic happenings of thirteen centuries ago – to weep over the deaths of Ali, the Prophet's son-in-law, and Ali's two sons, Hasan and Husayn – seemed to them more important than to consider

The Grand Sanusi

what Islam stood for and what direction it wanted to give to men's lives . . .

On many evenings, in many towns, you could see groups of men and women assembled in a street around a wandering dervish, a religious mendicant clad in white, with a panther skin on his back, a long-stemmed axe in his right hand and an alms-bowl carved from a coconut in his left. He would recite a half-sung, half-spoken ballad about the struggles for succession to the Caliphate that followed the death of the Prophet in the seventh century – a mournful tale of faith and blood and death – and it would always run somewhat like this:

Listen, O people, to what befell God's chosen ones, and how the blood of the Prophet's seed was spilled over the earth.

There was once a Prophet whom God had likened unto a City of Knowledge; and the Gate to that City was the most trusted and valiant of his followers, his son-in-law Ali, Light of the World, sharer of the Prophet's Message, called the Lion of God.

When the Prophet passed away, the Lion of God was his rightful successor. But wicked men usurped the Lion's God-ordained right and made another the Prophet's khalifa; *and after the first usurper's death, another of his evil ilk succeeded him; and after him, yet another.*

And only after the third usurper perished did the Will of God become manifest, and the Lion of God attained to this rightful place as Commander of the Faithful.

But Ali's and God's enemies were many; and one day, when he lay prostrated before his Lord in prayer, an assassin's sword struck him dead. The earth shook in anguish at the blasphemous deed, and and the mountains wept and the stones shed tears.

Oh, God's curse be upon the evildoers, and may everlasting punishment consume them!

And again an evil usurper came to the fore and denied the Lion of God's sons, Hasan and Husayn, sons of Fatima the Blessed, their right of succession to the Prophet's Throne. Hasan was foully poisoned; and when Husayn rose in defence of the Faith, his beautiful life was extinguished on the field of Karbala as he knelt down by a pool of water to quench his thirst after the battle.

Oh, God's curse be upon the evildoers, and may the angels' tears forever water the sacred soil of Karbala!

The head of Husayn – the head the Prophet had once kissed – was cruelly cut off and his headless body was brought back to the tent where his weeping children awaited their father's return.

And ever since, the Faithful have invoked God's curse on the transgressors and wept over the deaths of Ali and Hasan and Husayn; and you, O Faithful, raise your voices in lament for their deaths – for God forgives the sins of those who weep for the Seed of the Prophet . . .

And the chanted ballad would bring forth passionate sobbing from the listening women, while silent tears would roll over the faces of bearded men . . .

Such extravagant 'laments' were a far cry indeed from the true, historical picture of those early happenings that had caused a never-healed schism in the world of Islam: the division of the Muslim community into Sunnites, who form the bulk of the Muslim peoples and stand firm on the principle of an *elective* succession to the Caliphate, and the Shiites, who maintain that the Prophet designated Ali, his son-in-law, as his rightful heir and successor. In reality, however, the Prophet died without nominating any successor, whereupon one of his oldest and most faithful Companions, Abu Bakr, was elected *khalifa* by the overwhelming majority of the community. Abu Bakr was succeeded by Umar and the latter by Uthman; and only after Uthman's death was Ali elected to the Caliphate. There was, as I knew well even in my Iranian days, nothing evil or wicked about Ali's three predecessors. They were undoubtedly the greatest and noblest figures of Islamic history after the Prophet, and had for many years been among his most intimate Companions; and they were certainly not 'usurpers', having been elected by the people in the free exercise of the right accorded to them by Islam. It was not their assumption of power but rather Ali's and his followers' unwillingness to accept wholeheartedly the results of those popular elections that led to the subsequent struggles for power, to Ali's death, and to the transformation – under the fifth Caliph, Mu'awiyya – of the original, republican form of the Islamic State into a hereditary kingship, and, ultimately, to Husayn's death at Karbala.

Yes, I had known all this before I came to Iran; but here I was struck by the boundless emotion which that old, tragic tale of thirteen centuries ago could still arouse among the Iranian people whenever the names of Ali, Hasan or Husayn were mentioned. I began to wonder: Was it the innate melancholy of the Iranians and their sense of the dramatic that had caused them to embrace the *Shia* doctrine? – or was it the tragic quality of the latter's origin that had led to this intense Iranian melancholy?

By degrees, over a number of months, a startling answer took shape in my mind.

When, in the middle of the seventh century, the armies of Caliph Umar conquered the ancient Sasanian Empire, bringing Islam with them, Iran's Zoroastrian cult had already long been reduced to rigid formalism and was thus unable to oppose effectively the dynamic new idea that had come from Arabia. But at the time when the Arab conquest burst upon it, Iran was passing through a period of social and intellectual ferment which seemed to promise a national regeneration. This hope of an inner, organic revival was shattered by the Arab invasion; and the Iranians, abandoning their own historic line of development, henceforth accommodated themselves to the cultural and ethical concepts that had been brought in from outside.

The advent of Islam represented in Iran, as in so many other countries, a tremendous social advance; it destroyed the old Iranian caste system and brought into being a new community of free, equal people; it opened new channels for cultural energies that had long lain dormant and inarticulate: but with all this, the proud descendants of Darius and Xerxes could never forget that the historical continuity of their national life, the organic connection between their Yesterday and Today, had suddenly been broken. A people whose innermost character had found its expression in the baroque dualism of the Zand religion and its almost pantheistic worship of the four elements – air, water, fire and earth – was now faced with Islam's austere, uncompromising monotheism and its passion for the Absolute. The transition was too sharp and painful to allow the Iranians to subordinate their deeply rooted national consciousness to the supranational concept of Islam. In spite of their speedy and apparently voluntary acceptance of the new religion, they subconsciously equated the victory of the Islamic idea with Iran's national defeat; and the feeling of having been defeated and irrevocably torn out of the context of their ancient cultural heritage – a feeling desperately intense for all its vagueness – was destined to corrode their national self-confidence for centuries to come. Unlike so many other nations to whom the acceptance of Islam gave almost immediately a most positive impulse to further cultural development, the Iranians' first – and, in a way, most durable – reaction to it was one of deep humiliation and repressed resentment.

That resentment *had* to be repressed and smothered in the dark folds of the subconscious, for in the meantime Islam had become Iran's own faith. But in their hatred of the Arabian conquest, the Iranians instinctively resorted to what psychoanalysis describes as 'overcompensation': they began to regard the faith brought to them by their Arabian conquerors as something that was exclusively their own. They did it by subtly transforming the rational, unmystical God-consciousness of the Arabs into its very opposite: mystical fanaticism and sombre emotion. A faith which to the Arab was presence and reality and a source of composure and freedom, evolved, in the Iranian mind, into a dark longing for the supernatural and symbolic. The Islamic principle of God's ungraspable transcendency was transfigured into the mystical doctrine (for which there were many precedents in pre-Islamic Iran) of God's physical manifestation in especially chosen mortals who would transmit this divine essence to their descendants. To such a tendency, an espousal of the *Shia* doctrine offered a most welcome channel: for there could be no doubt that the Shiite veneration, almost deification, of Ali and his descendants concealed the germ of the idea of God's incarnation and continual reincarnation – an idea entirely alien to Islam but very close to the Iranian heart.

It had been no accident that the Prophet Muhammad died without having nominated a successor and, indeed, refused to nominate one when a suggestion to that effect was made shortly before his death. By his attitude he intended to convey, firstly, that the spiritual quality of Prophethood was not something that could be 'inherited', and, secondly, that the future leadership of the community should be the outcome of free election by the people themselves and not of an 'ordination' by the Prophet (which would naturally have been implied in his designation of a successor): and thus he deliberately ruled out the idea that the community's leadership could ever be anything but secular or could be in the nature of an 'apostolic succession'. But this was precisely what the *Shia* doctrine aimed at. It not only insisted – in clear contradiction to the spirit of Islam – on the principle of apostolic succession, but reserved that succession exclusively to 'the Prophet's seed', that is, to his cousin and son-in-law Ali and his lineal descendants.

This was entirely in tune with the mystical inclinations of the Iranians. But when they enthusiastically joined the camp of those who claimed that Muhammad's spiritual essence lived on in Ali and the latter's descendants, the Iranians did not merely satisfy a mystical desire: there was yet another, subconscious motivation for their choice. If Ali was the rightful heir and successor of the Prophet, the three Caliphs who preceded him must obviously have been usurpers – and among them had been Umar, that same Umar who had conquered Iran! The national hatred of the conqueror of the Sasanian Empire could now be rationalized in terms of religion – the religion that had become Iran's own: Umar had 'deprived' Ali and his sons Hasan and Husayn of their divinely ordained right of succession to the Caliphate of Islam and, thus, had opposed the will of God; consequently, in obedience to the will of God, Ali's party was to be supported. Out of a national antagonism, a religious doctrine was born.

In the Iranian enthronement of the *Shia* doctrine I discerned a mute protest against the Arabian conquest of Iran. Now I understood why the Iranians cursed Umar with a hatred far more bitter than that reserved for the other two 'usurpers', Abu Bakr and Uthman: from the doctrinal point of view, the first Caliph, Abu Bakr, should have been regarded as the principal transgressor – but it was Umar who had conquered Iran . . .

This, then, was the reason for the strange intensity with which the House of Ali was venerated in Iran. Its cult represented a symbolic act of Iranian revenge on Arabian Islam (which stood so uncompromisingly against the deification of any human personality including that of Muhammad). True, the *Shia* doctrine had not originated in Iran; there were Shiite groups in other Muslim lands as well: but nowhere else had it achieved so complete a hold over the people's emotions and imagination. When the Iranians gave passionate vent to their mourning over the deaths of Ali, Hasan and Husayn, they wept not merely over the destruction of the House of Ali but also over themselves and the loss of their ancient glory ...

.   .   .   .

THEY WERE A MELANCHOLY people, those Iranians. Their melancholy was reflected even in the Iranian landscape – in the endless stretches of fallow land, the lonely mountain paths and highways, the widely scattered villages of mud houses, the flocks of sheep which were driven in the evening in grey-brown waves to the well. In the cities life dripped in slow, incessant drops, without industry or gaiety; everything seemed to be shrouded in dreamy veils, and each face had a look of indolent waiting. One never heard music in the streets. If in the evening a Tatar stable boy broke into song in a caravanserai, one involuntarily pricked up one's ears in astonishment. Publicly only the many dervishes sang: and they always sang the same ancient, tragic ballads about Ali, Hasan and Husayn. Death and tears wove around those songs and went like heavy wine to the heads of the listeners. A terror of sadness, but of a willingly, almost greedily accepted sadness, seemed to lie over these people.

On summer evenings in Tehran you could see men and women crouching motionless by the watercourses that ran along both sides of the streets under the shadow of the huge elm trees. They sat and stared into the flowing water. They did not talk to one another. They only listened to the gurgling of the water and let the rustling of the tree branches pass over their heads. Whenever I saw them I had to think of David's psalm: *By the rivers of Babylon, there we sat down, yea, we wept ...*

They sat by the side of the watercourses like huge, dumb, dark birds, lost in silent contemplation of the flowing water. Were they thinking a long, long-drawn-out thought which belonged to them, and to them alone? Were they waiting? ... for what?

And David sang: *We hanged our harps upon the willows in the midst thereof ...*

— 3 —

'COME, ZAYD, let us go' – and I put Ali Agha's letter into my pocket and rise to say good-bye to Az-Zughaybi. But he shakes his head:

'No, brother, let Zayd stay here with me for a while. If thou art too niggardly to tell me all that has befallen thee during these past months, let him tell me the story in thy stead. Or dost thou think thy friends no longer care about what happens to thee?'

X
DAJJAL

ENTER THE winding alleys of the oldest part of Medina: house-walls of stone rooted in shadow, bay windows and balconies hanging over lanes that resemble gorges and are so narrow in places that two people can barely pass one another; and find myself before the grey stone façade of the library built about one hundred years ago by a Turkish scholar. In its courtyard, behind the forged bronze grill of the gate, an inviting silence. I cross the stone-flagged yard, past the single tree that stands with motionless branches in its middle, and step into the domed hall lined with glass-covered bookcases – thousands of hand-written books, among them some of the rarest manuscripts known to the Islamic world. It is books like these that have given glory to Islamic culture: a glory that has passed away like the wind of yesterday.

As I look at these books in their tooled-leather covers, the discrepancy between the Muslim Yesterday and Today strikes me like a painful blow . . .

'What ails thee, my son? Why this bitter look on thy face?'

I turn toward the voice – and behold, sitting on the carpet between one of the bay windows, a folio volume on his knees, the diminutive figure of my old friend, Shaykh Abdullah ibn Bulayhid. His sharp, ironical eyes greet me with a warm flicker as I kiss his forehead and sit down by his side. He is the greatest of all the *ulama* of Najd and, in spite of a certain doctrinaire narrowness peculiar to the Wahhabi outlook, one of the keenest minds I have ever met in Muslim countries. His friendship for me has contributed greatly to making my life in Arabia easy and pleasant, for in Ibn Saud's kingdom his word counts more than that of any other man except the King himself. He closes his book with a snap and draws me to himself, looking at me inquiringly.

'I was thinking, O Shaykh, how far we Muslims have travelled from this' – and I point toward the books on the shelves –'to our present misery and degradation.'

'My son,' answers the old man, 'we are but reaping what we have sown. Once we were great: and it was Islam that made us great. We were the bearers of a message. As long as we remained faithful to that message, our hearts were inspired and our minds illumined; but as soon as we forgot for what ends we had been chosen by the Almighty, we fell. We have travelled far away from this'– and the *shaykh* repeats my gesture toward the books –'because we have travelled far away from what the Prophet – may God bless him and give him peace – taught us thirteen centuries ago . . .'

'And how goes thy work?' he inquires after a pause; for he knows that I am engaged in studies connected with early Islamic history.

'I must confess, O Shaykh, not very well. I cannot find rest in my heart and do not know why. And so I have taken again to wandering in the desert.'

Ibn Bulayhid looks at me with smilingly squinting eyes – those wise, penetrating eyes – and twirls his henna-dyed beard: 'The mind will have its due and the body will have its due . . . Thou shouldst marry.'

I know, of course, that in Najd marriage is considered to be the solution for almost every sort of perplexity, and so I cannot hold back my laughter:

' But, Shaykh, thou art well aware that I have married again only two years ago, and this year a son has been born to me.'

The old man shrugs his shoulders: 'If a man's heart is at rest with his wife, he stays at home as much as he can. Thou dost not stay that much at home . . . And, moreover, it has never yet hurt a man to wed a second wife.' (He himself, in spite of his seventy years, has three at present, and I am told that the youngest one, whom he married only a couple of months ago, is barely sixteen years old.)

'It may be,' I rejoin, 'that it doesn't hurt a man to take a second wife; but what of the first wife? Does not her hurt matter as well?'

'My son: if a woman holds the whole of her man's heart, he will not think of, nor need, marrying another. But if his heart is not entirely with her – will she gain anything by keeping him thus half-heartedly to herself alone?'

There is certainly no answer to that. Islam recommends, to be sure, single marriages, but allows a man to marry up to four wives under exceptional circumstances. One might ask why the same latitude has not been given to woman as well; but the answer is simple. Notwithstanding the spiritual fact of love that has entered human life in the course of man's development, the underlying *biological* reason for the sexual urge is, in both sexes, procreation: and while a woman can, at one time, conceive a child from one man only and has to carry it for nine months before she is able to conceive another, man is so constituted that he may beget a child every time he embraces a woman. Thus, while nature would have been merely wasteful to produce a poly-gamous instinct in woman, man's undoubted polygamous in-clination is, from nature's point of view, biologically justified. It is, of course, obvious that the biological factor is only one – and by no means always the most important – of the aspects of love: none the less, it is a basic factor and, therefore, decisive in the social institution of marriage as such. With the wisdom that al-ways takes human nature fully into account, Islamic Law under-takes no more than the safeguarding of the socio-biological function of marriage (which includes, of course, care for the progeny as well), allowing a man to marry more than one wife and not allowing a woman to have more than one husband at one time; while the spiritual problem of marriage, being impon-derable and therefore outside the purview of law, is left to the discretion of the partners. Whenever love is full and complete, the question of another marriage naturally does not arise for either of them; whenever a husband does not love his wife with all his heart but still well enough not to want to lose her, he may take another wife, provided the first one is agreeable to thus sharing his affection; and if she cannot agree to this, she may obtain a divorce and is free to remarry. In any case – since marriage in Islam is not a sacrament but a civil contract – re-course to divorce is always open to either of the marriage part-ners, the more so as the stigma which elsewhere attaches to divorce with greater or lesser intensity is absent in Muslim society (with the possible exception of the Indian Muslims, who have been influenced in this respect by centuries of contact with Hindu society, in which divorce is utterly forbidden).

The freedom which Islamic Law accords to both men and women to contract or dissolve a marriage explains why it con-

siders adultery one of the most heinous of crimes: for in the face
of such latitude, no emotional or sensual entanglement can ever
serve as an excuse. It is true that in the centuries of Muslim decline, social custom has often made it difficult for a woman to
exercise her prerogative of divorce as freely as the Law-Giver
had intended: for this, however, not Islam but custom is to
blame – just as custom, and not Islamic Law, is to be blamed for
the seclusion in which woman has been kept for so long in so
many Muslim countries: for neither in the Koran nor in the life-
example of the Prophet do we find any warrant for this practice,
which later found its way into Muslim society from Byzantium.

. . . .

SHAYKH IBN BULAYHID INTERRUPTS my introspection with
a knowing look: 'There is no need to hurry a decision. It will
come to thee, my son, whenever it is to come.'

— 2 —

THE LIBRARY IS SILENT; the old *shaykh* and I are alone in
the domed room. From a little mosque nearby we hear the call to
the sunset prayer; and a moment later the same call reverberates
from the five minarets of the Prophet's Mosque which, now invisible to us, watch so solemnly and so full of sweet pride over
the green cupola. The *mu'azzin* on one of the minarets begins his
call: *Allahu akbar* . . . in a deep, dark, minor key, slowly ascending and descending in long arcs of sound: *God is the Greatest, God is the Greatest* . . . Before he has finished this first
phrase, the *mu'azzin* on the minaret nearest us falls in, in a
slightly higher tone, . . . *the Greatest, God is the Greatest!* And
while on the third minaret the same chant grows up slowly, the
first *mu'azzin* has already ended the first verse and begins – now
accompanied by the distant contrapuntal sounds of the first
phrase from the fourth and fifth minarets – the second verse: *I
bear witness that there is no God but God!* – while the voices from
the second and then from the third minaret glide down on soft
wings: . . . *and I bear witness that Muhammad is God's Messenger!*
In the same way, each verse repeated twice by each of the five
mu'azzins, the call proceeds: *Come to prayer, come to prayer.
Hasten to everlasting happiness!* Each of the voices seems to
awaken the others and to draw them closer together, only to

glide away itself and to take up the melody at another point, thus carrying it to the closing verse: *God is the Greatest, God is the Greatest! There is no God but God!*

This sonorous, solemn mingling and parting of voices is unlike any other chant of man. And as my heart pounds up to my throat in excited love for this city and its sounds, I begin to feel that all my wanderings have always had but one meaning: to grasp the meaning of this call . . .

'Come,' says Shaykh Ibn Bulayhid, 'let us go to the mosque for the *maghrib* prayer.'

.   .   .   .

THE HARAM, OR HOLY MOSQUE, of Medina was brought into its present shape in the middle of the last century, but parts of it are much older – some dating back to the time of the Egyptian Mamluk dynasty and some even earlier. The central hall, which contains the tomb of the Prophet, covers exactly the same ground as the building erected by the third Caliph, Uthman, in the seventh century. Over it rises a large green cupola, adorned on its inner side with colourful ornamental painting. Many rows of heavy marble columns support the roof and harmoniously divide the interior. The marble floor is laid with costly carpets. Exquisitely wrought bronze candelabras flank each of the three *mihrabs*, semicircular niches oriented toward Mecca and decorated with delicate faïence tiles in blue and white: one of them is always the place of the *imam* who leads the congregation in prayer. On long brass chains hang hundreds of glass and crystal globes; at night they are lighted from within by small lamps that are fed with olive oil and spread a soft shimmer over the rows of praying people. During the day a greenish twilight fills the mosque and makes it resemble the bottom of a lake; as through water human figures glide on bare feet over the carpets and marble slabs; as if separated by walls of water the voice of the *iman* sounds at the time of prayer from the end of the large hall, muffled and without echo.

The Prophet's tomb itself is invisible, for it is covered with heavy brocade hangings and enclosed by a bronze grill presented in the fifteenth century by the Egyptian Mamluk sultan, Qa'it Bey. In reality, there is no tomb structure as such, for the Prophet was buried under the earthen floor in the very room of the little house in which he lived and died. In later times a doorless wall was built around the house, thus entirely sealing it off from the outer world. During the Prophet's lifetime the mosque was immediately adjacent to his house; in the course of centuries, however, it was extended above and beyond the tomb.

Long rows of rugs are spread over the gravel of the open quadrangle inside the mosque; rows of men crouch on them, reading the Koran, conversing with each other, meditating or simply idling, in anticipation of the sunset prayer. Ibn Bulayhid seems to be lost in a wordless prayer.

From the distance comes a voice reciting, as always before the sunset prayer, a portion of the Holy Book. Today it is the ninety-sixth *sura* – the first ever revealed to Muhammad – beginning with the words: *Read in the name of thy Sustainer* . . . It was in these words that God's call came for the first time to Muhammad in the cave of Hira near Mecca.

He had been praying in solitude, as so often before, praying for light and truth, when suddenly an angel appeared before him and commanded, 'Read!' And Muhammad, who, like most of the people of his environment, had never learned to read and, above all, did not know what it was he was expected to read, answered: 'I cannot read.' Whereupon the angel took him and pressed him to himself so that Muhammad felt all strength leave him; then he released him and repeated his command: 'Read!' And again Muhammad replied: 'I cannot read.' Then the angel pressed him again until he became limp and he thought he would die; and once more came the thundering voice: 'Read!' And when, for the third time, Muhammad whispered in his anguish, 'I cannot read . . .' the angel released him and spoke:

> *Read in the name of thy Sustainer, Who created*
> *– created man from a germ-cell!*
> *Read, and thy Sustainer is the most bountiful:*
> *He who taught the use of the pen,*
> *Taught man what he knew not . . .*

And thus, with an allusion to man's consciousness, intellect and knowledge, began the revelation of the Koran, which was to continue for twenty-three years until the Prophet's death in Medina at the age of sixty-three.

This story of his first experience of divine revelation reminds one, in some ways, of Jacob's wrestling with the angel as narrated in the Book of Genesis. But whereas Jacob resisted, Muhammad surrendered himself to the angel's embrace with awe and anguish until 'all strength left him' and nothing remained in him but the ability to listen to a voice of which one could no longer say whether it came from without or from within. He did not know yet that henceforth he would have to be full and empty at one and the same time: a human being filled with human urges and desires and the consciousness of his own life – and, at the same time, a passive instrument for the reception of a Message. The unseen book of Eternal Truth – the truth that alone gives meaning to all perceptible things and happenings – was being laid bare before his heart, waiting to be understood; and he was told to 'read' out of it to the world so that other men might understand 'what they knew not' and, indeed, could not know by themselves.

The tremendous implications of this vision overwhelmed Muhammad; he, like Moses before the burning bush, thought himself unworthy of the exalted position of prophethood and trembled at the thought that God might have selected him. We are told that he went back to town and to his home and called out to his wife Khadija: 'Wrap me up, wrap me up!'– for he was shaking like a branch in a storm. And she wrapped him up in a blanket, and gradually his trembling subsided. Then he told her what had happened to him, and said: 'Verily, I fear for myself'. But Khadija, with the clearsightedness that only love can give, knew at once that he was afraid of the magnitude of the task before him; and she replied: 'No, by God! Never will He confer a task upon thee which thou art unable to perform, and never will He humiliate thee! For, behold, thou art a good man: thou fulfillest thy duties toward thy kin, and supportest the weak, and bringest gain to the destitute, and art generous toward the guest, and helpest those in genuine distress.' To comfort him, she took her husband to Waraqa, a learned cousin of hers who had been a Christian for many years and, according to tradition, could read the Bible in Hebrew; at that time he was an old man and had become blind. And Khadija said: 'O my uncle's son, hark to this thy kinsman!' And when Muhammad recounted what he had experienced, Waraqa raised his arms in awe and said: 'That was the Angel of Revelation, the same whom God had sent to His earlier prophets. Oh, would I were a young man! Would that I be alive, and able to help thee when thy people drive thee away!' Whereupon Muhammad asked in astonishment: 'Why should they drive me away?' And the wise Waraqa replied: 'Yes, they will. Never yet came a man to his people with the like thou hast come with but was persecuted.'

And persecute him they did, for thirteen years, until he forsook Mecca and went to Medina. For the Meccans had always been hard of heart ...

. . . .

BUT, AFTER ALL, IS IT so difficult to understand the hardness of heart most of the Meccans displayed when they first heard Muhammad's call? Devoid of all spiritual urges, they knew only practical endeavours: for they believed that life could be widened only by widening the means by which outward comfort might be increased. To such people, the thought of having to surrender themselves without compromise to a moral claim – for *Islam* means, literally, 'self-surrender to God'– may well have seemed unbearable. In addition, the teaching of Muhammad threatened the established order of things and the tribal conventions so dear to the Meccans. When he started preaching the Oneness of God and denounced idol worship as the supreme sin, they saw in it not merely an attack on their traditional beliefs but also an attempt to destroy the social pattern of their lives. In particular, they did not like Islam's interference with what they regarded as purely 'mundane' issues outside the purview of religion – like economics, questions of social equity, and people's behaviour in general – for this interference did not agree too well with their business habits, their licentiousness and their views about the tribal good. To them, religion was a personal matter – a question of attitude rather than of behaviour.

Now this was the exact opposite of what the Arabian Prophet had in mind when he spoke of religion. To him, social practices and institutions came very much within the orbit of religion, and he would surely have been astonished if anyone had told him that religion was a matter of personal conscience alone and had nothing to do with social behaviour. It was this feature of his message that, more than anything else, made it so distasteful to the pagan Meccans. Had it not been for his interference with social problems, their displeasure with the Prophet might well have been less intense. Undoubtedly they would have been annoyed by Islam in so far as its theology conflicted with their own religious views; but most probably they would have put up with it after some initial grumbling – just as they had put up, a little earlier, with the sporadic preaching of Christianity – if only the Prophet had followed the example of the Christian priests and confined himself to exhorting the people to believe in God, to pray to Him for salvation and to behave decently in their personal concerns. But he did not follow the Christian example, and did not confine himself to questions of belief, ritual and personal morality. How could he? Did not his God command him to pray: *Our Lord, give us the good of this world as well as the good of the world to come?*

In the very structure of this Koranic sentence, 'the good of this world' is made to precede 'the good of the world to come': firstly, because the present precedes the future and, secondly, because man is so constituted that he must seek the satisfaction of his physical, worldly needs before he can listen to the call of the spirit and seek the good of the Hereafter. Muhammad's message did not postulate spirituality as something divorced from or opposed to physical life: it rested entirely on the concept that spirit and flesh are but different aspects of one and the same reality – human life. In the nature of things, therefore, he could not content himself with merely nursing a moral attitude in individual persons but had to aim at translating this attitude into a definite social scheme which would ensure to every member of the community the greatest possible measure of physical and material well-being and, thus, the greatest opportunity for spiritual growth.

He began by telling people that *Action is part of faith:* for God is not merely concerned with a person's beliefs but also with his or her doings – especially such doings as affect other people besides oneself. He preached, with the most flaming imagery that God had put at his disposal, against the oppression of the weak by the strong. He propounded the unheard-of thesis that men and women were equal before God and that all religious duties and hopes applied to both alike; he even went so far as to declare, to the horror of all right-minded pagan Meccans, that a

woman was a person in her own right, and not merely by virtue
of her relationship with men as mother, sister, wife or daughter,
and that, therefore, she was entitled to own property, to do
business on her own and to dispose of her own person in marriage! He condemned all games of chance and all forms of intoxicants, for, in the words of the Koran, *Great evil and some
advantage is in them, but the evil is greater than the advantage*. To
top it all, he stood up against the traditional exploitation of man
by man; against profits from interest-bearing loans, whatever the
rate of interest; against private monopolies and 'corners';
against gambling on other people's potential needs – a thing we
today call 'speculation'; against judging right or wrong through
the lens of tribal group sentiment – in modern parlance, 'nationalism'. Indeed, he denied any moral legitimacy to tribal feelings and considerations. In his eyes, the only legitimate – that is,
ethically admissible – motive for communal groupment was not
the accident of a common origin, but a people's free, conscious
acceptance of a common outlook on life and a common scale of
moral values.

In effect, the Prophet insisted on a thorough revision of almost all the social concepts which until then had been regarded
as immutable, and thus, as one would say today, he 'brought
religion into politics': quite a revolutionary innovation in those
times.

The rulers of pagan Mecca were convinced, as most people at
all times are, that the social conventions, habits of thought and
customs in which they had been brought up were the best that
could ever be conceived. Naturally, therefore, they resented the
Prophet's attempt to bring religion into politics – that is, to make
God-consciousness the starting point of social change – and condemned it as immoral, seditious and 'opposed to all canons of
propriety'. And when it became evident that he was not a mere
dreamer but knew how to inspire men to action, the defenders of
the established order resorted to vigorous counteraction and began to persecute him and his followers . . .

In one way or another, all prophets have challenged the 'established order' of their times; is it therefore so surprising that almost all of them were persecuted and ridiculed by their kinsfolk?
– and that the latest of them, Muhammad, is ridiculed in the
West to this day?

— 3 —

AS SOON AS the *maghrib* prayer is over, Shaykh Ibn Bulayhid becomes the centre of an attentive circle of Najdi beduins and townsmen desirous of profiting from his learning and world-wisdom; while he himself is always eager to hear what people can tell him of their experiences and travels in distant parts. Long travels are nothing uncommon among the Najdis; they call themselves *ahl ash-shidad* –'people of the camel-saddle'– and to many of them the camel-saddle is indeed more familiar than a bed at home. It must certainly be more familiar to the young Harb beduin who has just finished recounting to the *shaykh* what befell him on his recent journey to Iraq, where he has seen, for the first time, *faranji* people – that is, Europeans (who owe this designation to the Franks with whom the Arabs came in contact during the Crusades).

'Tell me, O Shaykh, why is it that the *faranjis* always wear hats that shade their eyes? How can they see the sky?'

'That is just what they do not want to see,' replies the *shaykh*, with a twinkle in my direction. 'Perhaps they are afraid lest the sight of the heavens remind them of God; and they do not want to be reminded of God on weekdays...'

We all laugh, but the young beduin is persistent in his search for knowledge. 'Then why is it that God is so bountiful toward them and gives them riches that He denies to the Faithful?'

'Oh, that is simple, my son. They worship gold, and so their deity is in their pockets... But my friend here,'– and he places his hand on my knee –'knows more about the *faranjis* than I do, for he comes from among them: God, glorified be His name, has led him out of that darkness into the light of Islam.'

'Is that so, O brother?' asks the eager young beduin. 'Is it true that thou hast been a *faranji* thyself?'– and when I nod, he whispers, 'Praise be unto God, praise be unto God, who guides aright whomsoever He wishes... Tell me, brother, why is it that the *faranjis* are so unmindful of God?'

'That is a long story,' I reply, 'and cannot be explained in a few words. All that I can tell thee now is that the world of the *faranjis* has become the world of the *Dajjal*, the Glittering, the Deceptive One. Hast thou ever heard of our Holy Prophet's prediction that in later times most of the world's people would follow the *Dajjal*, believing him to be God?'

And as he looks at me with a question in his eyes, I recount, to the visible approval of Shaykh Ibn Bulayhid, the prophecy about the appearance of that apocalyptic being, the *Dajjal*, who would be blind in one eye but endowed with mysterious powers conferred upon him by God. He would hear with his ears what is spoken in the farthest corners of the earth, and would see with his one eye things that are happening in infinite distances; he would fly around the earth in days, would make treasures of gold and silver suddenly appear from under ground, would cause rain to fall and plants to grow at his command, would kill and bring to life again: so that all whose faith is weak would believe him to be God Himself and would prostrate themselves before him in adoration. But those whose faith is strong would read what is written in letters of flame on his forehead: *Denier of God* – and thus they would know that he is but a deception to test man's faith . . .

And while my beduin friend looks at me with wide-open eyes and murmurs, 'I take my refuge with God,' I turn to Ibn Bulayhid:

'Is not this parable, O Shaykh, a fitting description of modern technical civilization? It is "one-eyed": that is, it looks upon only one side of life – material progress – and is unaware of its spiritual side. With the help of its mechanical marvels it enables man to see and hear far beyond his natural ability, and to cover endless distances at an inconceivable speed. Its scientific knowledge causes "rain to fall and plants to grow" and uncovers unsuspected treasures from beneath the ground. Its medicine brings life to those who seem to have been doomed to death, while its wars and scientific horrors destroy life. And its material advancement is so powerful and so glittering that the weak in faith are coming to believe that it is a godhead in its own right; but those who have remained conscious of their Creator clearly recognize that to worship the *Dajjal* means to deny God . . .'

'Thou art right, O Muhammad, thou art right!' cries out Ibn Bulayhid, excitedly striking my knee. 'It has never occurred to me to look upon the *Dajjal* prophecy in this light; but thou art right! Instead of realizing that man's advancement and the progress of science is a bounty from our Lord, more and more people in their folly are beginning to think that it is an end in itself and fit to be worshipped.'

•　　　•　　　•　　　•　　　•　　　•　　　•

YES, I THINK TO MYSELF, Western man has truly given him-self up to the worship of the *Dajjal*. He has long ago lost all in-nocence, all inner integration with nature. Life has become a puzzle to him. He is sceptical, and therefore isolated from his brother and lonely within himself. In order not to perish in this loneliness, he must endeavour to dominate life by outward means. The fact of being alive can, by itself, no longer give him inner security: he must always wrestle for it, with pain, from moment to new moment. Because he has lost all metaphysical orientation, and has decided to do without it, he must continu-ously invent for himself mechanical allies: and thus the furious, desperate drive of his technique. He invents every day new mach-ines and gives each of them something of his soul to make them fight for his existence. That they do indeed; but at the same time they create for him ever new needs, new dangers, new fears – and an unquenchable thirst for newer, yet artificial allies. His soul loses itself in the ever bolder, ever more fantastic, ever more powerful wheelwork of the creative machine: and the machine loses its true purpose – to be a protector and enricher of human life – and evolves into a deity in its own right, a devouring Moloch of steel. The priests and preachers of this insatiable deity do not seem to be aware that the rapidity of modern tech-nical progress is a result not only of a positive growth of know-ledge but also of spiritual despair, and that the grand material achievements in the light of which Western man proclaims his will to attain to mastery over nature are, in their innermost, of a defensive character: behind their shining façades lurks the fear of the Unknown.

Western civilization has not been able to strike a harmonious balance between man's bodily and social needs and his spiritual cravings; it has abandoned its erstwhile religious ethics without being able to produce out of itself any other moral system, how-ever theoretical, that would commend itself to reason. Despite all its advances in education, it has not been able to overcome man's stupid readiness to fall a prey to any slogan, however absurd, which clever demagogues think fit to invent. It has raised the technique of 'organization' to a fine art – and nevertheless the nations of the West daily demonstrate their utter inability to control the forces which their scientists have brought into being, and have now reached a stage where apparently unbounded scientific possibilities go hand in hand with world-wide chaos. Lacking all truly religious orientation, the Westerner cannot morally benefit by the light of the knowledge which his – undoubtedly great – science is shedding. To him might be applied the words of the Koran:

Their parable is the parable of people who lit a fire: but when it had shed its light around them, God took away their light and left them in darkness in which they cannot see – deaf, dumb, blind: and yet they do not turn back.

And yet, in the arrogance of their blindness, the people of the West are convinced that it is *their* civilization that will bring light and happiness to the world . . . In the eighteenth and nineteenth centuries they thought of spreading the gospel of Christianity all over the world; but now that their religious ardour has cooled so much that they consider religion no more than soothing background music – allowed to accompany, but not to influence, 'real' life – they have begun to spread instead the materialistic gospel of the 'Western way of life': the belief that all human problems can be solved in factories, laboratories and on the desks of statisticians.

And thus the *Dajjal* has come into his own . . .

— 4 —

FOR A LONG TIME there is silence. Then the *shaykh* speaks again: 'Was it the realization of what the *Dajjal* means that made thee embrace Islam, O my son?'

'In a way, I think, it must have been; but it was only the last step.'

'The last step . . . Yes: thou hast told me once the story of thy way to Islam – but when and how, exactly, did it first dawn upon thee that Islam might be thy goal?'

'When? Let me see . . . I think it was on a winter day in Afghanistan, when my horse lost a shoe and I had to seek out a smith in a village that lay off my path; and there a man told me, "But thou art a Muslim, only thou dost not know it thyself . . ." That was about eight months before I embraced Islam . . . I was on my way from Herat to Kabul . . .'

.   .   .   .

I WAS ON MY WAY from Herat to Kabul and was riding, accompanied by Ibrahim and an Afghan trooper, through the snow-buried mountain valleys and passes of the Hindu-Kush, in central Afghanistan. It was cold and the snow was glistening and on all sides stood steep mountains in black and white.

I was sad and, at the same time, strangely happy that day. I was sad because the people with whom I had been living during the past few months seemed to be separated by opaque veils from the light and the strength and the growth which their faith could have given them; and I was happy because the light and the strength and the growth of that faith stood as near before my eyes as the black and white mountains – almost to be touched with the hand.

My horse began to limp and something clinked at its hoof: an iron shoe had become loose and was hanging only by two nails.

'Is there a village nearby where we could find a smith?' I asked our Afghan companion.

'The village of Deh-Zangi is less than a league away. There is a blacksmith there and the *hakim* of the Hazarajat has his castle there.'

And so to Deh-Zangi we rode over glistening snow, slowly, so as not to tire my horse.

The *hakim*, or district governor, was a young man of short stature and gay countenance – a friendly man who was glad to have a foreign guest in the loneliness of his modest castle. Though a close relative of King Amanullah, he was one of the most unassuming men I had met or was ever to meet in Afghanistan. He forced me to stay with him for two days.

In the evening of the second day we sat down as usual to an opulent dinner, and afterward a man from the village entertained us with ballads sung to the accompaniment of a three-stringed lute. He sang in Pashtu – a language which I did not understand – but some of the Persian words he used sprang up vividly against the background of the warm, carpeted room and the cold gleam of snow that came through the windows. He sang, I remember, of David's fight with Goliath – of the fight of faith against brute power – and although I could not quite follow the words of the song, its theme was clear to me as it began in humility, then rose in a violent ascent of passion to a final, triumphant outcry.

When it ended, the *hakim* remarked: 'David was small, but his faith was great . . .'

I could not prevent myself from adding: 'And you are many, but your faith is small.'

My host looked at me with astonishment, and, embarrassed by what I had almost involuntarily said, I rapidly began to explain myself. My explanation took the shape of a torrent of questions:

'How has it come about that you Muslims have lost your self-confidence – that self-confidence which once enabled you to spread your faith, in less than a hundred years, from Arabia westward as far as the Atlantic and eastward deep into China – and now surrender yourselves so easily, so weakly, to the thoughts and customs of the West? Why can't you, whose fore-fathers illumined the world with science and art at a time when Europe lay in deep barbarism and ignorance, summon forth the courage to go back to your own progressive, radiant faith? How is it that Ataturk, that petty masquerader who denies all value to Islam, has become to you Muslims a symbol of "Muslim revivial"?'

My host remained speechless. It had started to snow outside. Again I felt that wave of mingled sadness and happiness that I had felt on approaching Deh-Zangi. I sensed the glory that had been and the shame that was enveloping these late sons of a great civilization.

'Tell me – how has it come about that the faith of your Prophet and all its clearness and simplicity has been buried beneath a rubble of sterile speculation and the hair-splitting of your scholastics? How has it happened that your princes and great land-owners revel in wealth and luxury while so many of their Muslim brethren subsist in unspeakable poverty and squalour – although your Prophet taught that *No one may call himself a Faithful who eats his fill while his neighbour remains hungry?* Can you make me understand why you have brushed woman into the background of your lives – although the women around the Prophet and his Companions took part in so grand a manner in the life of their men? How has it come about that so many of you Muslims are ignorant and so few can even read and write – although your Prophet declared that *Striving after knowledge is a most sacred duty for every Muslim man and woman* and that

*The superiority of the learned man over the mere pious is like the
superiority of the moon when it is full over all other stars?'*

Still my host stared at me without speaking, and I began to
think that my outburst had deeply offended him. The man with
the lute, not understanding Persian well enough to follow me,
looked on in wonderment at the sight of the stranger who spoke
with so much passion to the *hakim*. In the end, the latter pulled
his wide yellow sheepskin cloak closer about himself, as if feeling
cold; then he whispered:

'But – you are a Muslim . . .'

I laughed, and replied: 'No, I am not a Muslim, but I have
come to see so much beauty in Islam that it makes me sometimes
angry to watch you people waste it . . . Forgive me if I have
spoken harshly. I did not speak as an enemy.'

But my host shook his head. 'No, it is as I have said: you are
a Muslim, only you don't know it yourself . . . Why don't you
say, now and here, "There is no God but God and Muhammad is
His Prophet" and become a Muslim in fact, as you already are in
your heart? Say it brother, say it now, and I will go with you tomorrow to Kabul and take you to the *amir*, and he will receive
you with open arms as one of us. He will give you houses and
gardens and cattle, and we all will love you. Say it, my brother . . .'

'If I ever do say it, it will be because my mind has been set at
rest and not for the sake of the *amir's* houses and gardens.'

'But,' he insisted, 'you already know far more about Islam
than most of us; what *is* it that you have not yet understood?'

'It is not a question of understanding. It is rather a question of
being convinced: convinced that the Koran is really the word of
God and not merely the brilliant creation of a great human
mind . . .'

But the words of my Afghan friend never really left me in the
months that followed.

From Kabul I rode for weeks through southern Afghanistan –
through the ancient city of Ghazni, from which nearly a thousand years ago the great Mahmud set out on his conquest of
India; through exotic Kandahar, where you could see the fiercest
warrior-tribesmen in all the world; across the deserts of Afghanistan's southwestern corner; and back to Herat, where my
Afghan trek had started.

It was in 1926, toward the end of the winter, that I left Herat on the first stage of my long homeward journey, which was to take me by train from the Afghan border to Marv in Russian Turkestan, to Samarkand, Bokhara and Tashkent, and thence across the Turkoman steppes to the Urals and Moscow.

My first (and most lasting) impression of Soviet Russia – at the railway station of Marv – was a huge, beautifully executed poster which depicted a young proletarian in blue overalls booting a ridiculous, white-bearded gentleman, clad in flowing robes, out of a cloud-filled sky. The Russian legend beneath the poster read: 'Thus have the workers of the Soviet Union kicked God out of his heaven! Issued by the *Bezbozhniki* (Godless) Association of the Union of Soviet Socialist Republics.'

Such officially sanctioned antireligious propaganda obtruded itself everywhere one went: in public buildings, in the streets and, preferably, in the vicinity of houses of worship. In Turkestan these were, naturally, for the most part mosques. While prayer congregations were not explicitly forbidden, the authorities did everything to deter people from attending them. I was often told, especially in Bokhara and Tashkent, that police spies would take down the name of every person who entered a mosque; copies of the Koran were being impounded and destroyed; and a favourite pastime of the young *bezbozhniki* was to throw heads of pigs into mosques; a truly charming custom.

It was with a feeling of relief that I crossed the Polish frontier after weeks of journeying through Asiatic and European Russia. I went straight to Frankfurt and made my appearance in the now familiar precincts of my newspaper. It did not take me long to find out that during my absence my name had become famous, and that I was now considered one of the most outstanding foreign correspondents of Central Europe. Some of my articles – especially those dealing with the intricate religious psychology of the Iranians – had come to the attention of prominent orientalist scholars and received a more than passing recognition. On the strength of this achievement, I was invited to deliver a series of lectures at the Academy of Geopolitics in Berlin – where I was told that it had never happened before that a man of my age (I was not yet twenty-six) had been accorded such a distinction. Other articles of more general interest had been reproduced, with the permission of the *Frankfurter Zeitung*, by many other newspapers; one article, I learned, had been reprinted nearly thirty

times. All in all, my Iranian wanderings had been extremely
fruitful . . .

•   •   •   •   •   •   •   •   •

IT WAS AT THIS TIME that I married Elsa. The two years I
had been away from Europe had not weakened our love but
rather strengthened it, and it was with a happiness I had never
felt before that I brushed aside her apprehensions about the great
difference in our ages.

'But how can you marry me?' she argued. 'You are not yet
twenty-six, and I am over forty. Think of it: when you will be
thirty, I will be forty-five; and when you will be forty, I will be
an old woman . . .'

I laughed: 'What does it matter? I cannot imagine a future
without you.'

And finally she gave in.

I did not exaggerate when I said that I could not imagine a
future without Elsa. Her beauty and her instinctive grace made
her so utterly attractive to me that I could not even look at any
other woman; and her sensitive understanding of what I wanted
of life illumined my own hopes and desires and made them more
concrete, more graspable than my own thinking could ever have
done.

On one occasion – it must have been about a week after we
had been married – she remarked: 'How strange that you, of all
people, should depreciate mysticism in religion . . . You are a
mystic yourself – a sensuous kind of mystic, reaching out with
your fingertips toward the life around you, seeing an intricate,
mystical pattern in everyday things – in many things that to
other people appear so commonplace . . . But the moment you
turn to religion, you are all brain. With most people it would be
the other way around . . .'

But Elsa was not really puzzled. She knew what I was searching for when I spoke to her of Islam; and although she may not
have felt the same urgency as I did, her love made her share my
quest.

Often we would read the Koran together and discuss its ideas;
and Elsa, like myself, became more and more impressed by the
inner cohesion between its moral teaching and its practical guidance. According to the Koran, God did not call for blind sub-

servience on the part of man but rather appealed to his intellect; He did not stand apart from man's destiny but was *nearer to you than the vein in your neck;* He did not draw any dividing line between faith and social behaviour; and, what was perhaps most important, He did not start from the axiom that all life was burdened with a conflict between matter and spirit and that the way toward the Light demanded a freeing of the soul from the shackles of the flesh. Every form of life-denial and self-mortification had been condemned by the Prophet in sayings like *Behold, asceticism is not for us,* and *There is no world-renunciation in Islam.* The human will to live was not only recognized as a positive, fruitful instinct but was endowed with the sanctity of an ethical postulate as well. Man was taught, in effect: You not only *may* utilize your life to the full, but you are *obliged* to do so.

An integrated image of Islam was now emerging with a finality, a decisiveness that sometimes astounded me. It was taking shape by a process that could almost be described as a kind of mental osmosis – that is, without any conscious effort on my part to piece together and 'systematize' the many fragments of knowledge that had come my way during the past four years. I saw before me something like a perfect work of architecture, with all its elements harmoniously conceived to complement and support each other, with nothing superfluous and nothing lacking – a balance and composure which gave one the feeling that everything in the outlook and postulates of Islam was 'in its proper place'.

Thirteen centuries ago a man had stood up and said: 'I am only a mortal man; but He who has created the universe has bidden me to bear His Message to you. In order that you might live in harmony with the plan of His creation, He has commanded me to remind you of His existence, omnipotence and omniscience, and to place before you a programme of behaviour. If you accept this reminder and this programme, follow me.' This was the essence of Muhammad's prophetic mission.

The social scheme he propounded was of that simplicity which goes together only with real grandeur. It started from the premise that men are biological beings with biological needs and are so conditioned by their Creator that they must live in *groups* in order to satisfy the full range of their physical, moral and intellectual requirements: in short, they are *dependent* on one another. The continuity of an individual's rise in spiritual stature (the fundamental objective of every religion) depends on whether he is helped, encouraged and protected by the people around him – who, of course, expect the same co-operation from him. This human interdependence was the reason why in Islam religion could not be separated from economics and politics. To arrange practical human relations in such a way that every individual might find as few obstacles and as much encouragement as possible in the development of his personality: this, and nothing else, appeared to be the Islamic concept of the true function of society. And so it was only natural that the system which the Prophet Muhammad enunciated in the twenty-three years of his ministry related not only to matters spiritual but provided a framework for all individual and social acitivity as well. It held out the concept not only of individual righteousness but also of the equitable society which such righteousness should bring about. It provided the outline of a political community – the outline only, because the details of man's political needs are time-bound and therefore variable – as well as a scheme of individual rights and social duties in which the fact of historical evolution was duly anticipated. The Islamic code embraced life in all its aspects, moral and physical, individual and communal; problems of the flesh and of the mind, of sex and economics had, side by side with problems of theology and worship, their legitimate place in the Prophet's teachings, and nothing that pertained to life seemed too trivial to be drawn into the orbit of religious thought – not even such 'mundane' issues as commerce, inheritance, property rights or ownership of land.

All the clauses of Islamic Law were devised for the equal benefit of all members of the community, without distinction of birth, race, sex or previous social allegiance. No special benefits were reserved for the community's founder or his descendants. High and low were, in a social sense, nonexistent terms; and nonexistent was the concept of class. All rights, duties and opportunities applied equally to all who professed faith in Islam. No priest was required to mediate between man and God, for *He knows what lies open in their hands before them and what they conceal behind their backs*. No loyalty was recognized beyond the loyalty to God and His Prophet, to one's parents, and to the community that had as its goal the establishment of God's kingdom on earth; and this precluded that kind of loyalty which says, 'right or wrong, my country' or 'my nation'. To elucidate this principle, the Prophet very pointedly said on more than one occasion: *He is not of us who proclaims the cause of tribal partisanship; and he is not of us who fights in the cause of tribal partisanship; and he is not of us who dies for the sake of tribal partisanship.*

Before Islam, all political organizations – even those on a theocratic or semi-theocratic basis – had been limited by the narrow concepts of tribe and tribal homogeneity. Thus, the god-kings of ancient Egypt had no thought beyond the horizon of the Nile valley and its inhabitants, and in the early theocratic state of the Hebrews, when God was supposed to rule, it was necessarily the God of the Children of Israel. In the structure of Koranic thought, on the other hand, considerations of descent or tribal adherence had no place. Islam postulated a self-contained political community which cut across the conventional divisions of tribe and race. In this respect, Islam and Christianity might be said to have had the same aim: both advocated an international community of people united by their adherence to a common ideal; but whereas Christianity had contented itself with a mere moral advocacy of this principle and, by advising its followers to give Caesar his due, had restricted its universal appeal to the spiritual sphere, Islam unfolded before the world the vision of a political organization in which God-consciousness would be the mainspring of man's practical behaviour and the sole basis of all social institutions. Thus – fulfilling what Christianity had left unfulfilled – Islam inaugurated a new chapter in the development of man: the first instance of an open, ideological society in contrast with the closed, racially or geographically limited, societies of the past.

The message of Islam envisaged and brought to life a civilization in which there was no room for nationalism, no 'vested interests', no class divisions, no Church, no priesthood, no hereditary nobility; in fact, no hereditary functions at all. The aim was to establish a theocracy with regard to God and a democracy between man and man. The most important feature of that new civilization – a feature which set it entirely apart from all other movements in human history – was the fact that it had been conceived in terms of, and arose from, a voluntary agreement of the people concerned. Here, social progress was not, as in all other communities and civilizations known to history, a result of pressure and counterpressure of conflicting interests, but part and parcel of an original 'constitution'. In other words, a genuine social contract lay at the root of things: not as a figure of speech formulated by later generations of power-holders in defence of their privileges, but as the real, historic source of Islamic civilization. The Koran said: *Behold, God has bought of the Faithful their persons and their possessions, offering them Paradise in return . . . Rejoice, then, in the bargain you have made, for this is the triumph supreme.*

I knew that this 'triumph supreme'– the one instance of a real social contract recorded by history – was realized only during a very short period; or, rather, only during a very short period was a large-scale attempt made to realize it. Less than a century after the Prophet's death, the political form of pristine Islam began to be corrupted and, in the following centuries, the original programme was gradually pushed into the background. Clannish wranglings for power took the place of a free agreement of free men and women; hereditary kingship, as inimical to the political concept of Islam as polytheism is to its theological concept, soon came into being – and with it, dynastic struggles and intrigues, tribal preferences and oppressions, and the usual degradation of religion to the status of a handmaiden of political power: in short, the entire host of 'vested interests' so well known to history. For a time, the great thinkers of Islam tried to keep its true ideology aloft and pure; but those who came after them were of lesser stature and lapsed after two or three centuries into a morass of intellectual convention, ceased to think for themselves and became content to repeat the dead phrases of earlier generations – forgetting that every human opinion is time-bound and fallible and therefore in need of eternal renewal. The original impetus of Islam, so tremendous in its beginnings, sufficed for a while to carry the Muslim commonwealth to great cultural heights – to that splendid vision of scientific, literary and artistic achievement which historians describe as the Golden Age of Islam; but within a few more centuries this impetus also died down for want of spiritual nourishment, and Muslim civilization became more and more stagnant and devoid of creative power.

.   .   .   .

I HAD NO ILLUSIONS as to the present state of affairs in the Muslim world. The four years I had spent in those countries had shown me that while Islam was still alive, perceptible in the world-view of its adherents and in their silent admission of its ethical premises, they themselves were like people paralyzed, unable to translate their beliefs into fruitful action. But what concerned me more than the failure of present-day Muslims to implement the scheme of Islam were the potentialities of that scheme itself. It was sufficient for me to know that for a short time, quite at the beginning of Islamic history, a successful attempt *had* been made to translate that scheme into practice; and what had seemed possible at one time might perhaps become really possible at another. What did it matter, I told myself, that the Muslims had gone astray from the original teaching and subsided into indolence and ignorance? What did it matter that they did not live up to the ideal placed before them by the Arabian Prophet thirteen centuries ago – if the ideal itself still lay open to all who were willing to listen to its message?

And it might well be, I thought, that we latecomers needed that message even more desperately than did the people of Muhammad's time. They lived in an environment much simpler than ours, and so their problems and difficulties had been much easier of solution. The world in which I was living – the whole of it – was wobbling because of the absence of any agreement as to what is good and evil spiritually and, therefore, socially and economically as well. I did not believe that individual man was in need of 'salvation': but I did believe that modern society was in need of salvation. More than any previous time, I felt with mounting certainty, this time of ours was in need of an ideological basis for a new social contract: it needed a faith that would make us understand the hollowness of material progress for the sake of progress alone – and nevertheless would give the life of this world its due; that would show us how to strike a balance between our spiritual and physical requirements: and thus save us from the disaster into which we were rushing headlong.

.   .   .   .

IT WOULD NOT BE too much to say that at this period of my life the problem of Islam – for it was a problem to me – occupied my mind to the exclusion of everything else. By now my absorption had outgrown its initial stages, when it had been no more than an intellectual interest in a strange, if attractive, ideology and culture: it had become a passionate search for truth. Compared with this search, even the adventurous excitement of the last two years of travel paled into insignificance: so much so that it became difficult for me to concentrate on writing the new book which the editor of the *Frankfurter Zeitung* was entitled to expect of me.

At first Dr Simon viewed indulgently my obvious reluctance to proceed with this book. After all, I had just returned from a long journey and deserved some sort of holiday; my recent marriage seemed also to warrant a respite from the routine of writing. But when the holiday and the respite began to extend beyond what Dr Simon regarded as reasonable, he suggested that I should now come down to earth.

In retrospect, it seems to me that he was very understanding; but it did not seem so at the time. His frequent and urgent inquiries about the progress of 'the book' had an effect contrary to what he intended: I felt myself unduly imposed upon; and I began to detest the very thought of the book. I was more concerned with what I had still to discover than with describing what I had found so far.

In the end, Dr Simon made the exasperated observation: 'I don't think you will ever write this book. What you are suffering from is *horror libri.*'

Somewhat nettled, I replied: 'Maybe my disease is even more serious than that. Perhaps I am suffering from *horror scribendi.*'

'Well, if you're suffering from that,' he retorted sharply, 'do you think the *Frankfurter Zeitung* is the proper place for you?'

One word led to another and our disagreement grew into a quarrel. On the same day I resigned from the *Frankfurter Zeitung* and a week later left with Elsa for Berlin.

I did not, of course, intend to give up journalism, for, apart from the comfortable livelihood and the pleasure (temporarily marred by 'the book') which writing gave me, it provided me with my only means of returning to the Muslim world: and to the Muslim world I wanted to return at any cost. But with the reputation I had achieved over the past four years, it was not difficult to make new press connections. Very soon after my break

Elsa and her Son

with Frankfurt, I concluded highly satisfactory agreements with three other newspapers: the *Neue Zürcher Zeitung* of Zurich, the *Telegraaf* of Amsterdam and the *Kölnische Zeitung* of Cologne. From now on my articles on the Middle East were to be syndicated by these three newspapers, which – though perhaps not comparable with the *Frankfurter Zeitung* – were among the most important in Europe.

For the time being Elsa and I settled down in Berlin, where I intended to complete my series of lectures at the Academy of Geopolitics and also to continue my Islamic studies.

My old literary friends were glad to see me back, but somehow it was not easy to take up the threads of our former relations at the point where they had been left dangling when I went to the Middle East. We had grown estranged; we no longer spoke the same intellectual language. In particular, from none of my friends could I elicit anything like understanding for my preoccupation with Islam. Almost to a man they shook their heads in puzzlement when I tried to explain to them that Islam, as an intellectual and social concept, could favourably compare with any other ideology. Although on occasion they might concede the reasonableness of this or that Islamic proposition, most of them were of the opinion that the old religions were a thing of the past, and that our time demanded a new, 'humanistic' approach. But even those who did not so sweepingly deny all validity to institutional religion were by no means disposed to give up the popular Western notion that Islam, being overly concerned with mundane matters, lacked the 'mystique' which one had a right to expect from religion.

It rather surprised me to discover that the very aspect of Islam which had attracted me in the first instance – the absence of a division of reality into physical and spiritual compartments and the stress on reason as a way to faith – appealed so little to intellectuals who otherwise were wont to claim for reason a dominant role in life: it was in the religious sphere alone that they instinctively receded from their habitually so 'rational' and 'realistic' position. And in this respect I could discern no difference whatever between those few of my friends who were religiously inclined and the many to whom religion had ceased to be more than an outmoded convention.

In time, however, I came to understand where their difficulty lay. I began to perceive that in the eyes of people brought up within the orbit of Christian thought – with its stress on the 'supernatural' allegedly inherent in every true religious experience – a predominantly rational approach appeared to detract from a religion's spiritual value. This attitude was by no means confined to believing Christians. Because of Europe's long, almost exclusive association with Christianity, even the agnostic European had subconsciously learned to look upon all religious experience through the lens of Christian concepts, and would regard it as 'valid' only if it was accompanied by a thrill of numinous awe before things hidden and beyond intellectual comprehension. Islam did not fulfill this requirement: it insisted on a co-ordination of the physical and spiritual aspects of life on a perfectly natural plane. In fact, its world-view was so different from the Christian, on which most of the West's ethical concepts were based, that to accept the validity of the one inescapably led to questioning the validity of the other.

As for myself, I knew now that I was being driven to Islam; but a last hesitancy made me postpone the final, irrevocable step. The thought of embracing Islam was like the prospect of venturing out onto a bridge that spanned an abyss between two different worlds: a bridge so long that one would have to reach the point of no return before the other end became visible. I was well aware that if I became a Muslim I would have to cut myself off from the world in which I had grown up. No other outcome was possible. One could not really follow the call of Muhammad and still maintain one's inner links with a society that was ruled by diametrically opposed concepts. But – *was Islam truly a message from God or merely the wisdom of a great, but fallible, man . . . ?*

.   .   .   .

ONE DAY – it was in September 1926 – Elsa and I found ourselves travelling in the Berlin subway. It was an upper-class compartment. My eye fell casually on a well-dressed man opposite me, apparently a well-to-do businessman, with a beautiful briefcase on his knees and a large diamond ring on his hand. I thought idly how well the portly figure of this man fitted into the picture of prosperity which one encountered everywhere in Central Europe in those days: a prosperity the more prominent as it had come after years of inflation, when all economic life had been topsy-turvy and shabbiness of appearance the rule. Most of the people were now well dressed and well fed, and the man opposite me was therefore no exception. But when I looked at his face, I did not seem to be looking at a happy face. He appeared to be worried: and not merely worried but acutely unhappy, with eyes staring vacantly ahead and the corners of his mouth drawn in as if in pain – but not in bodily pain. Not wanting to be rude, I turned my eyes away and saw next to him a lady of some elegance. She also had a strangely unhappy expression on her face, as if contemplating or experiencing something that caused her pain; nevertheless, her mouth was fixed in the stiff semblance of a smile which, I was certain, must have been habitual. And then I began to look around at all the other faces in the compartment – faces belonging without exception to well-dressed, well-fed people: and in almost every one of them I could discern an expression of hidden suffering, so hidden that the owner of the face seemed to be quite unaware of it.

This was indeed strange. I had never before seen so many unhappy faces around me: or was it perhaps that I had never before looked for what was now so loudly speaking in them? The impression was so strong that I mentioned it to Elsa; and she too began to look around her with the careful eyes of a painter accustomed to study human features. Then she turned to me, astonished, and said: 'You are right. They all look as though they were suffering torments of hell . . . I wonder, do they know themselves what is going on in them?'

I knew that they did not – for otherwise they could not go on wasting their lives as they did, without any faith in binding truths, without any goal beyond the desire to raise their own 'standard of living', without any hopes other than having more material amenities, more gadgets, and perhaps more power . . .

When we returned home, I happened to glance at my desk on which lay open a copy of the Koran I had been reading earlier. Mechanically, I picked the book up to put it away, but just as I was about to close it, my eye fell on the open page before me, and I read:

You are obsessed by greed for more and more
Until you go down to your graves.

Nay, but you will come to know!
Nay, but you will come to know!
Nay, if you but knew it with the knowledge of certainty,
You would indeed see the hell you are in.
In time, indeed, you shall see it with the eye of certainty:
And on that Day you will be asked what you have done
with the boon of life.

For a moment I was speechless. I think the book shook in my hands. Then I handed it to Elsa. 'Read this. Is it not an answer to what we saw in the subway?'

It was an answer: an answer so decisive that all doubt was suddenly at an end. I knew now, beyond any doubt, that it was a God-inspired book I was holding in my hand: for although it had been placed before man over thirteen centuries ago, it clearly anticipated something that could have become true only in this complicated, mechanized, phantom-ridden age of ours.

At all times people had known greed: but at no time before this had greed outgrown a mere eagerness to acquire things and become an obsession that blurred the sight of everything else: an irresistible craving to get, to do, to contrive more and more – more today than yesterday, and more tomorrow than today: a demon riding on the necks of men and whipping their hearts forward toward goals that tauntingly glitter in the distance but dissolve into contemptible nothingness as soon as they are reached, always holding out the promise of new goals ahead – goals still more brilliant, more tempting as long as they lie on the horizon, and bound to wither into further nothingness as soon as they come within grasp: and that hunger, that insatiable hunger for ever new goals gnawing at man's soul: *Nay, if you but knew it you would see the hell you are in* . . .

This, I saw, was not the mere human wisdom of a man of a distant past in distant Arabia. However wise he may have been, such a man could not by himself have foreseen the torment so peculiar to this twentieth century. Out of the Koran spoke a voice greater than the voice of Muhammad . . .

— 5 —

DARKNESS HAS FALLEN over the courtyard of the Prophet's Mosque, broken through only by the oil lamps which are suspended on long chains between the pillars of the arcades. Shaykh

Abdullah ibn Bulayhid sits with his head sunk low over his chest and his eyes closed. One who does not know him might think that he has fallen asleep; but I know that he has been listening to my narrative with deep absorption, trying to fit it into the pattern of his own wide experience of men and their hearts. After a long while he raises his head and opens his eyes:

'And then? And what didst thou do then?'

'The obvious thing, O Shaykh. I sought out a Muslim friend of mine, an Indian who was at that time head of the small Muslim community in Berlin, and told him that I wanted to embrace Islam. He stretched out his right hand toward me, and I placed mine in it and, in the presence of two witnesses, declared: "I bear witness that there is no God but God and that Muhammad is His Messenger."* A few weeks later my wife did the same.'

'And what did thy people say to that?'

'Well, they did not like it. When I informed my father that I had become a Muslim, he did not even answer my letter. Some months later my sister wrote, telling me that he considered me dead . . . Thereupon I sent him another letter, assuring him that my acceptance of Islam did not change anything in my attitude toward him or my love for him; that, on the contrary, Islam enjoined upon me to love and honour my parents above all other people . . . But this letter also remained unanswered.'

'Thy father must indeed be strongly attached to his religion. . .'

'No, O Shaykh, he is not; and that is the strangest part of the story. He considers me, I think, a renegade, not so much from his faith (for that has never held him strongly) as from the community in which he grew up and the culture to which he is attached.'

'And has thou never seen him since?'

'No. Very soon after our conversion, my wife and I left Europe; we could not bear to remain there any longer. And I have never gone back . . .'†

* This declaration of faith is the only 'ritual' necessary to become a Muslim. In Islam, the terms 'Messenger' and 'Prophet' are interchangeable when applied to major Prophets bearing a new Message, like Muhammad, Jesus, Moses, Abraham.

† Our relationship was resumed in 1935, after my father had at last come to understand and appreciate the reasons for my conversion to Islam. Although we never met again in person, we remained in continuous correspondence until 1942, when he and my sister were deported from Vienna by the Nazis and subsequently died in a concentration camp.

XI

JIHAD

— 1 —

AS I AM LEAVING the Prophet's Mosque, a hand grips mine: and as I turn my head, I meet the kind old eyes of Sidi Muhammad az-Zuwayy, the Sanusi.

'O my son, how glad I am to see thee after all these months. May God bless thy step in the blessed City of the Prophet . . .'

Hand in hand, we walk slowly over the cobbled street leading from the mosque to the main bazaar. In his white North African *burnus*, Sidi Muhammad is a familiar figure in Medina, where he has been living for years; and many people interrupt our progress to greet him with the respect due not only to his seventy years but also to his fame as one of the leaders of Libya's heroic fight for independence.

'I want thee to know, O my son, that Sayyid Ahmad is in Medina. He is not in good health, and it would give him much pleasure to see thee. How long wilt thou remain here?'

'Only until the day after tomorrow,' I reply, 'but I shall certainly not leave without seeing Sayyid Ahmad. Let us go to him now.'

In the whole of Arabia there is no man whom I love better than Sayyid Ahmad, for there is no man who has sacrificed himself so wholly and so selflessly for an ideal. A scholar and a warrior, he has devoted his entire life to the spiritual revival of the Muslim community and to its struggle for political independence, knowing well that the one cannot be brought about without the other.

How well I remember my first meeting with Sayyid Ahmad, many years ago, in Mecca . . .

To the north of the Holy City rises Mount Abu Qubays, the centre of many ancient legends and traditions. From its summit, crowned by a small, whitewashed mosque with two low minarets, there is a wonderful view down into the valley of Mecca with the

312

square of the Mosque of the Kaaba at its bottom and the colourful, loose amphitheatre of houses climbing up the naked, rocky slopes on all sides. A little below the summit of Mount Abu Qubays, a complex of stone buildings hangs over narrow terraces like a cluster of eagles' nests: the Meccan seat of the Sanusi Fraternity. The old man whom I met there – an exile to whom all ways to his home in Cyrenaica were closed after thirty years' fight and his seven-year odyssey between the Black Sea and the mountains of Yemen – bore a name famous throughout the Muslim world: Sayyid Ahmad, the Grand Sanusi. No other name had caused so many sleepless night to the colonial rulers of North Africa, not even that of the great Abd al-Qadir of Algeria in the nineteenth century, or of the Moroccan Abd al-Karim who had been so powerful a thorn in the side of the French in more recent days. Those names, however unforgettable to the Muslims, had only a political import – while Sayyid Ahmad and his Order had for many years been a great spiritual power as well.

I was introduced to him by my Javanese friend Hajji Agos Salim, who held a position of leadership in Indonesia's struggle for political emancipation and had come to Mecca on pilgrimage. When Sayyid Ahmad learned that I was a recent convert to Islam, he stretched out his hand toward me and said gently:

'Welcome among thy brethren, O young brother of mine . . .'

Suffering was engraved on the beautiful brow of the aging fighter for faith and freedom. His face, with its little grey beard and sensually-shrewd mouth between painful grooves, was tired; the lids fell heavily over the eyes and made them appear drowsy; the tone of his voice as soft and weighted with sorrow. But sometimes it flared up in him. The eyes assumed a glittering sharpness, the voice grew into resonance, and out of the folds of his white *burnus* an arm rose like an eagle's wing.

Heir to an idea and a mission which, had it reached fulfilment, might have brought about a renascence of modern Islam: even in the decay of age and illness and in the breakdown of his life's work, the North African hero had not lost his glow. He had the right not to despair; he knew that the longing after religious and political revival in the true spirit of Islam – which was what the Sanusi movement stood for – could never be wiped out of the hearts of the Muslim peoples.

.   .   .   .

IT WAS SAYYID AHMAD'S GRANDFATHER, the great Algerian scholar Muhammad ibn Ali as-Sanusi (thus surnamed
after the clan of Banu Sanus, to which he belonged), who in the
first half of the century conceived the idea of an Islamic fraternity which might pave the way to the establishment of a truly
Islamic commonwealth. After years of wandering and studying
in many Arab lands, Muhammad ibn Ali founded the first
zawiya, or lodge, of the Sanusi Order at Mount Abu Qubays in
Mecca and rapidly gained a strong following among the beduins
of the Hijaz. He did not remain in Mecca, however, but returned
to North Africa, ultimately to settle at Jaghbub, an oasis in the
desert between Cyrenaica and Egypt, from where his message
spread like lightning all over Libya and far beyond. When he
died in 1859, the Sanusi (as all members of the Order came to be
known) held sway over a vast state stretching from the shores of
the Mediterranean deep into equatorial Africa and into the
country of the Tuareg in the Algerian Sahara.

The term 'state' does not precisely describe this unique creation, for the Grand Sanusi never aimed at establishing a personal
rule for himself or for his descendants: what he wanted was to
prepare an organizational basis for a moral, social and political
revival of Islam. In accordance with this aim, he did nothing to
upset the traditional tribal structure of the region, nor did he
challenge the nominal suzerainty over Libya of the Turkish
Sultan – whom he continued to recognize as the Caliph of Islam
– but devoted all his efforts to educating the beduins in the
tenets of Islam, from which they had deviated in the past, and to
bringing about among them that consciousness of brotherhood
which had been envisaged by the Koran but had been largely
obliterated by centuries of tribal feuding. From the many
zawiyas which had sprung up all over North Africa, the Sanusi
carried their message to the remotest tribes and wrought within a
few decades an almost miraculous change among Arabs and
Berbers alike. The old intertribal anarchy gradually subsided,
and the once unruly warriors of the desert became imbued with
a hitherto unknown spirit of co-operation. In the zawiyas their
children received education – not only in the teachings of Islam
but also in many practical arts and crafts that previously had
been disdained by the warlike nomads. They were induced to
drill more and better wells in areas which for centuries had lain

barren, and under Sanusi guidance prosperous plantations began to dot the desert. Trade was encouraged, and the peace engendered by the Sanusi made travel possible in parts where in past years no caravan could move unmolested. In short, the influence of the Order was a powerful stimulus to civilization and progress, while its strict orthodoxy raised the moral standards of the new community far above anything which that part of the world had ever experienced. Almost to a man, the tribes and their chieftains willingly accepted the spiritual leadership of the Grand Sanusi; and even the Turkish authorities in Libya's coastal towns found that the moral authority of the Order made it vastly easier for them to deal with the once so 'difficult' beduin tribes.

Thus, while the Order concentrated its efforts on a progressive regeneration of the indigenous people, its influence became in time almost indistinguishable from actual governmental power. This power rested on the Order's ability to rouse the simple beduins and the Tuareg of North Africa out of their erstwhile sterile formalism in matters religious, to fill them with a desire to live truly in the spirit of Islam and to give them the feeling that all of them were working for freedom, human dignity and brotherhood. Never since the time of the Prophet had there been anywhere in the Muslim world a large-scale movement as closely approximating the Islamic way of life as that of the Sanusi.

This peaceful era was shattered in the last quarter of the nineteenth century, when France began to advance southward from Algeria into equatorial Africa, and to occupy, step by step, regions that previously had been independent under the spiritual guidance of the Order. In defence of their freedom, the founder's son and successor, Muhammad al-Mahdi, was forced to take to the sword and was never able to lay it down. This long struggle was a true Islamic *jihad* – a war of self-defence, thus defined by the Koran: *Fight in the way of God against those who fight against you, but do not yourselves be aggressors; for, verily, God does not love aggressors . . . Fight against them until there is no longer oppression and all men are free to worship God. But if they desist, all hostility shall cease . . .*

But the French did not desist; they carried their tricolour on their bayonets deeper and deeper into Muslim lands.

When Muhammad al-Mahdi died in 1902, his nephew Sayyid Ahmad followed him in the leadership of the Order. From the age of nineteen, during his uncle's lifetime and later when he himself became Grand Sanusi, he was engaged in the fight against French encroachment in what is now French Equatorial Africa. When the Italians invaded Tripolitania and Cyrenaica in 1911, he found himself fighting on two fronts; and this new and more immediate pressure forced him to transfer his main attention to the north. Side by side with the Turks and, after the latter abandoned Libya, alone, Sayyid Ahmad and his Sanusi *mujahidin* – as these fighters for freedom called themselves – waged war against the invaders with such success, that in spite of their superior armaments and numbers, the Italians could keep only a precarious foothold in a few coastal towns.

The British, then solidly entrenched in Egypt and obviously none too anxious to see the Italians expand into the interior of North Africa, were not hostile to the Sanusi. Their neutral attitude was of utmost importance to the Order since all the supplies of the *mujahidin* came from Egypt, where they enjoyed the sympathy of practically the whole population. It is quite probable that this British neutrality would in the long run have enabled the Sanusi to drive the Italians entirely out of Cyrenaica. But in 1915 Turkey entered the Great War on the side of Germany, and the Ottoman Sultan, as Caliph of Islam, called upon the Grand Sanusi to assist the Turks by attacking the British in Egypt. The British, naturally more than ever concerned about safeguarding the rear of their Egyptian possession, urged Sayyid Ahmad to remain neutral. In exchange for his neutrality, they were prepared to accord political recognition to the Sanusi Order in Libya, and even to cede to it some of the Egyptian oases in the Western Desert.

Had Sayyid Ahmad accepted this offer, he would only have followed what common sense categorically demanded. He did not owe any particular loyalty to the Turks, who had signed away Libya to the Italians some years earlier, leaving the Sanusi to fight on alone; the British had not committed any act of hostility against the Sanusi but, on the contrary, had allowed them to receive supplies from Egypt – and Egypt was their sole avenue of supply. Moreover, the Berlin-inspired 'jihad' which the Ottoman Sultan had proclaimed certainly did not fulfill the requirements laid down by the Koran: the Turks were not fighting in self-defence but rather had joined a non-Muslim power in an aggressive war. Thus, religious and political considerations alike pointed to one course alone for the Grand Sanusi: to keep out of a war which was not his. Several of the most influential Sanusi leaders – my friend Sidi Muhammad az-Zuwayy among them – advised Sayyid Ahmad to remain neutral. But his quixotic sense of chivalry toward the Caliph of Islam finally outweighed the dictates of reason and induced him to make the wrong decision: he declared himself for the Turks and attacked the British in the Western Desert.

This conflict of conscience and its eventual outcome were the more tragic as in the case of Sayyid Ahmad there was not merely a question of personal loss or gain but also, possibly, of doing irreparable harm to the great cause to which his whole life, and the lives of two generations before him, had been devoted. Knowing him as I do, there is no doubt in my mind that he was prompted by a most unselfish motive – the desire to safeguard the unity of the Muslim world; but I have as little doubt that, from a political point of view, his decision was the worst he could ever have made. By waging war against the British, he sacrificed, without fully realizing it at the time, the entire future of the Sanusi Order.

From then on he was forced to fight on three fronts: in the north against the Italians, in the southwest against the French, and in the east against the British. In the beginning he met with some success. The British, hard pressed by the German-Turkish advance toward the Suez Canal, evacuated the oases in the Western Desert, which were immediately occupied by Sayyid Ahmad. Flying Sanusi columns mounted on dromedaries, led by Muhammad az-Zuwayy (who in his wisdom had so strongly opposed this venture), penetrated to the vicinity of Cairo. At that moment, however, the fortunes of war suddenly shifted: the swift advance of the German-Turkish army was halted in the Sinai Peninsula and turned into a retreat. Shortly thereafter, the British counterattacked the Sanusi in the Western Desert, reoccupied the frontier oases and wells, and thus cut off the sole supply route of the *mujahidin*. The interior of Cyrenaica could not alone nourish a population engaged in a life-and-death struggle; and the few German and Austrian submarines that secretly landed arms and ammunition brought no more than token help.

In 1917 Sayyid Ahmad was persuaded by his Turkish advisers to go by submarine to Istanbul and there arrange for more effective support. Before he left, he entrusted the leadership of the Order in Cyrenaica to his cousin, Sayyid Muhammad al-Idris.* Being of a more conciliatory disposition than Sayyid Ahmad, Idris almost at once attempted to come to terms with the British and the Italians. The British – who had disliked the conflict with the Sanusi from the very beginning – readily agreed to make peace; and they exerted pressure on the Italians to do the same. Shortly afterward, Sayyid Idris was officially recognized by the Italian government as 'Amir of the Sanusi', and was able to maintain a precarious quasi independence in the interior of Cyrenaica until 1922. When it became obvious, however, that the Italians did not really mean to abide by their agreements but were bent on subjecting the entire country to their rule, Sayyid Idris, in protest, left for Egypt at the beginning of 1923, handing over leadership of the Sanusi to a trusted old follower, Umar al-Mukhtar. The anticipated breach of agreements by the Italians followed almost immediately, and the war in Cyrenaica was resumed.

Meanwhile in Turkey, Sayyid Ahmad met with disappointment after disappointment. It had been his intention to return to Cyrenaica as soon as he had achieved his purpose; but the purpose was never achieved. For, once in Istanbul, strange intrigues forced him to delay his return from week to week, from month to month. It would almost appear that the circles around the Sultan did not really desire the Sanusi to succeed. The Turks had always been fearful lest one day the resurgent Arabs try to regain the leadership of the Muslim world; a victory of the Sanusi would of necessity have heralded such an Arab resurgence and made the Grand Sanusi, whose fame was almost legendary even in Turkey, the obvious successor to the Caliphate. That he himself had no such ambitions did not assuage the suspicions of the High Porte; and although he was treated with utmost respect and all honours due to his position, Sayyid Ahmad was politely but effectively detained in Turkey. The Ottoman breakdown in 1918 and the subsequent occupation of Istanbul by the Allies signalled the end of his misplaced hopes – and at the same time closed all avenues of return to Cyrenaica.

* King of Libya since 1952.

But the urge to work for the cause of Muslim unity did not allow Sayyid Ahmad to remain inactive. As the Allied troops were landing at Istanbul, he crossed over to Asia Minor to join Kemal Ataturk – then still known as Mustafa Kemal – who had just begun to organize the Turkish resistance in the interior of Anatolia.

One should remember that, in the beginning, the heroic struggle of Kemal's Turkey stood in the sign of Islam, and that it was religious enthusiasm alone that gave the Turkish nation in those grim days the strength to fight against the overwhelming power of the Greeks, who were backed by all the resources of the Allies.

Placing his great spiritual and moral authority in the service of the Turkish cause, Sayyid Ahmad travelled tirelessly through the towns and villages of Anatolia, calling upon the people to support the *Ghazi*, or 'Defender of the Faith', Mustafa Kemal. The Grand Sanusi's efforts and the lustre of his name contributed immeasurably to the success of the Kemalist movement among the simple peasants of Anatolia, to whom nationalist slogans meant nothing, but who for countless generations had deemed it a privilege to lay down their lives for Islam.

But here again the Grand Sanusi had committed an error of judgment – not with regard to the Turkish people, whose religious fervour did lead them to victory against an enemy many times stronger, but with regard to the intentions of their leader: for no sooner had the *Ghazi* attained to victory than it became obvious that his real aims differed widely from what his people had been led to expect. Instead of basing his social revolution on a revived and reinvigorated Islam, Ataturk forsook the spiritual force of religion (which alone had brought him to victory) and made, quite unnecessarily, a rejection of all Islamic values the basis of his reforms. Unnecessarily even from Ataturk's viewpoint: for he could easily have harnessed the tremendous religious enthusiasm of his people to a positive drive for progress without cutting them adrift from all that had shaped their culture and made them a great race.

In bitter disappointment with Ataturk's anti-Islamic reforms, Sayyid Ahmad withdrew completely from all political activity in Turkey and finally, in 1923, left for Damascus. There, in spite of his opposition to Ataturk's internal policies, he tried to serve the cause of Muslim unity by attempting to persuade the Syrians to reunite with Turkey. The French mandatory government viewed him, naturally, with utmost distrust and when, toward the end of 1924, his friends learned that his arrest was imminent, he escaped by car across the desert to the frontier of Najd and thence proceeded to Mecca, where he was received warmly by King Ibn Saud.

— 2 —

'AND HOW ARE the *mujahidin* faring, O Sidi Muhammad?' I ask – for I have been without news from Cyrenaica for nearly a year.

The round, white-bearded face of Sidi Muhammad az-Zuwayy darkens: 'The news is not good, O my son. The fighting has ended some months ago. The *mujahidin* have been broken; the last bullet has been spent. Now only God's mercy stands between our unhappy people and the vengeance of their oppressors ...'

'And what about Sayyid Idris?'

'Sayyid Idris,' replies Sidi Muhammad with a sigh, 'Sayyid Idris is still in Egypt, powerless, waiting – for what? He is a good man, God bless him, but no warrior. He lives with his books, and the sword does not sit well in his hand ...'

'But Umar al-Mukhtar – he surely did not surrender? Did he escape to Egypt?'

Sidi Muhammad stops in his tracks and stares at me in astonishment: 'Umar ... ? So thou hast not heard even that?'

'Heard what?'

'My son,' he says gently, 'Sidi Umar, may God have mercy on him, has been dead for nearly a year ...'

Umar al-Mukhtar – dead ... That lion of Cyrenaica, whose seventy-odd years did not prevent him from fighting, to the last, for his country's freedom: dead ... For ten long, grim years he was the soul of his people's resistance against hopeless odds – against Italian armies ten times more numerous than his – armies equipped with the most modern weapons, armoured cars, aeroplanes and artillery – while Umar and his half-starved *mujahidin* had nothing but rifles and a few horses with which to wage a desperate guerrilla warfare in a country that had been turned into one huge prison camp ...

I can hardly trust my own voice as I say: 'For the last year and a half, ever since I returned from Cyrenaica, I have known that he and his men were doomed. How I tried to persuade him to retreat into Egypt with the remnants of the *mujahidin*, so that he might remain alive for his people . . . and how calmly he brushed aside my attempts at persuasion, knowing well that death, and nothing but death, awaited him in Cyrenaica: and now, after a hundred battles, that long-waiting death has at last caught up with him . . . But, tell me, when did he fall?'

Muhammad az-Zuwayy shakes his head slowly; and as we emerge from the narrow bazaar street into the open, dark square of Al-Manakha, he tells me:

'He did not fall in battle. He was wounded and captured alive. And then the Italians killed him . . . hanged him like a common thief . . .'

'But how could they!' I exclaim. 'Not even Graziani would dare to do such a terrible thing!'

'But he did, he did,' he replies, with a wry smile. 'It was General Graziani himself who ordered him to be hanged. Sidi Umar and a score of his men were deep in Italian-held territory when they decided to pay their respects to the tomb of Sidi Rafi, the Prophet's Companion, which was in the vicinity. Somehow the Italians learned of his presence and sealed off the valley on both sides with many men. There was no way to escape. Sidi Umar and the *mujahidin* defended themselves until only he and two others remained alive. At last his horse was shot dead under him and, in falling, pinned him to the ground. But the old lion continued firing his rifle until a bullet shattered one of his hands; and then he continued firing with the other hand until his ammunition ran out. Then they got hold of him and carried him, bound, to Suluq. There he was brought before General Graziani, who asked him: "What wouldst thou say if the Italian government, in its great clemency, would allow thee to live? Art thou prepared to promise that thou wilt spend thy remaining years in peace?" But Sidi Umar replied: "I shall not cease to fight against thee and thy people until either you leave my country or I leave my life. And I swear to thee by Him who knows what is in men's hearts that if my hands were not bound this very moment, I would fight thee with my bare hands, old and broken as I am. . . ." Thereupon General Graziani laughed and give the order that

Sidi Umar be hanged in the market place of Suluq; which they
did. And they herded together many thousands of Muslim men
and women from the camps in which they were imprisoned and
forced them to witness the hanging of their leader . . .'*

— 3 —

STILL HAND IN HAND, Muhammad az-Zuwayy and I pro-
ceed in the direction of the Sanusi *zawiya*. Darkness lies over the
vast square, and the noises of the bazaar have been left behind.
The sand crunches under our sandals. Here and there a group of
resting load-camels can be discerned, and the line of houses on
the distant periphery of the square shows indistinctly against the
cloudy night sky. It reminds me of the fringe of a distant forest –
like those juniper forests on the tableland of Cyrenaica where I
first encountered Sidi Umar al-Mukhtar: and the memory of
that fruitless journey wells up within me with all its tragic
flavour of darkness and danger and death. I see the sombre face
of Sidi Umar bent over a small, flickering fire and hear his
husky, solemn voice: 'We have to fight for our faith and our
freedom until we drive the invaders away or die ourselves . . .
We have no other choice . . .'

.   .   .   .

IT WAS A STRANGE MISSION that brought me to Cyrenaica
in the late January of 1931. Some months earlier – to be precise,
in the autumn of 1930 – the Grand Sanusi came to Medina. I
spent hours in his and Muhammad az-Zuwayy's company, discussing the desperate straits of the *mujahidin* who were carrying
on the struggle in Cyrenaica under the leadership of Umar
al-Mukhtar. It was evident that unless they received quick and
effective help from outside, they would not be able to last out
much longer.

The situation in Cyrenaica was roughly this: all the towns on
the coast and several points in the northern part of the Jabal
Akhdar – the 'Green Mountains' of central Cyrenaica – were
firmly held by the Italians. Between these fortified points they
maintained continuous patrols with armoured cars and considerable numbers of infantry, mostly Eritrean *askaris*, sup-

* This act of Italian chivalry took place on 16 September, 1931.

ported by an air squadron which made frequent sorties over the countryside. The beduins (who constituted the core of the Sanusi resistance) were unable to move without being spotted immediately and strafed from the air. It often happened that a reconnaissance plane reported the presence of a tribal encampment by wireless to the nearest post; and while the machine guns of the plane prevented the people from dispersing, a few armoured cars would come up, driving straight through tents, camels and people, indiscriminately killing everyone within range – men, women, children and cattle; and whatever people and animals survived were herded together and driven northward into the huge barbed-wire enclosures which the Italians had established near the coast. At that time, toward the end of 1930, about eighty thousand beduins, together with several hundred thousand head of cattle, were herded together into an area which did not provide sufficient nourishment for a quarter of their number; in result, the death rate among man and beast was appalling. In addition to this, the Italians were erecting a barbed-wire barrier along the Egyptian border from the coast southward to Jaghbub in order to make it impossible for the guerrillas to obtain supplies from Egypt. The valiant Maghariba tribe under their indomitable chieftain, Al-Ataywish – Umar al-Mukhtar's right-hand man – were still putting up a stiff resistance near the western coast of Cyrenaica, but most of the tribe had already been overwhelmed by the superior numbers and equipment of the Italians. Deep in the south, the Zuwayya tribe, led by ninety-year-old Abu Karayyim, were still fighting desperately despite the loss of their tribal centre, the Jalu oases. Hunger and disease were decimating the beduin population in the interior.

All the fighting forces which Sidi Umar could deploy at any one time amounted to hardly more than a thousand men. This, however, was not entirely due to lack of men. The kind of guerrilla warfare which the *mujahidin* were waging did not favour large groupments of warriors but depended rather on the speed and mobility of small striking forces which would suddenly appear out of nowhere, attack an Italian column or outpost, capture its arms and disperse without trace into the tangled juniper forests and broken-up *wadis* of the Cyrenaican plateau. That such small bands, however brave and death-despising, could never win a decisive victory over an enemy who commanded al-most unlimited resources of men and armaments was obvious. The question was, therefore, how to increase the strength of the *mujahidin* so as to enable them not only to inflict sporadic losses on the invaders but to wrest from them the positions in which they were entrenched and hold those positions in the face of re-newed enemy attacks.

Such an increase of Sanusi strength depended on several fac-tors: a steady influx of badly needed food supplies from Egypt; weapons with which to meet the onslaughts of aeroplanes and armoured cars – especially antitank rifles and heavy machine guns; trained technical personnel to employ such weapons and to instruct the *mujahidin* in their use; and, lastly, the establish-ment of reliable wireless communications between the various groups of *mujahidin* in Cyrenaica and secret supply depots with-in Egyptian territory.

For about a week, evening after evening, the Grand Sanusi, Sidi Muhammad and I held council on what might be done. Sidi Muhammad expressed the opinion that an occasional reinforce-ment of the *mujahidin* in Cyrenaica would not solve the problem. It was his belief that the oasis of Kufra, far to the south in the Libyan Desert, which had been the headquarters of the Sanusi Order under Sayyid Ahmad, should again be made the focal point of all future warfare: for Kufra was still beyond the reach of Italian troops. It lay, moreover, on the direct (if very long and difficult) caravan route to the Egyptian oases of Bahriyya and Farafra, and therefore could be more effectively provisioned than any other point in the country. It could also be made a rallying centre for the many thousands of Cyrenaican refugees who were living in camps in Egypt, and thus form a steady re-servoir of manpower for Sidi Umar's guerrilla forces in the north. Properly fortified and equipped with modern weapons, Kufra could hold off machine-gun attacks by low-flying aircraft, while bombing from great heights would not really endanger such a widely dispersed group of settlements.

The Grand Sanusi suggested that if such a reorganization of the struggle were possible, he himself would return to Kufra to direct future operations from there. I, for my part, insisted that for the success of such a plan it was imperative for Sayyid Ahmad to re-establish good relations with the British, whom he had so bitterly, and so unnecessarily, antagonized by his attack on them in 1915. Such an improvement of relations might not be impossible, for Britain was not very happy about Italy's expansionist mood, especially now that Mussolini was trumpeting to all the world his intention of 're-establishing the Roman Empire' on both shores of the Mediterranean, and was casting covetous glances on Egypt as well.

My deep interest in the fate of the Sanusi was due not only to my admiration of the extreme heroism in a righteous cause; what concerned me even more was the possible repercussion of a Sanusi victory on the Arab world as a whole. Like so many other Muslims, I had for years pinned my hopes on Ibn Saud as the potential leader of an Islamic revival; and now that these hopes had proved futile, I could see in the entire Muslim world only one movement that genuinely strove for the fulfilment of the ideal of an Islamic society: the Sanusi movement, now fighting a last-ditch battle for survival.

And it was because Sayyid Ahmad knew how intensely my own emotions were involved with the Sanusi cause that he now turned to me and, looking straight into my eyes, asked:

'Wouldst thou, O Muhammad, go to Cyrenaica on our behalf and find out what could be done for the *mujahidin*? Perhaps thou wilt be able to see things with clearer eyes than my people can...'

I looked back at him and nodded, without a word. Although I was aware of his confidence in me and, therefore, not completely surprised by his suggestion, it nevertheless took my breath away. The prospect of an adventure of such magnitude exhilarated me beyond words; but what thrilled me even more was the thought of being able to contribute something to the cause for which so many other men had given their lives.

Sayyid Ahmad reached toward a shelf above his head and drew out a copy of the Koran wrapped in a silken cloth. Placing it on his knees, he took my right hand between both of his and laid it on the Book:

'Swear, O Muhammad, by Him who knows what is in the hearts of men, that thou wilt always keep faith with the *mujahidin* . . .'

I took the oath; and never in my life have I been surer of what I pledged than at that moment.

.   .   .   .

THE MISSION WHICH SAYYID AHMAD entrusted to me required extreme secrecy. Since my relations with the Grand Sanusi were well known and could not have escaped the notice of the foreign missions in Jidda, it was not advisable to travel openly to Egypt and run the risk of being trailed there. My recent uncovering of the intrigues behind Faysal ad-Dawish's rebellion had certainly not enhanced my standing with the British, and it was only too probable that they would watch me closely from the moment I set foot on Egyptian soil. We decided, therefore, that even my going to Egypt should be kept in the dark. I would cross the Red Sea in one of those Arabian sailing ships and land surreptitiously, without passport or visa, at some secluded point on the coast of Upper Egypt. In Egypt I would be able to move about freely in the guise of a Hijazi townsman, for the many Meccans and Medinese who went there in pursuit of trade or in search of prospective pilgrims were a familiar sight in Egyptian towns and villages – and as I spoke the Hijazi dialect with perfect ease, I could pass anywhere for a native of one of the two Holy Cities.

Several weeks of preparation were required to complete the arrangements which involved secret exchanges of letters with Sidi Umar in Cyrenaica as well as with Sanusi contacts in Egypt; and so it was only in the first week of January 1931, that Zayd and I made our way out of the Hijazi port-town of Yanbu to a little-frequented part of the shore. It was a moonless night, and walking over the uneven path in sandals was most unpleasant. Once, when I stumbled, the butt of the Luger pistol tucked under my Hijazi *kaftan* struck my ribs; and this brought vividly to my mind the dangerous nature of the adventure on which I was embarking.

Here I was, walking toward a rendezvous with an obscure Arabian skipper who was to take me in his *dhow* across the sea and land me secretly somewhere on the Egyptian coast. I had no papers with me which could betray my identity and so, if I were caught in Egypt, it would not be an easy matter to prove who I was. But even the risk of spending a few weeks in an Egyptian jail was nothing as compared with the dangers that lay farther ahead. I would have to make my way across the entire width of the Western Desert, avoiding detection by Italian spotter planes and possibly also armoured car patrols, into the heart of a

country in which only weapons spoke. Why was I doing this? – I
asked myself.

Although danger was not unknown to me, I had never sought
it out for the sake of a possible thrill. Whenever I had gone into
it, it was always in response to urges, conscious or unconscious,
connected in a very personal way with my own life. Then what
about the present undertaking? Did I really believe that my intervention could turn the tide in favour of the *mujahidin*? I
wanted to believe it: but in my innermost I knew that I was setting out on a quixotic errand. Then why, in God's name, was I
risking my life as I had never risked it before, and with so little
promise ahead?

But the answer was there before the question was even consciously formulated.

When I had come to know Islam and accepted it as my way of
life, I had thought that all my questioning and searching had
come to an end. Only gradually, very gradually, did I become
aware that this was not the end: for to accept a way of life as
binding for oneself was, to me at least, inextricably bound up
with a desire to pursue it among like-minded people – and not
only to pursue it in a personal sense but also to work for its social
fruition within the community of my choice. To me, Islam was a
way and not an end – and the desperate guerrillas of Umar al-
Mukhtar were fighting with their lifeblood for the freedom to
tread that way, just as the Companions of the Prophet had done
thirteen centuries ago. To be of help to them in their hard and
bitter struggle, however uncertain the outcome, was as personally necessary to me as to pray . . .

And there was the shore. In the soft swell of the wavelets that
lapped against the pebbles rocked the rowboat that was to take
us to the ship anchored in the dark distance beyond. As the
solitary oarsman rose from the waiting boat, I turned to Zayd:

'Zayd, my brother, dost thou know that we are going into a
venture which may prove more threatening to thee and me than
all of Ad-Dawish's *Ikhwan* put together? Dost thou not look
back with yearning to the peace of Medina and thy friends?'

'Thy way is my way, O my uncle,' he replied. 'And hast thou
not told me thyself that water which stands motionless becomes
stale and foul? Let us go – and may the water run until it becomes clear . . .'

The ship was one of those large, clumsy *dhows* which ply all around the coasts of Arabia: built entirely of wood, smelling of dried fish and seaweed, with a high poop, two Latin-rigged masts and a large, low-ceilinged cabin between them. The *rais*, or skipper, was a wizened old Arab from Muscat. The small, beady eyes that peered at me from beneath the folds of a voluminous, multicoloured turban bore a wary expression that spoke of long years spent in illicit hazards and adventures; and the curved, silver-encrusted dagger in his sash did not seem to be mere ornament.

'*Marhaba, ya marhaba*, O my friends!' he cried as we clambered aboard. 'This is an hour of good augury!'

How many times, I mused, had he given the same hearty welcome to poor *hajjis* whom he surreptitiously took on board in Egypt and, without any further thought to their welfare, landed on the coasts of the Hijaz, so that they might avoid paying the heavy pilgrimage tax which the Saudi government had imposed on those who wish to make the pilgrimage to the House of God? And how many times had he used exactly these words to the slave traders who, in sharp violation of the Law of Islam, had captured some wretched Ethiopians to sell in the slave markets of Yemen? But then, I consoled myself, the experience which our *rais* must have gained – however questionable its background – could be only to our advantage: for he knew his way around the Red Sea as few other sailors did, and could be relied upon to set us down on a safe shore.

.   .   .   .

AND INDEED, FOUR NIGHTS after we had embarked on the *dhow*, we were landed, again in the small rowboat, north of the port of Qusayr on the coast of Upper Egypt. To our astonishment, the *rais* refused to accept payment, 'for,' he said with a grin, 'I have been paid by my masters. May God be with you.'

As I had expected, it was not difficult to make ourselves inconspicuous in Qusayr, for the town was accustomed to seeing men in Hijazi garb. On the morning after our arrival we booked seats in a ramshackle bus bound for As-Siyut on the Nile; and, sandwiched between an alarmingly fat woman who carried a basket full of chickens in her vast lap and an old *fellah* who, upon observing our attire, immediately started reminiscing about the *hajj* he had performed ten years earlier, Zayd and I started on the first stage of our African journey.

I had always thought that any man engaged in a surreptitious and risky undertaking was bound to feel as though he were the object of suspicion on the part of everyone he encountered, and that his disguise could easily be seen through. But, strangely enough, I did not have that feeling now. During my past years in Arabia I had entered the life of its people so fully that somehow it did not occur to me to regard myself as anything but one of them; and although I had never shared the peculiar business interests of the Meccans and Medinese, I now felt so entirely at home in my role of pilgrim tout that I promptly became involved in an almost 'professional' discussion with several other passengers on the virtues of performing the *hajj*. Zayd fell into the spirit of the game with great zest, and so the first hours of our journey were spent in lively conversation.

After changing to a train at As-Siyut, we finally arrived at the small town of Bani Suef and went straight to the house of our Sanusi contact, Ismail adh-Dhibi – a short, stout man of merry countenance, speaking the resonant Arabic of Upper Egypt. Being only a clothier of moderate means, he was not one of the notables of the town; but his allegiance to the Sanusi Order had been proved on many occasions, and his personal devotion to Sayyid Ahmad made him doubly trustworthy. Although the hour was late, he aroused a servant to prepare a meal for us, and while we waited for it, he recounted the arrangements he had made.

First of all, immediately on receipt of Sayyid Ahmad's message, he had contacted a well-known member of the Egyptian royal family who for many years had been an ardent and active supporter of the Sanusi cause. The Prince was fully apprised of the purpose of my mission; he had readily consented to place the necessary funds at my disposal and also to provide mounts and two reliable guides for the desert journey to the Cyrenaican border. At this moment, our host informed us, they were awaiting us in one of the palm orchards outside Bani Suef.

Zayd and I now discarded our Hijazi dress, which would arouse too much curiosity on the Western Desert routes. In its place we were provided with cotton trousers and tunics of North African cut as well as with woollen *burnuses* such as are worn in western Egypt and Libya. From the basement of his house Ismail produced two short cavalry carbines of Italian pattern – 'for it will be easier to replenish your ammunition for this kind of rifle among the *mujahidin*.'

On the following night, guided by our host, we made our way out of the town. Our two guides proved to be beduins from the Egyptian tribe of Awlad Ali, among whom the Sanusi had many supporters; one of them, Abdullah, was a vivacious young man who had participated a year earlier in the fighting in Cyrenaica and could thus give us a good deal of information about what we might expect there. The other, whose name I have forgotten, was a gaunt, morose fellow who spoke only rarely but showed himself no less trustworthy than the more personable Abdullah. The four camels they had with them – strong, speedy dromedaries of Bisharin breed – had obviously been chosen for their quality; they carried saddles not much different from those to which I had been accustomed in Arabia. As we were to move rapidly, without long halts, cooked food would be out of the question most of the way; consequently, our provisions were simple: a large bagful of dates and a smaller bag filled to bursting with hard, sweetened biscuits made of coarse wheat flour and dates; and three of the camels had waterskins attached to their saddles.

Shortly before midnight, Ismail embraced us and invoked God's blessing on our enterprise; I could see that he was deeply moved. With Abdullah leading, we left the palm orchard behind us and soon, under the light of a bright moon, ambled at a brisk pace over the gravelly desert plain toward the northwest.

Owing to the necessity of avoiding any encounter with the Egyptian Frontier Administration – whose cars and camel-mounted constabulary might, for all we knew, patrol this part of the Western Desert – we took care to keep as far as possible from the main caravan tracks; but as almost all traffic between Bahriyya and the Nile valley went via Fayyum, far to the north, the risk was not too great.

During the first night out we covered about thirty miles and stopped for the day in a clump of tamarisk bushes; on the second and following nights we did much better, so that before dawn of the fourth day we arrived at the rim of the deep depression within which lay the oasis of Bahriyya.

While we encamped under cover of some boulders outside the

oasis – which consisted of several separate settlements and plantations, the chief of them being the village of Bawiti – Abdullah made his way on foot down the steep, rocky incline into the palm-covered depression to seek out our contact man at Bawiti. He would not be able to return before nightfall, and so we lay down to sleep in the shadow of the rocks: a pleasant rest after the strain and cold of our night-long ride. Nevertheless, I did not sleep much, for too many ideas occupied my mind.

Ruminating on our plans, it seemed to me that it would not be too difficult to maintain a permanent line of communications between Bani Suef and Bahriyya; even large caravans would be able, I was certain, to proceed undetected between these two points if sufficient care was taken. Despite the fact that a Frontier Administration post was situated at Bawiti (we could see its white buildings from our hiding place above the oasis), it might be possible to establish a secret wireless transmitter in one of the more isolated villages in the south of Bahriyya. On this point I was reassured some hours later by Abdullah and the old Berber – our contact man – who accompanied him. It appeared that, on the whole, the oasis was only loosely supervised by the government; and, what was even more important, the population was overwhelmingly pro-Sanusi.

Five more nights of strenuous riding: first over gravel and broken ground and then through flat sand dunes; past the uninhabited Sitra oasis and its lifeless, dark-blue salt lake fringed by reeds and thickets of wild palms; over the Arj depression with its fantastic, craggy chalk rocks, to which the moonlight imparted a ghostly, other-worldly appearance; and, toward the end of the fifth night, our first view of the oasis of Siwa . . .

For years it had been one of my most cherished desires to visit this remote oasis which once had been the seat of an Ammon temple and an oracle famous throughout the ancient world; but somehow my desire had never been fulfilled. And now it lay before me in the rising dawn: a vast expanse of palm groves surrounding a solitary hill on which the houses of the town, rooted in the rock like cave dwellings, rose tier upon tier toward a tall, conical minaret that topped the flat summit. It was a bizarre conglomeration of crumbling masonry such as one might behold in a dream . . . I was seized with an urge to enter its mysterious confines and to wander through lanes that had witnessed the times of the Pharaohs, and to see the ruins of the temple in which Croesus, King of Lydia, heard the oracle that spelt his doom, and the Macedonian Alexander was promised conquest of the world.

But once again my longing was to remain unfulfilled. Although so near, the town of Siwa must needs remain closed to me. To visit a place so remote from contacts with the outer world and so unaccustomed to strangers that every new face was bound to be noticed at once would indeed have been foolhardy: for, situated almost on the Libyan border, Siwa was most closely watched by the Frontier Administration and also, beyond any doubt, full of informers in Italian pay. And so, regretfully consoling myself with the thought that it was not my portion to see it on this trip, I dismissed Siwa from my mind.

We skirted the town in a wide circle to the south and finally made camp in a grove of wild palms. Without allowing himself to rest – for we had no intention of stopping so close to the border any longer than was absolutely necessary – Abdullah immediately rode off to the neighbouring hamlet to find the man whom Sayyid Ahmad had entrusted with seeing us across the frontier. After a few hours, he returned with the two new guides and the four fresh camels that were to take us onward. The guides, Bara'sa beduins from the Jabal Akhdar, were Umar al-Mukhtar's men, sent especially by him to lead us through the gap between the Italian-occupied oases of Jaghbub and Jalu onto the Cyrenaican plateau, where I was to meet Umar.

Abdullah and his friend took leave of us to return to their village in Egypt; and under the guidance of the two *mujahidin*, Khalil and Abd ar-Rahman, we started on our week's trek across the almost waterless desert steppe that gently ascends toward the Jabal Akhdar. It was the hardest desert journey I had ever experienced. Although there was not much danger of discovery by Italian patrols if one took care to hide in daytime and travel only by night, the necessity of avoiding the widely spaced wells made the long march a nightmare. Only once were we able to water our camels and refill our waterskins from a desolate well in Wadi al-Mra; and this almost proved our undoing.

We had arrived at the well later than we had expected – in fact, dawn was breaking when we started to draw water for the animals, and the sun stood above the horizon when we finished.

We had still, as Khalil told us, two good hours to go before we would reach the rocky depression that was to be our hiding place for the day. But hardly had we resumed our march when the ominous drone of an aeroplane broke the desert silence: and a few minutes later a small monoplane appeared over our heads, banked steeply, and began to circle in a steadily lowering spiral. There was no place to take cover, and so we jumped down from the camels and scattered. At that moment the pilot opened fire with his machine gun.

'Down, down on the ground!' I shouted. 'Don't move – play dead!'

But Khalil, who must have experienced many such encounters in his long years with the *mujahidin*, did not 'play dead'. He lay down on his back, his head against a boulder, and, resting his rifle on one raised knee, started firing at the oncoming plane – not at random, but taking careful aim before every shot, as if at target practice. It was an extremely daring thing to do, for the plane went straight for him in a flat dive, spraying the sand with bullets. But one of Khalil's shots must have hit the plane, for suddenly it swerved, turned its nose upward and rapidly gained altitude. The pilot had probably decided that it would not be worthwhile to shoot up four men at the risk of his own safety. He circled once or twice above us, and then disappeared toward the east, in the direction of Jaghbub.

'Those Italian sons of dogs are cowards,' Khalil announced calmly as we reassembled. 'They like to kill – but they do not like to expose their own skins too much.'

None of us had been injured, but Abd ar-Rahman's camel was dead. We transferred his saddlebags to Zayd's animal, and henceforth he rode pillion behind Zayd.

Three nights later we reached the juniper forests of the Jabal Akhdar and gratefully exchanged our exhausted camels for the horses that had been waiting for us at a secluded spot in the custody of a group of *mujahidin*. From now on the desert lay behind us; we rode over a hilly, rocky plateau criss-crossed by innumerable dry stream beds and dotted with juniper trees which in places formed almost impenetrable thickets. This wild and pathless land in the heart of Italian-occupied territory was the hunting ground of the *mujahidin*.

FOUR MORE NIGHTS BROUGHT us to Wadi at-Taaban – the 'Valley of the Tired One', as it was most appropriately named – where we were to meet Umar al-Mukhtar. Safely ensconced in a thickly wooded gulley, with our horses hobbled in the lee of a rock, we awaited the coming of the Lion of the Jabal Akhdar. The night was cold and starless and filled with a rustling silence.

It would still be some hours until Sidi Umar arrived; and as the night was exceedingly dark, our two Bara'sa beduins saw no reason why we should not replenish our supply of water from the wells of Bu Sfayya, a few miles to the east. True, there was a fortified Italian post less than half a mile from Bu Sfayya–

' – but,' said Khalil, 'those curs will not dare to leave their walls in so dark a night.'

Thus Khalil, accompanied by Zayd, set out on horseback with two empty waterskins, having wrapped rags around the hooves of their horses to prevent any sound on the rocky ground. They disappeared into the darkness while Abd ar-Rahman and I huddled together for warmth against the low rocks. It would have been too risky to light a fire.

After an hour or so, some twigs crackled among the junipers; a sandal struck softly against a stone. My companion, instantly alert, stood straight for a while, the rifle in his hands, and peered into the darkness. A subdued call, not unlike the wail of a jackal, came from the thicket, and Abd ar-Rahman, cupping his hand before his mouth, answered with a similar sound. The figures of two men appeared before us. They were on foot and carried rifles. When they came closer, one of them said, 'The way of God,' and Abd ar-Rahman replied, 'There is no might and no power beside Him' – which seemed to be a kind of password.

Of the two new arrivals – both of them clothed in ragged *jards*, the wraps of Libyan beduins – one apparently knew Abd ar-Rahman, for he gripped both his hands and greeted him affectionately. I was introduced, and the two *mujahidin* clasped hands with me in turn. One of them said:

'May God be with thee. Sidi Umar is coming.'

We stood listening. After perhaps ten minutes, the twigs again crackled in the juniper bushes and three more men emerged from the shadows, each from a different direction, converging upon us with rifles ready. When they had convinced themselves that we were indeed those whom they expected to meet, they immedi-

ately fanned out into the thicket, again in different directions, obviously intending to keep good watch over their leader's safety.

And then he came, riding a small horse whose hooves were
muffled in cloth. Two men walked on each side and several more
followed him. When he reached the rocks by which we were
waiting, one of his men helped him to dismount, and I saw that
he moved with difficulty (later I learned that he had been
wounded in a skirmish some ten days earlier). In the light of the
rising moon I could now see him clearly; a man of middle size,
strong of bone; a short, snow-white beard framed his sombre,
deeply lined face; the eyes lay deep in their sockets; from the
creases around them one could guess that in different circumstances they might have readily laughed, but now there was
nothing in them but darkness and suffering and courage.

I stepped forward to meet him and felt the strong pressure of
his gnarled hand.

'Welcome, my son' – and as he spoke his eyes swept over me,
keenly, appraisingly: the eyes of a man to whom danger was
daily bread.

One of his men spread a blanket on the ground and Sidi Umar
sat down heavily. Abd ar-Rahman bent over to kiss his hand and
then, after asking the leader's permission, set himself to lighting
a small fire under the protective overhang of a rock. In the faint
glow of the fire, Sidi Umar read the letter from Sayyid Ahmad
which I had brought with me. He read it carefully, folded it, held
it for a moment over his head – a gesture of respect and devotion one almost never sees in Arabia but often in North Africa
– and then turned toward me with a smile:

'Sayyid Ahmad, may God lengthen his life, has good words to
say about thee. Thou art ready to help us. But I do not know
where help could come from, save from God, the Mighty, the
Bountiful. We are indeed reaching the end of our allotted time.'

'But this plan which Sayyid Ahmad has evolved', I interposed,
'could it not be a new beginning? If steady supplies could be
arranged and Kufra made the base of future operations, could
not the Italians be held?'

I had never seen a smile so bitter, so hopeless as that with
which Sidi Umar answered me: 'Kufra . . . ? Kufra is lost. It was
occupied by the Italians about a fortnight ago . . . '

This news stunned me. Throughout all the past months,

Sayyid Ahmad and I had been building our plans on the supposition that Kufra could be made a rallying point for intensified resistance. With Kufra gone, nothing remained to the Sanusi but the tortured plateau of the Jabal Akhdar – nothing but the steadily tightening vice of Italian occupation, loss of point after point, a slow, relentless strangulation . . .

'How did Kufra fall?'

With a weary gesture, Sidi Umar motioned to one of his men to come closer: 'Let this man tell thee the story . . . He is one of the few who have escaped from Kufra. He came to me only yesterday.'

The man from Kufra sat down on his haunches before me and pulled his ragged *burnus* around him. He spoke slowly, without any tremor of emotion in his voice; but his gaunt face seemed to mirror all the horrors he had witnessed.

'They came upon us in three columns, from three sides, with many armoured cars and heavy cannon. Their aeroplanes came down low and bombed houses and mosques and palm groves. We had only a few hundred men able to carry arms; the rest were women and children and old men. We defended house after house, but they were too strong for us, and in the end only the village of Al-Hawari was left to us. Our rifles were useless against their armoured cars; and they overwhelmed us. Only a few of us escaped. I hid myself in the palm orchards waiting for a chance to make my way through the Italian lines; and all through the night I could hear the screams of the women as they were being raped by the Italian soldiers and Eritrean *askaris*. On the following day an old woman came to my hiding place and brought me water and bread. She told me that the Italian general had assembled all the surviving people before the tomb of Sayyid Muhammad al-Mahdi; and before their eyes he tore a copy of the Koran into pieces, threw it to the ground and set his boot upon it, shouting, "Let your beduin prophet help you now, if he can!" And then he ordered the palm trees of the oasis to be cut down and the wells destroyed and all the books of Sayyid Ahmad's library burned. And on the next day he commanded that some of our elders and *ulama* be taken up in an aeroplane – and they were hurled out of the plane high above the ground to be smashed to death . . . And all through the second night I heard from my hiding place the cries of our women and the laughter of the soldiers, and their rifle shots . . . At last I crept out into the desert in the dark of night and found a stray camel and rode away . . .'

When the man from Kufra had concluded his terrible tale, Sidi Umar gently drew me to himself and repeated: 'So thou canst see, my son, we have indeed come close to the end of our allotted time.' And, as if in reply to the unspoken question in my eyes, he added: 'We fight because we have to fight for our faith and our freedom until we drive the invaders out or die ourselves. We have no other choice. To God we belong and unto Him do we return. We have sent away our women and children to Egypt, so that we should not have to worry about their safety when God wills us to die.'

A muffled drone became audible somewhere in the dark sky. With almost a reflex movement, one of Sidi Umar's men threw sand on the fire. The plane, no more than a vague shape against the moonlit clouds, passed fairly low over us on its eastward flight, and the sound of its engine slowly died away.

'But, Sidi Umar,' I said, 'would it not be better for thee and thy *mujahidin* to withdraw into Egypt while there is still a way open? For in Egypt it would perhaps be possible to bring together the many refugees from Cyrenaica and to organize a more effective force. The struggle here ought to be halted for a time, so that the people might regain some of their strength . . . I know that the British in Egypt are not too happy at the thought of having a strong Italian position on their flank; God knows, they might perhaps close their eyes to your preparations if you could convince them that you do not regard them as enemies . . .'

'No, my son, it is too late for that. What thou speakest of was possible fifteen, sixteen years ago, before Sayyid Ahmad, may God lengthen his life, took it upon himself to attack the British in order to help the Turks – who did not help us . . . Now it is too late. The British will not move a finger to make our lot easier; and the Italians are determined to fight us to the finish and to crush all possibility of future resistance. Should I and my followers go now to Egypt, we would never be able to return. And how could we abandon our people and leave them leaderless, to be devoured by the enemies of God?'

'What about Sayyid Idris? Does he share thy views, Sidi Umar?'

'Sayyid Idris is a good man, a good son of a great father. But God has not given him the heart to sustain such a struggle . . .'

There was a deep earnest, but no despondency, in Sidi Umar's voice, as he thus discussed with me the inevitable outcome of his long struggle for freedom: he knew that nothing awaited him but death. Death held no terror for him; he did not seek it; but neither did he try to evade it. And, I am sure, even if he had known what kind of death lay before him, he would not have tried to avoid it. He seemed to be conscious in every fibre of his body and mind that each man carries his destiny within himself, wherever he goes and whatever he does.

A soft commotion became audible from within the brush, so soft that one might have remained unaware of it under ordinary circumstances; but these were no ordinary circumstances. With my ears tensed in anticipation of all manner of danger from unexpected quarters, I could clearly distinguish the faint sounds of stealthy movement that had stopped abruptly, to be resumed a few moments later. The bushes parted and out stepped Zayd and Khalil, accompanied by two of the sentries; the horses they led were loaded with bulging waterskins. At the sight of Sidi Umar, Khalil rushed forward to kiss the leader's hand, whereupon I introduced Zayd. The sharp eyes of Sidi Umar rested with obvious approval on Zayd's austere face and spare figure; placing his hand on Zayd's shoulder, he said:

'Welcome to thee, O brother from the land of my fathers. Of which Arabs art thou?' – and when Zayd told him that he belonged to the tribe of Shammar, Umar nodded smilingly: 'Oh, then thou art of the tribe of Hatim at-Tayyi, the most generous of men. . . .'*

Some dates wrapped in a piece of cloth were placed before us by one of Sidi Umar's men; and he invited us to the simple fare. When we had eaten, the old warrior stood up:

'It is time to move on, brothers. We are too close to the Italian post at Bu Sfayya to allow daybreak to find us here.'

We broke our improvised camp and rode on behind Sidi Umar, while the rest of his men followed on foot. As soon as we emerged from the gulley, I saw that Sidi Umar's company was

* Pre-Islamic Arabian warrior and poet famous for his generosity. His name has become synonymous for this virtue, to which the Arabs attach the utmost importance. The Shammar tribe, to which Zayd belonged, traces its descent from Hatim's tribe, the Tayy.

Author, 1932

much larger than I had thought: one by one, dark shadows darted from behind rocks and trees and joined our column, while several more men were strung out in loose pickets far to its right and left. No casual observer would have guessed that there were about thirty men around us, for each of them moved with the silence of a Red Indian scout.

Before dawn we reached the main encampment of Umar al-Mukhtar's own *dawr* (guerrilla band), which at that time consisted of a little over two hundred men. It was sheltered in a deep, narrow gorge, and several small fires were burning under overhanging rocks. Some men were sleeping on the ground; others, blurred shadows in the greyness of early dawn, were busy with various camp tasks – cleaning their arms, fetching water, cooking meals, or tending to the few horses that were tethered to trees here and there. Almost all seemed to be clothed in rags, and neither then nor later did I see a single whole *jard* or *burnus* in the entire group. Many of the men wore bandages which spoke of recent encounters with the enemy.

To my surprise, I perceived two women – one old and one young – in the camp; they sat near one of the fires, apparently engrossed in repairing a torn saddle with crude bodkins.

'These two sisters of ours go with us wherever we go,' said Sidi Umar in reply to my mute astonishment. 'They have refused to seek the safety of Egypt together with the rest of our women and children. They are mother and daughter. All their men have been killed in the struggle.'

For two days and a night – during which the camp was shifted to another place within the forests and gorges of the plateau – Sidi Umar and I went over every possibility of arranging more regular supplies for the *mujahidin*. A trickle was still coming from Egypt. Ever since Sayyid Idris had reached an understanding with them during the period of his armistice with the Italians, the British authorities seemed to be willing to look, once again, with a certain tolerance upon Sanusi activities within Egyptian territory so long as they remained limited to local moves. In particular, they took no official notice of the small groups of warriors who occasionally succeeded in breaking through the Italian lines and came to Sallum, the nearest Egyptian town on the coast, to sell their war booty – mostly Italian mules – in exchange for badly needed food stores. Such expeditions, however, were extremely hazardous for the *mujahidin* and could not often be undertaken, the more so since the Italians were making rapid progress with the barbed-wire entanglements that ran along the Egyptian border. Sidi Umar agreed with me that the only alternative could be a supply route along the way I had come, with secret depots in the Egyptian oases of Bahriyya, Farafra and Siwa; but he was very doubtful whether this scheme could long elude the vigilance of the Italians.

(Umar's apprehensions proved only too well founded. A few months later one such supply caravan did reach the *mujahidin*, but was spotted by the Italians while passing through the 'gap' between Jaghbub and Jalu. Soon afterward a fortified Italian post was established at Bir Tarfawi, about halfway between the two oases, and this, in addition to almost continuous air patrols, made further enterprises of this kind far too risky.)

I had now to think of my return. Not being very keen on retracing the long, arduous trail I had pursued on my westward journey, I inquired of Sidi Umar whether any shorter route was feasible. There was, he told me, but a dangerous one: through the barbed-wire entanglements, to Sallum. As it happened, a band of *mujahidin* were ready to set out on a venture of this kind in order to bring flour from Sallum; if I wanted, I could join them. I decided that I wanted.

Zayd and I took leave of Umar al-Mukhtar, never to see him again: less than eight months later he was captured and executed by the Italians.

. . . .

AFTER ABOUT A WEEK'S MARCH – only by night – over the rough terrain and through the juniper thickets of the eastern Jabal Akhdar, our band of some twenty men reached the Egyptian-Cyrenaican border near the point where we planned to make our break-through. This point had not been selected at random. Although the barbed-wire barrier already covered the greater part of the frontier, it was in those days not quite completed. At some places, as here, there was only a single entanglement about eight feet high and four feet wide, while in other places there were already as many as three separate rows strung in heavy, multiple coils over poles embedded in concrete foundations. The spot we had chosen was only half a mile or so from a fortified outpost in which, we knew, there were armoured cars as well; but it had been a choice between this sector of the border or another which might perhaps be less well fortified but guarded by a double or even triple line of wire.

Arrangements had been made for us to be met a few miles inside Egyptian territory by Sanusi supporters with transport animals. Thus, it would not be necessary to endanger our own horses; they were sent back in the charge of a few of the *mujahidin*, while the rest – Zayd and I among them – approached the wire on foot shortly before midnight. Darkness was our only protection, for the Italians had cut down all trees and bushes along the frontier.

With pickets posted at a distance of several hundred yards to the north and south, six of our men – armed with wire-cutters and heavy leather gloves captured in previous raids on Italian working parties – crept forward on all fours; we others covered their advance with our rifles. It was a tense moment. Straining my ears for the slightest sound, I could hear only the crunch of gravel under the weight of the advancing bodies and the occasional call of a night bird. Then came the screech of the first shears biting into the wire – it sounded like an explosion to my ears – followed by a subdued staccato of snapping metal strands . . . *snap, snap, snap* . . . grating and snapping, deeper and deeper into the entanglement . . .

Another bird call broke through the night; but this time it was not a bird but a signal: a signal from one of our pickets in the north announcing the approach of danger . . . and almost at the same moment we heard the drone of a motor coming toward us. A searchlight swept obliquely into the air. Like one man, we threw ourselves to the ground, except for the wire cutters who went on with their work in desperate haste, no longer bothering about stealth but cutting, hacking into the wire with shears and rifle butts, like men possessed. A few seconds later a shot rang out: our northern sentry. The crew of the armoured car must have sighted him, for the beam of the searchlight suddenly swept downward and we heard the ominous rattle of a machine gun. The roar of the engine increased in volume and the black silhouette bore down upon us, its beam catching us squarely on the ground. A blast of machine-gun fire followed; the gunner had apparently aimed too high: I could hear the whizz and whine of the bullets as they passed over our heads. Lying on our bellies, we answered the fire with our rifles.

'The searchlight, the searchlight!' someone shouted. 'Aim at the searchlight!' – and the searchlight went out, apparently shattered by the bullets of our sharpshooters. The armoured car came to an abrupt halt, but its machine gunner continued firing blindly. At that instant a shout from ahead of us announced that the break-through was completed – and, one by one, we squeezed ourselves through the narrow opening, ripping our clothes and our flesh on the barbed wire. A sound of running steps – and two more *jard*-clad figures threw themselves into the gap in the entanglement: our sentries rejoining us. The Italians were apparently loath to leave the car and engage us in open fight . . .

And then we stood on Egyptian soil – or, rather, we continued to run, followed for a while by erratic firing from across the border, taking cover behind boulders, sand ridges and isolated bushes.

Dawn found us well inside Egyptian territory and out of danger. Of our twenty-odd men, five were missing, presumably dead, and four wounded, though none seriously.

'God has been merciful to us,' said one of the wounded *mujahidin*. 'Sometimes we lose half of our men in crossing the wire. But, then, none ever dies whom God, exalted be His name, has not willed to die . . . And does not the Holy Book say, *Speak not of those who are slain in the way of God as dead: for they are alive . . . ?*'

Two weeks later, returning by way of Marsa Matruh and Alexandria to Upper Egypt and thence, as pre-arranged, by *dhow* back to Yanbu, Zayd and I found ourselves once again in Medina. The entire venture had taken about two months, and our absence from the Hijaz had hardly been noticed . . .

. . . .

AS I STEP WITH SIDI Muhammad az-Zuwayy over the threshold of the humble Sanusi *zawiya* of Medina, those dim echoes of death and despair linger in my mind, and the smell of juniper trees, and the contraction of my heart at the sound of bullets passing over my head, and the pain of a hopeless quest; and then the memory of my Cyrenaican adventure fades away and only the pain remains.

— 4 —

AND ONCE AGAIN I stand before the Grand Sanusi and look upon the old warrior's tired face; and once again I kiss the hand that has held a sword so long that it cannot hold it any longer.

'God bless thee, my son, and make thy way secure . . . It is over a year since we last met; and the year has seen the end of our hopes. But praise be unto God, whatever He may decree . . .'

It must indeed have been a sorrowful year for Sayyid Ahmad: the furrows around his mouth are deeper and his voice is lower than ever. The old eagle is broken. He sits huddled on the carpet, his white *burnus* wrapped tightly about him as if for warmth, staring wordlessly into an endless distance.

'If we could only have saved Umar al-Mukhtar,' he whispers. 'If we could only have persuaded him to escape to Egypt while there was yet time . . .'

'Nobody could have saved Sidi Umar,' I comfort him. 'He did not want to be saved. He preferred to die if he could not be victorious. I knew it when I parted from him, O Sidi Ahmad.'

Sayyid Ahmad nods heavily: 'Yes, I too knew it, I too knew it . . . I knew it too late. Sometimes it occurs to me that I was wrong to heed the call from Istanbul, seventeen years ago . . . Was not that perhaps the beginning of death not only for Umar but for all the Sanusi?'

To this I have no reply, for I have always felt that Sayyid Ahmad's decision to start his unnecessary war against the British was the most fatal mistake of his life.

'But,' adds Sayyid Ahmad, 'how could I have done otherwise when the Caliph of Islam asked me for help? Was I right or was I foolish? But who, except God, can say whether a man is right or foolish if he follows the call of his conscience?'

Who can say, indeed?

The Grand Sanusi's head sways slowly from side to side in a perplexity of pain. His eyes are veiled behind drooping lids; and with sudden certainty I know that they will never again flare up with a flame of hope.*

* Sayyid Ahmad died at Medina in the following year (1933).

XII

END OF THE ROAD

— 1 —

WE LEAVE MEDINA late at night, following the 'eastern' route – the one the Prophet followed on his last pilgrimage to Mecca, a few months before his death.

We ride through the rest of the night and through the approaching dawn. After a short stop for our morning prayer we proceed into the day, which is grey and cloudy. In the forenoon it begins to rain, and soon we are wet to our skins. Finally we espy a small beduin encampment far to our left and decide to take shelter in one of the black tents.

The camp is small and belongs to a group of Harb beduins, who receive us with a loud, 'May God give you life, O strangers, and be you welcome.' I spread my blanket over the mats of goat hair in the tent of the *shaykh*, whose wife – unveiled like most of the beduin women in this region – repeats her husband's gracious welcome. After my sleepless night, sleep overcomes me speedily under the drumming of the rain on the tent roof.

The rain drums into my awakening several hours later. Nightly darkness lies over me – oh, no, it is not the night, only the dark canopy of the tent; and it smells of wet wool. I stretch my arms and my hand strikes against a camel-saddle standing on the ground behind me. The smoothness of the old wood is good to the touch; it is pleasant to play on it with one's fingers, up the pommel, until they meet the iron-hard, sharp-edged camel-gut with which it is laced together. There is nobody in the tent but me.

After a while I rise and step into the tent opening. The rain is hammering holes into the sand – myriads of tiny holes which suddenly appear and as suddenly disappear to make room for new holes – and turns to spray over the blue-grey granite boulders to my right. There is nobody in sight, for at this time of day the men must have gone out to look after their camels; the

344

many black tents near the acacia tree down below in the valley are silent in the silence of the rainy afternoon. From one of them a grey wisp of smoke winds upward – herald of the evening meal; it is too thin and too humble to assert itself against the rain, and creeps sidewise, fluttering helplessly, like a woman's hair in the wind. Behind the moving veil of silver-grey water-ribbons the hillocks seem to sway; the air is full of the scent of water and wild acacia trees and damp tent-wool.

Gradually the splashing and dripping ceases and the clouds begin to break up under the rays of the evening sun. I walk toward one of the low granite boulders. In it is a depression as large as one of the platters on which a whole roasted sheep and rice are offered to guests on festive occasions; now it is filled with rain water. When I put my arms into it, it reaches up to the elbows, lukewarm, strangely caressing; and as I move my arms about in it, it feels as if my skin were drinking. From one of the tents emerges a woman with a big copper vessel on her head, evidently intending to fill it from one of the many pools in the rocks; she holds her arms stretched outward, sideward and upward, gripping with her hands the hems of her wide red garment like wings, and sways softly as she approaches. She sways like water when it slowly flows down from the rocks, I think to myself; she is beautiful like water . . . From the distance I can hear the bellowing of the returning camels: and here they are, appearing in a spread-out group from behind the rocks, solemnly shuffling with loose legs. The herdsmen drive them on with sharp, short calls into the middle of the valley, then they call 'Ghrr . . . ghrr . . . ,' to make the animals kneel down; and the many brown backs swing down in wavy movements toward the ground. In the growing dusk the men hobble the camels' forelegs and then disperse to the tents, each to his own.

And here is the night with its soft darkness and coolness. Before most of the tents glow fires; the clattering of cooking-pots and pans and the laughter of the women mingle with the occasional calls of the men and the fragments of their talk which the wind carries to me. The sheep and goats that have come after the camels continue to bleat for a while, and sometimes a dog barks – just as he barks in all the nights in all the tent-camps of Arabia.

Zayd is nowhere to be seen; he is probably still asleep in one of the tents. I walk slowly down to the resting camels. With their great bodies they have burrowed for themselves hollows in the sand and now lie comfortably, some of them chewing their cud and others stretching their necks long on the ground. One or another lifts its head and grunts as I pass by and playfully grasp its fat hump. A very young foal is tightly pressed against its mother's side; frightened by my hands, it jumps up, while the mother turns her head toward me and softly bellows with wide-open mouth. I take hold of the foal's neck with my arms and hold it fast and press my face into the warm wool of its back: and all at once it stands quite still and seems to have lost all fear. The warmth of the young animal body penetrates my face and my chest; under the palm of my hand I sense the blood pounding in its neck-vein; it merges with the beat of my own blood and awakens in me an overwhelming sense of closeness to life itself, and a longing to lose myself in it entirely.

— 2 —

WE RIDE, AND EVERY STEP of the dromedaries brings us nearer to the end of our road. We ride for days through the sun-lit steppe; we sleep at night under the stars and awake in the coolness of dawn; and slowly I approach the end of my road.

There has never been any other road for me; although I did not know it for many years, Mecca has always been my goal. It called to me, long before my mind became aware of it, with a powerful voice: 'My Kingdom is in this world as well as in the world to come: My Kingdom waits for man's body as well as for his soul and extends over all that he thinks and feels and does – his commerce as well as his prayer, his bedchamber as well as his politics; My Kingdom knows neither end nor limits.' And when, over a number of years, all this became clear to me, I knew where I belonged: I knew that the brotherhood of Islam had been waiting for me ever since I was born; and I embraced Islam. The desire of my early youth, to belong to a definite orbit of ideas, to be part of a community of brethren, had at last been fulfilled.

Strangely enough – but perhaps not so strange if one considers what Islam stands for – my very first experience as a Muslim among Muslims was one of brotherhood . . .

In the first days of January 1927, I set out again, this time accompanied by Elsa and her little son, for the Middle East; and this time, I sensed, it would be for good.

For days we voyaged through the Mediterranean, through a shimmering circle of sea and sky, sometimes greeted by distant coasts and by the smoke of ships that glided past. Europe had disappeared far behind us and was almost forgotten.

I often went down from the comfort of our cabin deck into the stale steerage with its tiered rows of iron bunks. Since the boat was going to the Far East, the majority of the steerage passengers were Chinese, small craftsmen and traders returning to the Middle Kingdom after years of hard labour in Europe. Besides these, there was a small group of Arabs from Yemen who had come on board at Marseilles. They also were returning home. The noises and smells of Western ports were still about them; they were still living in the afterglow of the days when their brown hands had shovelled coal in the stokeholds of English, American or Dutch steamers; they were still speaking of strange foreign cities: New York, Buenos Aires, Hamburg. Once, caught by a sudden longing for the shining unknown, they had let themselves be hired in the port of Aden as stokers and coal trimmers; they had gone out of their familiar world and thought that they were growing beyond themselves in the embrace of the world's incomprehensible strangeness: but soon the boat would reach Aden and those times would recede into the past. They would exchange the Western hat for a turban or a *kufiyya*, retain the yesterday only as a memory and, each man for himself, return to their village homes in Yemen. Would they return the same men as they had set out – or as changed men? Had the West caught their souls – or only brushed their senses?

The problem of these men deepened in my mind into a problem of wider import.

Never before, I reflected, have the worlds of Islam and the West come so close to one another as today. This closeness is a struggle, visible and invisible. Under the impact of Western cultural influences, the souls of many Muslim men and women are slowly shrivelling. They are letting themselves be led away from their erstwhile belief that an improvement of living standards should be but a means to improving man's spiritual perceptions; they are falling into the same idolatry of 'progress' into which the Western world fell after it reduced religion to a mere melodious tinkling somewhere in the background of happening; and are thereby growing smaller in stature, not greater: for all cultural imitation, opposed as it is to creativeness, is bound to make a people small . . .

Not that the Muslims could not learn much from the West, especially in the fields of science and technology. But, then, acquisition of scientific notions and methods is not really 'imitation': and certainly not in the case of a people whose faith commands them to search for knowledge wherever it is to be found. Science is neither Western nor Eastern, for all scientific discoveries are only links in an unending chain of intellectual endeavour which embraces mankind as a whole. Every scientist builds on the foundations supplied by his predecessors, be they of his own nation or of another; and this process of building, correcting and improving goes on and on, from man to man, from age to age, from civilization to civilization: so that the scientific achievements of a particular age or civilization can never be said to 'belong' to that age or civilization. At various times one nation, more vigorous than others, is able to contribute more to the general fund of knowledge; but in the long run the process is shared, and legitimately so, by all. There was a time when the civilization of the Muslims was more vigorous than the civilization of Europe. It transmitted to Europe many technological inventions of a revolutionary nature, and more than that: the very principles of that 'scientific method' on which modern science and civilization are built. Nevertheless, Jabir ibn Hayyan's fundamental discoveries in chemistry did not make chemistry an 'Arabian' science; nor can algebra and trigonometry be described as 'Muslim' sciences, although the one was evolved by Al-Khwarizmi and the other by Al-Battani, both of whom were Muslims: just as one cannot speak of an 'English' Theory of Gravity, although the man who formulated it was an Englishman. All such achievements are the common property of the human race. If, therefore, the Muslims adopt, as adopt they must, modern methods in science and technology, they will do not more than follow the evolutionary instinct which causes men to avail themselves of other men's experiences. But if they adopt – as there is no need for them to do – Western forms of life, Western manners and customs and social concepts, they will not gain thereby: for what the West can give them in this respect will not be superior to what their own culture has given them and to what their own faith points the way.

If the Muslims keep their heads cool and accept progress as a means and not as an end in itself, they may not only retain their own inner freedom but also, perhaps, pass on to Western man the lost secret of life's sweetness . . .

.   .   .   .

AMONG THE YEMENIS on the boat was a thin, short man with an eagle's nose and so intense a face that it seemed to be on fire; but his gestures were quiet and measured. When he learned that I was a newcomer to Islam, he showed a special affection for me; for hours we would sit together on deck while he spoke to me of his mountain village in Yemen. His name was Muhammad Salih.

One evening I visited him below deck. One of his friends lay ill with fever on his iron bunk, and I was told that the ship's doctor would not bother to come down to the steerage. As he appeared to be suffering from malaria, I gave him some quinine. While I was thus busy with him, the other Yemenis gathered in a corner around little Muhammad Salih and, with sideglances at me, took whispered counsel. In the end one of them advanced – a tall man with an olive-brown face and hot black eyes – and offered me a bundle of crumpled franc notes:

'We have collected this among ourselves. Unfortunately it is not much; grant us the favour and accept it.'

I stepped back, startled, and explained that it was not for money that I had given medicine to their friend.

'No, no, we know it; but do nevertheless accept this money. It is not a payment but a gift – a gift from thy brethren. We are happy about thee, and therefore we give thee money. Thou art a Muslim and our brother. Thou art even better than we others: for we have been born as Muslims, our fathers were Muslims and our grandfathers; but thou hast recognized Islam with thine own heart . . . Accept the money, brother, for the sake of the Prophet of God.'

But I, still bound by my European conventions, defended myself. 'I could not possibly accept a gift in return for a service to a sick friend . . . Besides, I have money enough; you surely need it more than I. However, if you insist on giving it away, give it to the poor at Port Said.'

'No,' repeated the Yemeni, 'thou accept it from us – and if thou dost not wish to keep it, give it in thine own name to the poor.'

And as they pressed me, and, shaken by my refusal, became sad and silent, as if I had refused not their money but their hearts, I suddenly comprehended: where I had come from people were accustomed to build walls between I and You: this, however, was a community without walls . . .

'Give me the money, brothers. I accept it and I thank you.'

— 3 —

'TOMORROW, *insha-Allah*, we will be in Mecca. The fire thou art lighting, Zayd, will be the last; our journey is coming to an end.'

'But surely, my uncle, there will be other fires to light, and there will always be another journey ahead of thee and me?'

'That may be so, Zayd, my brother: but somehow I feel those other journeys will not be in this land. I have been wandering in Arabia so long that it has grown into my blood; and I fear if I do not leave now, I never shall . . . But I have to go away, Zayd: dost thou not remember the saying that water must move and flow if it is to remain clear? I want, while I am still young, to see how our Muslim brethren live in other parts of the world – in India, in China, in Java . . .'

'But, O my uncle,' replies Zayd with consternation, 'surely thou hast not ceased to love the land of the Arabs?'

'No, Zayd, I love it as much as ever; perhaps even a little too much – so much that it hurts me to think of what the future might bring to it. I am told that the King is planning to open up his country to *faranjis*, so that he may gain money from them: he will allow them to dig for oil in Al-Hasa, and for gold in the Hijaz – and God alone knows what all this will do to the beduins. This country will never be the same again . . .'

Out of the hush of the desert night sounds the beat of a galloping camel. A lonely rider rushes with flying saddle-tassels and flowing *abaya* out of the darkness into the light of our campfire, brings his dromedary to an abrupt standstill and, without waiting for it to kneel, jumps down from the saddle. After a short 'Peace be with you' he starts, without uttering another word, to unsaddle the beast, tosses his saddlebags near the campfire and sits down on the ground, still silent, with face averted.

'May God give thee life, O Abu Said,' says Zayd, who evidently knows the stranger. But the stranger remains silent, whereupon Zayd turns to me: 'He is one of Ibn Saud's *rajajil*, the devil.'

The morose Abu Said is very dark; his thick lips and crinkly hair, worn carefully plaited in two long tresses, betray African ancestry. He is extremely well dressed; the dagger in his belt – probably a gift from the King – is sheathed in gold; and his mount is an excellent, honey-coloured dromedary of the 'northern' race, slim-limbed, narrow of head, with powerful shoulders and hind-quarters.

'What is the matter with thee, O Abu Said? Why dost thou not speak to thy friends? Art thou possessed by a jinn?'

'It is Nura . . .' whispers Abu Said – and after a while, when the hot coffee has loosened his tongue, he tells us about Nura, a girl from the Najdi town of Ar-Rass (he mentions her father's name and it happens that I know him well). He had observed her secretly over the garden wall when she was drawing water in the company of other women – 'and I felt as if a glowing coal had fallen into my heart. I love her, but her father, that dog, wouldn't give me his daughter in marriage, the beggar – and said that she was afraid of me! I offered a lot of money as her dower, also a piece of my land; but he always refused and in the end married her off to her cousin, God's curse be upon him and her!'

His strong, dark face is illuminated from one side by the campfire, and the shadows which flicker across it are like the shadows of a hell of torment. He cannot bear to remain sitting for long; driven by his restlessness, he jumps up, busies his hands for a moment with his saddle, returns to the fire and, suddenly, dashes off into the empty night. We can hear him as he runs in wide circles around our camping place and shouts, shouts:

'Nura's fire burns me! Nura's fire burns in my breast!' – and again, with a sob: 'Nura, Nura!'

He approaches the campfire again and runs in circles around it, with his *kaftan* fluttering like a ghostly night bird in the light and darkness of the flickering fire.

Is he mad? I do not think so. But it may be that out of the dark recesses of his soul rise up some primeval, atavistic emotions – ancestral memories of the African bush, the memories of people who lived in the midst of demons and weird mysteries, still very close to the time when the divine spark of consciousness changed the animal into man; and the spark is not yet strong enough to bind the unchained urges together and to weld them into a higher emotion . . . For a second it seems to me that I can really see Abu Said's heart before me, a lump of flesh and blood smoking in the fire of passion as if in real fire – and somehow it appears quite natural to me that he should cry so terribly, cry and run in circles like a madman until the hobbled camels raise themselves, frightened, on three legs . . .

Then he returns to us, and throws himself on the ground. I can discern the repugnance in Zayd's face at the sight of such an unrestrained outburst – for to the aristocratic disposition of a true Arab there is nothing more contemptible than such an unleashing of the emotions. But Zayd's good heart soon gets the better of him. He tugs Abu Said by the sleeve, and while the other lifts his head and stares at him with blank eyes, Zayd gently pulls him closer to himself:

'O Abu Said, how canst thou forget thyself like this? Thou art a warrior, Abu Said . . . Thou has killed men and often have men nearly killed thee – and now a woman strikes thee down? There are other women in the world besides Nura. . . . O Abu Said, thou warrior, thou fool . . .'

And as the African groans softly and covers his face with his hands, Zayd continues:

'Be silent, O Abu Said . . . Look up: dost thou see that lighted path in the heavens?'

Abu Said looks up in astonishment, and I involuntarily follow Zayd's pointing finger and turn my eyes to the pale, uneven path that runs across the sky from one horizon to the other horizon. You would call it the Milky Way: but the beduins in their desert wisdom know that it is nothing but the track of that heavenly ram which was sent to Abraham when, in obedience to his God and in his heart's despair, he raised the knife to sacrifice his firstborn son. The path of the ram remained visible in the heavens for time eternal, a symbol of mercy and grace, remembrance of the rescue sent to heal the pain of one human heart – and thus a solace to those who were to come after: to those who are lonely or lost in the desert, and to those others who stumble, weeping and desolate, through the wilderness of their own lives.

And Zayd goes on, his hand raised toward the sky, speaking solemnly and at the same time unassumingly, as only an Arab can speak:

'This is the path of the ram which God sent to our Master Abraham when he was about to kill his first-born; thus God showed mercy to His servant . . . Dost thou think He will forget thee?'

Under Zayd's soothing words Abu Said's dark face softens in childlike wonderment and becomes visibly quieter; and he looks attentively, like a pupil following his teacher, toward the sky, trying to find in it an answer to his despair.

— 4 —

ABRAHAM AND HIS heavenly ram: such images come easily to one's mind in this country. It is remarkable how vivid the memory of that ancient patriarch is among the Arabs – far more vivid than among the Christians in the West who, after all, base their religious imagery in the first instance on the Old Testament; or even among the Jews, to whom the Old Testament is the beginning and the end of God's word to man. The spiritual presence of Abraham is always felt in Arabia, as in the whole Muslim world, not only in the frequency with which his name (in its Arabic form *Ibrahim*) is given to Muslim children, but also in the ever-recurring remembrance, both in the Koran and in the Muslims' daily prayers, of the patriarch's role as the first conscious preacher of God's Oneness: which also explains the great importance given by Islam to the annual pilgrimage to Mecca, which since earliest times has been intimately connected with the story of Abraham. He was not – as so many Westerners mistakenly assume – brought into the orbit of Arab thought by Muhammad in an attempt, as it were, to 'borrow' elements of religious lore from Judaism: for it is historically established that Abraham's personality was well known to the Arabs long before the birth of Islam. All references to the patriarch in the Koran itself are so worded as to leave no doubt that he had been living in the foreground of the Arabian mind ages before Muhammad's time: his name and the outline of his life are always mentioned without any preliminaries or explanations – as something, that is, with which even the earliest listeners to the Koran must have been thoroughly familiar. Indeed, already in pre-Islamic times

Abraham had an outstanding place in the genealogies of the Arabs as the progenitor, through Ishmael (*Ismail*), Hagar's son, of the 'northern' Arab group which today comprises more than half of the entire Arabian nation, and to which Muhammad's own tribe, the Quraysh, belonged.

Only the beginning of the story of Ishmael and his mother is mentioned in the Old Testament, for its later development does not bear directly on the destinies of the Hebrew nation, to which the Old Testament is mainly devoted; but pre-Islamic Arab tradition has much more to say on the subject.

According to this tradition, Hagar and Ishmael were abandoned by Abraham at the place where Mecca stands today – which, on the face of it, is by no means improbable if one remembers that to a camel-riding nomad a journey of thirty days or more was and is nothing out of the ordinary. At any rate, Arab tradition says that it was to this valley that Abraham brought Hagar and their child – to this gorge between rocky hills, naked and barren under the Arabian sun, swept by flaming desert winds and avoided even by birds of prey. Even today, when the valley of Mecca is filled with houses and streets and people of many tongues and races, the desert solitude cries out from the dead slopes around it, and over the crowds of pilgrims who prostrate themselves before the Kaaba hover the ghosts of those long-past millenniums in which silence, unbroken and devoid of all life, hung over the empty valley.

It was a proper setting for the despair of that Egyptian bondwoman who had borne a son to her master and thus had become the object of so much hatred on the part of her master's wife that she and her son Ishmael had to be cast away. The patriarch must have been grieved indeed when he did this to placate his implacable wife; but one should remember that he, who was so close to God, was convinced that His mercy was without limit. We are told in the Book of Genesis that God had thus comforted him: 'Let it not be grievous in thy sight because of the child and because of thy bondwoman . . . Of her son will I make a nation because he is of thy seed.' And so Abraham forsook the weeping woman and the child in the valley, leaving with them a waterskin and a skin filled with dates; and went away northward through Midian to the land of Canaan.

A solitary wild *sarha* tree stood in the valley. In its shadow sat Hagar with the child on her lap. Around her there was nothing but swimming, waving heat, glaring light on sand and rocky slopes. How good was the shadow of the tree ... But the silence, this horrible silence without the breath of any living thing! As the day was slowly passing Hagar thought: If only something living would come here, a bird, an animal, yes – even a beast of prey: what a joy it would be! But nothing came except the night, comforting like all desert nights, a cooling vault of darkness and stars that softened the bitterness of her despair. Hagar felt new courage. She fed her child some dates and both drank from the waterskin.

The night passed, and another day, and another night. But when the third day came with fiery breath, there was no more water in the skin, and despair outgrew all strength, and hope became like a broken vessel. And when the child cried in vain, with an ever weaker voice, for water, Hagar cried out to the Lord; but He did not show Himself. And Hagar, distraught by the suffering of her dying child, ran to and fro with uplifted hands through the valley, always over the same stretch between two low hills: and it is in remembrance of her despair that the pilgrims who now come to Mecca run seven times between these two hillocks, crying out, as she once cried: 'O Thou Bountiful, Thou Full of Grace! Who shall have mercy on us unless Thou hast mercy!'

And then came the answer: behold, a stream of water gushed forth and began to flow over the sand. Hagar shouted with joy and pressed the child's face into the precious liquid so that he might drink; and she drank with him, calling out imploringly between her gasps, 'Zummi, zummi!' – which is a word without meaning, merely imitating the sound of the water as it welled up from the earth, as if to say, 'Gush forth, gush forth!' Lest it run out and lose itself in the ground, Hagar heaped a little wall of sand around the spring: whereupon it ceased to flow and became a well, which henceforth came to be known as the Well of Zemzem and exists to this day.

The two were now saved from thirst, and the dates lasted them a little longer. After a few days a group of beduins, who with their families and chattels had abandoned their homelands in South Arabia and were seeking new pastures, happened to pass by the mouth of the valley. When they saw flocks of bird circling over it, they concluded that there must be water. Some of their men rode into the valley to explore it and found a lonely woman with a child sitting by the rim of an abundant well. Peacefully disposed as they were, the tribesmen asked Hagar's permission to settle in her valley. This she granted, with the condition that the well of Zemzem forever remain the property of Ishmael and his descendants.

As for Abraham, tradition says he returned to the valley after some time and found Hagar and their son alive, as he had been promised by God. From then on he visited them often, and saw Ishmael grow to manhood and marry a girl from the South Arabian tribe. Years later the patriarch was commanded in a dream to build next to the Well of Zemzem a temple to his Lord; and thereupon, helped by his son, he built the prototype of the sanctuary which stands in Mecca to this day and is known as the Kaaba. As they were cutting the stones for what was to become the first temple ever raised to the worship of the One God, Abraham turned his face toward heaven and exclaimed, '*Labbayk, Allahumma, labbayk!*' – 'For Thee am I ready, O God, for Thee am I ready!': and that is why on their pilgrimage to Mecca – the pilgrimage to the first temple of the One God – Muslims raise the cry, '*Labbayk, Allahumma, labbayk!*' when they approach the Holy City.

— 5 —

'LABBAYK, ALLAHUMMA, LABBAYK...'

How many times have I heard this cry during my five pilgrimages to Mecca. I seem to hear it now, as I lie near Zayd and Abu Said by the fire.

I close my eyes and the moon and the stars vanish. I lay my arm over my face, and not even the light of the fire can now penetrate my eyelids; all sounds of the desert go under, I hear nothing but the sound of *labbayk* in my mind and the humming and throbbing of blood in my ears: it hums and throbs and pounds like the pounding of sea waves against the hull of a ship and like the throbbing of engines: I can hear the engines throb and feel the quiver of the ship's planks under me and smell its smoke and oil and hear the cry '*Labbayk, Allahumma, labbayk*' as it sounded from hundreds of throats on the ship which bore me on my first pilgrimage, nearly six years ago, from Egypt to Arabia over the sea that is called the Red, and nobody knows why. For the water was grey as long as we sailed through the Gulf of Suez, enclosed on the right side by the mountains of the African continent and on the left by those of the Sinai Peninsula – both of them naked, rocky ranges without vegetation, moving with the progress of our voyage farther and farther apart into a hazy distance of misty grey which let the land be sensed rather than seen. And when, in the later afternoon, we glided into the open width of the Red Sea, it was blue like the Mediterranean under the strokes of a caressing wind.

There were only pilgrims on board, so many that the ship could hardly contain them. The shipping company, greedy for the profits of the short *hajj* season, had literally filled it to the brim without caring for the comfort of the passengers. On the decks, in the cabins, in all passageways, on every staircase, in the dining rooms of the first and second class, in the holds which had been emptied for the purpose and equipped with temporary ladders: in every available space and corner human beings were painfully herded together. They were mostly pilgrims from Egypt and North Africa. In great humility, with only the goal of the voyage before their eyes, they bore uncomplainingly all that unnecessary hardship. How they crouched on the deck planks, in tight groups, men, women and children, and with difficulty managed their household chores (for no food was provided by the company); how they always struggled to and fro for water with tin cans and canvas canteens, every movement a torture in this press of humanity; how they assembled five times a day around the water taps – of which there were too few for so many people – in order to perform their ablutions before prayer; how they suffered in the stifling air of the deep holds, two stories below the deck, where at other times only bales and cases of goods travelled: whoever saw this had to recognize the power of faith which was in these pilgrims. For they did not really seem to feel their suffering, so consumed were they with the thought of Mecca. They spoke only of their *hajj*, and the emotion with which they looked toward the near future made their faces shine. The women often sang in chorus songs about the Holy City, and again and again came the refrain: '*Labbayk, Allahumma, labbayk!*'

At about noon of the second day the ship siren sounded: this was a sign that we had reached the latitude of Rabigh, a small port north of Jidda, where, in accordance with an old tradition, the male pilgrims coming from the north are supposed to put away their everyday clothes and don the *ihram*, or pilgrim's garment. This consists of two unsewn pieces of white woollen or cotton cloth, of which one is wound around the waist and reaches below the knees, while the other is slung loosely around one shoulder, with the head remaining uncovered. The reason for this attire, which goes back to an injunction of the Prophet, is that during the *hajj* there should be no feeling of strangeness between the Faithful who flock together from all the corners of the world to visit the House of God, no difference between races and nations, or between rich and poor or high and low, so that all may know that they are brethren, equal before God and man. And very soon there disappeared from our ship all the colourful clothing of the men. You could no longer see the red Tunisian *tarbushes*, the sumptuous *burnuses* of the Moroccans, or the gaudy *gallabiyyas* of the Egyptian *fellahin:* everywhere around you there was only this humble white cloth, devoid of any adornment, draped over bodies which were now moving with greater dignity, visibly affected by this change to the state of pilgrimage. Because the *ihram* would expose too much of their bodies, women pilgrims keep to their usual garments; but as on our ship these were only black or white – the black gowns of the Egyptian and the white ones of the North African women – they did not bring any touch of colour into the picture.

At dawn of the third day the ship dropped anchor before the coast of Arabia. Most of us stood at the railing and gazed toward the land that was slowly rising out of the mists of the morning.

On all sides one could see silhouettes of other pilgrim ships, and between them and the land pale-yellow and emerald-green streaks in the water: submarine coral reefs, part of that long, inhospitable chain which lies before the eastern shore of the Red Sea. Beyond them, toward the east, there was something like a hill, low and dusky; but when the sun rose behind it, it suddenly ceased to be a hill and became a town by the sea, climbing from its rim toward the centre with higher and higher houses, a small delicate structure of rose and yellow-grey coral stone: the port-town of Jidda. By and by you could discern the carved, latticed windows and the wooden screens of balconies, to which the humid air had in the course of years imparted a uniform grey-green colour. A minaret jutted up in the middle, white and straight like an uplifted finger.

Again the cry, '*Labbayk, Allahumma, labbayk!*' was raised – a joyful cry of self-surrender and enthusiasm that swept from the tense, white-garbed pilgrims on board over the water toward the land of their supreme hopes.

Their hopes, and mine: for to me the sight of the coast of Arabia was the climax of years of search. I looked at Elsa, my wife, who was my companion on that pilgrimage, and read the same feeling in her eyes . . .

And then we saw a host of white wings darting toward us from the mainland: Arabian coastal boats. With Latin sails they skimmed over the flat sea, softly and soundlessly winding their way through fords between invisible coral reefs – the first emissaries of Arabia, ready to receive us. As they glided closer and closer and, in the end, flocked together with swaying masts at the side of the ship, their sails folded one after another with a rush and a swishing and flapping as if a flight of giant herons had alighted for feeding, and out of the silence of a moment ago there arose a screeching and shouting from their midst: it was the shouting of the boatmen who now jumped from boat to boat and stormed the ship's ladder to get hold of the pilgrims' baggage; and the pilgrims were so filled with excitement at the sight of the Holy Land that they allowed things to happen to them without defending themselves.

The boats were heavy and broad; the clumsiness of their hulls contrasted strangely with the beauty and slimness of their high masts and sails. It must have been in such a boat, or perhaps in a somewhat larger one of the same kind, that the bold seafarer Sindbad set out to run into unasked-for adventures and to land on an island which in truth – oh horror! – was the back of a whale . . . And in similar ships there sailed, long before Sindbad, the Phoenicians southward through this same Red Sea and on through the Arabian Sea, seeking spices and incense and the treasures of Ophir . . .

And now we, puny successors of those heroic voyages, sailed across the coral sea, skirting the undersea reefs in wide curves: pilgrims in white garments, stowed between cases and boxes and trunks and bundles, a dumb host trembling with expectation.

I, too, was full of expectation. But how could I foresee, as I sat in the bow of the boat, the hand of my wife in my hand, that the simple enterprise of a pilgrimage would so deeply, and so completely, change our lives? Again I am compelled to think of Sindbad. When he left the shores of his homeland, he – like myself – had no inkling of what the future would bring. He did not foresee, nor desire, all those strange adventures that were to befall him, but wanted only to trade and to gain money; while I wanted no more than to perform a pilgrimage: but when the things that were to happen to him and to me really happened, neither of us was ever again able to look upon the world with his old eyes.

True, nothing so fantastic ever came my way as the jinns and the enchanted maidens and the giant bird Roc that the sailor from Basra had to contend with: but, none the less, that first pilgrimage of mine was destined to cut deeper into my life than all his voyages together had done to him. For Elsa, death waited ahead; and neither of us had any premonition how near it was. And as to myself, I knew that I had left the West to live among the Muslims; but I did not know that I was leaving my entire past behind. Without any warning, my old world was coming to an end: the world of Western ideas and feelings, endeavours and imageries. A door was silently closing behind me, so silently that I was not aware of it; I thought it would be a journey like all the earlier journeys, when one wandered through foreign lands, always to return to one's past: but the days were to be changed entirely, and with them the direction of all desire.

.   .   .   .

BY THAT TIME I HAD already seen many countries of the East. I knew Iran and Egypt better than any country of Europe; Kabul had long since ceased to be strange; the bazaars of Damascus and Isfahan were familiar to me. And so I could not but feel, 'How trivial,' when I walked for the first time through a bazaar in Jidda and saw only a loose mixture and formless repetition of what elsewhere in the East one could observe in far greater perfection. The bazaar was covered with planks and sackcloth as protection against the steaming heat; out of holes and cracks thin, tamed sun rays shone through and gilded the twilight. Open kitchens before which Negro boys were roasting small pieces of meat on spits over glowing charcoal; coffee shops with burnished brass utensils and settees made of palm fronds; meaningless shops full of European and Eastern junk. Everywhere sultriness and smell of fish and coral dust. Everywhere crowds of people – innumerable pilgrims in white and the colourful, worldly citizens of Jidda, in whose faces, clothes and manners met all the countries of the Muslim world: perhaps a father from India, while the mother's father – himself probably a mixture of Malay and Arab – may have married a grandmother who on her father's side descended from Uzbegs and on her mother's side possibly from Somalis: living traces of the centuries of pilgrimage and of the Islamic environment which knows no colour bar and no distinction between races. In addition to this indigenous and pilgrim-borne confusion, Jidda was in those days (1927) the only place in the Hijaz in which non-Muslims were allowed to reside. You could occasionally see shop signs in European writing and people in white tropical dress with sun helmets or hats on their heads; over the consulates fluttered foreign flags.

All this belonged, as it were, not yet so much to the mainland as to the sea: to the sounds and smells of the port, to the ships riding at anchor beyond the pale coral streaks, to the fishing boats with white triangular sails – to a world not much unlike that of the Mediterranean. The houses, though, were already a little different, open to the breeze with richly moulded façades, carved wooden window frames and covered balconies, thinnest screens of wood that permitted the inmates to look out without hindrance into the open but prevented the passerby from seeing the interior; all this woodwork sat like grey-green lace on the walls of rose coral stone, delicate and extremely harmonious. This was no longer the Mediterranean and not yet quite Arabia; it was the coastal world of the Red Sea, which produces similar architecture on both its sides.

Arabia, however, announced itself already in the steely sky, the naked, rocky hills and sand dunes toward the east, and in that breath of greatness and that bare scarcity which are always so strangely intermingled in an Arabian landscape.

. . . .

IN THE AFTERNOON OF the next day our caravan started on the road to Mecca, winding its way through crowds of pilgrims,

beduins, camels with and without litters, riding-camels, gaily
caparisoned donkeys, toward the eastern gate of the town. Off
and on motorcars passed us – Saudi Arabia's earliest motorcars
– loaded with pilgrims and noisy with their claxon horns. The
camels seemed to sense that the new monsters were their enemies,
for they shied every time one approached, frantically veering
toward house walls and moving their long necks hither and
thither, confused and helpless. A new time was threateningly
dawning for these tall, patient animals, filling them with fear and
apocalyptic forebodings.

After a while we left the white city walls behind and found ourselves all at once in the desert – in a wide plain, greyish-brown,
desolate, dotted with thorny bushes and patches of steppe grass,
with low, isolated hills growing out of it like islands in a sea, and
hedged in to the east by somewhat higher, rocky ranges, bluish-
grey, jagged of outline, barren of all life. All over that forbidding
plain there plodded caravans, many of them, in long processions
– hundreds and thousands of camels – animal behind animal in
single file, loaded with litters and pilgrims and baggage, sometimes disappearing behind hills and then reappearing. Gradually
all their paths converged onto a single, sandy road, created by
the tracks of similar caravans over long centuries.

In the silence of the desert, which was underlined rather than
broken by the plopping of the camels' feet, the occasional calls of
the beduin drivers and the low-toned singing of a pilgrim here and
there, I was suddenly overcome by an eerie sensation – so overwhelming a sensation that one might almost call it a vision: I saw
myself on a bridge that spanned an invisible abyss: a bridge so
long that the end from which I had come was already lost in a
misty distance, while the other end had hardly begun to unveil
itself to the eye. I stood in the middle: and my heart contracted
with dread as I saw myself thus halfway between the two ends of
the bridge – already too far from the one and not yet close
enough to the other – and it seemed to me, for long seconds, that
I would always have to remain thus between the two ends, always above the roaring abyss –

– when an Egyptian woman on the camel before mine suddenly sounded the ancient pilgrim's cry, 'Labbayk, Allahumma,
labbayk!' – and my dream broke asunder.

From all sides you could hear people speaking and murmuring

in many tongues. Sometimes a few pilgrims called out in chorus, *'Labbayk, Allahumma, labbayk!'* – or an Egyptian *fellah* woman sang a song in honour of the Prophet, whereupon another uttered a *ghatrafa*, that joyful cry of Arab women (which in Egypt is called *zaghruta*): a shrill, very high-pitched trill which women raise on all festive occasions – like marriage, childbirth, circumcision, religious processions of all kinds and, of course, pilgrimages. In the knightly Arabia of earlier times, when the daughters of chieftains used to ride to war with the men of their tribe in order to spur them on to greater bravery (for it was regarded as extreme dishonour to allow one of these maidens to be killed, or, still worse, to be captured by the enemy), the *ghatrafa* was often heard on a field of battle.

Most of the pilgrims rode in litters – two on each camel – and the rolling motion of these contraptions gradually made one dizzy and tortured the nerves, so unceasing was the pitching and rocking. One dozed exhausted for a few moments, was awakened by a sudden jolt, slept again, and awoke again. From time to time the camel drivers, who accompanied the caravan on foot, called to their animals. One or another of them occasionally chanted in rhythm with the long-drawn-out step of the camels.

Toward morning we reached Bahra, were the caravan stopped for the day; for the heat permitted travel only during the night.

This village – in reality nothing but a double line of shacks, coffee shops, a few huts of palm fronds and a very small mosque – was the traditional halting-place for caravans halfway between Jidda and Mecca. The landscape was the same as it had been all the way since we left the coast: a desert with isolated hills here and there and higher, blue mountains in the east which separated the coastal lowlands from the plateau of Central Arabia. But now all this desert around us resembled a huge army camp with innumerable tents, camels, litters, bundles, a confusion of many tongues – Arabic, Hindustani, Malay, Persian, Somali, Turkish, Pashtu, Amhara, and God knows how many more. This was a real gathering of nations; but as everyone was wearing the all-leveling *ihram*, the differences of origin were hardly noticeable and all the many races appeared almost like one.

The pilgrims were tired after the night march, but only very few among them knew how to utilize this time of rest; to most of them travelling must have been a very unusual enterprise, and to many it was the first journey of their lives – and such a journey, toward such a goal! They had to be restless; they had to move about; their hands had to search for something to do, even if it was no more than opening and retying their bags and bundles: otherwise one would have become lost to the world, would have entirely lost oneself in unearthly happiness as in a sea . . .

This seemed to have happened to the family in the tent next to mine, apparently pilgrims from a Bengal village. They hardly exchanged a word, sat cross-legged on the ground and stared fixedly toward the east, in the direction of Mecca, into the desert that was filled with shimmering heat. There was such a faraway peace in their faces that you felt: they were already before the House of God, and almost in His Presence. The men were of a remarkable beauty, lean, with shoulder-long hair and glossy black beards. One of them lay ill on a rug: by his side crouched two young women, like colourful little birds in their voluminous red-and-blue trousers and silver-embroidered tunics, their thick black tresses hanging down their backs; the younger of the two had a thin gold ring in one nostril.

In the afternoon the sick man died. The women did not raise a lament as they so often do in Eastern countries: for this man had died on the pilgrimage, on sacred soil, and was thus blest. The men washed the corpse and wrapped it in the same white cloth which he had worn as his last garment. Thereafter one of them stood before the tent, cupped his hands to his mouth and called out loudly the call to prayer: 'God is the Greatest, God is the Greatest! There is no God but God, and Muhammad is God's Messenger! . . . Prayer for the dead! May God have mercy upon you all!' And from all sides the *ihram*-clad men flocked together and lined up in rows behind an *imam* like soldiers of a great army. When the prayer was over, they dug a grave, an old man read a few passages from the Koran, and then they threw sand over the dead pilgrim, who lay on his side, his faced turned toward Mecca.

. . . .

BEFORE SUNRISE ON THE SECOND morning the sandy plain narrowed, the hills grew closer together; we passed through a gorge and saw in the pale light of dawn the first buildings of

Mecca; then we entered the streets of the Holy City with the rising sun.

The houses resembled those in Jidda with their carved oriel windows and enclosed balconies; but the stone of which they were built seemed to be heavier, more massive than the light-coloured coral stone of Jidda. It was still very early in the morn-in, but already a thick, brooding heat was growing. Before many of the houses stood benches on which exhausted men were sleeping. Narrower and narrower became the unpaved streets through which our rocking caravan moved toward the centre of the city. As only a few days remained before the festival of the *hajj*, the crowds in the streets were very large. Innumerable pilgrims in the white *ihram*, and others who had temporarily changed again into their everyday clothes – clothes from all countries of the Muslim world; water carriers bent under heavy waterskins or under a yoke weighted by two old petroleum cans used as buckets; donkey drivers and riding-donkeys with tinkling bells and gay trappings; and, to make the confusion complete, camels coming from the opposite direction, loaded with empty litters and bellowing in various tones. There was such a hubbub in the narrow streets that you might have thought the *hajj* was not a thing that had taken place annually for centuries but a surprise for which the people had not been prepared. In the end our caravan ceased to be a caravan and became a disorderly tangle of camels, litters, baggage, pilgrims, camel drivers and noise.

I had arranged from Jidda to stay in the house of a well-known *mutawwif*, or pilgrim's guide, by name of Hasan Abid, but there seemed to be little chance of finding him or his house in this chaos. But suddenly someone shouted, 'Hasan Abid! Where are you pilgrims for Hasan Abid?' – and, like a jinn from out of a bottle, a young man appeared before us and, with a deep bow, requested that we follow him; he had been sent by Hasan Abid to lead us to his house.

After an opulent breakfast served by the *mutawwif*, I went out, led by the same young man who had received us earlier, to the Holy Mosque. We walked through the teeming, buzzing streets, past butcher shops with rows of skinned sheep hanging before them; past vegetable vendors with their goods spread on straw mats on the ground; amidst swarms of flies and the smell of vegetables, dust and perspiration; then through a narrow, covered bazaar in which only clothiers had their shops: a festival of colour. As elsewhere in the bazaars of Western Asia and North Africa, the shops were only niches about one yard above ground level, with the shopkeeper sitting cross-legged, surrounded by his bolts of cloth of all materials and colours, while above him there hung in rows all manner of dress articles for all the nations of the Muslim world.

And, again, there were people of all races and garbs and expressions, some with turbans and others bareheaded; some who walked silently with lowered heads, perhaps with a rosary in their hands, and others who were running on light feet through the crowds; supple, brown bodies of Somalis, shining like copper from between the folds of their toga-like garments; Arabs from the highlands of the interior, lean figures, narrow of face, proud of bearing; heavy-limbed, thickset Uzbegs from Bokhara, who even in this Meccan heat had kept to their quilted *kaftans* and knee-high leather boots; sarong-clad Javanese girls with open faces and almond-shaped eyes; Moroccans, slow of stride and dignified in their white *burnuses;* Meccans in white tunics, their heads covered with ridiculously small white skullcaps; Egyptian *fellahin* with excited faces; white-clad Indians with black eyes peering from under voluminous, snow-white turbans, and Indian women so impenetrably shrouded in their white *burqas* that they looked like walking tents; huge Fullata Negroes from Timbuktu or Dahomey in indigo-blue robes and red skullcaps; and petite Chinese ladies, like embroidered butterflies, tripping along on minute, bound feet that resembled the hooves of gazelles. A shouting, thronging commotion in all directions, so that you felt you were in the midst of breaking waves of which you could grasp some details but never an integrated picture. Everything floated amid a buzz of innumerable languages, hot gestures and excitement – until we found ourselves, suddenly, before one of the gates of the *Haram*, the Holy Mosque.

It was a triple-arched gate with stone steps climbing up to it; on the threshold sat a half-naked Indian beggar, stretching his emaciated hand toward us. And then I saw for the first time the inner square of the sanctuary, which lay below the level of the street – much lower than the threshold – and thus opened itself to the eye like a bowl: a huge quadrangle surrounded on all sides by many-pillared cloisters with semicircular arches, and in its centre a cube about forty feet high, draped in black, with a broad band of gold-embroidered verses from the Koran running around the upper portion of the covering: the Kaaba . . .

This, then, was the Kaaba, the goal of longing for so many millions of people for so many centuries. To reach this goal, countless pilgrims had made heavy sacrifices throughout the ages; many had died on the way; many had reached it only after great privations; and to all of them this small, square building was the apex of their desires, and to reach it meant fulfilment.

There it stood, almost a perfect cube (as its Arabic name connotes) entirely covered with black brocade, a quiet island in the middle of the vast quadrangle of the mosque: much quieter than any other work of architecture anywhere in the world. It would almost appear that he who first built the Kaaba – for since the time of Abraham the original structure has been rebuilt several times in the same shape – wanted to create a parable of man's humility before God. The builder knew that no beauty of architectural rhythm and no perfection of line, however great, could ever do justice to the idea of God: and so he confined himself to the simplest three-dimensional form imaginable – a cube of stone.

I had seen in various Muslim countries mosques in which the hands of great artists had created inspired works of art. I had seen mosques in North Africa, shimmering prayer-palaces of marble and white alabaster; the Dome of the Rock in Jerusalem, a powerfully perfect cupola over a delicate understructure, a dream of lightness and heaviness united without contradiction; and the majestic buildings of Istanbul, the Sulaymaniyya, the Yeni-Valide, the Bayazid Mosque; and those of Brussa, in Asia Minor; and the Safavid mosques in Iran – royal harmonies of stone, multicoloured majolica tiles, mosaics, huge stalacite portals over silver-embossed doors, slender minarets with alabaster and turquoise-blue galleries, marble-covered quandrangles with fountains and age-old plantain trees; and the mighty ruins of Tamerlane's mosques in Samarkand, splendid even in their decay.

All these had I seen – but never had I felt so strongly as now, before the Kaaba, that the hand of the builder had come so close to his religious conception. In the utter simplicity of a cube, in the complete renunciation of all beauty of line and form, spoke this thought: 'Whatever beauty man may be able to create with his hands, it will be only conceit to deem it worthy of God; therefore, the simplest that man can conceive is the greatest that he can do to express the glory of God.' A similar feeling may have been responsible for the mathematical simplicity of the Egyptian pyramids – although there man's conceit had at least found a vent in the tremendous dimensions he gave to his buildings. But here, in the Kaaba, even the size spoke of human renunciation and self-surrender; and the proud modesty of this little structure had no compare on earth.

.   .   .   .

THERE IS ONLY ONE entrance into the Kaaba – a silver-sheathed door on the northeast side, about seven feet above ground level, so that it can only be reached by means of a movable wooden staircase which is placed before the door on a few days of the year. The interior, usually closed (I saw it only on later occasions), is very simple: a marble floor with a few carpets and lamps of bronze and silver hanging from a roof that is supported by heavy wooden beams. Actually, this interior has no special significance of its own, for the sanctity of the Kaaba applies to the whole building, which is the *qibla* – that is, the direction of prayer – for the entire Islamic world. It is toward this symbol of God's Oneness that hundreds of millions of Muslims the world over turn their faces in prayer five times a day.

Embedded in the eastern corner of the building and left uncovered is a dark-coloured stone surrounded by a broad silver frame. This Black Stone, which has been kissed hollow by many generations of pilgrims, has been the cause of much misunderstanding among non-Muslims, who believe it to be a fetish taken over by Muhammad as a concession to the pagan Meccans. Nothing could be farther from truth. Just as the Kaaba is an object of reverence but not of worship, so too is the Black Stone. It is revered as the only remnant of Abraham's original building; and because the lips of Muhammad touched it on his Farewell Pilgrimage, all pilgrims have done the same ever since. The Prophet was well aware that all the later generations of the Faithful would always follow his example: and when he kissed the stone he knew that on it the lips of future pilgrims would forever meet the memory of his lips in the symbolic embrace he thus offered, beyond time and beyond death, to his entire community. And the pilgrims, when they kiss the Black Stone, feel that they are embracing the Prophet and all the other Muslims who have been here before them and those who will come after them.

No Muslim would deny that the Kaaba had existed long before the Prophet Muhammad; indeed, its significance lies precisely in this fact. The Prophet did not claim to be the founder of a new religion. On the contrary: self-surrender to God – *Islam* – has been, according to the Koran, 'man's natural inclination' since the dawn of human consciousness; it was this that Abraham and Moses and Jesus and all the other Prophets of God had been teaching – the message of the Koran being but the last of the Divine Revelations. Nor would a Muslim deny that the sanctuary had been full of idols and fetishes before Muhammad broke them, just as Moses had broken the golden calf at Sinai: for, long before the idols were brought into the Kaaba, the True God had been worshipped there, and thus Muhammad did no more than restore Abraham's temple to its original purpose.

.   .   .   .

AND THERE I STOOD before the temple of Abraham and gazed at the marvel without thinking (for thoughts and reflections came only much later), and out of some hidden, smiling kernel within me there slowly grew an elation like a song.

Smooth marble slabs, with sunlight reflections dancing upon them, covered the ground in a wide circle around the Kaaba, and over these marble slabs walked many people, men and women, round and round the black-draped House of God. Among them were some who wept, some who loudly called to God in prayer, and many who had no words and no tears but could only walk with lowered heads . . .

It is part of the *hajj* to walk seven times around the Kaaba: not just to show respect to the central sanctuary of Islam but to recall to oneself the basic demand of Islamic life. The Kaaba is a symbol of God's Oneness; and the pilgrim's bodily movement around it is a symbolic expression of human activity, implying that not only our thoughts and feelings – all that is comprised in the term 'inner life' – but also our outward, active life, our doings and practical endeavours must have God as their centre.

And I, too, moved slowly forward and became part of the

circular flow around the Kaaba. Off and on I became conscious of a man or woman near me; isolated pictures appeared fleetingly before my eyes and vanished. There was a huge Negro in a white *ihram*, with a wooden rosary slung like a chain around a powerful, black wrist. An old Malay tripped along by my side for a while, his arms dangling, as if in helpless confusion, against his batik sarong. A grey eye under bushy brows – to whom did it belong? – and now lost in the crowd. Among the many people in front of the Black Stone, a young Indian woman: she was obviously ill; in her narrow, delicate face lay a strangely open yearning, visible to the onlooker's eye like the life of fishes and algae in the depths of a crystal-clear pond. Her hands with their pale, upturned palms were stretched out toward the Kaaba, and her fingers trembled as if in accompaniment to a wordless prayer . . .

I walked on and on, the minutes passed, all that had been small and bitter in my heart began to leave my heart, I became part of a circular stream – oh, was this the meaning of what we were doing: to become aware that one is a part of a movement in an orbit? Was this, perhaps, all confusion's end? And the minutes dissolved, and time itself stood still, and this was the centre of the universe . . .

.   .   .   .

NINE DAYS LATER ELSA DIED.

She died suddenly, after less than a week's illness which at first had seemed to be no more than an indisposition due to heat and the unusual diet, but later turned out to be an obscure tropical ailment before which the Syrian doctors at the hospital of Mecca stood helpless. Darkness and utter despair closed around me.

She was buried in the sandy graveyard of Mecca. A stone was placed over her grave. I did not want any inscription on it; thinking of an inscription was like thinking of the future: and I could not conceive of any future now.

Elsa's little son, Ahmad, remained with me for over a year and accompanied me on my first journey into the interior of Arabia – a valiant, ten-year-old companion. But after a time I had to say good-bye to him as well, for his mother's family finally persuaded me that he must be sent to school in Europe; then nothing remained of Elsa except her memory and a stone in a Meccan graveyard and a darkness that was not lifted until long afterward, long after I had given myself up to the timeless embrace of Arabia.

— 6 —

THE NIGHT IS FAR ADVANCED, but we continue to sit around the glimmering campfire. Abu Said has now emerged from the raging tempest of his passion; his eyes are sad and somewhat tired; he speaks to us of Nura as one might speak of a dear person that has died long ago.

'She was not beautiful, you know, but I loved her . . .'

The moon above us is full with the fullness of a living being. No wonder the pre-Islamic Arabs thought it to be one of the 'daughters of God' – the long-haired Al-Lat, goddess of fertility, who was said to communicate her mysterious powers of procreation to the earth and thus to beget new life in humans and animals. In her honour, the young men and women of ancient Mecca and Taïf used to celebrate the nights of the full moon in open-air revels and unrestrained love-making and poetic contests. Out of earthenware pitchers and leathern bottles flowed the red wine; and because it was so red and so full of excitement, the poets likened it in their wild dithyrambs to the blood of women. This proud and passionate youth poured its exuberance into the lap of Al-Lat, 'whose loveliness is like the shine of the moon when it is full, and whose loftiness is like the flight of black herons' – the ancient, youthfully mighty goddess who had spread her wings from South Arabia to the north and had reached even distant Hellas in the shape of Leto, the mother of Apollo.

From the diffuse, vague nature worship of Al-Lat and a host of other deities to the sublime concept of the One God of the Koran: it was a long road that the Arabs had to travel. But, after all, man has always loved to travel far on the roads of his spirit, here in Arabia no less than in the rest of the world: he has loved it so much that all his history may indeed be described as the history of a quest for faith.

With the Arabs, this quest has always aimed at the Absolute. Even in their earliest times, when their imagination filled the world around them with a multitude of gods and demons, they were ever conscious of the One who dwelt in majesty over all the deities – an invisible, ungraspable Omnipotence far above the humanly conceivable – the Eternal Cause above all effects. The goddess Al-Lat and her divine sisters, Manat and Uzza, were no more than 'God's daughters', mediators between the Unknowable One and the visible world, symbols of the incomprehensible forces that surrounded the childhood of man: but deep in the background of Arabian thought, knowledge of the One was always present, always ready to flare up into conscious faith. How else could it have been? They were a people that had grown up in silence and solitude between a hard sky and a hard earth; hard was their life in the midst of these austere, endless spaces; and so they could not escape the longing after a Power that would encompass all existence with unerring justice and kindness, severity and wisdom: God the Absolute. He dwells in infinity and radiates into infinity – but because *you* are within His working, *He is closer to you than the vein in your neck* . . .

.   .   .   .

THE CAMPFIRE HAS DIED down. Zayd and Abu Said are asleep, and nearby our three dromedaries lie on the moon-blanched sand and chew their cud with soft, crunching sounds, pausing from time to time. Good animals . . . Sometimes one of them shifts its position and rubs with the horny surface of its chest against the ground and occasionally blows snortingly, as if sighing. Good animals. They are without a definite expression, quite different from horses, which are always so clearly outlined in their characters; yes, different from all the other animals which man uses – just as the desert steppe to which they belong is different from all other landscapes: without a definite expression, swinging between contradictions, moody, and nevertheless infinitely modest.

I cannot sleep, and so I wander away from the camp and climb one of the hillocks close by. The moon hangs low over the western horizon and lights up the low, rocky hills which rise like phantoms out of the dead plain. From here onward, the coastal lowlands of the Hijaz flow toward the west in a soft incline: a series of valleys torn up by many winding, dry stream beds, barren of all life, without villages, without houses, without trees – rigid in their nakedness under the moonlight. And yet it was from this desolate, lifeless land, from amidst these sandy valleys and naked hills, that the most life-affirming faith of man's history sprang forth . . .

Warm and still is the night. Half-light and distance make the hills waver and sway. Under the shine of the moon a pale, blue shimmer vibrates, and through this pale blueness glides an opalescent hint, a ghostly remembrance, of all the colours on earth; but the unearthly blueness subdues them all, melting without transition into what should be the horizon, and is like a summons to unfathomable, unknowable things.

Not far from here, hidden from my eyes in the midst of this lifeless wilderness of valleys and hills, lies the plain of Arafat, on which all the pilgrims who come to Mecca assemble on one day of the year as a reminder of that Last Assembly, when man will have to answer to his Creator for all he has done in life. How often have I stood there myself, bareheaded, in the white pilgrim garb, among a multitude of white-garbed, bareheaded pilgrims from three continents, our faces turned toward the Jabal ar-Rahma – the 'Mount of Mercy' – which rises out of the vast plain: standing and waiting through the noon, through the afternoon, reflecting upon that inescapable Day, 'when you will be exposed to view, and no secret of yours will remain concealed' . . .

And as I stand on the hillcrest and gaze down toward the invisible Plain of Arafat, the moonlit blueness of the landscape before me, so dead a moment ago, suddenly comes to life with the currents of all the human lives that have passed through it and is filled with the eerie voices of the millions of men and women who have walked or ridden between Mecca and Arafat in over thirteen hundred pilgrimages for over thirteen hundred years. Their voices and their steps and the voices and the steps of their animals reawaken and resound anew; I see them walking and riding and assembling – all those myriads of white-garbed pilgrims of thirteen hundred years; I hear the sounds of their passed-away days; the wings of the faith which has drawn them together to this land of rocks and sand and seeming deadness beat again with the warmth of life over the arc of centuries, and the mighty wingbeat draws me into its orbit and draws my own passed-away days into the present, and once again I am riding over the plain—

– riding in a thundering gallop over the plain, amidst thousands and thousands of *ihram*-clad beduins, returning from

Arafat to Mecca – a tiny particle of that roaring, earth-shaking, irresistible wave of countless galloping dromedaries and men, with the tribal banners on their high poles beating like drums in the wind and their tribal war cries tearing through the air: '*Ya Rawga, ya Rawga!*' by which the Atayba tribesmen evoke their ancestor's name, answered by the '*Ya Awf, ya Awf!*' of the Harb and echoed by the almost defiant, '*Shammar, ya Shammar!*' from the farthest right wing of the column.

We ride on, rushing, flying over the plain, and to me it seems that we are flying with the wind, abandoned to a happiness that knows neither end nor limit . . . and the wind shouts a wild paean of joy into my ears: 'Never again, never again, never again will you be a stranger!'

My brethren on the right and my brethren on the left, all of them unknown to me but none a stranger: in the tumultuous joy of our chase, we are one body in pursuit of one goal. Wide is the world before us, and in our hearts glimmers a spark of the flame that burned in the hearts of the Prophet's Companions. They know, my brethren on the right and my brethren on the left, that they have fallen short of what was expected of them, and that in the flight of centuries their hearts have grown small: and yet, the promise of fulfilment has not been taken from them . . . from us . . .

Someone in the surging host abandons his tribal cry for a cry of faith: 'We are the brethren of him who gives himself up to God!' – and another joins in: '*Allahu akbar!*' – 'God is the Greatest! – God alone is Great!'

And all the tribal detachments take up this one cry. They are no longer Najdi beduins revelling in their tribal pride: they are men who know that the secrets of God are but waiting for them . . . for us . . . Amidst the din of the thousands of rushing camels' feet and the flapping of a hundred banners, their cry grows up into a roar of triumph: '*Allahu akbar!*'

It flows in mighty waves over the heads of the thousands of galloping men, over the wide plain, to all the ends of the earth: '*Allahu akbar!*' These men have grown beyond their own little lives, and now their faith sweeps them forward, in oneness, toward some uncharted horizons . . . Longing need no longer remain small and hidden; it has found its awakening, a blinding sunrise of fulfilment. In this fulfilment, man strides along in all his God-given spendour; his stride is joy, and his knowledge is freedom, and his world a sphere without bounds . . .

The smell of the dromedaries' bodies, their panting and snorting, the thundering of their innumerable feet; the shouting of the men, the clanking of the rifles slung on saddle-pegs, the dust and the sweat and the wildly excited faces around me; and a sudden, glad stillness within me.

I turn around in my saddle and see behind me the waving, weaving mass of thousands of white-clad riders and, beyond them, the bridge over which I have come: its end is just behind me while its beginning is already lost in the mists of distance.